LILLYWHITE'S LEGACY

A History of
The Cheltenham Cricket Festival

To David

with best wishes

Grenville Simons.

Cheltenham 2004.

Two Leg Sir

W.J.SUTER.   CHELTENHAM.

Jim Lillywhite

James Lillywhite

LILLYWHITE'S LEGACY

A History of
The Cheltenham Cricket Festival

Grenville Simons

Foreword by
David Morgan

So shall my tale not be of dust
Chilled in a common urn,
While proudly through your younger lust
My testament shall burn.

JOHN DRINKWATER
(from *Legacy*)

Wisteria Books
Birtsmorton

First published in 2004

by
Wisteria Books
Wisteria Cottage
Birt Street
Birtsmorton
Malvern
Worcs. WR13 6AW

British Library Cataloguing in Publication Data

ISBN 0 9527760 1 4

Design and Typesetting by George Simons.

Set in Times 10/9

Printed by Goodman Baylis Ltd., Worcester

Bound by MPG Books Ltd., Bodmin

To George, Edward, Barnaby and Emily, with love

FOREWORD

by David Morgan
Chairman of the England and Wales Cricket Board

In his Foreword to Nico Craven's "County Cricket's Castaways", Michael Henderson wrote, "Every year Nico Craven revisits Cheltenham, and every year he sees what he likes". The same could be said of Grenville Simons: Wisteria Books and Grenville and his family have a special place in the life of the Cheltenham Cricket Festival with the Festival an integral part of their summers. And so this book bears the stamp of authority and provides an insider's perspective.

The book is therefore a must for cricketers and lovers of the game particularly those who have played and watched cricket at the College Ground.

Readers will be reminded of the changes which have taken place in the game, both social and structural, and will enjoy accounts of the achievements of Gloucestershire players as well as those of their opponents. There are fitting reminders of the great names of the past - Grace, Jessop, Hammond, Goddard, Barnett, Milton, Allen and Graveney, to mention but a few - and of Gloucestershire's success in recent times in the limited over format of the game under Mark Alleyne's leadership with expert guidance from John Bracewell. Reminders, too, of entertainment with no shortage of style provided by the county's well-chosen overseas players: stars such as Procter, Zaheer, Sadiq and Walsh.

The Festival itself has done well to survive significant threats which came late in both the 19th and 20th centuries. In his book, "Famous Cricket Grounds" published in 1951, Laurence Meynell wrote of Gloucestershire cricket in the late 19th century "having no recognised home with county matches played at Clifton College ('a bumping pitch and a blinding light'), Gloucester, Cheltenham, Cirencester and Moreton-in-Marsh; but there was all the time a strong and a growing feeling that the team . . . should have an established headquarters of its own. So it came about that some 26 acres of land at Ashley Down became the centre of county cricket in Gloucestershire, and the first county match was played there against Warwickshire in 1889". Thus, having survived the establishment of Bristol as the county's headquarters, Cheltenham and Festival cricket in general, came under renewed pressure about a hundred years later with the advent of the four-day game and a reduction in the number of championship matches from as many as thirty to sixteen. That the Cheltenham Cricket Festival continues to this day to provide competitive county cricket in such a beautiful setting is a tribute to those who have worked so hard and effectively to maintain its charm and, not least, its economic competitiveness.

The prosperity of the Cheltenham Cricket Festival is in no small way due to Cheltenham seeking to be the best in festivals rather than it pretending to be something else. It sets a fine example along with Scarborough for others to follow and in so doing helps maintain the attractiveness of the county cricket circuit.

Such is the charm of Cheltenham and the glorious Cotswolds that county members search the newly published county fixtures each pre-season in the hope that their club will be scheduled to play against Gloucestershire during the Festival. With the 2004 fixtures not providing for a visit from Glamorgan, I know of many here in Wales who will regret missing the unique atmosphere of the College ground not to mention the hospitality of the Montpellier Wine Bar at its marquee situated as ever on the edge of the playing area on a prime site.

This book has been put together with much care by Grenville Simons who has combined his love of the game with a genuine appreciation for the written word.

Christchurch
Newport
UK

January 2004

CONTENTS

Foreword by David Morgan   7

List of illustrations   11

Acknowledgements   13

Preface   15

1   LILLYWHITE LEADS THE WAY   17
    (1855-1871)

2   COUNTY CRICKET COMES TO CHELTENHAM   25
    (1872-1877)

3   THE CRICKET WEEK   35
    (1878-1882)

4   TOURIST ATTRACTION   55
    (1883-1889)

5   THE DAWNING OF A NEW AGE   66
    (1890-1894)

6   UPS AND DOWNS   76
    (1895-1899)

7   FAREWELL TO THE WEEK   94
    (1900-1905)

8   THE FESTIVAL ARRIVES   105
    (1906-1909)

9   THE 'GENTLEMAN'S PERSONAL GENTLEMAN'   114
    (1910-1914)

10 A NEW ERA   124
    (1919-1927)

11 HATS OFF TO HAMMOND AND LYON   146
    (1928-1934)

12 UNDERTONES OF WAR   167
    (1935-1939)

13 IN A FESTIVAL SPIRIT   183
    (1946-1949)

14 'BORE' DRAWS   195
    (1950-1954)

15 MACKINTOSH AND SANDWICHES   212
    (1955-1959)

16 THE SWINGING SIXTIES   226
    (1960-1969)

17 GLORIOUS GLOSTERS   251
    (1970-1975)

18 RECORDS, RAIN AND THE CORPORATE GAME   268
    (1976-1979)

19 THE WINNER TAKES IT ALL   277
    (1980-1986)

20 SALUTE WALSH AND ALLEYNE   295
    (1987-1997)

21 APPROACHING THE FESTIVAL CENTENARY   330
    (1998-2003)

BIBLIOGRAPHY   360

STATISTICAL APPENDIX Compiled by Keith Gerrish   363

INDEX   391

LIST OF ILLUSTRATIONS

James Lillywhite *(Reproduced by kind permission
of Nicholas Sharp, Private Collection)*   Frontispiece

Maps showing evolution of Cheltenham College ground   20

The College Playground *c.* 1870 *(Reproduced by kind
permission of Cheltenham Art Gallery and Museum)*   22

The first poster for a county match played on the College ground   33

The Plough Hotel in Cheltenham High Street   38

Baron de Ferrières *(Reproduced by kind permission
of Cheltenham Art Gallery and Museum)*   40

The loving cup *(Reproduced by kind permission of
Cheltenham Borough Council)*   40

Lillywhite's emporium *(Reproduced by kind permission
of Aylwin Sampson)*   53

A family day out at the Cricket Week *(Reproduced by kind
permission of Roger Mann, from the Roger Mann Collection)*   68

W. G. Grace *(Reproduced by kind permission of
Cheltenham College Archives)*   80

Cheltenham Cricket Week 1898 *(Reproduced by kind permission
of Cheltenham College Archives)*   90

Charles Townsend in conversation *(Reproduced by kind
permission of Roger Mann, from the Roger Mann Collection)*   90

The end of Kent's first innings in 1903 *(Gloucestershire Graphic)*   100

Iredale, Woof, Hill and McLeod *(Gloucestershire Graphic)*   102

Gloucestershire v Australians *(Reproduced by kind permission
of John Hawkins, Private Collection)*   112

Jessop speaking to Dr Dighton *(Gloucestershire Graphic)*   112

Gloucestershire v Kent *(Gloucestershire Graphic)*   117

A view of the ground in 1913   120

A queue outside the ground in 1921 *(Gloucestershire Graphic)*   130

The grandstand in 1921 *(Gloucestershire Graphic)*   130

Gloucestershire v Australians in 1926 *(Gloucestershire Graphic)*   142

A view of the ground in 1929 *(Gloucestershire Graphic)*   150

Close of play 1930 *(Gloucestershire Graphic)*   156

The crowd in 1935 *(Gloucestershire Graphic)*   169
Spectator Herbert Champney *(Gloucestershire Graphic)*   175
At the mayor's lunch *(Gloucestershire Graphic)*   179
A last glimpse of the Festival before the war
    (Gloucestershire Graphic)   179
Hospital patients with a grandstand view *(Getty Images)*   188
Cartoon *(Gloucestershire Echo)*   202
Gloucestershire v New Zealand, 1958   220, 221
Ken Graveney watches Gloucestershire batsmen in action   233
Cartoon *(Gloucestershire Echo)*   242
Mike Bissex being awarded his county cap *(Glos.CCC Yearbook)*   254
John Mortimore *(Reproduced by kind permission of Bill Smith)*   261
Cheltenham Cricket Festival *(Reproduced by kind permission
    of Aylwin Sampson)*   283
Courtney Walsh in action against Lancashire
    (Reproduced by kind permission of NI Syndication)   302, 303
'The Pavilion, Cheltenham College' by Jack Russell
    (Reproduced by kind permission of the Jack Russell Gallery)   318
Cheltenham Cricket Festival by Jocelyn Galsworthy
    (Reproduced by kind permission of Jocelyn Galsworthy)   327
Jocelyn Galsworthy at work
    (Reproduced by kind permission of Chris Bentall)   328

The following colour photographs
    (Reproduced by kind permission of Tony Hickey)
Sunday, Monday or All Days book launch   328
Chris Coley listening to Lord Vestey   328
Jack Russell becomes a jockey   333
Gurhkas entertain the crowd   333
Parachutists landing on the ground   333
Shirt sleeves and sunhats   334
View towards the pavilion   334
View from the balcony   339
The Chapel end   339
Tom and Ken Graveney   340
The groundstaff   340
A familiar Festival view   345
Umbrellas up, as the old enemy returns   345
Cheltenham collage   346

ACKNOWLEDGEMENTS

I would like to thank all those who have helped me in gathering material for this book through their advice, encouragement and kindness.

I am most grateful to the following players and officials who gave their time to talk or write about their Festival memories: David Allen, Mark Alleyne, Bill Athey, Sir Derrick Bailey, Martyn Ball, Mike Bissex, John Bracewell, Andy Brassington, 'Podge' Brodhurst, Dennis Brookes, Tony Brown, George Chesterton, Hugh Davis, Geoff Edrich, John Emburey, David Gower, David Graveney, Tom Graveney, David Green, Mark Hardinges, Graeme Hick, Ray Julian, Frank McHugh, Bill Merry, Arthur Milton, Tom Moody, John Mortimore, Don Oslear, Roy Palmer, Jonty Rhodes, Barry Richards, Kevin Sharp, Rt Revd Lord Sheppard of Liverpool, Mike Smith, Andy Stovold, Martin Stovold, Peter Walker, Bryan 'Bomber' Wells, Stuart Westley, Richard Whiley, Andy Wilson and Matthew Windows.

I wish to acknowledge, with gratitude, the following for their valuable personal contributions: Bert Avery, David Bridle, Chris Coley, Ken Faulkner, Derek Goddard, Andrew Hignell, Percy Howse, Marie Journeaux, Bill Lewis, John Light, Bob McInroy, Joan Milton, Geoffrey Need, Jean Ough, Lisa Oversby, Don Perry, Tom Richardson, Jim Ruston, Colin Sexstone, Richard Sharp, Michael Simpson, David Smith, Geoff Swift, Lord Vestey, Norman Walters and Kit Wright.

For reading through the text and making valuable suggestions, I am very grateful to John Mace, Aylwin Sampson and Andrew Fraser. To Roy Arnold I owe a special debt, for generously providing the use of his library for much of my research. With his keen auditor's eyes he proofed the text, checking scores and figures in particular and I only wish that he had lived to see the finished product.

I would like to thank David Morgan very much for writing the foreword. I am indebted to Keith Gerrish for compiling the statistics which provide an invaluable appendix. I am also deeply grateful to Nico Craven for setting me completion dates (and allowing me to break them) and for passing on so many of his Festival tales; but above all for his constant support and encouragement.

My grateful thanks go to the following for providing information and assistance in a variety of ways: Chris Bentall, Jane Blackstock, Steven Blake, Robert Brooke, Adrian Burton, Stephen Chalke, Carol Cole, Bill Coleman, Chris Ellsmore, David Foot, Gloucestershire County Cricket Club, Maggie Hanson, Tim Harman, Murray Hedgcock, Liz Ihre, Joanne Lampen, Adam Lillywhite, George Lillywhite, Charles Merullo, Emma Sangeelee, Nicholas Sharp, Stephen Sidders, Mary Wells and Derek West.

I would like to thank the following who have kindly given permission to reprint copyright material: Macmillan for an extract from *Legacy,* taken from *Tides,* by John Drinkwater; John Murray for the use of *Cheltenham,* by John Betjeman from his *Collected Poems*; John Wisden and Co Ltd. for permission to quote from *Wisden Cricketers' Almanack* and the *Gloucestershire Echo* for permission to reproduce photographs and extracts from the *Gloucestershire Graphic, Gloucestershire Echo* and *Cheltenham Chronicle.*

I acknowledge and thank all those who have kindly given permission for photographs and illustrations to be reproduced. I am also very grateful to all the staff in the Reference Department of Cheltenham Library, for guiding me towards various publications and helping me when needed with the microfilm screen. Also, my thanks go to Tim Pearce, Christine Leighton and Phillipa Davies at Cheltenham College for all their assistance.

Huge thanks go to my family without whose good humour, help, encouragement, and appreciation of the Festival, the book would never have been completed. I am indebted to George for his expertise and many hours of hard work on the entire book layout and dust jacket design. Edward and Barnaby have given tremendous support proofing and word processing and have offered many constructive suggestions, while Emily has provided soothing music when needed. Finally, my thanks go to Manda, my wife, who has given me wholehearted support throughout the project and gently imparted much sound advice and constructive criticism as she scrutinized the text.

While every effort has been made to locate copyright holders, my apologies go to anyone I have inadvertently failed to acknowledge.

PREFACE

Since 1872, Gloucestershire cricketers have scored over one hundred and nine thousand runs and taken nearly five thousand wickets on the College ground. No wonder it is a popular venue for the county's players and supporters alike.

My introduction to this unique festival setting of College buildings and their surroundings was in the summer of 1987, selling cricket books from the back of our car. It did not take long to realise that, although cricket was the central theme, the Festival was a social occasion rejoicing beneath the English summer sky.

Over the years, I listened, along with my family, to the tales of those who had attended the event numerous times. Nostalgia overflowed - this Festival folklore needed to be chronicled.

While gathering material for this book, I have been most fortunate to meet, talk to and correspond with many people, all of whom have a deep affection for the event and, like me, would find it hard to imagine a summer without it. Much of the attraction lies in Cheltenham's familiar pattern, always falling at the start of the summer holidays, with its customary ground layout and a seemingly perpetual free flow of runs and regular fall of wickets.

In *Gloucestershire Road,* Grahame Parker treats us to this vignette:

'There are few scenes in cricket to compare with the Cheltenham Festival on a sunny day. It embodies the very best traditions of the game. Business and Club marquees around the ground, rows of temporary stands, strong local and municipal involvement, receptions and functions, all against the backdrop of that superb Victorian architecture and a cricket pitch that is no place for the negative or faint hearted.'

It is against that setting of Victorian England that the story begins . . .

Grenville Simons
Birtsmorton

March 2004

CHAPTER ONE (1855-1871)

LILLYWHITE LEADS THE WAY

A year before he died, former Sussex cricketer, Frederick William Lillywhite, visited the thriving spa town of Cheltenham. This pioneer of round-arm bowling, dubbed the 'Nonpareil' for his outstanding ability, made his way to the College and came across a large grassy area next to the gymnasium called the Playground. Here he talked to the boys and watched them practising cricket, soon noticing that the standard of their game was somewhat lacking. He realised they were in need of a permanent coach and his thoughts turned to his eldest son, James. Before leaving the College, he sowed seeds in the minds of the senior pupils that a cricket professional should be found, pointing out that with good coaching their results would improve.

The boys acted swiftly on the advice of 'Old Lilly' and the *Minute Book* reports that a letter was read out from a senior pupil at a meeting of the College board of directors on 9 October 1855. The pupil, referred to as 'Mr Hamilton Pasley, opening batsman and keen cricketer', had written 'on behalf of the young gentlemen of the College' requesting 'the employment of Mr James Lillywhite as Manager of the Playground and instructor in cricket'.

No time was wasted and a fortnight later the College discipline committee reported that they had 'entered into an engagement with James Lillywhite to commence from the 1st day of March 1856 to teach the pupils cricket and generally superintend the Playground at a salary of fifty-two guineas per annum, terminable by either party on a notice of three months'. His employers were keen for success for they knew, as did an 'Old Collegian' who later wrote of those early days, that 'cricket thrived but poorly'. He did not disappoint them and unbeknown to the committee members his appointment would have enormously far-reaching repercussions.

James Lillywhite quickly influenced school life and turned cricket into a major and successful sport at the College. Furthermore, he made use of his astute cricket and business mind to lay the early foundations for the great institution of Gloucestershire cricket, the Cheltenham Cricket Festival.

* * * * * *

On Lillywhite's arrival, the College was still very much in its infancy. A site for its establishment had been found some fifteen years earlier on land purchased for £4,000 from the wealthy Lord Northwick. The first mention of a land transaction is recorded in the *Minute Book* when a special meeting of the board of directors took place in April 1842. The ground known as Sandford Fields, formerly Sandford Tithing, appeared 'most admirably adapted' for almost everything that they required. It was 'high in position and most healthful as to air', standing on a 'stratum of sand said to be above 50 feet in depth and supplied with an abundance of the purest spring water'.

Initially, Lord Northwick agreed to sell half the field which amounted to around twelve acres, and was made up of two parts. The larger area, some of which would be for playing fields, was the land nearest to Charlton Park, while a space at the western end of the field would be for the site of the College itself. This plot included five villa allotments on the Bath Road, with a road frontage of three hundred feet and a depth of one hundred and eighty feet.

Living at nearby Thirlestaine House, undoubtedly the most magnificent residence in Cheltenham, Lord Northwick housed his large, valuable collection of paintings. In order to retain some form of privacy from the noisy schoolboys in their play area, the eccentric bachelor reserved for 'himself and his own enjoyment' the sites of sixteen villa allotments and a small strip of land on which he grazed his cows.

Eventually, in 1855, his lordship decided to sell the sixteen allotments, an area of some six acres, for which he received a further £3,000. The ground, which had been carefully cultivated, had become a fertile area of market garden, celebrated for growing excellent raspberries along with other fruit, vegetables and flowers. Once the newly-appointed Playground manager and cricket coach had levelled and prepared the site, he would have ample space in which to develop his work.

James Lillywhite was thirty when he took up this challenging new post. He had already experienced school life as a cricket coach at Westminster School in 1849, Eton in 1852, Marlborough the following year and most recently, in 1854, had been employed by the Clydesdale

Club in Glasgow. He appeared to be tailor-made for the job, his sense of humour and 'love of honest sport' making him popular with the staff and pupils. 'Jim', or 'Jem' as he became known, could keep order when 'temper and rivalry' were high and calm the 'quick anger of youth'. He seemed to know instinctively the position of the narrow line between 'frolic and mischief' so enabling him to maintain a friendly spirit in the Playground when discipline was a problem. It was here that he channelled his unflagging energy as an inspirational coach, groundsman and provider of pastoral care.

The spacious area of the Playground provided a central meeting point for recreation and amusement for the continually increasing number of boys. There were parallel bars, gymnastic ladders and ropes and the hugely popular 'tuck stalls'. Meat pies, macaroons, toffee, ices and raspberries and cream were just some of the tasty fare available to the ever-hungry, growing youths. But the greatest favourite of all were Mrs Tyler's 'twopennies', delicious raised pastry pies filled with gooseberries, apples or plums. Members of the First XI were allowed 'tick' at Tyler's which doubtless made boys try even harder to get into the team.

A little business venture such as this would have appealed to Lillywhite's entrepreneurial mind, for in 1850 his father had set him up in business with his younger brothers, John and Fred, selling sports goods under the name 'Lillywhite and Sons'. Once settled in Cheltenham, he saw an opportunity for selling sports equipment at school and later established his own 'emporium' in Queen's Circus. Supplying the well-to-do residents of the town, members of the armed forces, schools and colleges, the business quickly thrived and his name and influence began to spread within the county of Gloucestershire.

On the College front things were looking good. The inaugural Cheltenham versus Marlborough cricket match ended with victory for Lillywhite's boys and the presence of this experienced cricketer and wise coach was starting to prove beneficial. Lillywhite had been a useful twisting, medium-paced, round-arm bowler and moderate batsman for both Sussex and Middlesex, but his career as a player had unfortunately been cut short as the result of 'an accident', most probably the incident in which he lost the sight in one eye.

Several professionals had been engaged before, but due to their temporary terms of employment they had not been totally dedicated to the interests of the First XI. They had been drafted in to help the head of the Military Department, Revd T. A. Southwood, who had laid the

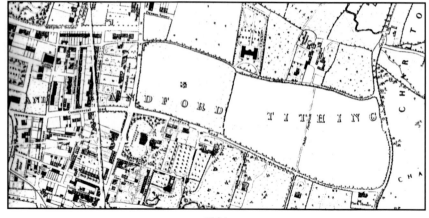

1834

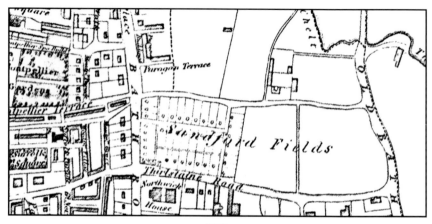

1840

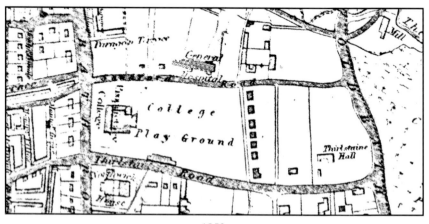

1853

Maps showing the evolution of the Cheltenham College cricket ground. The open land of Sandford Tithing becomes the Sandford Fields allotments and finally the College buildings and Playground.

foundation of cricket at the College by levelling a playing area, organising coaching for the boys and forming the first cricket team. Lillywhite was now moving it on to another level.

Lillywhite played in several internal games, batting 'rather gingerly with his one eye', on one occasion scoring 62* for the Modern against the Classical Department. He bowled accurately in school trial matches, usually helping the Second XI against the First. By now he was ably assisted by James Grundy during the months of April and May. Grundy, a former Nottinghamshire player and one of the best medium-paced round-arm bowlers of his day, was the ideal man to bowl at the boys, as he was unfailingly accurate and could 'land 'em on a cheese-plate' for hour after hour.

In 1861, eleven years before Gloucestershire were to play their first game on the College ground, Jem made a real scoop. He arranged for the United All-England XI to come and play Twenty-two Past and Present Cheltonians. In order for this to take place he had to consult long and hard with the College board who were 'dreadfully afraid of admitting all sorts of riff-raff into the College grounds'. Eventually he convinced them of the benefits the game would bring to the College. Excited spectators witnessed the big names of Robert Carpenter, John Wisden, William Caffyn, Heathfield Harman Stephenson, Tom Lockyer and John Lillywhite playing for the visitors. These men were the luminaries of the cricket world, having just returned home from the first ever overseas cricket tour, the historic trip to Canada and the United States organised and run by Fred Lillywhite, James' younger brother. But on this occasion the mighty fell, with the strong College Twenty-two, including Lillywhite and Grundy, winning by an innings and 85 runs.

Lillywhite's first cricket match business venture did not turn out to be very profitable, despite various subscriptions from resident gentry and staff and friends of the College. The attendance was rather poor and costs had to be met. But the seed was sown, for great cricketers and entertainers had set foot on the Playground; Lillywhite's mind was set and glorious things would soon follow.

The hard-working Revd Alfred Barry became headmaster in 1862, and under his guidance the College continued to grow and develop with more emphasis placed on sport. Public school educationalists saw this kind of physical activity as character-building, developing leadership qualities and teaching moral standards. This suited Lillywhite.

By 1865 an imposing new building had been constructed on the southern side of the Playground, comprising a gymnasium with racquets

The College Playground *c*. 1870

courts at each end. Already coaching fives and football, in addition to his cricket commitments and responsibility for the upkeep of some seventeen acres of cricket ground, Lillywhite now instructed the boys racquets in the new courts.

The following year James' younger brother, Fred, died aged only thirty-seven. A busy man, variably engaged as a scorer, chronicler, printer and sports outfitter, he had also been in and out of a partnership with John Wisden. His hunger for work seemed at times to have rebounded on him and caused business difficulties and he had a habitual knack of upsetting people.

James, on the other hand, was of 'unfailing good temper and kindliness of heart', while his house, Boswell Cottage in Suffolk Square, was 'free to cricketers at all times'. His business in Queen's Circus thrived. As an importer and manufacturer of 'all articles used in British sports and games' he capitalised on the period of Victorian prosperity.

Over a decade earlier the Great Exhibition had ushered in an age of affluence, great riches coming to some, although many remained poor. Despite reflecting these extremes of wealth and poverty, Cheltenham had recently received a seal of approval from Charles Dickens. After delivering one of his many public readings in the town, the author commented that 'all sorts of long visaged prophets' had told him that the people of the town were 'dull, stolid and slow', but he found them 'exactly the reverse in all aspects'.

Dickens' old friend, the actor-manager and great tragedian William Charles Macready, had already informed the eminent novelist, 'I do not think there is a town in England, or out of it, laid out with so much taste, such a continual intermixture of garden, villa, street and avenue . . . that with the shops and clubs and various institutions, gives the promise of a residence answering the demands of the most fastidious.'

Jem could see the opportunity that lay ahead of him. In a busy, enlightened town of some 40,000 inhabitants, that attracted a substantial number of well-to-do people for their holidays, there was a market for mixing sport and entertainment on a grand scale. In his youth he had witnessed the fun, popularity and growing interest that surrounded the well-established Canterbury Cricket Week. Now he could envisage creating a similar scene of multi-coloured tents, military bands and theatrical performances around first-class cricket in Cheltenham. He set about the task with enthusiasm and the finishing touch to his plan came in 1870 when, after much hard work, in particular the untiring efforts of Dr H. M. Grace, Gloucestershire cricket became organised on a county basis. Lillywhite now had access to a magnificent, large ground and close contacts with the ambitious, newly-formed Gloucestershire County Cricket Club which, in turn, had the greatest crowd-puller of all, the inimitable W. G. Grace.

CHAPTER TWO (1872-1877)

COUNTY CRICKET COMES TO CHELTENHAM

—— 1872 ——

On 18 July 1872, as foot and mouth disease spread throughout farms in the county, Gloucestershire began their first match on the College ground. The opposition was Surrey and the home side 'won in a canter'.

Two months earlier these two counties had played at the Oval. Gloucestershire should have won the contest by one run but, due to a dropped catch, lost by one wicket instead in a thrilling finish. Understandably both teams were equally keen to win the return fixture.

The first day's play, scheduled to commence at midday, was delayed by an hour until the players had all assembled. W.G. won the toss and decided to bat in front of a small, expectant crowd of several hundred spectators.

Surrey's Anstead quickly removed Dr E. M. Grace for a duck with a sharpshooter, then soon after bowled G. F. Grace. By the time W.G. walked in to bat, some 500 spectators had gathered and they cheered him loudly as he approached the wicket. Gloucestershire's champion played himself in and was starting to score runs when, on 15, he was lbw to a slower ball from the visitors' England bowler, James Southerton. The *Cheltenham Looker-On* reports that the Gloucestershire spectators 'were greatly disappointed as the "Hamlet" of the play was now removed', going on to say that the Surrey followers were 'exhuberant with delight, feeling sure that without "Grace" Gloucestershire would be defeated easily'.

But the home side was made of sterner stuff and went on to make a total of 221, largely thanks to half-centuries by the schoolmaster, Frank Townsend (father of the celebrated Charles), and George Strachan. Prestbury-born Strachan, one of the products of Jem's coaching, had captained the College XI in 1870 and bowled splendidly when

Cheltenham played Marlborough, his match haul of eleven wickets helping to steer the Cheltonians to a six wicket victory. Earlier in the season Strachan had captained Surrey. Now playing for the county of his birth, and back under the watchful eye of his mentor, the young all-rounder played a faultless innings, and in a splendid spell of bowling destroyed any hopes that Surrey might have had of winning. An even younger product of Jem's coaching also played for the home county. J. H. A. Tremenheere, had left College only a week earlier, his presence helping to build an association between school and county.

The Surrey reply was unconvincing and by two o'clock on the second day they had been bowled out for 108. Lunch was taken in a tent in front of the gymnasium, with the band of the 3rd Gloucestershire Artillery entertaining around 1500 spectators. At half past three, after a leisurely meal, play recommenced with Surrey needing 113 to avoid an innings defeat. In just under two and a half hours, W.G. (7 for 38) and Strachan (3 for 36), bowling unchanged, dismissed the visitors for 76.

With the contest ending so unexpectedly there was obvious disappointment amongst the crowd. Appreciating his responsibility as the event manager, Lillywhite organised a 'fun' game for the third day. Some of the Gloucestershire players were unable to stay, but the Surrey players remained in Cheltenham and formed a South of England XI with the inclusion of G. F. Grace and Strachan. The opposition was a Town Eighteen with the recent school-leaver Tremenheere. Alas, because the game had been arranged at the eleventh hour only a small group of onlookers had gathered at midday to watch play commence. The XI won easily and both Old Cheltonians made important contributions, as did a certain Mr E. Lawrence for the Eighteen. In the future he would play an important role in helping Lillywhite's plans to materialize. Meanwhile, three days of cricket had been played and Jem could look forward to the following year.

W.G. was to play for the county at Cheltenham every year until 1898. With other members of the Grace family, he gave the early matches their legendary quality, an invaluable commodity for Lillywhite as he planned for the future. Lillywhite's interest in Gloucestershire cricket would not falter from now until his untimely death in 1882.

Earlier in the year, with the publication of *James Lillywhite's Cricketers' Annual,* Jem had added yet another string to his bow. Edited by Charles Alcock, author, cricket administrator and later founder of the weekly magazine *Cricket*, the annual ran to three editions in its first year. Known as 'Red Lilly' because of the colour of its covers, its founder was following in the footsteps of other members of his family. In 1849, his brother Fred had compiled and edited the first edition of *Lillywhite's Guide to Cricketers*. It lasted until 1866, amalgamating the following year with the newly published *John Lillywhite's Cricketers' Companion*, which in its green paper covers was known as 'Green Lilly'. These popular annuals provided the cricket enthusiast with match reports, detailed statistics and a variety of charming sporting advertisements including one for the family sports equipment business.

—— 1873 ——

It is not clear what the financial arrangements were for Lillywhite's responsibilities in 1872, but there is no doubt that in 1873 he was paid the sum of £10 for managing the Cheltenham match. The visiting team, Sussex, contained none other than Jem's cousin, James Lillywhite junior, resulting in a conflict of allegiance for members of the family. Jem's brother John Lillywhite came to watch and stayed at the fashionable Queen's Hotel, along with James junior and other members of the two teams.

The first day of scheduled play was a disaster, being completely washed out by rain and high winds. The summer was proving to be rather sunless and wet, resulting in a poor corn harvest. The depression which sat over the College ground that day was insignificant compared to the feeling of gathering gloom that was starting to affect the whole country.

It was universally agreed that Britain was beginning to experience the onset of an economic depression, confined to no particular business but affecting trade and industry in general. Its strange feature was that production did not drop, but prices and profits started to fall: an anxious time for Lillywhite to be launching his planned speculative cricket venture.

At the College ground the gloom was forgotten the following day, with the opening period of play being dominated by the Graces. Hitting freely, E.M. and W.G. started the innings with a flourish, producing a partnership of 95 in the first hour. The rest of the day belonged to Frank Townsend, who became the first Gloucestershire player to score a century at Cheltenham. He was eventually dismissed the following day having scored 136, an innings described in *Wisden* as a 'masterly performance'. The pun aptly described the schoolmaster's score, which remained his highest for the county. He received a great ovation from the crowd and was later presented with a silver mounted bat by the delighted match manager.

From lunch until stumps were drawn, lively music was played by the band of the 3rd Gloucestershire Artillery, making a welcome return from the previous year. Gloucestershire amassed a total of 424 and by six o'clock when the game finished, Sussex had exhibited fine batting skills in reaching 212 for 5.

The match was drawn and after this, their last game of the season, acclaim was showered on the Gloucestershire cricketers. The youngest of the leading counties, with four victories and no defeats, they were awarded the title of joint champions with Nottinghamshire.

—— **1874** ——

Two people returned to Cheltenham the following year in different capacities from previous visits. Over a decade earlier William Caffyn, arguably the most elegant batsman of his generation, had made his appearance for the United All-England XI at the College. On his return from coaching cricket in Australia, Jem had persuaded this 'crack' to join him for the season and pass on some of his skill and knowledge of the game to the boys. While he was coaching the youngsters that May, a short way down the road the eleventh child of a Cheltenham doctor was born. Gilbert Jessop, destined to be a future Festival hero, took his first breath of Cotswold air.

The other reappearance at Cheltenham was that of George Strachan. Two years earlier he had helped to steer Gloucestershire to victory against Surrey. In 1874 Strachan returned as captain of the Surrey team and the Old Cheltonian was given a good trouncing as Gloucestershire propelled themselves to become outright county champions.

In early June at the Oval, Surrey had beaten Gloucestershire by an innings. Now, on a rather suspect Cheltenham wicket, the home side more than made amends for this earlier defeat. In only fifty-five minutes, the visitors were bowled out in one hundred balls for 27, and to this day it remains the lowest innings total made by any opponents on the ground. Gloucestershire's batting was a little more impressive and they gained a lead of 97. At the close of play on the first day, with Surrey following on, having already lost 2 wickets, a thousand disappointed spectators left. The next day, a hollow feeling hung over the ground and by lunch-time the game was over. Gloucestershire had won by an innings and 24 runs, with W.G. returning match figures of 14 for 66, a portent of the years to follow when he would often excel with a bowling performance if he had failed to middle with the bat.

In order to appease the disillusioned crowd, Lillywhite, who was again being paid £10 to manage the match, arranged for a scratch game to be played that afternoon. Townsend's XI scored 129 and W.G.'s XI replied with 77 for 2. Much to the amusement of players and spectators, batting with a broomstick, W.G. scored 35 and according to *M.C.C. Cricket Scores and Biographies,* 'his vast superiority to other cricketers was thus still more "strikingly" apparent.'

Two months later John Lillywhite died aged forty-eight. Nicknamed 'The Mud Bowler', he was the most talented cricketer of Old Lilly's progeny and was, according to *Wisden,* 'a right good fellow'. He was buried in Highgate Cemetery in the same grave as his father, mother and wife. James was at the graveside with other members of the family and friends from the cricketing fraternity.

Before his brother's death, James was already the senior partner in the firm of James Lillywhite, Frowd and Company. Now the sole survivor of his generation of the family, he would soon be joined in business, dealing in sporting goods and producing annual cricket publications, by his cousin James Lillywhite junior. This competent cricketer, who was to captain England in the first two Test matches in 1877, would later assist his cousin at the College, coaching the boys in the springtime before their important annual match against Marlborough.

—— **1875** ——

Jem took little notice of the contentious proposal put forward by Revd J. Greene, the county committee member from Clifton, and seconded by the club secretary E. M. Grace, that there should be no 'musical band' playing at Cheltenham. They objected to the 'noise and jovial atmosphere' on the ground. To them, cricket was an incorruptible Victorian pastime and they did not wish to allow an opening for the game to slip back to the sinful, boisterous gambling days of former times. The motion was defeated by just one vote and Jem immediately arranged for the Town Band to appear at the 1875 match against Sussex. They performed lively music during the lunch interval just after James Lillywhite junior had dismissed both W.G. and E.M. But the game belonged to Gloucestershire, who went on to win by 40 runs thanks to a splendid all-round performance by E.M., who scored 65 and 71 and took 5 wickets. Meanwhile, W.G.'s contribution to the dismissal of Sussex in their second innings had been to take up a position fielding right in front of the crease, just out of the bowler's line. He took three catches helped by this stance which intimidated and embarrassed the batsmen.

—— **1876** ——

The large crowd that gathered at Cheltenham for the 1876 match against Yorkshire was able to watch the final scene of one of the finest batting sagas ever witnessed. The hero was W.G. who was enjoying an *annus mirabilis*. During one week of August, in seventeen and a half hours at the crease, he piled up 839 runs in three innings, one of which was not out. He had begun by pasting the Kent bowlers at Canterbury while making 344 for the MCC. Then at Clifton his 177 made the renowned Nottinghamshire bowling attack look rather ordinary. Finally 'The Champion' came to Cheltenham. This was more than Lillywhite could have ever hoped for and it ensured that his future plans were fully justified and would soon be realised.

For their first visit to the College ground, the Yorkshire players were greeted by perfect weather conditions, hot sunshine tempered by a gentle breeze coming from the hills. The match started at noon; having won the toss, W.G. elected to bat and opened the innings with E.M. who was dismissed early on. The *Looker-On* reported, 'The fact that "the greatest cricketer of the age" was in, quickly spread over the town, and crowds of spectators hurried to the ground. So by lunch the largest crowd ever seen at Cheltenham were dispersed over the Playground, the Grand Stand in front of the gym crowded with fashionably dressed ladies and others of our residents not yet lingering by the sad sea waves.'

W.G. did not disappoint them. He batted, untroubled, reaching his century soon after lunch with a huge hit over square-leg onto the gymnasium roof off the bowling of Tom Emmett. More sixes crashed into the grandstand and onto the main tent while he mercilessly plundered the north country bowlers for eight hours, making 318* in the Gloucestershire total of 528. His innings remains the highest individual score ever made for the county and his fifth wicket partnership of 261 with Moberly, who scored 103, also stands as a record.

When last man J. A. Bush came to the crease, W.G. still needed a few more runs to get to 300. Bush, in his characteristic good humour, reassured his captain, remarking, 'All right, old man, I'll stay in until you get your runs,' and he did. Grace complimented the groundsman on the excellent condition of the wicket and modestly acknowledged that the runs were there in store just waiting for someone to score them. From this moment of masterly magic, Cheltenham never looked back.

During W.G.'s superlative performance, the Yorkshire fielders became totally demoralised. Having tried eight bowlers, the captain, Ephraim Lockwood, could not persuade anybody to bowl. When asked to bowl again, Hill declined, whereupon Emmett shouted to Lockwood, 'Why don't you make him bowl? You're captain!'

Hill tauntingly replied, 'Why don't you bowl yourself? You're frightened!'

These words incensed Emmett who had already bowled over fifty overs. He cussedly took the ball and promptly bowled three wides in succession. After the dust had settled the great Yorkshire bowler, with his customary wit, remarked, 'It was Grace before lunch, Grace after lunch, Grace all day.'

Rain meant that the match ended as a draw, but Jem had just what he wanted: records and publicity. To top it all, a fortnight later, the members of the famous coterie of Gloucestershire amateurs were crowned county champions again.

—— **1877** ——

In the spring, plans for a 'Cricket Week' began to unfold. Lillywhite wrote a letter to the county committee, supported by one from Revd T. A. Southwood who was now nearing retirement from the College, proposing a week of cricket instead of just one match. Lillywhite attended the meeting at the Grand Hotel in Bristol and explained and elaborated on his ideas, but after a prolonged discussion the committee decided that, as the 1877 matches had already been organised, nothing could be arranged for that year. The committee were in favour of Jem's innovative plan, looking to carry it out the following year. They requested that the secretary should ask Lord Fitzhardinge to write to Lord Redesdale seeking permission from the Cheltenham College Council to use the Playground for a week's cricket during the summer holidays.

At a meeting held at the House of Lords on 16 May 1877 the minutes reveal:

'An application from the Gloucestershire Cricket Club for permission to play their Annual Matches on the College Ground was granted, the Council reserving to itself the power of suspending the permission should circumstances require it. The Club to pay any sum that may be considered reasonable by the Council, towards the wear and tear of the Grand Stand on the occasions of the Club Meetings the Club also to communicate with the Finance Committee as to the necessary arrangements.'

With permission now granted by the Council, it was decided to put the matter on hold until after the end of the current season. Meanwhile Lillywhite started to make plans for the visit of Nottinghamshire that August.

For the first time a poster was printed to advertise the Cheltenham match. It revealed the interesting difference between the sides: Nottinghamshire had two amateurs and nine professionals in contrast to Gloucestershire's ten amateurs (although arguably the Graces were paid to perform) along with one professional. The latter was W. E. Midwinter, the county's first full-time professional, who was paid £8 a match. Billy Midwinter was born at St Briavels in the Forest of Dean, but at an early age had emigrated with his parents to Australia. Here he had learned his cricket and played against W.G. during the English tour of 1873/4. Grace was impressed and when Midwinter decided to try his luck playing cricket on English soil, he coaxed him to Gloucestershire.

Batting first, the home side lost early wickets, but the innings was propped up with a fine 83 by G. F. Grace. Rumours had arisen before the match that W.G. intended retiring from playing cricket at the end of the season, possibly an early example of sporting 'spin'. This concern had attracted a larger than usual crowd who were disappointed to see him struggle to make runs and eventually lose his wicket when on seventeen.

An excellent cold lunch was set out in a large marquee on the hospital side of the ground, supplied by Mr George, the cook and confectioner, who ran the Steam Bread and Biscuit Works in the High Street. His fine foods were always in demand by the town residents and he was the acclaimed manufacturer of the Royal Cheltenham Wafer, under the patronage of HRH the Princess of Wales.

After lunch the Gloucestershire innings progressed and the attendance increased, especially in the gymnasium enclosure, the *Looker-On* reporting that it became filled with 'the youth, beauty and fashion of Cheltenham and the neighbourhood'.

In reply to the county's total of 235, the visitors were bowled out for 111 and 79, with Arthur Shrewsbury top-scoring in both innings. Heavy

The first poster for a county match played on the College ground rain had fallen on the morning of the final day, and when play eventually started there followed an extraordinary finish. The remaining eight Nottinghamshire wickets were removed in fifty minutes for only 10 runs. W.G.'s match bowling analysis (76-36-89-17) was outstanding and remains a record bowling performance for Gloucestershire at Cheltenham.

Lillywhite had advertised the fact that, should there be an early finish to the county match, another contest would then be staged. The promise was fulfilled with a game that afternoon between the Gloucester XI with broomsticks and a Cheltenham XI with bats. The spectators were entertained by E.M. scoring 103 and Billy Midwinter making 58 in the 'broomsticks' total of 290 runs. At the close of play the 'batsmen' had replied with 50 for 2.

Gloucestershire's triumph was one of their seven victories of the season. Undefeated again, they had done even better than the previous year, thus retaining the county championship. The year 1877 saw the county at peak performance, but achievements in the following decade would be disappointingly moderate.

The committee kept to their word and at a meeting in the autumn they agreed to pay Lillywhite £120 to run two games over six days the following season. He was to be responsible for covering all the local expenses and would have to shoulder the risk of bad weather and therefore the possible loss of revenue from reduced gate money. Meanwhile, the committee decided to obtain tenders to put canvas around the College ground in order to prevent bystanders from watching the proceedings without paying.

CHAPTER THREE (1878-1882)

THE CRICKET WEEK

—— 1878 ——

The entrepreneur's plans materialized and with Sussex and Yorkshire the scheduled visitors, the 'Cricket Week' had arrived. Lillywhite worked hard organising a variety of social events for the Week. He planned musical concerts, theatrical performances and a special celebratory banquet. Such entertainments resembled the popular treats that annually awaited the pilgrims to the Canterbury Week and there was no reason why they should not succeed in Cheltenham. Accessibility and means of transport to the town continued to improve; visitor numbers were increasing, educational establishments were flourishing and there were many fashionable facilities on offer. The town was still reverberating with excitement at having recently been given Borough status and the wealthy mayor, Charles Conrad Adolphus de Ferrières, was more than willing to give the Week his full backing.

As he watched the twilight settle over the College buildings on the eve of the inaugural match against Sussex, Jem's expectations for the following six days must have been high. Doubtless he anticipated similar excitement to that experienced during the highlights of the Canterbury Week. He would also have recalled the visit he had organised to this very ground of the All-England XI. It was fortunate he was not to know Sussex would be incapable of challenging Gloucestershire, and the game would finish well before time on the second day.

On Monday 19 August, the first day of the Cricket Week, the weather was perfect and Jem had the ground looking in excellent condition. The match started at noon. W.G. won the toss, chose to bat and opened the innings with his cousin, W. R. Gilbert, who outshone the great man and helped the home side to a total of 198. Batting low down in the order, Revd Percy Hattersley-Smith, a member of the College teaching staff, made a valuable 51*, while Jesse Hide, the young Sussex fast bowler, returned impressive figures of 7 for 48. There were only a few spectators in the morning, but by the afternoon their numbers had increased. A large throng of Cheltenham's gentry had assembled in the grandstand and enclosure and there was strong support for the visitors in front of the tents and elsewhere around the ground.

With admission one shilling a day and entrance to the grandstand an extra sixpence (with various allowances for schools, colleges and subscribers), there would have to have been exceptional circumstances for Lillywhite not to break even. Better still, with six days of cricket scheduled he might easily make a profit.

That evening a large audience, including the cricketers and their friends, were entertained in the theatre by the 'Philo-Thespians', a group of 'distinguished lady and gentlemen amateurs'. Various comedy acts received rapturous applause, but the *crème de la crème* was the performance of Mr Edgar Manning, in cricketing attire, imitating W.G. while singing a comic song.

Before lunch the following day, the two Gloucestershire opening batsmen, with help from a little overnight rain, had bowled out the visitors for 29 in just thirty-one overs. W.G. took 6 for 18 and Gilbert 4 for 8; James Lillywhite junior had made nought. The growing number of spectators then witnessed Sussex reach 51 for 2 by the lunchbreak, during which Mr Pollock's Town Band played a choice selection of music, while many of those present enjoyed one of Mr George's delicious luncheons for 2*s*. 6*d*. The crowd had grown by the start of the afternoon and were looking forward to an entertaining session of play. But by five o'clock W.G., bowling unchanged, took 7 for 88, and in skittling out the visitors steered his team to victory by an innings and 24 runs.

While a 'large and fashionable company of people' enjoyed another splendid evening of music and comedy at the theatre, Lillywhite hastily arranged a scratch game for the following day. He dropped the idea of the advertised contest between Gloucestershire with broomsticks versus Cheltenham with bats. Instead he invited players from both county sides to join together and form a United South of England team to play his tried and trusted friends, the Eighteen of Cheltenham. A reasonable crowd watched an entertaining day's play which ended unresolved when stumps were drawn at six o'clock. An hour later saw the onset of what was arguably the highlight of the Week.

Earlier in the year, while Lillywhite had been planning the event, he had contacted the popular Mayor de Ferrières who had generously pledged his support for the occasion by offering to host a banquet. The grandson of a Napoleonic general, de Ferrières, who had been naturalized as an Englishman, lived in the new Bayshill House, built on the site of Fauconberg House where King George III once stayed.

Just before seven o'clock on Wednesday evening, in the middle of this first Cricket Week, the mayor made his way from his fine residence to the Plough Hotel to welcome his invited guests. The seventeenth century coaching inn, situated on the High Street in the heart of the town, overlooked the piece of ground once used for a five hour Cudgel Match. As recently as a century ago, contests took place in which participants were encouraged by the advertisement: 'He that breaks the most heads in three bouts, and comes off clear, to receive a good hat, and a guinea in money'. Tonight's proceedings would be more genteel, befitting the gracious and elegant spa town of Cheltenham. For several years the Plough had been the venue for a celebratory supper attended by Jem after the College 'Old v. Present' match, an excellent evening where champagne flowed freely and the masters kept a low profile. This occasion would be somewhat grander.

The mayor's complimentary banquet for W.G. and other members of the Gloucestershire XI also included invitations to other cricketers, the members of Cheltenham Town Council, local clergy, other local mayors and a number of Alderman Baron de Ferrières' personal friends. A small number of tickets priced at 7s. 6d. each were sold to members of the general public. Many more could have been sold, but space was limited. Just over a hundred guests, including Lillywhite and his right-hand man Edwin Lawrence, sat down in the Yeomanry Mess Room. The mayor was supported on his right by W.G., the Mayor of Gloucester and the Member of Parliament Mr Agg-Gardner. On his left were seated the Sussex captain, Revd F. F. Greenfield, the Mayor of Tewkesbury and Revd E. S. Carter, captain of the Yorkshire team who would be competing the following day.

When all those present had been well wined and dined, the mayor handed the claret-filled 'loving cup' to the Gloucestershire captain. The magnificent cup, which had recently been presented to the Corporation by de Ferrières, was being used for the first time at a public banquet and W.G. drank from it to the sound of loud applause. Amidst cheers and laughter, speeches were delivered and toasts proposed to 'The Health of the Queen and Royal Family'; 'Success to the Cricket Week'; 'The Gloucestershire Eleven'; 'The Sussex and Yorkshire Elevens'; 'The Health of the Mayor of Cheltenham' and 'The Press'.

Throughout the speeches fond references were made to Lillywhite's hard work, determination to overcome difficulties and ambition to hold

The Plough Hotel in Cheltenham High Street where the
Cricket Week dinner was held in 1878

the Cricket Week. It was not surprising, therefore, that he received the loudest and warmest ovation of the evening when he rose to speak. He thanked everyone who had helped him organise the event and the mayor for his support and generosity, in particular the splendid banquet he had hosted. He went on to thank the College Council for granting the use of their magnificent ground and acknowledged Gloucestershire CCC, and finally his 'old friend', W. G. Grace, for the help he had given.

He then touched on the business side of cricket match management, telling the audience that his profit from the 1872 game had been £4, reasoning that this was partly because in those days Cheltenham knew little about cricket. He went on to report that to date the subscription list had already reached £150 and the total continued to grow as people he met in the town kept asking him to add their names. He concluded by saying he felt strongly that they had every reason to be 'thankful for the present and hopeful for the future'. As the clock approached midnight, the toasts, which had been interspersed with 'comic and sentimental songs', came to an end. The mayor and many of the guests departed, but a small group remained in the hotel room until the early hours of the morning, leaving little time for sleep before the start of the Yorkshire match.

Two months earlier Yorkshire had beaten the county at Sheffield and it was evident by the strength of the team they had brought to Cheltenham that they were aiming to complete the double. With strong competition in the air, a large crowd had assembled by the start of play. The visitors won the toss and two of the best batsmen in England, Lockwood and Ulyett, opened their innings. Throughout the day an ever-increasing number of spectators, including many members of 'the fair sex', watched with interest from the grandstand and saw the game fluctuate. At lunch Yorkshire were 68 for 6, but by the close of play they had fought back to 212 for 9. Stubborn opening bat, Louis Hall, made 82* and W.G. bowled 86 overs taking 6 for 77.

Later, many of the afternoon's onlookers made their way to the newly-constructed 'Winter Garden', prettily decorated and illuminated, to attend a Grand Promenade Concert given by the Town Band under the direction of Mr Pollock. They had already given great pleasure when playing earlier in the day at the College ground and were only half way through their evening programme when the heavens opened and the concert abruptly ended. The rain continued that night and at intervals during the next day, preventing a ball from being bowled. This left too much to be squeezed into the last day and the game ended as a draw. It

Baron de Ferrières who hosted the first Cricket Week
dinner in 1878 at the Plough Hotel

The loving cup from which W.G. Grace took the first sip

was the only disappointment in an entertaining six days. Jem was praised in the press and the initial Cheltenham Week was pronounced 'a social success'.

—— 1879 ——

Heavy rain clouds returned again the following August creating an unwelcome presence throughout the 1879 Week. During thirty-six hours before the start of the first match, three and a half inches of rain fell over Cheltenham. Saturday evening's violent thunderstorm was accompanied by heavy rain which continued throughout the night and most of Sunday. That day, roads flooded and the normally quiet and gentle flowing River Chelt burst its banks close to the ground at Sandford and raged through the town.

Early on Monday morning, the first day of the match against Yorkshire, ominous clouds were blowing in from the west, but by noon, when play started, the sun was shining brightly. W.G., Midwinter and G.F. bowled the visitors out for 135 and by the close of play a considerable crowd had watched Gloucestershire reach 57 for 4.

The following day the rain returned and continually hampered play leaving too much to be completed on the final day and the game finished as a draw. This was not before the home side reached 269 with useful contributions by G.F., Midwinter and Moberley.

James Lillywhite's Cricketers' Annual reported that 'the Yorkshire bowlers could not get a foothold in the mud', but everything slid into place on the social scene. After the frustrating day's play on Tuesday, a hilarious evening had been enjoyed by a very large audience at the Theatre Royal. The Royal Cheltenham Comedians performed the comedietta *Cut off with a Shilling* and the farce *Whitebait at Greenwich*. The evening concluded with the comic operetta *The Blind Beggars* which received much loud applause.

The new mayor, Alderman H. Willmott, held a Grand Banquet at the Plough Hotel on Wednesday evening, following the example of his predecessor. Numbers were slightly down compared with the inaugural year, but the format was similar and at the end everyone agreed it had been another 'jolly' evening.

The second match was against a strong and well-organised Nottinghamshire team. Despite inclement weather, there was a good crowd for the game which dealt a surprise to the home side. The

Gloucestershire players, watched by a number of smartly dressed ladies wearing new style 'pinafores', battled their way to 123 by the end of the first afternoon.

That evening's entertainment was a Grand Ballad Concert at the Winter Garden. A group of well-known vocalists, with Madame Edith Wynne as the 'prima donna', performed various compositions 'admirably', as did the talented instrumentalists. There was some doubt as to whether the event would be well-attended due to the time of year. It was generally recognised that many of the town's concert goers were 'by the salt sea waves' throughout the summer holidays. There was no need for concern; the Cricket Week and all its attractions had more devotees than might have been realised.

Next morning, with warm sunshine drying a damp wicket, Nottinghamshire quickly lost their way against the bowling of W.G. (6 for 37) and Midwinter (4 for 23), and they were all out for 65 in sixty-eight overs. Enthusiastic supporters gathered in and around Mr George's tent for lunch to congratulate the Gloucestershire team, seemingly on course for victory, but the visitors had other ideas.

By the close of play, bowling and fielding splendidly, they had dismissed their hosts for 119. England's foremost bowler of the time, Alfred Shaw, had taken 5 for 14 and the visitors needed 178 to win the next day. The concluding entertainment of the week took place that evening with a Promenade Concert, Athletic Sports and Display of Fireworks in Montpellier Gardens.

There were more fireworks on the cricket field the following day as the visitors tackled what seemed like a rather stiff task. But a sparkling second wicket partnership of 140 between the brilliant young batsman Arthur Shrewsbury (87) and William Barnes (53), steered Nottinghamshire to a splendid 6 wicket victory which meant that Gloucestershire lost their unbeaten record for inter-county matches on the ground.

The season had been a poor one for the county, with only one victory. The summer weather was disastrous, bringing one of the worst harvests of the century and increasing illness and disease amongst farm livestock. From early May to late August there were probably no more than three consecutive days of hot, dry, settled conditions and the adverse weather had undoubtedly limited the attendance during the Week.

In Bristol the success of Lillywhite's Cheltenham venture was not being so well received, and at a committee meeting the astonishing proposal was made that all five of the county's home matches should be played at Clifton. It was a disheartening time with fears there might be no more cricket at Cheltenham. Thankfully for Lillywhite, and all those who have enjoyed the subsequent matches on the College ground, the proposal was defeated - by one vote.

—— **1880** ——

The new decade treated spectators at Cheltenham with two of the finest batting performances of the year. Although the sun shone only spasmodically, such was the growing attractiveness and popularity of the Week, attendances were larger than at anytime before.

Proceedings opened on Monday 16 August with the return of Nottinghamshire. The side included many players from the previous year and the team, enjoying a very successful season, was close to winning the county championship. Following on, Gloucestershire just managed to score enough runs to force a draw, largely thanks to the stubborn resistance of William Moberly. Given a little more time, the visitors would have won comfortably. The feature of the match was a chanceless five and three quarter hour innings of 143 by the outstanding William Barnes. This was the first century of the Week, and Barnes was becoming increasingly familiar with the charming Cotswold setting. During his short innings William Gunn managed to hit the ball onto the clock tower, while Fred Morley, one of the great left-handed bowlers of this time, ended with the heroic match figures of 132-66-155-10.

After play on the second day, the entertainment started. A large expectant audience gathered at the Theatre Royal for *A Dramatic Performance*. The evening opened with the reading of a prologue especially written for the occasion and liberally laced with topical puns:

> 'I come to bid you welcome, none the less
> That Chelt'nam's in her August emptiness.
> A hundred ways her fickle children range,
> Spending their *cash* in seeking some *small change,*
> So much the more for you - she spreads her charms;
> For you she opens wide her ample arms,
> And welcomes all who come to taste the fare
> Our stout *Jim Lillywhite* has made his care;
> He'll try to give you what you come to seek,
> And hopes the teams are strong for all the *week.*
> In your applause may his reward be found,-

The *Play* to-night - the *Play* upon the ground.
May the *brave* cricketers (the joke is old,
That every *batsman* must of needs be *bowled*)
Show you, ere either does to other yield,
An even fight upon a well-fought field!
Then, whether Fortune smile whilst those accost her
Who form the pride of our rich vales of Glo'ster,
And crown again with victory's wreath eternal
The prowess of the Graces and "the Colonel";
Or aid fair Surrey's Captain (Cheltenham born),
And give once more *extr'or'nary* luck to *Strachan;*
Or make those drawers of the winning lots
Who should be Titans (tight uns) bound to live in (k)Notts,
The friendly rivalry none shall annoy.
But, oft these pleasant days of wholesome joy
Shall come to memory when drear Winter's nights
Send other *bats* upon their noiseless flights,
When *balls* come quick (though from no bowler's arm),
When jailors *keep the wicke* (*d, t,*) and the charm
Of *Fielding* lights the quiet reader's path, -
The only cricket - *Cricket on the hearth.*
Till once more jocund Summer in her train
Shall bring you here for welcome once again.
To-night our actors - I won't call them *stars* -
Will first present you with their "Family Jars".'

Mr E. H. Hudson, the 'celebrated comedian', was joined by 'London theatre performers' Miss Lizzie Henderson and Miss Kate Carlyon. A handful of amateur players helped to make up the cast for the performances of Lunn's comedy *Family Jars* and the two farces *Turn Him Out* and *To Paris and Back for Five Pounds*. The popular county cricketer W. R. Gilbert took to the stage in *Turn Him Out,* his performance as 'Nicodemus Nobbs' causing roars of laughter from the 'amused and contented' audience. A reliable batsman and useful slow round-arm bowler, Walter Gilbert was often overshadowed on the field by the Grace brothers, his cricketing cousins. On stage, however, he was unchallenged by them: there was no possibility whatsoever of the Graces changing from greensward to greenroom.

This year, the similarity between entertainment at Cheltenham and that performed at the Canterbury Cricket Week was clear to see. Gilbert was doing what many of the Kentish players had done for years, exchanging daytime cricketing attire for Thespian apparel in the evenings. The Old Stagers, by now a well-established company, had been formed almost forty years earlier to provide amusement after the close of the day's play and to encourage visitors to stay in the cathedral city for the whole week. Performances by Tom Taylor, Nicholas Felix and William Yardley, together with other Kent cricketers and professional actors and actresses, epitomized the spirit of the Week. There was no reason why Cheltenham could not mirror these productions. The ingredients were present with a vibrant theatre, fashionable life in town and the growing appeal of the event.

The third Grand Banquet took place at the Plough Hotel on Wednesday evening. The mayor, Alderman W. N. Skillicorne, invited the three competing teams, their staff and some of his personal friends, along with a small number of paying guests. Numbers were depleted because the Nottinghamshire team had to leave Cheltenham and travel north as soon as play was over, so they would be ready to entertain Middlesex the following morning. The Surrey eleven did not arrive in time, having finished their match at Brighton an hour before the dinner started. So between sixty and seventy people sat down to eat their way through a mouthwatering bill of fare.

MENU

Clear Mock-Turtle Soup   Pea Soup

Boiled Salmon   Lobster Sauce   Fried Whiting   Stewed Eels

Lobster Patties   Sweetbreads à la Mushrooms
Stewed Kidneys   Curried Veal

Fore-quarter of Lamb   Boiled Chickens   Sirloin of Beef
York Ham   Ducks   Venison.

Berkeley Hunt Pudding   Fruit Tarts
Boiled Custards
Apricot Cream   Wine Jelly   Anchovy Toast

Dessert.

His worship the mayor presided at the top table with local dignitaries and the Gloucestershire players nearby. At the end of the meal the mayor rose to speak and toasted the Queen and other members of the royal family and he was followed by Sir Brook Kay who proposed 'Success to the Cricket Week'. He then toasted Jem who acknowledged the compliment and reported that even now, only half-way through the Week, it was already a financial success.

Prominent amongst the diners were the celebrated 'Three Graces' who were thoroughly enjoying themselves; but soon tragedy was to follow. After the Cheltenham fixture the triumverate of Graces played for England against Australia at the Oval in the first ever home-staged Test match. Fred collected a pair, did not bowl, but took a magnificent running catch to dismiss the bearded giant hitter, George Bonnor. A fortnight later, following a severe cold with 'congestion of the lungs', dearly loved Fred, aged only thirty, died. Tall and well-built, and the youngest of the five brothers, this stylish, middle-order batsman and round-arm fast bowler had been considered by W.G. to be 'the best of them all'.

Fred Grace's last Cheltenham match was against Surrey starting the morning after the mayor's banquet. For an all-round performance this was Midwinter's game, while Fred took his leave quietly - run out for nought and taking no wickets. Surrey batted first and made 285, thanks largely to the contribution from the prolific W. W. Read (93), while Midwinter (87-52-81-5) worked hard for his money. Gloucestershire replied with 351, Midwinter (103) leading the way with what was regarded as one of the finest batting performances of the year, and the visitors started their second innings 68 runs in arrears around lunch time on the final day. Then followed some outstanding bowling by W.G. (7 for 65) which paved his way, assisted by Gilbert, to knock off the 52 runs needed for victory in only twenty-six of the remaining forty minutes. This ten wicket win was sweet revenge, for the county's only defeat of the season had been earlier in the summer by Surrey at the Oval.

—— **1881** ——

A cloud hung over the county at the start of the 1881 season. For the last decade, the side had been built around the Grace brothers, so Fred's departure left a huge gap. Fortunately new faces emerged with W. A. Woof and A. D. Greene making their Cheltenham debuts, by which time the side was enjoying a reasonably successful season.

The Week was growing in prominence. The results of Jem's conscientious efforts and his determination to overcome difficulties were there for all to see. Ever-increasing attendances, a good profit margin and complimentary coverage in the national press illustrated the popularity of this event. Some members of the public were starting to have more leisure time and were enjoying the excitement of watching championship county cricket. But continuous hard work was beginning to have a seriously detrimental effect on Jem's health.

Everything scheduled was much the same as before, with Yorkshire the old rivals and Somerset the new ones. The weather was familiarly unpredictable, but it did not stop the military band from playing or large crowds gathering for Mr George's refreshments, especially his two o'clock 2s. 6d. lunches. Mr Brookes' scorecard business thrived, re-printing at the fall of every wicket and charging 2d. for each up-to-date issue.

As usual, there were beneficial arrangements offered to passengers by the Midland and Great Western Railway companies. Cheap return tickets were available and excursion trains at low fares ran from London, South Wales, Bristol, Birmingham and many of the smaller intermediate stations. The Theatre Royal was poised ready with its planned production and three nights of Promenade Concerts at Montpellier Gardens were arranged. Available from James Lillywhite's Emporium at 3, Queen's Circus were tickets at 21s. each for the Grand Banquet, admission tickets to the College ground and weekly subscriptions.

The eleven professionals of Yorkshire reached 267 in their first innings. The Lockwood brothers - the visitors' answer to the Graces - batted admirably in a partnership of 76 when early wickets fell. By mid-afternoon on the second day, with the hosts building their reply, heavy rain ended play.

Luckily a treat was in store. The cricketers and many visitors converged on the theatre that evening to see performances of *Nine Points of the Law* and the drama *Robert Macaire!* An appreciative full house was well entertained by a talented cast including the regulars, Mr Shenton and the Misses Henderson and Carlyon. The latter also delivered a specially arranged interlogue, during which loud applause 'broke out' when Miss Carlyon mentioned the founder's name:

> 'True cricketers no cogging practice know,
> No tricks to make a friend nor mar a foe.

"May the best man win," for an example bright
Comes Cheltenham to the fore with Lillywhite.'

Finishing the popular verse . . .

'And now a word of pardon for the time
I've tried your patience with my foolish rhyme.
May cricket flourish, and with rapid pace
Advance in popularity and *Grace;*
And *Lillywhite* reward substantial gain,
To prove his efforts have not been in vain.
Adieu! I really now must disappear,
With hopes to meet you all again, next year.'

The following morning bright sunshine bathed the ground while preparations went ahead for the final day's play. As mid-morning approached, so too did uninvited dark clouds, blown in by prevailing winds. After heavy showers, play started at noon, and Gloucestershire proceeded to a total of 254 thanks to the middle-order batsmen Gilbert (53), Cranston (63), Moberly, Townsend and Midwinter. In two hours of play, from tea until six o'clock when the match was declared a draw, Yorkshire galloped along to 194 for 3, despite having to compete against Bush who, for the first time in a county match, bowled some of his 'fast underhands'.

As was customary, the players were invited to the mayor's banquet that night. It was held for the first time at the fashionable Queen's Hotel. Opened in 1838 on the site of the old Imperial Spa, the hotel was in an ideal situation described in the *Looker-On* as being 'at the end of one of the finest carriage drives in this, or perhaps in any other, country upon rising ground, and commanding, consequently, the most extensive and picturesque views'. The imposing building, with its six Corinthian columns, attracted a different clientele from the Plough, 'once the town's leading hotel', which was still very much a traditional coaching inn.

The Yorkshire team snubbed their invitation. Times were changing and they were not the first group of independent minded professionals to place money before merriment; they left the town immediately the match was over to prepare for their fixture the following day. The *Looker-On* reported that 'the gentlemen of Somersetshire, however, behaved more courteously' attending the dinner along with the Gloucestershire players and other guests. After an excellent meal, washed down with a plentiful supply of wine from the Queen's Hotel cellars, the format followed the same as in previous years, with customary toasts loyally received.

This was going to be the last banquet that Jem would attend and it was his final response to the 'Success to the Cricket Week' toast. To hearty cheers, he explained how he had once thought that this was his most difficult task. Now, he felt, it had become one of his most pleasant undertakings because it gave him the opportunity to thank his friends for their loyal support. He then thanked the College Council for lending the ground and the county club for their patronage and workable business arrangement. Amidst further cheers he praised the Graces, lamenting the absence of Fred, and then thanked the residents of Cheltenham who were 'away on holiday at the moment', but who had supported the event with their subscriptions. His final words, according to the *Cheltenham Examiner,* were that he hoped 'he had done something to promote a love of the game in Cheltenham'. He certainly had, for attendances were growing and over one hundred and twenty years later the event would still be flourishing.

The local derby match started the following morning. Settled weather encouraged a large crowd and by early afternoon the grandstand was nearly full. Winning the toss, Somerset chose to bat and by mid-afternoon they were all out for 198 as a result of steady bowling by the Gloucestershire professionals Midwinter and Woof. Left-armer 'Woofie' - bowler, errand runner and baggage man - was only in his second year of employment for the county and his 4 for 56 helped to put the neighbours in their place. In the home team's reply of 184, new boy Greene, the previous summer's captain of Oxford University, made nought and was one of four dismissals made by wicket-keeper F. J. Sainsbury. Midwinter (5 for 35) and W.G. skittled out Somerset in their second innings and the hosts won comfortably by 7 wickets.

Lillywhite had always ensured that the press were warmly toasted and courted at the mayor's banquet. He had many friends in the profession through his own involvement in the world of publishing with his annual, so subsequent glowing reports that appeared in *The Field* and *Bell's Life* must have delighted him. The former stated that the event 'though young in years, has already attained to a degree of importance little short of that held by the Canterbury Week'. The article went on:

'In many respects the two Weeks form a strong contrast, and some of the faults found with the older institution are not to be met with in the new . . . At Cheltenham, for instance, the cricket is county cricket, pure and simple, and the interest in the results of the matches is far greater than that felt at Canterbury, where people assemble to watch the play of individuals rather than of combined elevens.'

Commenting about the fact that the month of August in Cheltenham was supposed to be quiet and the town deserted, *The Field* confirmed there had been large attendances each day 'in spite of unpropitious weather . . . The grandstand has been filled with ladies who, through sunshine and rain, have watched the matches with evident delight, and applauded with a degree of warmth seldom heard on a cricket ground.' The report concluded that none of this would have been possible without the efforts of James Lillywhite who 'in spite of many drawbacks and difficulties, has worked the week up to its present state of popularity'.

Bell's Life made the point that originally 'Cheltenham was not what one might term a cricketing town . . . the worthy inhabitants were not exactly mad on the subject'. It went on to point out that the town had now developed 'the taste for cricket . . . owing to the capital displays which have been exhibited'. The report further emphasised the part played by Jem in the success of the Week, highlighting the 'energy displayed' in overcoming difficulties:

'It is only those, however, who have undertaken to carry out such matters that can fully realise the difficulties that beset the path of one who has taken upon himself the task. Petty jealousies are at once aroused, and more often than not the prime mover in the business gives way in despair. Mr Lillywhite says that his path has not been strewn with roses. Indifferent to coldness and apathy, he has persevered, and we are happy to say that he has come off triumphantly, having created an institution in their midst which must ultimately prove a great benefit to the town. In years to come we hope the honoured name of the son of one of England's greatest exponents of cricket will become a "household word" in the county of Gloucestershire and Cheltenham for having established one of the most successful of cricket weeks.'

—— **1882** ——

Over the following months Jem's health began to deteriorate and by the summer he was visibly declining. Responsibility for running the Cricket Week gradually moved to Edwin Lawrence, by now his son-in-law, who, amongst many other things, ran the Montpellier Coal Exchange and had already been involved with the event for many years. A keen and skilful player in scratch matches, he had assisted his father-in-law preparing the ground, supplying tickets and collecting subscriptions. Engrossed in business and public affairs in the town, Lawrence, who had achieved great renown as a local cricketer, had abandoned his personal participation in outdoor sports some twenty years earlier, but had kept in touch as a committee member, honorary officer, or prominent supporter of local cricket, football, cycling and athletic clubs.

The weather for the fifth annual Week was unsettled and the illness of James Lillywhite added further gloom, although he remained the event promoter and was involved with all the arrangements, with his son-in-law's valuable support. Off-the-field entertainment was planned to include theatre performances of Dance's well known comedy *Naval Engagements* and the farce *Chisselling*.

Talk before the match against Middlesex was about W.G. who had gone through the season without scoring a hundred. The Cheltenham crowd would have loved to see his form improve and his fortune change, but, for the time being, it did not. He scored only 47 runs in three innings.

Gloucestershire batted first and by lunch, when both sides were entertained in a marquee by the mayor, they were already in trouble and were soon all out in the afternoon for 144. Middlesex replied confidently and gained a first innings lead of just over 80. The hosts then collapsed to some admirable bowling by C. T. Studd (8 for 71) and the visitors went on to win comfortably by 8 wickets. During the match a new gadget was on show for the first time: a scoreboard. The *Looker-On* reported that this 'novelty in telegraph' was exhibited by a Mr Denning of Chard with 'the board being quickly manipulated'. It was considered 'decidedly a great improvement on the present style of marking'.

Another new attraction on the ground was Pooley's malt bread supplied by Mr George, who had recently been appointed an agent for the manufacture of this popular product at the Steam Bread and Biscuit Works in town. More easily digested and agreeable to the palate, being 'sweet, moist and nutritious' - and boasting laxative qualities - the malt bread had also been the subject of many glowing testimonials from members of the medical profession.

With regard to results, it was becoming a disastrous season for the club, so Lillywhite, whose health had temporarily taken a 'favourable turn', must have been delighted with the performance of the sixteen-year-old William Wade Fitzherbert Pullen. Facing a strong Yorkshire attack which included six magnificent bowlers - Peate, Ulyett, Bates, Hill, Emmett and Hall - the 'colt' played a faultless innings (71) before being run out. The visitors' reply to the Gloucestershire total of 256 was disappointing. They were dismissed for 115, then following on they slumped to 96 all out, with Townsend taking four catches, giving the hosts victory by an innings and 45 runs. Once again, Woof showed his ability ending up with match analysis of 9 for 66.

Soon after the Week had finished Lillywhite went to London to see if the physicians there could halt his deteriorating condition. There was nothing that could be done and on his return to Cheltenham he became confined to bed. Yet such was the nature of the man that he bore his affliction 'with patient, cheerful resignation'.

During this distressing time, at a committee meeting on 27 October it was resolved that 'in the event of the death of James Lillywhite before the matches at Cheltenham in 1883, his son-in-law, Mr Lawrence, or the representatives of the family, shall have the management of the Week'. Wise men look ahead and make preparations for the future, but this tactless presumption that Lillywhite would not survive until the following Week left an uneasy feeling festering between both family and committee.

But sadly the presumption proved to be founded and on 24 November, at his home 3, Queen's Circus, James Lillywhite died at the age of fifty-seven.

There were many heartfelt tributes. One read, 'Unpretentious and unostentatious in all he did, it is only natural that he became immensely popular with all classes of cricketers.' Another described his attitude to the game saying, 'He had the welfare of the game thoroughly and conscientiously at heart - his passion for it was undying.' This had been demonstrated earlier in the year in an article he had written entitled 'A Good Natured Growl' in which he shared his concern over such matters as unfair bowling and inadequate umpiring. His large 'troop of friends' paid tribute to his 'unvarying amiability and good humour', recalling his gentle rebukes of 'Oh, deary, deary' in coaching sessions at the College and his exhortation to 'Play gentlemen, play!'

The funeral was held on Wednesday 29 November. Many of the shops in the town closed for part of the day and most of the houses in Montpellier displayed signs of respect. At the town cemetery, overlooked by Cleeve Hill, the mourners included his widow and two daughters. His son-in-law, Edwin Lawrence, and cousin, James Lillywhite, were present together with other members of the family, while E. M. Grace and W. R. Gilbert attended, with several business associates and many other friends. As a mark of respect for their mentor, between fifty and sixty senior

A contemporary view of the building which housed Lillywhite's 'emporium' at
3, Queen's Circus, and where he died in November 1882.
Illustration by Aylwin Sampson

College boys walked bareheaded in front of the hearse from the cemetery gates and formed a guard of honour on either side of the entrance to the chapel. Several College masters were present and the graveside ceremony was concluded with a reading by the principal Revd Dr Kynaston. Over his grave a plain white cross, topped by a dove of peace, was erected by 'past and present Cheltonians' in recognition of his twenty-five years as cricket professional at the College. Fourteen years later his wife, Eliza, was laid to rest beside him, followed only two years later by Winifred Mary their six-year-old granddaughter.

James Lillywhite had lived and worked in the town for over a quarter of a century. As Playground manager and cricket coach at the College he had made many warm and longstanding friendships. With his sports equipment business he had won the respect of his fellow townsmen as a persevering and upright retailer. As co-lessee of the Montpellier Rotunda and Gardens, his capable and cheery management skills were invaluable. However, the real gem, his *pièce de résistance*, was to establish the Cricket Week. He was lucky enough to witness the start and early development of his creation, but his untimely death prevented him from observing the full fruit of his labours, the Cheltenham Cricket Festival: Lillywhite's legacy.

CHAPTER FOUR (1883-1889)

TOURIST ATTRACTION

—— 1883 ——

Since its establishment in 1878, the Cricket Week had not experienced a spell of splendid weather equal to that enjoyed in 1883, the prolonged sunshine encouraging a large crowd. Edwin Lawrence shouldered the responsibility of organising the event, the proceeds from which were donated by the committee to Jem's widow as a token of the esteem in which her late husband had been held.

Lawrence was the right man for the challenging position. Educated at the Grammar School, he had been the acknowledged 'dux' at the time of the bitter 'black-tassel controversy' with the Collegians. The latter resented Grammar School boys wearing mortar-boards and 'Homeric combats' arose in which young Lawrence featured prominently. Recently he had taken a leading part in the formation of the Conservative Club in Albion Street and was voted the first secretary in its palmy days, while in another role, as secretary of the Poor Relief Committee, he was able to do much work on behalf of the underprivileged. He was universally liked and respected and he understood both the business and playing aspects of the game.

By 20 August, when the match against Surrey started, an exceptional harvest was being gathered in around the county. A fine yield of potatoes was reported and an excellent gathering of apples 'free from grubs'. There was a bulky hay harvest and the corn crops on the Cotswold Hills had never been better. Conversely, the county's fortunes on the cricket field were poor, but when W.G. (5 for 91) and Woof (4 for 42) dismissed the visitors for 261, hopes started to rise. They had been closely watched by Surrey's Edward Barratt who stood in as umpire at the start of his team's innings until he was needed to bat, because one of the nominated umpires had failed to arrive. Then came Gloucestershire's feeble reply. In two and a half hours they were bowled out for 109 despite the 'vigorous and plucky' batting of H. V. Page. A recent recruit to the side, having captained the College XI the previous year, Page, now an Oxford blue, had gone in to bat with the county on 32 for 5 and doggedly scored 50 out of the next 77. Following on, the hosts were all out for 171, mesmorized by the fine, slow, left-arm bowling of the erstwhile umpire Barratt. This great spinner of the ball took 7 for 74 and finished with a match analysis of 12 for 121, forming part of the huge haul of 176 wickets which he took for Surrey during the season.

The visitors won by 9 wickets before lunch on the final day. This was a big disappointment for the Wednesday half-holiday residents of the town, and for a large party of excursionists who arrived from Cardiff and other places en route only to find the cricket was over. In the Assembly Room that evening a party of Tyrolese Minstrels played Swiss and Tyrolean melodies, while the county's cricketers awaited the arrival of a strong Nottinghamshire side on course to win the championship.

Glorious weather greeted the midlanders who batted first and reached 276 thanks to Barnes (86). Gloucestershire's batting was fragile; W.G. failed again and over half the side were out before the total reached 100. Then followed a magnificent, record-setting, ninth wicket stand of 129 between Page (93) and W. O. Vizard (49*). This was undoubtedly young Page's week, for when he was given out lbw seven short of his century, he was carried triumphantly into the pavilion shoulder high, and presented with a handsome travelling clock by fellow Old Cheltonians in recognition of his fine scores. The tail-enders partnership averted the follow-on and the large crowd were then treated to a feast of Nottinghamshire runs. Arthur Shrewsbury made 57 in his best style and Flowers (73), Gunn (77) and Selby (100) all punished the tired Gloucestershire bowlers, before rain washed out the last day and the match ended as a draw.

—— **1884** ——

When the fixtures for this season were announced there had been great excitement on discovering that the Australian touring team were 'coming to town'. Local businessmen were overjoyed for it had long been the case that August was a quiet month in the town, the residents migrating to the seaside; the tourist trade needed a boost and the Australians might provide it.

Ten days before the touring team arrived, they had drawn a high scoring game with the county at Clifton in which W.G. made an unbeaten hundred. So great interest surrounded the return fixture, especially as former county professional Billy Midwinter was now playing for the tourists. He made a modest return to the ground taking one wicket, that of E.M. (56), and fell victim to his former fellow professional Woofie who took 5 for 138.

The ground looked beautiful when Billy Murdoch led his team onto the field and the weather was glorious, befitting a team from the southern hemisphere. How unjust it seemed that Lillywhite should not be there to witness the event; he would have been proud of his son-in-law's organisation. In a supporting role, great public spirit was shown by residents and shopkeepers whose efforts ensured the centre of town was colourfully decorated, while visitors gathered from many parts of the country and contributed to a happy holiday atmosphere.

Gloucestershire's batting disappointed the large crowd. W.G. was dismissed for a duck and George Giffen took 6 for 58. But this did not spoil the day for forty fortunate employees from Postlip Mills, Winchcombe. With an early example of corporate hospitality, their employer, Mr Adlard, treated them to a day at the cricket, including the cost of the 'brakes and four' from the Plough Hotel, collecting the party from Winchcombe and returning them home again.

That evening a Promenade Concert and firework display was held at Montpellier Gardens. Players, umpires and officials were courteously invited by Lillywhite's former business partner, Mr Sweeting, the lessee of the Gardens. It was well attended, while many more were able to get a view of the spectacular pyrotechnic display from the streets and pavements of the town. A set-piece display entitled the 'Australians v. Gloucestershire - May the Best Team Win' went off without a hitch, as did the grande finale, a fort being bombarded by a ship either side.

The Australian batsmen continued to illuminate the town, despite rather dull weather, as they raced to a total of 402 in reply to the county's 183. With Murdoch (89) clean bowled by a lob from Townsend, Giffen scoring 91 and fifties from Bonnor and Scott, a large task faced the hosts in their second innings. On a worn wicket, freshened up by a drop of rain, Palmer (7 for 31) from the College end and Spofforth (3 for 47) together bowled Gloucestershire out for a meagre 83. At one stage they lost 7 wickets for 38 runs and the tourists ultimately won comfortably by an innings and 136 runs.

With the cricketers came Wood's Australian Glass Working Exhibition set out in the Assembly Rooms, with a challenge issued by the Wood brothers for anyone to produce glass products to equal theirs. In the evenings, at the same venue, Fay's Company staged *American Wonders*, a show consisting of ventriloquism, thought-reading and a dark and light seance, but it was poorly attended despite being billed as 'sensational'.

On Thursday, the match against Middlesex started. The Londoners batted first and thanks to an attractive century from Oxford undergraduate T. C. O'Brien they reached 255. He was given solid assistance by I. D. Walker (50), youngest of the seven Walker brothers who were to Middlesex what the Graces were to Gloucestershire. Woof (6 for 96) shouldered the responsibility of the bowling and Gloucestershire's reply of 388 pleased the home supporters. The highlight of the innings was a magnificent contribution of 161 by Pullen in a 190 run, record, fourth wicket partnership with E. M. Grace. Pullen's score was the best for the county during the season and remained the highest of his career. The Middlesex reply of 295 contained more dashing batting from O'Brien (58), but time ran out and the match was drawn.

—— **1885** ——

At last W.G. produced 'something out of the bag' for the faithful Cheltenham crowd to cheer. It was a good thing he did because there was a feeling of anticlimax in the town after the highly successful events of the previous year. With no 'tourist' attraction this year, many residents went off on their holidays and certain well-to-do parts of the town felt somewhat empty.

However, as always, the cricket attracted people from all walks of life and the diverse crowd of onlookers present at the first fixture of the Week saw Sussex, making a welcome reappearance, win a high-scoring match by 4 wickets. Over 1,000 runs were scored in three days, no doubt making those who had taken flight from the town rue their departure when they read the reports. In reply to the visitors' total of 300, Gloucestershire made only 159. Following on, runs by Gilbert (95) and Townsend (69) and fifties from Brain and Page enabled them to reach 376. A thrilling finish developed on the final day as Sussex reached their target of 236 with five minutes to spare, thanks to William Newham (141*) batting 'in grand style'.

Surrey provided the opposition for the second fixture and Gloucestershire duly completed the double for the season over the southerners. With a cold, north-easterly wind sweeping down from Cleeve Hill, Surrey's batsmen, apart from Robert Abel (88*), crumpled to the slow round-arm bowling of Gilbert (6 for 51). Then W.G., who was having a good season with the bat, made his long-awaited first century (104) at the Week, helping Gloucestershire to reach 277. Trailing by 79 runs, Surrey batted steadily at the start of their second innings and it looked as if the game was heading for a draw. Heavy rain on Friday night, coupled with hot sunshine the following morning, changed the plot. On a treacherous wicket the visitors were bowled out for 116, scuppered by the labours of W.G. (41-17-55-4) and Woof (40-23-43-6), giving the county victory by nine wickets. By now Woof had followed in Lillywhite's footsteps as coach at the College, so limiting the number of games he could play for the county; but he was able to manage the Cheltenham fixture for a number of years as it coincided with school holidays. By the time he retired in 1925, he had coached many fine cricketers among them Duleepsinhji, Du Boulay and the Champain brothers.

—— 1886 ——

As the church-going residents of Cheltenham returned home after evensong on Sunday 15 August, the Australian touring team checked in at the Queen's Hotel. Bannerman, Bonnor, Cooper, McDonnell, Midwinter and Murdoch from the previous tour were replaced in the party by Evans, Garrett, Jarvis, Jones, McIlwraith and Trumble.

The tourists must have been quite concerned that once again they were up against W.G., who had shown fine form earlier in the month when scoring 110 against them at Clifton. Moreover, in the recent Test match at the Oval, Grace had scored a majestic 170 as England hammered the visitors by an innings and 217 runs.

The Week opened inauspiciously with a layer of grey cloud hanging over the College ground after heavy, overnight rain, but the freshly mown and rolled pitch was in better condition than might have been expected. Having watched the groundstaff at work, a small group of spectators began an impromptu game beside the grandstand, while alongside them two Gloucestershire professionals, Woof and Painter, were warming up. The Australians rested Jarvis who had injured his foot, and Giffen stood down having just received news from home of his elder brother's death.

By noon the sun had broken through and the large number of people who had travelled by train from Swansea, Birmingham, Oxford and Gloucester had arrived on the ground. Edwin Lawrence must have afforded a little smile to himself as a crowd of around 3,000 people were gathered, eager for the match to start. There followed a small delay while the canvas screens were erected on the perimeter railings and play finally commenced at just after half past twelve.

The Australians won the toss and elected to bat, and to sporting applause, Jones and Palmer walked to the wicket. W.G. opened the bowling from the 'Villas' end and Woof from the College end, with the batting cautious and the scoring rather slow, partly because of some smart Gloucestershire fielding. Throughout the match, conditions favoured bowlers. In their first innings the visitors were dismissed for 119 and the county for only 74. Excellent bowling by Woof (7 for 32) in Australia's second innings, in which six batsmen failed to score any runs, left his side needing 160 to win. The Grace brothers batted well together (W.G. 30, E.M. 50) on a wicket very much the worse for wear, but they received little support from their team-mates. It was 'The Demon' bowler Spofforth, arguably the greatest of all fast bowlers, who finally removed both batsmen as the game approached an exciting climax and his impressive match analysis (73-32-106-10) helped to steer his team to a 26 run victory.

For some time, trouble had been brewing over the proposed double English tour to Australia that winter. It had been planned for Shaw and Shrewsbury to take out a strong professional eleven, while the Melbourne Club had invited an English side of gentlemen and players. The matter came to a head during the tourists' match at Cheltenham, with *Wisden* reporting that the Australian manager, Major Wardill, had decided 'in compliance with instructions received from the Melbourne Club' to abandon their idea.

The main entertainment of the Week was a Grand Evening Fete at Montpellier Gardens. The Cheltenham Military Band played as visitors and players wandered through the gardens which were attractively lit up by '5,000 Chinese lanterns and 20,000 variegated lamps', before being treated to a grand firework display by James Pain of London. Meanwhile, at The New Club, a private gentleman's club housed in a handsome building alongside The Promenade, visiting 'gentlemen amateur' cricketers were able to enjoy the honorary membership status extended to them during the Week.

County cricket commenced on Thursday morning with the arrival of Yorkshire, hotfoot from the first Scarborough Festival. These two fashionable spa towns could both now be proud of staging important cricket gatherings.

Positioned near the bottom of the table, Gloucestershire were having a poor season and their performance over the next two days did little to help their cause. In front of a small crowd, in disappointing weather, the visitors won a low-scoring match by 5 wickets. Bowlers enjoyed the conditions, with W.G. (5 for 65) somewhat upstaged by Yorkshire's Tom Emmett (5 for 35) and their slow spinner Saul Wade (33-18-56-11).

—— **1887** ——

Fine weather ushered in the Week. Throughout the country there were many celebrations for Queen Victoria's Jubilee, but the county's cricketers were less jubilant as they battled through another season of poor results.

Captained by Albert Hornby, Lancashire were enjoying a successful season and their first appearance at Cheltenham proved to be a great attraction. They won the toss and the famous opening batsmen of the time, Hornby and Barlow, made their way to the wicket. The latter's solid defence and his captain's brilliance combined to fascinate cricket lovers, and crowds flocked to the College ground to witness their partnership.

Their dreams were short-lived. Both men were quickly dismissed by twenty-five-year old Gloucestershire 'new boy', fast left-arm bowler Fred Roberts. The local lad from Mickleton showed scant regard for the two heroes of Francis Thompson's famous poem *At Lord's*. But the honours of the day went to Joseph Eccles, who was warmly congratulated on reaching his maiden first-class hundred (113) out of a total of 252. Left-armers Briggs (5 for 63) and Barlow (4 for 55), the latter bowling lobs, dismissed their hosts for 132, then in front of a large crowd Gloucestershire started the follow-on with dogged resistance coming from their batsmen, particularly Herbert Page (53). Heavy rain throughout Tuesday night and Wednesday morning delayed the start of play until three o'clock that afternoon, when the hosts were quickly bowled out and the visitors reached 103 for 4 to give them a 6 wicket victory.

West Country neighbours Somerset arrived for the next match bringing twenty-one-year old Sammy Woods and rainfall more typical of Exmoor. At the start of what was to be an outstanding career, Woods made an unpromising first visit to Cheltenham. By winning the toss, Gloucestershire won the match. W.G. (92), who was enjoying a productive season with the bat, received good support from his team-mates and the total of 272 was too much for the visitors on a damp, rapidly deteriorating pitch. They were bowled out for 132 and 125 largely by Roberts (65-31-84-11), who must have enjoyed his first week's work on the College ground, helping to give his side an easy win by an innings and 15 runs.

—— **1888** ——

This year Cheltenham was celebrating the centenary of King George III's visit to the town. In 1788, the royal party had stayed at Lord Fauconberg's Bayshill House for five weeks so the King could take the Cheltenham waters following a 'smart bilious attack'. Having mingled with residents of the town and ridden out to meet local farmers, George III had come away with very favourable impressions of Cheltenham and the surrounding countryside. This royal seal of approval had secured the town's reputation as a fashionable spa and helped assure its future prosperity.

One of the most exciting events organised was the return match against the Australians, who were hoping to avenge a 257 run defeat that Gloucestershire had inflicted upon them a week earlier at Clifton. According to the *Gloucestershire Echo,* 'the meadow, so delightfully situated' was 'carefully mowed and rolled' to resemble 'a green carpet which had been neatly laid'. On Monday morning just a few hundred spectators gathered in the drizzle, but their hopes were given a boost when some of the players from both teams went out to practise. By midday the sun was shining and the small number of onlookers 'demonstrated their impatience' at the game's delay. Proceedings got underway: Australian captain Percy McDonnell, a Greek scholar, won the toss and elected to bat, and soon after half past twelve W.G. led out his team. Despite being without Woof, who was unwell, Gloucestershire's bowlers troubled the visitors on a hard, drying wicket. Roberts bowled unchanged (31.1-12-51-6) partnered by fast right-armer Edward Peake (3 for 47) and the Australians were dismissed for a meagre 118. Rain prevented the hosts from starting their innings, so at half past four stumps were drawn.

On the second day, in glorious weather, 3,500 spectators gathered to watch the morning's play. They were duly rewarded and enjoyed a splendid opening partnership between the Grace brothers. After lunch, the crowd, now almost doubled in size and basking in magnificent sunshine, willed W.G. towards another century. He fell eight short but had steered his side into a strong position with a first innings lead of 91 runs.

For the rest of the day eyes turned to the final preparations being made for a Centenary Fete in Montpellier Gardens. Celebrations started at half past six, with the Mayor of Cheltenham, local dignitaries and the Australian and Gloucestershire cricketers in attendance. A Grand Promenade Concert was performed from the bandstand. Paying 6*d.* for admission and an extra 6*d.* for a seat on the grandstand, the large number of visitors who were staying for the Week, along with town residents, enjoyed lively music and many attractive decorations, including Chinese lanterns suspended from tree to tree. Just after nine o'clock a loud explosion marked the start of Messrs Pain and Son's firework display and very quickly the whole neighbourhood was illuminated. The earlier rainfall had dampened some of the set pieces, but it did not stop 'the magnificent high flying rockets, rich, colourful showers of fire-balls and many revolving displays'. Celebrating the tercentenary of the Spanish Armada, 'The Destruction of the Spanish Armada' was 'the pyrotechnic Pain's *chef d'oeuvre*'. The set piece, representing a large ship with its masts, sails and ropes, was particularly impressive when coloured fire-balls started to blaze off. Amidst loud cheers the display was rounded off with a sparkling illumination of the Gardens and a set piece spelling out: 'Floreat Cheltonia. Population 1788, 5000; 1888, 50,000.'

If the residents had not seen the fireworks, then they would certainly have heard them exploding over the town. Further loud noises erupted from the College ground the following day, when Gloucestershire charged to an 8 wicket victory with W.G. driving the ball over the boundary amidst raucous cheering.

Brimming with confidence, Gloucestershire batted first against their next visitors, Middlesex, but rain interrupted play and the hosts were bowled out cheaply for 115. Despite the return of Woof, Middlesex replied strongly with 295, then bowled out the county by mid-afternoon on the Saturday to win by an innings and 33 runs. In spite of this anticlimax after Wednesday's handsome victory, the Week was described as an 'unqualified success' and great credit attributed to Edwin Lawrence, who must have been particularly pleased with Tuesday's 'bumper' crowd.

—— 1889 ——

With the centenary celebrations behind them, the loyal Cheltenham spectators had to settle for two rain-affected draws, albeit with exciting finishes. During the first match against reigning county champions Surrey, there were several notable moments. Going to the crease with the score on 13 for 3, Gloucestershire left-hander, James Cranston (111*), rescued his team after they had sunk into even further trouble at 45 for 6. His magnificent innings, 'hit with great vigour', helped his side to a total of 201.

The backbone of Surrey's 183 was 93 by Maurice Read, while the stalwart William Woof returned figures of 38-13-71-7 in what had now become five ball overs. Heavy rainfall affected the wicket on the final day and Gloucestershire were bowled out for 107, fast-medium paced bowler William Brockwell (15-6-24-5) leading the rout, playing as a replacement for John Shuter who was suffering from a heavy cold. Dismissing E.M. for nought in the second innings meant that for the first time in his forty years of playing first-class cricket the Gloucestershire man had 'bagged a brace' in a match. Trudging back to the pavilion, he must have wondered if it was time to relinquish his place in the team for a younger man, but he immediately had to think more positively and prevent Surrey from scoring the 126 needed for victory. In just over an hour and a half they reached 112 for 4, before stumps were drawn.

Middlesex were the next opposition in a game that see-sawed as much as the unsettled weather. On a cold, cloudy day, only two and a half hours of cricket was played. W.G was in fine form assisted by the lower order batsmen and the following day, when Gloucestershire were all out for 282, the maestro had made 127*. Middlesex, bowled out for 178, failed to save the follow-on but turned the game on Saturday, declaring their second innings at 240 for 7. This was largely brought about by the tall, elegant left-hander Francis Ford who made a brilliant 108 at a run-a-minute. Webbe's sporting declaration left the hosts needing 137 in seventy minutes, but accurate bowling by Stoddart and Ford limited the home side to 48 for 5 at the close.

In the *Echo* further praise was showered upon the hard-working Edwin Lawrence who had done 'all that human foresight could suggest towards providing for the comfort and accommodation of the public'. There had been record receipts for the Australian match in 1888 and despite this year's unsettled weather, the takings were higher than previous years, including totals of £90 on Tuesday and £70 on the Friday. Residents were starting to think twice before going away on holiday during the Week and more visitors were coming to stay for the event. A local publication, *The Garden Town of England,* confirmed this: 'The Annual Cricket Week is a firmly established attraction of the town . . .

Its record is one of continuous and steady progress, and its popularity may be judged from the fact that in favourable weather the attendance of spectators averages 3,000 daily, many being visitors from a distance.'

Lawrence had certainly followed in his father-in-law's footsteps and the event continued to grow, just as the founder would have wished. Cricket was flourishing at Canterbury, soon to celebrate its 'Jubilee Week' under the watchful eye of Lord Harris, and in Scarborough the managerial efforts of C. I. 'Buns' Thornton, renowned for his hitting of balls high into the sea air, ensured a successful cricketing occasion there.

Cheltenham might lack sea air, but it still had W.G.'s exhilarating influence. Author J. M. Kilburn described Grace as being 'more than a cricketer'. He was 'the game personified . . . one of the wonders of his world, and the surest guarantee of spectators cricket has ever known'. Gloucestershire had his services for one more decade.

CHAPTER FIVE (1890-1894)

THE DAWNING OF A NEW AGE

—— 1890 ——

Gloucestershire's last county match of the summer ended with a convincing victory against Middlesex at the College ground after a rather mediocre start to the season. At Cheltenham over the next ten years their fortunes would ebb and flow. While losing legendary established players, they would gain exciting new ones and records would be set both on and off the field.

Winning the toss for the eleventh successive time in county matches, W.G. elected to bat and his side scored 164. This was largely thanks to the captain's faultless innings of 57, during which he and John Painter added 89 for the fifth wicket in just half an hour. The partnership greatly influenced the match, for *Wisden* reported that both before and after the stand 'the ball held a mastery over the bat'. Middlesex were bowled out for 83 in their first innings by Woof (5 for 38) and Roberts (4 for 20). In just under one and a half hours the same two bowlers dismissed the visitors once more, this time for 59. Woof (6 for 32) and Roberts (3 for 25) gave Gloucestershire victory by an innings and 22 runs before lunch on the second day.

With no play on Wednesday, extra time could be devoted to preparations before welcoming the Australians. They arrived in town having just been defeated by Nottinghamshire, but quickly put these memories behind them, overcoming the unsettled weather and their hosts to win the contest comfortably by eight wickets. Once again, it was Woof (6 for 81) and Roberts (4 for 40) who broke down the visitors. In front of a large crowd, Australian, J. J. Ferris, soon to agree terms and qualify to play for Gloucestershire, helped the visitors to reach 184 with a dogged 54*. Then, taking the ball, left-armer Ferris (4 for 30) and his fellow fast bowler C. T. B. Turner (6 for 42) dispatched the county for 77. Rain spoiled the continuity of the game, but nevertheless £218. 5s. was taken in gate money on the second day. With Gloucestershire following on, the last morning began with the Cotswold hounds running round the ground and remaining on display by the pavilion until the close of play. Ferris, completing his all-round, match-winning performance with further impressive figures (30-18-35-6), bowled out his future team-mates for 130 and the visitors quickly knocked off the runs needed for victory.

No doubt the committee was delighted with the new find as much as it would have been with the fifth Annual Cricket Week Fete arranged by Webb Bros, had it not been ruined by rain towards the end of the evening. After play on Thursday, the players from both teams made their way to the Montpellier Gardens, illuminated again by Chinese lanterns, and with a large number of fellow guests they were entertained by the Town Band, and by the Cheltenham Cyclist Club who pedalled through the gardens and journeyed on around the town. Many of the cycles were decorated with lights, one in particular looking most effective having a fishing rod with a cross piece at the end from which lanterns were angled. With rain falling, some people made their way to the large marquee while others took shelter under the trees to watch the fireworks. Contrary to the usual custom, the display was arranged on the south side of the grounds and despite the rather overcast conditions, the Queen's Hotel made a striking backcloth. The only casualties were W.G. and Billy Murdoch, gigantic fire portraits of the rival captains fizzling out beneath a damp sky.

—— **1891** ——

This year gloom surrounded the Week. Gloucestershire, experiencing a poor season, were heading for the foot of the county championship table and spirits were further dampened by more rain to add to an already miserable summer. A drenched Cotswold harvest lay on the ground but excitement surrounded the forthcoming visit of Somerset.

As neighbours, and now first-class opposition, it was earnestly hoped Somerset would be beaten, especially as they had just defeated Surrey, the county champions, at Taunton. Rain prevented any play until mid-afternoon on Monday, but the visitors quickly made up for lost time, reaching 142 for 2 in under two hours. Gloucestershire's fielders had to put up with plenty of 'leather hunting' forced upon them by the free scoring of L. C. H. Palairet (100), making his maiden first-class century. Challen made 79 and together the pair put on 139 for the second wicket. The next day belonged to the bowlers of both teams; Somerset were all out for 255, with Woof returning splendid figures of 53.2-15-125-8, in

what was to be his last impressive performance for the county at Cheltenham. Disaster then struck for the hosts with five batsmen failing to score, one of them being H. V. Page now a master at the College. They were bowled out for 25, the smallest total of the year in first-class cricket, and batting again they slumped to 47 for 3 by the close of play and were staring an early, heavy defeat in the face. This was disappointing for Edwin Lawrence after all his hard work and painstaking care. The grandstand was in place as usual, under the sheltering wall of the gymnasium, but he had made several alterations to the ground layout, siting a luncheon and refreshment tent on the north side, with accommodation for the press, postal services and scorers at the Villas end.

Dismissed for 100, Gloucestershire lost by an innings and 130 runs. Woods (23.2-6-46-8) had made much more of an impression than he had on his Cheltenham debut, while ultra slow left-armer Edwin Tyler (27-5-70-10), with a somewhat dubious action, had bowled unchanged throughout both innings.

Only four and a half hours of play took place in the second match. Short spells were possible on the first two days against Middlesex, but persistent rain meant not a ball was bowled on the final day. In *Wisden* a report about the season stated: 'In no first-class county match, was so little progress made.' W.G. batted masterfully making 72* in a total of 145 for 6 on a wretched pitch that dealt W. R. Moon, the Middlesex wicket-keeper, two painful blows. The famous England goalkeeper was struck in the eye by one of the bails when E.M. became the first of J. T. Hearne's five wickets. On the final day he badly injured his hand, but his services were no longer required as his team did not bat and the game petered out into a draw.

—— 1892 ——

A large crowd gathered in excellent weather to greet Nottinghamshire at the opening of the fifteenth Week. It had been another disastrous season for the West Country team who were going into this game with one win and seven defeats, in stark contrast to Nottinghamshire's ten victories.

The visitors lived up to their reputation, scoring 287 for 4 on the opening day. Arthur Shrewsbury was at his very best. The small, delicate master of all wickets delighted the Cheltenham crowd by playing a faultless innings of 127 and was ably assisted by Gunn, Barnes and

Attewell who took advantage of some rather inept bowling. The hosts were in the field for almost six and a half hours and had bowled 168 overs by the time they had taken the final Nottinghamshire wicket with the total on 429. The addition of Ferris (44-8-131-1) to the Gloucestershire attack had not brought the intended results and rather a disappointing career with the county was to follow.

From the start of their innings the hosts looked shaky. The Grace brothers scored one run between them and omens for a large total were not good. With the ground bathed in sunshine, Gloucestershire were bowled out for 146 before lunch on the third day, six-foot Frank Shacklock (46.1-23-66-8) placing his side in a very strong position. Batting again, Gloucestershire provided sterner opposition. A valuable innings from Painter (70) helped to steer them to safety and at the close of play Ferris and W.G. were cheered off the ground with the total on 196 for 5.

Champions Surrey, on a West Country tour, arrived fresh from a victory over Somerset at Taunton. After rain held up play on the first day, the hosts struggled against Lockwood (19.3-8-42-7) on a bowler's wicket. They were dismissed for 93, and in reply Surrey comfortably reached 264, Read (107) punishing the Gloucestershire attack with some powerful hitting. Lockwood (38.1-20-73-5) caused further damage in the home side's second innings of 197 and Surrey moved to a comfortable 10 wicket victory. This had been a discouraging week for two Gloucestershire newcomers, the promising young wicket-keeper, Jack Board, and the Old Cheltonian, Capt A. H. Luard, neither of whom were to feature in the somewhat extraordinary events of the following year.

—— 1893 ——

Countrywide, cricket was in its heyday, flourishing with an abundance of players and spectators. It was disappointing that at this time Gloucestershire CCC was passing through a rather unhappy and difficult period. Morale was low and by the end of the season they were bottom of the championship table. The anguish of two defeats at Cheltenham was softened by a sensational incident that was witnessed on the second afternoon.

In reply to Somerset's 197, Gloucestershire, who were without W.G. for the first time at Cheltenham, made a respectable 166. 'The Doctor', who had appeared for an unbroken run of twenty-one years in the town, was away captaining the England team against Australia at the Oval. He was replaced by his eldest son, William Gilbert, who later must have enjoyed telling his father about the historic event that ended Somerset's second innings.

The first part of the August afternoon passed without incident. Lionel Palairet had made a graceful 72 with useful contributions from the rest of his team, taking the visitors to a rather formidable 270 for 7.

At this point, Charles Townsend, only sixteen and still a pupil at Clifton College, playing in his second match for Gloucestershire, performed a hat trick. The tall, slender leg-spinner was assisted by the handiwork of wicket-keeper W. H. Brain, whose unique contribution was to stump each of the batsmen, so the tail-end of the scorecard read:

Mr A. E. Newton	st Brain b Townsend	4
G. B. Nichols	st Brain b Townsend	0
E. J. Tyler	st Brain b Townsend	0

Son of the former county player Frank Townsend, Charles would later develop into an outstanding left-handed batsman who would play a major role in gradually bringing about a splendid revival for the county over the next two years. For now, four consecutive defeats at Cheltenham lay ahead of Gloucestershire.

Somerset bowled their hosts out for 174, winning by 127 runs. Tyler (69.2-22-110-10) had taken 20 wickets in just two matches on the College ground.

W.G. returned from London with a large smile on his face, having helped England beat the Australians by an innings and 43 runs. Recently there had been little for him to smile about in Gloucestershire cricket circles since he had become the subject of criticism over his methods and motives of team selection. When the county played at Cheltenham, in order to fill vacancies, he would invariably select boys and masters not necessarily on their merits, but because of their links to the College, in preference to local club cricketers with undisputed talent. Doubtless his justification was that the continuing success of the Week depended on fostering the county's bond with the College, but when county committee members voiced their disapproval he responded angrily seeing it as a pert challenge to the way he ran Gloucestershire cricket. He penned his disgust in a letter, resigning from the committee and captaincy. The committee begged him to rethink, which he did, carrying on both roles;

but the fuse had been lit, sparking off a gradual and irreversible deterioration in relationships.

The Australians followed W.G. to Cheltenham and made their way to the luxurious Queen's Hotel. Here they were carefully cosseted by the staff, under the watchful and experienced eye of the manageress Miss J. Hill. She was proud of the fine cuisine, wines and excellent services that the hotel offered, particularly the recently-constructed lift running from ground to top floor. This would be a welcome luxury, suggested the *Looker-On*, for 'rich and famous celebrities, notable names in society, retired military stouthearts and mothers and daughters, husbands and wives', not to mention tired young cricketers with aching limbs after a day's play.

As always, when the Australians were in town they added extra colour and excitement to the atmosphere. This was reflected in a burlesque performance at the theatre, a celebratory evening with fireworks, a performance by the Corporation Band playing during the afternoon at the College and the luxury of luncheon and refreshments of all kinds supplied on the ground by Mr King of the Clarence Hotel.

By mid-afternoon on the first day a crowd of 5,000 had gathered, paying one shilling ground admission and an extra shilling to enter the grandstand. Many had arrived by train, taking advantage of the favourable rates offered by rail companies. Tickets were issued at a fare and a quarter for a double journey from all stations within a reasonable distance of Cheltenham, while spectators from the Swindon area were able to remain at the ground until the close of play knowing they could catch the half past eight 'Special Train' which would call at all stations en route.

Gloucestershire were without William Murch, suffering a strained leg, but included Ferris playing against his former team, while W.G. junior retained his place and took the field with his father. In a low-scoring match, with nobody making over 50, the tourists proved to be too strong for the county. The Townsend and Brain combination carried on from where they had left off against Somerset, the leg-spinner taking 5 for 70, two wickets of which were the work of the speedy, agile stumper.

The hosts collapsed to the flight and guile of George Giffen (23-5-41-7), and were all out for 109 in reply to the visitors' total of 207. Batting again, on a wearing wicket, they fared only a little better reaching 131, which led to an 8 wicket defeat. This time it was Charles Turner (16-8-25-6) who caused their downfall; the large crowd were fortunate to see this splendid, thickset, medium-paced bowler, 'Turner the Terror', at his very best in a year when he took 160 wickets at an average of just under fourteen each.

—— 1894 ——

The top county of this era was Surrey; their batting and bowling was strong, and off the field they had a large membership generating a hefty income of over £10,000 a year. During the evening of Sunday 12 August the Londoners arrived in wet weather and settled in at the Royal Hotel. The old-established hotel, situated opposite the Assembly Rooms, was proving to be very successful since the recent appointment of Mrs Potter as manageress. Formerly of the Swan Hotel in Birmingham, she had quickly created 'a home from home' atmosphere and her organization and running of the cuisine was gaining an admirable reputation.

The following morning, in a confident mood, with ten wins out of twelve matches so far in the season, the Londoners took to the field. On a soft wicket, the lithe, supple, unflagging fast bowler Tom Richardson (17-5-27-6), who once when asked if he approved of increasing the number of balls in an over from five to six, replied, 'Give me ten!', bowled out his bottom-of-the-championship table hosts for 52.

Without the valuable partnership between Hayward (43) and Brockwell (72), Surrey would have been in similar trouble, but helped by a certain amount of luck they steered the visitors to a respectable total of 201. Old heads in the grandstand turned and watched with interest as a young fast bowler, G. L. Jessop (11-3-24-3), took the first of his nine wickets for the Week in his maiden appearance at the event. With the county suffering from a lack of dependable batting, and with only a moderate bowling attack, Jessop was a much needed tonic: the 'discovery of the summer'. There was no question of selection bias for this strong, agile boy from a local medical family who had been educated at the Grammar School.

A crowd of about 2,500 witnessed the humiliation of the hosts on Monday, the *Echo* maintaining, 'As long as the Graces are there, whether Gloucestershire do well or not, the crowds will come.' This was an organiser's dream and the following day a gathering of 2,000 watched Surrey cruise to an innings victory before lunch. Richardson (20.1-7-34-7) rolled over the Gloucestershire team who offered little resistence in making their total of 100, while the crowd relished the undeviating dexterity of the Surrey bowler at his best.

The early finish was a great frustration to the hundreds of enthusiasts who were still making their way to the ground, hoping for an afternoon session of play. W.G.'s captaincy was criticized, the charge being that he was wrong to have batted first on Monday and that he should have included the experienced and popular Woof in his team.

There was further opportunity to chew over the allegations after play had finished on Tuesday afternoon at 'The Earthstoppers for the Cotswold Hunt Annual Dinner', held at the Corn Exchange. A hundred huntsmen, gamekeepers and hunt followers enjoyed the feast, toasted the Queen and agreed how much they were looking forward to the new season, hoping that plenty of foxes would be found. The *Echo* reported that after a toast had been drunk, a voice chirped up, 'Tally-ho for Gretton; we have got plenty of foxes.'

When the laughter had subsided, the chairman reminded everyone how it had been customary for many years to hold the dinner during the Cricket Week because of the fondness those present had for the game. In the past, many a diner had left the meal in a merry state and enjoyed an afternoon's cricket. The chairman informed everyone that the match on the College ground was already over and he suggested that next year their gathering should be held on the first day of play to guarantee some cricket. This brought loud laughter and cheers of agreement. He finally floated the idea that if two of those present, appropriately named Dance and Ferrett, were picked for the county team there would be more of a chance of the game running its full course. Amidst the chortling one of them chirped up, 'I don't think we should make a much worse show.' Gloucestershire's cricketers were being mocked by their own folk, Cotswold country stock, who cherished the game of cricket. As their banter wafted up over the hills, preparations were already underway for the first visit of Kent, a fixture destined to bring further disappointment.

Rain affected the start of the game, but on winning the toss Kent chose to bat first on a wet wicket and made 161. The hosts replied with 97, somewhat overwhelmed by the Hearnes, Walter taking 4 for 53 from 26 overs and Alec returning impressive figures of 3.4-2-1-3. In their second innings, Kent made 105 and the Gloucestershire contingent amongst the crowd of over 3,000 enjoyed watching Jessop, with his easy delivery, pick up 3 wickets, giving him a match analysis of 20.2-11-22-6. The home side never looked as if they would get anywhere near the 170 needed to win and on Saturday morning, after Townsend was bowled on the second ball of the day by W. Hearne (22-8-40-6), it took just a further thirty minutes for the visitors to sweep to an 84 run victory.

As they left the ground, the faithful spectators might well have glanced at the steadily growing new chapel. The foundation stone had been laid the previous year and the building was beginning to grow as Gloucestershire's fortunes would the following season.

CHAPTER SIX (1895-1899)

UPS AND DOWNS

—— 1895 ——

This was the start of cricket's 'Golden Age', described by J. M. Kilburn as 'an era of misty glow', and said to have run from 1895 to 1914, starting with W.G.'s 'Indian Summer' and halted by the horrors of the First World War.

In May, W.G. reasserted himself on a pedestal above all others when, aged forty-seven, and enjoying his twenty-fifth year of captaincy, he made his century of centuries against Somerset. Throughout the season more runs flowed from his bat and by mid-August, when Gloucestershire came to play at Cheltenham, there were signs of a fine come-back after some disappointingly lean years. It was the start of the county's own mini-golden age brought about by their remarkable captain, together with strong support from Charles Townsend and rising star Gilbert Jessop.

Edwin Lawrence must have rubbed his hands with delight at the sight of the Gloucestershire players, buoyant and successful, now fourth in the championship table, arriving in the town during a spell of beautiful weather. He had the College ground looking first-class with a flat green outfield and an excellent wicket. Surrounding this were spacious marquees for the press and the players and also for Mr Chambers to serve his '2s. 6d. luncheons and other refreshments'. There was an air of expectancy, with good crowds anticipated and the hope of favourable results against the visiting teams, Nottinghamshire and Yorkshire.

The midlanders, who were bottom of the table, arrived that morning just having been heavily defeated by Middlesex. To the disappointment of spectators they were without Shrewsbury and Gunn, but they were given a warm welcome as they took to the field, closely followed by Ferris and W.G., who had won the toss and chosen to bat first. Gloucestershire had already beaten their rivals earlier in the season and W.G., described in the *Echo* as the 'inimitable master of the game', intended to complete the double. By mid-afternoon, Nottinghamshire, now without Flowers who had left the ground when hearing of his father's sudden death, were wilting in front of a packed grandstand and a thick ring of spectators circling the boundary. Over £100 had been taken at the gate, the highest receipts for an inter-county match at Cheltenham, but the record would be eclipsed twice more during the Week.

It was six years since W.G.'s last century on the ground so admirers were delighted to watch him occupy the crease all day scoring 113*, his eighth century of the season. They poured back on Tuesday morning, hoping for more. Their pleasure was short-lived, the 'Champion' adding only 6 to his overnight score. Gloucestershire were soon all out for 257, 'Dick' Attewell, renowned for his Trojan-like spells of bowling, finishing with the remarkable figures of 64-35-52-6.

Nottinghamshire were immediately overwhelmed by the bowling of Townsend (20.3-6-43-5) and Jessop (15-12-9-4), managing only 65 in their first innings. Townsend, bowling his leg-breaks, ended any hopes of the game lasting three days by skittling out the opposition for 99 and his figures (19-2-67-8) gave Gloucestershire victory by an innings and 93 runs.

The crowd were thrilled, for it was five years since the county had won at Cheltenham. Four days later there was further delight when, by defeating Yorkshire, they recorded their first ever two victories during the Week.

Earlier in the season at Bradford, Yorkshire had leathered Gloucestershire by eight wickets. Since then the West Country men had improved significantly and a large, hopeful crowd gathered for the first day's play. A total of £189 was taken on the gate and the paying public witnessed a splendid day's cricket.

Yorkshire batted enterprisingly making 221, despite the impressive bowling of Townsend (32.4-4-130-8). Throughout the day much muttering had rumbled around the ground as people thought that W.G. had kept the youngster on too long, but swiftly the discontent turned to wholehearted support for his decision to promote Jessop in the batting order after the captain himself had failed with the bat. Jessop responded by delivering one of his whirlwind innings, making 63 out of 65 from only twenty hits in just half an hour. 'For clean, well-timed, accurate hitting it took the cake,' wrote Wanderer in the *Echo*. Two of the talented amateurs who had emerged during the season, C. O. H. Sewell and R. W. Rice, partnered Jessop and helped steer Gloucestershire to 219. Everything depended upon both teams' second innings.

Townsend (24-5-54-7) routed Yorkshire, leaving his team needing 146 for victory. In five scintillating days at Cheltenham, the youngster, in his first full season for the county, had taken 28 wickets for 294 runs, including his one hundredth wicket for the summer. This was the stuff of heroes and even at this early stage of his career it placed him firmly behind the great Richardson of Surrey as the country's second most dangerous bowler.

On the last day of the Week, an excited crowd witnessed the county cruise to an historic seven wicket victory in their penultimate game of the season. They were particularly pleased to see the Cheltenham-born professional batsman Harry Wrathall, who had emerged during the season, featuring in the successful run-chase.

Despite the absence on the field of the fifty-three-year-old E.M. for the first time ever at Cheltenham, there had been many highlights. After a poor start to the season, they were now fourth out of fourteen in the championship. Wicket-keeper Jack Board was elated by his ten dimissals in five days and W.G. and Townsend led the national batting and bowling averages. As local supporters made their way home, their faces must have gleamed like Cheltenham's wrought ironwork on the porches and balconies they passed.

—— 1896 ——

After the previous year's success, the visit of Kent and the Australians brought the inevitable downfall. It was not on a level of the nose-dive that agriculture within the county was experiencing. In the countryside a whole way of life was starting to decline, while Gloucestershire were simply losing two more games of cricket.

For the first time in his illustrious career, Lord Harris, leading light of Kent cricket in the previous two decades, appeared at Cheltenham. After an interval of seven years, while Governor General of Bombay, he chose to make his reappearance in Kent's team on the College ground. Nobody more than Lord Harris enjoyed a Cricket Week. He had experienced the ambience of Canterbury on many occasions, leading Kent against some of the strongest sides in the land and engaging in the social chatter and frivolities of theatrical performances by the Old Stagers in the evenings.

After a poor start to the season, during which Kent had already beaten Gloucestershire by nine wickets, W.G.'s side had recently put together a string of good results. So there was little to choose between the teams as the 'hop' men left the Royal Hotel and made their way to the ground on a warm, sunny morning with, according to the *Echo* 'just a few clouds scudding across a brilliant blue sky'. The players 'preliminary canter' before the start of the game displayed much hard hitting, which continued once play commenced.

Loud cheers greeted W.G. as he led his team onto the field, closely followed by Kent's Mason and Burnup. The openers kept the scoreboard rattling along during their 122 run partnership. Useful contributions from Patterson and Lord Harris followed, but the rest of the team collapsed to Townsend. Throughout the season he had been suffering from 'tennis elbow' and had not produced his previous season's form, but there were signs that he was climbing back to the top of the tree with his figures of 24-3-74-7. By mid-afternoon the visitors had been dismissed for 190 and the interval between innings gave 'lovers of the fragrant weed' the opportunity to visit the gigantic cigar-box stand of Mr Fred Wright, a well-known Cheltenham tobacconist whose High Street shop displayed a life-sized model of a Highlander. A prominent local business man, with his intimate knowledge of tobacco and cigars, Mr Wright was also the manufacturer of the popular 'Cheltenham' cigarette, a great favourite in clubs all over the country.

Before the smokers had settled down, the hosts lost their opener, Rice, the Tewkesbury amateur, but Grace (64) and Hemingway (78) steadied the ship. As their partnership gained momentum, cheers of delight greeted a pavilion-side boundary by W.G. which brought up his run-total of the season to 2,000 and prompted a flurry of activity in the newly-sited press tent.

Much excitement and speculation surrounded the decision of Edwin Lawrence to move the members of the 'Fourth Estate' to a tent at the chapel end of the ground. The *Echo* reported that it was to improve efficiency, getting their copies away more quickly as the carriers would not have the temptation of lingering and 'looking lovingly upon the game' while on their delivery run. There were rumours that the new position had nothing to do with the transmission of news but had been brought about in answer to a request from the reporters and scorers to be nearer to the refreshment bar, for 'bending the arm' had always been one of their 'reprehensible practices'. Alternatively, it was suggested that Lawrence may have had their spiritual needs in mind and placed them near the newly completed chapel so they could easily retire for 'silent meditation'. Most importantly, from a commercial point of view, there was now additional stand accomodation for spectators which would be much needed during the forthcoming visit of the Australians.

Hemingway was hitting particularly powerfully and outscoring his

captain, and at one stage cut a ball hard towards Bradley fielding at point; before he could move, the ball bounced off the fielder's forehead and sped to the boundary. 'Bill' Bradley was unhurt and responded to this, and the mocking laughter of the home spectators at his peculiar bowling action, by taking the wickets of both batsmen before the close of play, leaving the home side on 151 for 3 overnight. Bradley (13.2-4-31-6) continued the assault the following day on a rain-affected pitch. He may have been a comical sight with both arms flung high above his thrown-back head but his aggressive bowling worried the Gloucestershire batsmen, causing them to slump to 202 all out, the last seven men scoring only 11 runs.

On a deteriorating wicket, Townsend took 6 for 68 and Kent made 178, too many runs for their hosts who were bowled out 25 runs short of their target. Bradley took four more wickets, ensuring he and the rest of the visitors had the last laugh.

The highest-ever attendance at Cheltenham was recorded the next day with just under 8,000 spectators flocking into the ground for the first day of the match against the Australians. Earlier on in the season at Bristol, Harry Trott's men had handed out an innings defeat to Gloucestershire. After this they had lost an exciting Test series 2-1, but had swept aside all other county opposition. Thousands of eager cricket lovers wanted to watch the entertaining colonial side and see how they would perform against Townsend's bowling. Furthermore, they might witness W.G. scoring his first century of the season. As a result, the gross receipts for the day were a record £374.15s., half of which went to the visitors.

Large, grey clouds billowed in the sky as people hurried along the pavements to reach the ground for the start of play. There was great disappointment when it was announced that the veteran George Giffen was not playing as he was away on leave of absence. Fourteen years earlier he had come to England for the first time and this current visit was considered to be the last for the great all-rounder, referred to as the 'W. G. Grace of Australia'.

Grace won the toss and just after midday he and Rice followed the Australians onto the field, amidst loud cheers. Gloucestershire's batsmen made only limited progress against the bowling of Trumble and McKibben. It was left to the cold luncheons, costing one shilling each at the King William in Bath Road, washed down with some of the medal-winning ales served by Thomas Coole, the proprietor, to help maintain the county supporters' spirits. Soon after lunch, Gloucestershire's innings, which had only lasted just under two hours, closed on 133. The cheerful, powerfully-built McKibben ended with figures of 21.2-8-48-6, but his right-arm medium slow deliveries did cause some eyebrows to be raised, as there was little doubt that he threw the ball when bowling his off-break.

On a somewhat difficult wicket the visitors batted steadily and a crowd of over 4,000 people gathered the following day to see their innings held together by Sydney Gregory, with an unbeaten 71. At one stage the crowd were treated to the rare sight of the Graces, father and son, bowling at opposite ends when the Champion rested Townsend. However, during the afternoon, Townsend's 'slows' proved hard to deal with and he took his one hundredth wicket of the season, ending with the remarkable figures of 28-5-79-8. At the close of play the game looked interestingly poised. Gloucestershire, on 3 for no wicket, were 68 runs behind as the teams made their way to the Assembly Rooms for a banquet, billed as the main feature of the Week.

Earlier in the century, the town's well-to-do social scene mainly revolved around the beautiful new Assembly Rooms, situated on the corner of the High Street and Rodney Road. Balls and card parties were frequently held here, attended by the 'youthful loveliness and grace of Britain'. The Duke of Wellington had once attended such a ball, enjoying the 'brilliant display of fashion and beauty'.

Those days had now passed and although this important Regency building was falling into disrepair, the attractively decorated large room was the perfect setting for what must have been one of its most memorable gatherings.

The aim of a number of Cheltenham residents and local 'votaries of the king of games', was to hold a celebration complimentary dinner to the 'hero of more than a hundred centuries' and also to the 'distinguished colonial visitors'. The tables were 'daintily and tastefully laid out' with attractive floral decorations, and large palm trees adorned the room, all of which presented 'an elegant and inviting appearance'. Mrs Potter, the hostess of the Royal, laid on 'a first-class epicurean menu for the dinner, served in her characteristic exemplary way and accompanied by several choice vintages'.

The mayor, Colonel Rogers, sat at the centre of the cross table, with Harry Trott on his right and W.G. on his left. Grace, in particularly fine form, was full of 'quips and cranks and wanton smiles'. The remainder of both teams sat intermingled on the same table. Baron de Ferrières took the vice-chair and Edwin Lawrence, along with many other guests, enjoyed the Town Band performing their programme of dance and light operatic music during the meal.

MENU

Hors d'oeuvres

Soups

Clear Ox Tail and Tomato

Fish

Turbot with Cardinal Sauce   Fillet of Sole

Entrees

Sweetbread and mushrooms   Curried Rabbit

Lobster Salad

Joints

Roast Beef with Horseradish Sauce

Lamb with Mint Sauce   Fillet of Veal

Poultry

Boiled Chicken with Cress

Roast Gosling with Apple Sauce

Ham

Sweets

Stewed Fruit   Peach Jelly   Ice Pudding

Savories

Marrow on Toast   Devilled Crab

Cheese Fingers

Dessert

An array of toasts and speeches were accompanied by much 'fun, laughter and applause'. The Australians received a warm welcome from the mellowing baron, followed by a banjo song from a Mr Harrison. The Australian captain rose to his feet and gave due thanks for the warm reception the tourists had received since arriving in Cheltenham and subjected W.G. to some playful taunting, taking his revenge on 'the old doctor' who had been 'badgering him about speech making and had made him nervous'. He pointed out that 'when the doctor started he could beat him at talking'. Mr Musgrove, the tourists' secretary, then offered more thanks for the kind way in which they had been treated and he was followed by Mr Feeney, who proposed the health of 'The Gloucestershire Team', and the great man of whom everyone was proud: 'The Champion'.

On rising to respond, the Gloucestershire captain had a magnificent reception. He described the Australian team as 'good cricketers and jolly good fellows', then quipped about cricket tours, Test matches and favouritism from umpires. His brother then spoke, giving a brief history of the club and commenting that although there had been many ups and downs, their position compared favourably with the northern teams 'who would pay men thirty bob and £2 a day just to see what they were made of - a thing Gloucestershire could not afford and did not choose to do, preferring to trust native ability'.

The loving cup was circulated and a toast was proposed to local cricket clubs by Mr O. J. Williams ('who also gave a clever whistling solo later on'). Regional teams were thriving, he said, and giving every chance to young cricketers to prepare themselves for distinction in the future, with locals Jessop, Lamb and Wrathall as obvious examples. Meanwhile, F. H. B. Champain, captain of the College XI for the last three years, had made his county debut against Kent at the start of the Week.

E.M. proposed a toast to the College authorities, expressing gratitude at the kindness of the Council 'in freely permitting the College ground to be used for the Cricket Week'. The county had always looked to Cheltenham to recoup their finances, and he announced that the five days of cricket in the previous year had yielded £700 and this year it looked as if the takings would exceed that figure. He concluded that Cheltenham not only provided excellent gates, but also 'enjoyable weeks' to which there were loud cheers.

Then followed a toast to 'The Ladies' seated in the gallery, on whom W.G. 'had showered many nods and becks and wreathed smiles throughout the evening'. Similarly, 'The Press', 'Mr Townsend' and 'The Dinner Committee' were all toasted and the mayor said he looked forward to the day when there would be two cricket weeks in the town, one at the beginning and the other, like the current one, at the close of the season. On the stroke of the 'witching hour' the national anthem was sung and the guests dispersed. The cricketers would only have a few hours sleep before the start of play. The Australians would cope, but for the tired and heavy-headed Gloucestershire players an ordeal was in store.

While the banquet had been in full swing, the heavens had opened and next morning the home side's batsmen were caught on a soft, sticky, drying wicket. By the time play started, nearly 2,000 spectators had gathered. An hour later the game was over, the visitors having won by an innings and 54 runs. Trumble (10-6-8-6) and McKibben (9.1-7-7-4) bowled in 'irresistible fashion' and Gloucestershire, whose batting was described by Jessop as 'extraordinarily feeble', were dismissed for just seventeen, the lowest innings total ever recorded at Cheltenham, and the lowest ever by Gloucestershire.

Two months later, the completed new College chapel was due to be dedicated by Archbishop Benson, but on the day he was meant to travel to Cheltenham he collapsed and died at Hawarden where he had been staying with the elderly statesman, William Gladstone. The Bishop of Gloucester officiated instead but the inaugural service was postponed. Lord Plunket, Archbishop of Dublin, eventually conducted the service in the middle of December and that evening a small earthquake shook the town causing cracks where the walls and roof join. This magnificent Perpendicular style building, the backcloth to many photographs and paintings of cricket at Cheltenham, still bears the scars of that tremor.

—— 1897 ——

Despite the club secretary's preference to 'trust native ability', the committee at the AGM in April was earnestly requested 'to review their efforts to introduce some young rising professionals into the county team', those present 'pledging to support the committee in any expenditure that may be necessary in this direction'.

On the cricket field that summer, as a fitting celebration of Queen Victoria's Diamond Jubilee, the county had a much better season. They ended up fifth in the championship winning both their games at Cheltenham, and it was generally agreed that W.G. had a 'fine band of young cricketers' around him. The outlook for the future was encouraging.

Three months before the doughty men of Kent checked in to the Queen's Hotel at the beginning of the Week, the establishment had been dusted from top to bottom, with every nook and cranny cleaned, every piece of silver polished, in preparation for the visit of Edward, Prince of Wales. Visiting the town to review the Royal Gloucestershire Hussars on the racecourse, the Prince had lunched at the hotel after leading a colourful procession up the Promenade.

Kent also were to make an impact on the town in their own way. With the first ball of the match Wright bowled Jessop, delighting the visitors but leaving the locals dejected. They had hoped to see the brilliant 'fearless hitter' at his very best. Jessop was having a splendid summer rivalling the feats of previous great hitters such as Thornton, Bonnor, Massie and Lyons. There was no more popular figure on a cricket field than the enthusiastic, cavalier all-rounder, who scored a thousand runs and captured one hundred wickets during the season. Wright again dismissed the Gloucestershire match-winner cheaply in the second innings and the game remained evenly balanced until the last day.

The highlight was a remarkable performance from the Malvern College captain, S. H. Day, who joined the select few to have scored a hundred in their first county match. His unbeaten 101 was over half his team's second innings total, but it was not enough and the hosts won by 63 runs.

Without Shrewsbury, Gunn and their regular wicket-keeper Pike, Nottinghamshire, the next visitors, were a weakened side. They introduced T. W. Oates, from Digby Colliery, behind the stumps, but he was unable to fuel his team with a match-winning performance.

Lawrence and his staff of assistants had everything running smoothly as usual. They had even taken notice of the complaints made by cyclists to the ground that in previous years bicycles had been stolen. Along with the grandstand and the tents for refreshments, the press and scorers, a special area had been set aside immediately opposite the entrance to the ground where all cycles could be numbered and stored safely for a charge of twopence.

Nearly 4,000 people gathered on the first day and saw the visitors bowled out for 198. Jessop failed to score again, but W.G. (131) and Townsend (66) put on 159 together, the crowd lapping it all up and thirsting for more. There was, indeed, more to come as the captain took 6 for 36 when the midlanders batted again, guiding his team to an innings and 40 run victory. He would not quench the thirst of the crowd again at the College ground, in this his penultimate Cheltenham Week. The following year his own personal performances were to be modest in comparison and there were also major upheavals on the horizon.

—— **1898** ——

In W.G.'s opinion, the finest county side he had ever captained was that of 1898. With a very strong batting line-up, a powerful and varied bowling attack and some very capable fielders, from May onwards they did not lose a match.

As in the previous year, Kent were the first visiting team. On a damp wicket, Grace won the toss and chose to bat, opening the innings with Walter Troup who was home on sick leave from the Indian Police Service. On hearing that Troup was in the country, W.G. had written asking him to play for the county throughout the season. Troup was still feeling unwell and replied declining the offer, giving the letter to his wife to post. Not wanting to encourage what she called 'his laziness', his wife destroyed the letter and wrote another one on his behalf saying that he would be 'delighted' to play. She obviously knew her husband well for, after a sticky start, runs began to flow from his bat and he had several large partnerships with the Champion during the season.

On the subject of communications, there were murmurings amongst spectators that a postal telegraph would be an asset on the ground. A large number of private messages emerged from the field and any sender had to go almost a mile to the nearest post office situated in the Promenade, engage a messenger, or beg a favour from the press to send it along with their dispatches. In the past Lawrence had contacted the Post Office management asking either for a wire to be connected, or to arrange for a service of telegraph boys operating to and from the ground, all to no avail.

Meanwhile, runs were difficult to score against some accurate Kent bowling and apart from a delightful 62 out of 93 in fifty-five minutes by Jessop, Gloucestershire were all out for 189. Heavy rain then stopped play and at the close the visitors were 75 for 6. Next day they continued to find Townsend (21-8-26-5) a handful and were bowled out for 103. On a rapidly deteriorating wicket, Kent immediately mounted a fine fight back, dismissing their hosts for just 80, with left-armer Frederick Martin now in the twilight of his career, taking 7 for 36. Needing 167 to win was always going to be a tall order for the visitors on a pitch that was favouring the bowlers. The wicket suited the Old Malvernian, C. J. Burnup; batting carefully and taking few risks, he made 66 out of his side's total of 139. Once again, Townsend (34-7-66-8) was indomitable, instigating a 27 run victory within two days and earning his side a day's rest.

The next fixture was against Warwickshire who were making their first appearance at Cheltenham. Local supporters were confident as Gloucestershire had already won an earlier encounter in the season at Edgbaston and further interest surrounded the game because of the recent remarkable batting of W. G. Quaife. Over the past fortnight his last six innings of 60, 117, 157, 24, 52 and 61 had been a series of not outs.

Batting first, the visitors made 290 with half-centuries coming from Devey, Lilley, Glover and Santall. George Quaife's impressive run came to an end when he fell victim to Townsend in his outstanding bowling performance of 46.4-8-128-9. The home team's batting showed strength in depth, with Sewell (71), back from South Africa, top scorer in a total of 346. Then Townsend immediately got down to wicket-taking. As in the first innings, he had Quaife neatly caught by his captain at backward point, and when the visitors were dismissed for 153 he had taken his one hundredth wicket of the season, and reaped another set of impressive figures (31-4-77-6). In five days of cricket, this accurate, teasing spinner had captured 28 wickets for 297 runs, the same number of dismissals as he had taken in 1895.

The hosts were poised for a victory which would place them third in the championship table. With the day's play over, there were practical jokes and all cricket talk was banned for the evening. Walter Troup explaining later in his memoirs, 'This rule was rigidly enforced, and if by any chance some enthusiast did forget himself sufficiently to talk "shop" he was immediately pounced upon and made to pay for a drinks round.'

Shortly after four o'clock on Saturday afternoon, Gloucestershire reached their target and won by five wickets. A small ceremony then took place in front of the pavilion, with W.G. presenting the match ball to Quaife and waggishly reminding him that it was he and Townsend who had ended his 471 run spree!

This was the precursor of another finale. Aged fifty, the Champion had made his last appearance at the Week. It could not have been described as his most lucky ground. In seventy-two innings he made only five centuries, so disappointing many of his ardent followers. His 318* in 1876 is immortal, but a Cricket Week is about batsmen consistently scoring large amounts of runs and by his own high standards he did not regularly produce the goods. He did, however, stage several splendid bowling displays; with his medium-fast or slow spin he was always quick to spot a batsman's weakness. For twenty-six years his presence was indispensible. Heading the cast list for every performance, W.G. entertained audiences of spellbound onlookers from all walks of life. There was never any regret at being late home for tea if you had seen the Champion, but his undisputed reign was over. It was time for 'The Croucher' to light the imagination and draw in crowds.

—— 1899 ——

In the spring it was requested that the committee should advertise for five additional professionals. Almost immediately Ted Spry arrived, followed by Harry Huggins and Percy Mills. They were to be followed in 1903 by a pair of great left-arm spinners in the shape of George Dennett and Cheltenham's irascible Charlie Parker.

After W.G. had captained the first four games of the season, Old Cheltonian, Walter Troup, took over. W.G.'s altercation with the committee had by now led to a deep rift following a letter he had written to them saying, 'I have the greatest affection for the county of my birth but for the committee as a body the greatest contempt.' Troup and 'Frizzie' Bush had tried in vain to get W.G. to put his pen through the offending words, but he would not. The Champion indicated that he wished to return to the side under Troup for the Cricket Week, but the new captain declined, pointing out that 'the dignity of the committee had been bitterly wounded and they would not hear of it'.

The tenth Australian touring team arrived in Cheltenham the day after their remarkable struggle for survival in a sensational Test match at the Oval. Hopes were high that Troup and his men might shrug off the drumming they had received from 'the Cornstalks' a few weeks earlier at Bristol and repeat Kent's success at the Canterbury Week, when they had beaten the tourists.

On a fine morning, with the College ground looking its very best, Troup won the toss and elected to bat on a splendidly prepared wicket. The *Echo* reported, 'Long before the time fixed upon for a start there was a good ring of ardent enthusiasts and the stands rapidly became filled and presented a most pleasing sight, the hundreds of ladies present for the most part being attired in their lightest and prettiest costumes.' A large cheer from the 3,000 spectators greeted Joe Darling as he led his team out.

For starters, Gloucestershire served up Champain and Rice, but disaster struck almost immediately when Ernest Jones removed the latter's leg stump on the fifth ball of the first over. Townsend, who had played in the recent Test, joined F. H. B. Champain and they progressed confidently. The opener, 'playing on his native heath, and before his own people', cut superbly, reaching his fifty at a run-a-minute but was out next ball. Jessop, playing carefully after being hit on the head by the lively bowling of Jones, held back the hurricane within him and also reached fifty. At lunch his side were 138 for 7, but by early afternoon they were all out for 203.

By the time the Australians began batting at four o'clock, over 5,000 people had paid for admission and watched the innings unfold to 97 for 3 by the close of play. That evening both teams were present in Montpellier Gardens, where the Australians admired 'the pretty scene and the pretty girls' at a concert and firework display organised by Mr A. W. Newton.

Before play the next morning, while the tourists were practising at the

The 1898 Cricket Week
From left to right, Sewell, Grace, Rice, Brown, Champain and Townsend

Charles Townsend in conversation. In 1899 he played one of the finest innings ever on the gr

nets, one of them spoke to Woofie. Unaware of his identity, the tourist asked the College coach if he could bowl, whereupon Woof gave the laconic reply, 'Just a bit,' took the ball and proceeded to demonstrate. At the end of the practice one of the Australians went and complimented him saying he showed promise. Woof thanked his admirer and must have still been chuckling to himself about the episode when, by popular demand, he was brought back to the county side to play against the Australians on the ground three years later.

The foundation of the visitors' innings was built around a faultless batting display by the tall, powerful 'Alf' Noble (77). Jessop bowled Iredale, sending his stump reeling nine yards, and the Gloucestershire attack shared the wickets; helped by some keen fielding they dismissed their guests for 228.

In ten minutes before lunch, Champain and Rice nonchalantly knocked off the deficit, but at a quarter to three, when play resumed in bad light, batting suddenly became difficult. Three wickets fell quickly and the faces of the spectators became 'as long as fiddles' as their team were only 16 runs ahead; but there was a surprise in store. On the second day, a crowd of over 5,000 was treated to one of the finest innings played on the College ground. It came from Charles Townsend, who had been in good form with the bat throughout the season. Dropped by Noble at point when he had made 5, the left-hander batted on ruthlessly, pulling and sweeping for just over five hours, scoring a magnificent 135*. Given solid support by his captain (51), the Cliftonian received a loud ovation when the Gloucestershire innings ended on 300. He had saved them from defeat and given them a chance of winning in the three and a half hours left for play.

With a little more time, victory might have been possible. The skilful, slow left-arm bowling of Arthur Paish reduced the Australians to 175 for 5, but at the finish this even contest ended in the home team enjoying the best of a drawn game. Afterwards Woof and his staff were congratulated by the tourists' secretary, Major Wardill, who commented that his team had not played on a better pitch throughout the tour: 'It was quite a Melbourne wicket!' This was high praise for the winning combination of the groundstaff's hard work and the surface deposit of Quaternary sand.

At the end of the game, two of the Australians, Laver and Iredale, tried to outdo their team mates by travelling what they thought would be a shorter and quicker route back to London. They disregarded the two carriages that had been reserved for the team on the half past seven train to the capital and went their own way. Unfortunately, their plan backfired due to a series of delays and by catching the wrong trains, so they spent several hours travelling around the Cotswolds. Having spent the night in Swindon, the two fugitives set off for London next morning. They finally arrived ten hours after the rest of the tour party and Laver later recalled that they received 'a severe gruelling' from their comrades for 'trying to save an hour's railway travelling!'

For the first time, a Sunday separated the two matches, so when the rich and well-supported Surrey team appeared on Monday morning the townsfolk were refreshed and ready for more cricket. The southerners were in excellent form and the knowledge that their 'crack' Tom Hayward was playing helped to draw the crowds.

Gloucestershire made one change from the team that played against the Australians. Popular Cheltenham professional Wrathall, who had recovered from illness, took the place of Champain who was still suffering from a knee injury sustained by a ball from Jones in the previous match. In bright sunshine, Abel and Brockwell opened the Surrey innings, facing the bowling of Jessop and Townsend. As one of the official umpires had failed to turn up, the Surrey bowler Tom Richardson stood in and must have enjoyed watching his team mates making a determined start. Brockwell (167), driving hard and hitting 21 fours, gave a magnificent display of all-round batting. In steering his team to a total of 292, one spectator was heard to remark, 'I'd rather have an hour of Brocky than all the Australians put together!'

Considering the large scores Surrey had been making recently, Gloucestershire had done well to dismiss them for under three hundred. This was due largely to Arthur Paish, the discovery of the year, who worked his way through the visitors, ending with figures of 31.4-4-93-7. He was rewarded the following afternoon when the executive of the club decided to allow a collection to be made on his behalf in recognition of his feat.

The feature of Gloucestershire's innings was the remarkable bowling of Lockwood (32-5-105-9) who restricted his hosts to 207. By the close of play Surrey had started to build a commanding lead and that evening both teams relaxed at the Opera House, watching a performance of *The White Heather*.

Appropriately each player was presented with a bunch of white heather and the gypsies' luck seemed to fall upon Paish and Lockwood the next day. The former, a sturdily built Gloucestershire man, who in seasons to come would have the fairness of his action questioned by umpires, bowled unchanged to return figures of 44.1-9-103-7. The visitors were all out for 211, but with their first innings lead this proved to be far too many runs for their hosts to chase. Lockwood (23-4-79-6) cleverly deceived the batsmen with subtle changes of pace, bowled his side to a 140 run victory and earned himself the record of the best bowling in a match for an opposition player at Cheltenham.

For Lawrence and the county committee, record attendances and takings for the Week proved their formula was spot-on and they could contemplate the new era with confidence.

CHAPTER SEVEN (1900-1905)

FAREWELL TO THE WEEK

—— 1900 ——

On 9 April Edwin Lawrence died aged 57. He was buried in Cheltenham cemetery close to his father-in-law, James Lillywhite, who had died at exactly the same age. Once a keen and skilful cricketer, he had managed the Week for seventeen years, consolidating Jem's work by maintaining his high standards, and introducing innovative ideas so increasing its popularity and cultivating financial success. A courteous and very popular figure in the town, the good-humoured Lawrence would be missed, not only by sportsmen, but also in political, municipal and social circles.

Local members of the county committee took over the running of the Week, led by Mr F. H. Harris, an experienced event organiser and a leading amateur cricketer in the district. The committee kept arrangements much the same, for they felt that no improvement could be made to Lawrence's successful management.

At the start of the season, Jessop left his job at the Stock Exchange and took over the reins from Troup who had returned to India. He thrived in his new role and by the time the Week started, he had already set a splendid example scoring over 2,000 runs and taking almost 100 wickets. Despite striving to engage more professionals, the county still had a large dependence on amateurs and when the team members were fully assembled towards the end of the season they made up a formidable side, winning five of their last eight matches.

Expectations were high as the first day of the Week dawned. There was the anticipation of the visit of mighty Yorkshire. As the county champions elect and a team bulging with great names, they were a tremendous attraction for spectators. Further appeal and fascination centred around the visit of Essex, making their first appearance on the ground later in the Week. Finally, attention was focused on the imminent arrival of the brilliant and unorthodox Gilbert Jessop, along with the

94

other local players in his team. 'Never have the Gloucestershire team been more welcome to the Garden Town than on the present occasion,' reported the *Echo*.

Dreams were shattered in the opening match when the county's eight amateurs were overwhelmed by Lord Hawke's team of hardened professionals, by an innings and 44 runs. Winning the toss, Jessop chose to bat first on one of Woof's well-prepared wickets. Opening the innings, Rice carried his bat for 38, while the rest of his team mates floundered in front of 4,000 spectators against the legendary Wilfred Rhodes (21.2-11-36-6), now bowling the statutory six ball over. They were dismissed in just two hours for 101. Gloucestershire's total was quickly passed, Lord Hawke celebrating his fortieth birthday by leading the charge with a fine 79 and George Hirst top-scoring with 108. Jessop (29-7-67-5) bowled well, but the visitors finished their first innings with a lead of over 200 runs. By the end of their innings the wicket had become 'somewhat difficult' and Gloucestershire were quickly bowled out for 160, Rhodes (27.4-7-67-7) making his first appearance on the ground, once again causing the damage.

During the Week, The White Viennese Band provided a great musical treat for the people of Cheltenham, and the famous instrumentalists were joined by 'a refined comedian, Mr Will Leslie' and 'the sweet, well-trained contralto, Miss Margaret A. Hicks Beach', niece of the Chancellor of the Exchequer.

The high class entertainment on stage was replicated on the cricket field where several players produced match-winning performances in an evenly-contested game. Batting first, the East Anglian side, despite missing Lucas, Kortright and McGahey, made 248, mainly due to a skilful innings of 134* by the tall, reliable Percy Perrin. A faultless three hour innings of 123 by Charles Townsend, who was nearing the end of his last regular season before departing into the legal profession, gave the hosts a lead of 37 at the half-way stage. Walter Mead demonstrated that he was in his element on a wearing wicket, taking 7 for 70 in forty overs, then a brilliant 'caught and bowled' by Jessop, to dismiss Perrin for nought in the second innings, was the talk of the town on Tuesday evening. Essex were routed by Jessop (26-10-29-8) with the best bowling performance of his career, and were all out for 118, leaving Gloucestershire 82 to win. On the last day, batting on an unpredictable wicket, Townsend steered his team to a narrow 2 wicket victory with a cool and determined 23*.

Noises were being made in the press that it would be beneficial to have a county match in Cheltenham during term time. Even though attendances on the College ground were still higher than at Bristol, it was nevertheless the case that the town was comparatively empty in August. It was not possible to use the Playground during the term, but in 1888 an experiment had been tried when Nottinghamshire appeared on the East Gloucestershire ground in June. The midlanders had won easily, assisted by William Barnes' strong, all-round performance. It had been generally agreed that the surrounding trees marred what would otherwise have been a suitable pitch, so the fixture was dropped. In 1903 the idea would be resurrected, this time as a match between Gloucestershire and the Philadelphians. No further fixture was to take place on the East Gloucestershire ground but the idea of a June festival in town would return to the agenda again in the mid 1920s.

—— 1901 ——

Lacking the services of the redoubtable Townsend and with Jessop hampered by the recurrence of a strain (which would end his career as a fast bowler) an irregular and unsettled Gloucestershire team had a disastrous season. In the past, new-found zest during the holiday month of August often led to a revival of fortunes, with Cheltenham the catalyst.

Middlesex, who had not appeared on the ground for ten years, had other thoughts. For the first two days, Gloucestershire held the upper hand, but staring defeat in the face on a broken wicket, the old Harrovian, W. P. Robertson, steered his team to a 4 wicket victory with an undefeated 110. Earlier in the game, Gloucestershire had earned themselves a 142 run first innings lead when Roberts and Paish, with 5 wickets each, had bowled out the visitors for 87. The only hitch was an injury picked up by wicket-keeper Board who received a nasty blow on the right hand, 'splitting his thumb' very badly, just before the end of play on the first day. Unfortunately, this prevented him from taking any further part in the match which had been assigned as his benefit, a ground collection that day having raised £11.18s on his behalf.

There were plenty of doctors around to treat the injured player, for a gathering of the British Medical Association was in full swing in town with over a thousand people attending the week-long 'scientific and social meeting'. The *Lancet* declared Cheltenham to be 'admirably adapted for both the festive and the serious side of a gathering of this sort'. The medics and their wives were enjoying the same atmosphere that cricket lovers had savoured for many years, no more so than when they mingled amidst the spectators before attending a delicious dinner at the College, served up by George's Ltd.

Dismissing their hosts for 148 left Middlesex needing 291 to win. Robertson, who coped admirably with deliveries that were 'flying about at different heights', was given solid assistance by the inventor of the googly or 'bosie', B. J. T. Bosanquet, who made 42. With an injured wicket-keeper and the dropping of seven catches by the Gloucestershire fieldsmen, the victory that looked so assured slipped out of the county's reach.

Rain interfered on all three days of the match against Kent, who had arrived directly from the Canterbury Week. One Hearne followed another, for the fine medium-pacer 'J.T.', with match figures of 8 for 77, had helped steer Middlesex to victory, while his cousin Alec, one of the best cricketers never to play for England, took to the field with 'the hoppers'. S. H. Day made a useful 60 for the visitors, but it was very much cricket between the showers and the game was abandoned as a draw on the third day.

The gates for the Week had been disappointing. The poor weather was a contributing factor, but the timing of the start to coincide with a Bank Holiday may have been unfortunate. Tradesmen would be under pressure to return to work after the break and would-be spectators might be running low on cash. Nationally there was also a gradual change in spectator preference taking place as football crowds began to swell, no doubt enticing away a number of cricket watchers.

—— 1902 ——

To celebrate the twenty-fifth anniversary of the Cricket Week, two very attractive matches were arranged, the first versus champions, Yorkshire, and the second against the Australians. The event started shortly after the crowning of King Edward VII in Westminster Abbey. The nation, which Queen Victoria had left with much to be proud of - materially rich and strategically powerful - was vibrant with celebrations.

Colourful decorations, musical bands and firework displays were amongst the many ways in which Cheltenham honoured the occasion, while it was agreed that the highly artistic display in the Colonnade, which had been erected for the Coronation, should remain for the Week.

The Hon. F. S. Jackson, George Hirst, Wilfred Rhodes and Gilbert Jessop travelled down to Cheltenham from the Oval after one of the most remarkable Test victories of all times. Australia had set England 263 to win on a difficult wicket and with the score on 48 for 5, Jessop went to the wicket. For the next one and a quarter hours he pulverized the Australian attack, making 104 out of the 139 runs that were added, with valuable support given by Jackson and Hirst. With 15 runs needed for victory when last man Rhodes came to the wicket, Hirst announced, 'Wilfred, we'll get 'em in singles'. They did, so giving England the first single wicket victory in Test cricket.

There was no time for sentiment the next day when the two Test players met. They were now on opposite sides and Yorkshire, formidable even without Lord Hawke, steamrollered over Gloucestershire in two days.

Leading up to the Week the weather had been poor. Woof and his staff had worked hard on the ground to get it looking good, but the wicket was slow and unpredictable. Winning the toss, Jessop batted first and was top-scorer with 42 out of a meagre total of 104. The visitors only needed to bat once, making 261, thanks to positive contributions from their long-established players. Taking advantage of a break from work, Townsend appeared in one of only three games he played all season and took 4 for 52, but he could not middle the ball any better than his team mates when he batted again. They were bowled out for 55, so receiving their second innings defeat from Yorkshire that season as the legendary Rhodes finished with match analysis of 10 for 60.

When the Australians arrived in Cheltenham on Sunday afternoon, a thunderstorm was raging and almost an inch of rain fell on the College ground. Only twenty minutes of play was possible the following day, but on Tuesday a large crowd feasted upon a Victor Trumper century. His innings of 125 was his ninth hundred of the tour and the mercurial master, arguably the greatest ever batsman, revelled on the treacherous wicket, toying with the bowling and experimenting with many daring and novel strokes. The Australians made 312, with Jessop taking 7 for 91, while Woof, playing his last game for the county on the ground, took the remaining 3 wickets. Apart from Jessop's exciting second innings score of 43 in forty minutes, which must have brought back memories of the Oval for the Australians, Gloucestershire, in front of a crowd of almost 5,000 spectators, found batting all too difficult against A. J. Hopkins (9 for 76) and Warwick Armstrong (8 for 109). Going down by an innings and 10 runs, for the first time in the history of the Week, the hosts lost both matches by an innings.

—— **1903** ——

In one of the wettest summers on record, the county gained only three victories in the whole of the season. Two of them were on the College ground and they were due to the wonderful new bowling combination of two left-armers, veteran Fred Roberts, in his last appearance at the Week, and Dorset-born new boy, George Dennett, making his Cheltenham debut.

Batting first, Gloucestershire made 258, with useful contributions coming from all the top order batsmen. Kent were then dismissed for 131 by Roberts (7 for 53) and Dennett (3 for 70), bowling twenty-five overs each. Making 220 when they batted again, the hosts set their guests a stiff target and when only two wickets were down at half past three on the last afternoon, it seemed as if Kent's rearguard action would ensure a draw. Young Dennett, raw to the first-class arena, had other ideas and just over an hour later the game was over. Dennett's figures (33-8-66-6), combined with Roberts' two wickets, earned Gloucestershire victory by 219 runs.

Worcestershire, appearing for the first time, were the visitors for the second match in which there were further fine bowling performances. On another well-timed holiday, Townsend enjoyed himself making a useful 52 out of 148. There was then a sensational ending to the Gloucestershire innings when Worcestershire's fast bowler Wilson (21-8-51-7) took the last four wickets in five balls without a run being hit from him. Anything their neighbours could do, Roberts (13-4-30-5) and Dennett (13-9-6-5) could do better, bowling their guests out for 46. A great innings of 73 by Wrathall, his highest score on the ground, helped his side to a second innings total of 114 as Wilson took a further 5 wickets. Roberts, however, finished his Cheltenham playing days in style, taking 8 for 64 and bowling his side to a 100 run victory.

—— **1904** ——

By the time the Week started, the new Town Hall was fully in use. Without the Assembly Rooms, which had been demolished, it was felt that the town needed a large, new venue for the numerous balls and concerts that were held. Cheltenham was still a very popular place for retired servicemen and civil servants, and the Town Hall lent a complementary air of grandeur and respectability to glamorous events.

However, there was unemployment and great poverty for an

The end of Kent's first innings in 1903

increasing number of the town's residents, not helped by a changing population trend. When James Lillywhite had first introduced cricket to the Playground, the majority of the country's population lived in rural areas, but due to the continuing growth and importance of industry and the migration of workers, the balance had changed and a majority of people now lived in urban areas. This trend suited the traders of the town, none more so than 'Barnett the Fishmonger'.

Edgar Barnett, captain of Cheltenham Town CC, was the first of the four Barnetts to play for the county. Against Yorkshire, he opened the batting with Wrathall. They made a promising start in reply to the visitors' 148, but when both of them were dismissed, followed by Jessop, the remaining eight Gloucestershire batsmen made just 14 runs between them and the county was all out for 84. Lord Hawke, with 52, was top scorer for the guests in their second innings total of 147, while Dennett added seven more wickets to his first innings haul of six, ending with a match analysis of 71.2-19-139-13.

Needing 212 to win, the home side was saved from the guile and mastery of Rhodes, who must have been itching to add to his first innings tally of 6 for 40, when heavy storms forced the game to be abandoned as a draw. In three consecutive appearances for Yorkshire on the ground, Rhodes had taken 29 wickets for 203 runs in five innings. In his next match at Cheltenham, in four years' time, he would be opening the batting for his team.

The ground had recovered enough for Gloucestershire to start their last scheduled first-class game of the season the following day. The visitors were Surrey who grabbed a 119 run win in two days on a bowler's wicket. England opener Tom Hayward made a resolute 53, enabling his team to reach 206. Once again Dennett was in fine form, taking 7 for 117, but he was then upstaged by the leg-break bowling of H. C. McDonell who took 7 for 44 as Gloucestershire slumped to 79 all out. Surrey's first innings lead proved invaluable because the sides were very even on the second day. Locals were delighted to see a young newcomer, Cheltenham-born professional Percy Mills, given another trial by the county. He obliged by taking 6 for 38 as the visitors were dismissed for 91, but it still left the hosts too stiff a task and they were bowled out for just 99. J. N. Crawford, a seventeen-year-old Repton schoolboy, bowled unchanged with McDonell in both innings; this time Crawford caused the main damage, taking 7 for 43, as both bowlers ended with 10 wickets in the match.

Lord Asquith, Mr. Lloyd George and the author, about 1905

—— 1905 ——

The final Cricket Week started at the end of August and ran into early September. Rain greatly interfered with proceedings, as summer slipped away and the cold and damp of autumn began to take hold. The end of the 'dull season' when residents were away on holiday, was recorded in the Cheltonian Chatter column of the *Chronicle*:

'One by one the blinds are drawn up in villa-dom, the obliging policeman is gradually released from the weight of responsibility of keeping his eye on numerous areas and back gardens after nightfall . . . Domestic pets return from their various temporary retreats and resume their customary eventide prowls, and other cheerful outward and visible signs bear witness that many highly-respectable and much-esteemed families are in residence once more.'

With life back to normal, the Australians arrived in town, to play their thirty-fourth match of the tour, having just defeated Kent by an innings. As they travelled westwards across the country, from one 'Garden of England' to another, the weather deteriorated. Notices on the town trams, promising to 'take you to the cricket ground', were all in vain as no play was possible on the first day.

Light relief was available through matinee and evening performances at the Montpellier Gardens. Back in town after six years, the original Blue Hungarian Band, conducted by Edouard Crosse, supported by soprano Miss Lydia Griffiths and 'the well known London humorist Mr Fred Daniels', put something of a smile back on the faces of those connected with cricket.

Proceedings eventually started at one o'clock next day. Darling, who had made a hundred at Canterbury, batted splendidly until one short of a century, when he skied the ball to long-on and was brilliantly caught in the outfield by Langdon after a considerable chase. Despite further overnight rain, play started on time on the final day. The visitors were quickly bowled out for 195, then Gloucestershire got off to a good start helped by the hard-hitting Wrathall (55) for whom a benefit fund collection was made that day. The home side was dismissed soon after lunch for 137. Laver and Howell had helped themselves to five wickets each and just when the game seemed to be heading for a tame draw, the Australians made a sporting declaration on 77 for 1 in their second innings. It left their hosts eighty minutes to score 136 for victory.

Reducing Gloucestershire to 64 for 9, their plan was very nearly successful, thwarted only by Jessop's stonewalling tactics and skill in securing the strike. In his fourteen overs, Cotter took 6 for 36 and Laver, who was not bowled in the innings, congratulated Jessop and his team for 'the sporting game they played'. In his book *An Australian Cricketer on Tour* he wrote, 'They did not unnecessarily waste time, nor appeal for the light, which was bad, partly due to the eclipse. Moreover, the incoming batsmen frequently crossed the outgoing batsman before he left the field. This is indeed playing cricket as it should be played.'

Having just managed to hold out against the tourists, the county bounced back and defeated a weakened Middlesex side in two days. Bright weather brought out the crowds on Thursday morning, but there was disappointment for some of them when they heard that Warner, McGregor, Beldham and Bosanquet were all absent from the metropolitan side.

Gloucestershire took advantage of the situation. On a bowler's wicket, twenty-two batsmen fell on the first day, with the hosts ending 100 runs ahead. Next day a 101 run, third wicket partnership between Board and Sewell proved to be a match-winning contribution. Needing 280 to win, Middlesex, according to *Wisden*, gave 'an inglorious display' and were all out in an hour and forty minutes losing by 174 runs.

Dennett's figures of 18.5-7-44-7 in the first innings and 18.2-4-46-5 in the second, created a new Gloucestershire record in inter-county matches. His season's haul of 131 wickets for 2,553 runs, at an average of 19.48, just beat Townsend's 1898 record of 130 wickets at twenty each. Gloucestershire ended their season on a high note and said farewell to the Cricket Week.

CHAPTER EIGHT (1906-1909)

THE FESTIVAL ARRIVES

—— 1906 ——

The inaugural Cheltenham Cricket Festival commenced quite by chance on 13 August 1906. The customary two matches allotted to the 'Week' were extended to three, simply because of difficulties that had arisen in making home fixtures fit in with the arrangements of visiting teams. Three games were scheduled to be played during nine weekdays. Providing the opposition were Kent, Sussex and Worcestershire. Despite some unsettled weather throughout the event, there were immediate rewards for cricket enthusiasts and local committee members, with over £700 of gate money going into the coffers of the county club.

At the end of July, Gloucestershire had been in a somewhat hopeless position, with eight defeats and only one victory to their name. *Wisden* records that this state of affairs was 'calculated to depress even the most sanguine of the county's supporters'. As in the past, August brought about an astonishing change. Availability of amateurs, who had not previously found time to play, enabled the side to finish the season in style, winning five out of eight matches.

It was clear that the number of visitors who came and stayed in the town in order to watch the cricket was on the decline. No obvious reason for this was apparent but there was the uncomfortable feeling that the attraction of cricket was on the wain. Undoubtedly the reputation of the home county was not as great as it once had been.

Locals remained defiantly loyal, and when play commenced on Monday morning the business streets of the town were, according to the *Chronicle*, 'so empty and silent that one might almost hear the grass grow between the chinks of the pavement'. It was as though a pact had been made 'from senior boss to junior errand-boy, on the principle if cricket interferes with business, give up business'.

Batting first, Gloucestershire made 220 with England slow left-armer Colin Blythe taking 6 for 100. Kent replied with 245 as Dennett

105

(46.2-5-113-6) collected his customary haul. An interesting finish was expected on the last day, with the visitors needing 132 to win and Dennett bowling on a deteriorating wicket. But Burnup and Dillon, batting with skill and confidence, scored the runs in under one and a half hours to give their team victory by ten wickets, so steering them towards becoming county champions for the first time.

A lively Gloucestershire performance over the following two days gave them victory over Sussex by an innings and 50 runs. No doubt matters would have been different if the visitors had been able to enjoy the presence of their two great batsmen of the time, Ranjitsinhji and Fry. Unfortunately, the former had returned to India, while three months earlier, at Lord's, Fry had injured his achilles tendon so badly that it completely ruled him out of playing for the rest of the season. In eighty minutes on Thursday morning Gloucestershire dismissed the southerners for 63 in twenty-six overs. Bowling unchanged, Dennett kept an immaculate length and collected 5 for 34, while Percy Ford, the six-foot seven-inch tall Gloucester city fast bowler, making his Cheltenham debut, got the ball to rise on a fiery wicket and took 5 for 29.

It looked as if the hosts would follow suit and also be bowled out cheaply, but on 56 for 4 a shower of rain caused half an hour's delay, after which conditions eased up. Taking advantage of the pitch, another Cheltenham newcomer, Frank Thomas, wrote himself into the record book by becoming the first player to make a hundred at the Festival. A contemporary of Townsend at Clifton College, Thomas had not played regularly and was now in his last season with the county. In a partnership of 150, made at the rate of a run-a-minute, Thomas (111) and Board (82) hit the Sussex bowling all over the field, and when stumps were drawn the hosts were in a strong position on 227 for 5.

Within an hour the following morning Gloucestershire were bowled out, adding 50 runs to their overnight total, but Sussex then quickly collapsed to the expertise of Dennett (18-2-75-4) and Ford (19-1-84-6) who, once again, bowled unchanged.

In the third match, Gloucestershire had even more to offer their supporters by playing the kind of cricket that gave the Festival instant appeal. On the first day, Worcestershire were overwhelmed by their hosts' score of 498 for 8 made in under five hours and they never recovered. Playing his first match of the season for the county, the holiday-spirited Townsend made an 'astonishingly brilliant' 214 in three and a half hours, going to the wicket with the score on one and returning to the pavilion fifth out with the total on 421. In two hours, he and Sewell

(107) put on 252, leaving the crowd with glowing memories and the committee with smiles on their faces.

Jessop described Townsend's driving as 'a revelation', going on to say that never before had he seen him hit 'with so much force . . . though he punched the ball in the air with the abandon of a mere slogger, quite foreign to the nature of the "Charles" of former days, not a chance went to hand'. He admitted that it had been a real eye opener for him and he wished that 'the "Old Man" had been there to have seen "Challey" slogging'.

The hosts then bowled and fielded superbly, throttling any fight back their guests might have mustered. Worcestershire were all at sea against Dennett's accuracy and he almost single-handedly bowled them out for 147 and 146, ending with a match analysis of 52.3-13-140-15, so giving his team victory by an innings and 230 runs.

At the end of what was to some now the 'Festival', but still referred to by many as the 'Week', a Grand Evening Fete and Firework Display took place at Pittville Park. In this delightful setting, the evening ended with the lighting of the firework portrait of Gilbert Jessop which provided far more sparks than he and other Cheltenham members of the Gloucestershire XI had produced on the cricket field over the past few days.

Townsend, Sewell and Thomas had batted wonderfully and Dennett had bowled magnificently. Conversely Jessop, Champain, Barnett and Wrathall, none of whom had made a hundred on the ground, had squandered the opportunity to impress their fellow townsmen.

Losing two out of the scheduled nine days of cricket as a result of easy victories was unsatisfactory to organisers and enthusiasts alike. Visiting the ground as usual at this time, E. M. Grace must have been reminded of what happened in this situation in the old days when W.G. and Lillywhite arranged for local cricketers to join the county players in a friendly game. Such a fixture failed to materialise, possibly because the county players feared a loss of dignity if locals were given a chance of distinguishing themselves. Inevitably business suffered along with a sense of occasion.

—— 1907 ——

It was hardly surprising that twelve months later, the two game Week was back. Week or Festival, Gloucestershire swept to victory in both matches. A rain-affected pitch produced a bowler's paradise on the first day when 22 wickets fell for a total of 313 runs. Batting first, Kent were spellbound by Dennett (25.5-7-75-7) and were dismissed for 135. Gloucestershire floundered too, and their meagre 111 would have been very drab if it had not been for Jessop who made a sparkling 33 out of 40 in thirteen minutes. At the close of play, Kent had worked themselves into a strong position, 91 ahead with 8 wickets in hand.

The following morning, gentle cunning and consistent accuracy from George Dennett (21-3-71-7) quickly finished off the visitors, leaving Gloucestershire needing 158 to win. In under two hours the hosts, led by Board (65) and Brownlee (47), scored the runs, winning the contest by 7 wickets.

A day of rest preceeded the start of an interesting game against Hampshire, who ended up losing by 83 runs on their first visit to the ground. An all-round performance by Henry Persse, taking 5 for 12 and scoring 50, gave the visitors a small first innings lead and they held the initiative until midway through Gloucestershire's second innings.

The turning point of the game was a fourth wicket stand of 147 between Jessop and Champain. Jessop's first 53 runs came in a breathtaking quarter of an hour as he made full use of his power, agility and marvellous eye. Here was that 'human catapult' in devastating action, the man who once was said to have pulled an off-side delivery from the College Lawn end with such ferocity that it sailed over Sandford Road and crashed against the hospital brickwork; and whose powerful hit on another occasion smashed the clockface on the pavilion. With many more tempting targets around the ground for him to aim at, Cheltenham spectators always lived in hope. Jessop's blows were tamed for the next fifty minutes of his innings, however, until he was finally out for 92; meanwhile Champain batted on skilfully for nearly two hours making 70.

F. H. Bateman-Champain was the best of the five cricket-loving brothers who represented Cheltenham College between 1883 and 1898. A member of the College XI for five seasons and captain for his last three, he was an impressive batsman who had scored a hundred against Joe Darling's Australian team of 1899 at Oxford. Champain would have been a highly successful first-class cricketer, but his schoolmaster duties at Wellington and Cheltenham prevented him playing regularly for the county. His opportunity to play came every August when the school holidays arrived, and in total he appeared eighty-three times for Gloucestershire over twenty years.

Dennett (17-4-43-5) and Mills (17-2-70-5) bowled unchanged and dismissed Hampshire for 120. By the end of the season, Dennett's match haul of 12 wickets had helped him become the first Gloucestershire bowler to take 200 wickets in a season.

—— **1908** ——

With the Week extended again to nine days, the Festival reappeared in 1908 and Champain made a match-winning hundred against Warwickshire, to become the first and only Old Cheltonian to score a century for Gloucestershire on the ground.

Without the services of Townsend, who had earlier promised to appear but was prevented from doing so by a strain, the county won their first match by 10 wickets. Warwickshire started badly, losing 6 wickets for 92 runs, before Quaife (89) and Stephens (74) saved the day by adding 128 for the seventh wicket, a record partnership for visitors to the ground. Harry Huggins, with 5 for 59, proved a valuable foil to the wily Dennett and the visitors were bowled out for 286. On 165 for 5, Jessop launched an assault upon the visiting bowlers making 72 out of 83 in just over half an hour. Champain (113) and 'Tommy' Langdon (108) steered Gloucestershire to a total of 473 before Warwickshire were bowled out for 206 and the required 23 runs were duly scored.

Fortunes were reversed in the next game against Hampshire who batted throughout the first day for 332. The backbone of their innings was a second wicket stand of 176 between Philip Mead (96), the tall, hard hitting left-hander with a cast-iron defence, and opener Alec Bowell (87). In reply, Gloucestershire (166 and 198) batted poorly and the visitors won by nine wickets.

On Thursday, a large crowd was expected to greet Yorkshire who were visiting after a lapse of four years. The Tykes, on top of the county championship table, were enjoying an undefeated season and by Saturday their 182 run victory made them absolutely certain of winning the competition. Jessop lost the third out of three Festival tosses and the visitors' new opener, Wilfred Rhodes, walked out to bat in Cotswold drizzle. Showers restricted play, and soon after five o'clock the game was abandoned for the day with Yorkshire on 192 for 6.

An improvement in the weather next day attracted many people to the ground. On a drying wicket, Yorkshire's bowlers were too good, and in reply to the visitors 219, Gloucestershire made a meagre 83. Opening the batting and making his Cheltenham debut was Alfred Dipper. Born into a long-established farming family a few miles away in Deerhurst, his rustic approach to the game had met with considerable success at nearby Tewkesbury CC, for whom he had made 132 earlier in the week. There were some armchair critics who thought he should have been playing at Cheltenham throughout the Festival, but the selectors had gone for a 'chopping and changing' policy.

With ground admission one shilling, grandstand and enclosure a shilling extra, and entry free for soldiers and sailors dressed in uniform, the ground was humming with almost 3,500 people by mid-afternoon. In their second innings, Yorkshire slowly tightened their grip on the game in front of a main stand full of ladies in colourful Edwardian dresses with resplendent hats, and gentlemen in shirts, ties and suits, boaters or top hats.

Setting Gloucestershire 359 to win in four hours on the last day, Yorkshire took just over half that time to bowl out their hosts. For once, Dennett's match figures of 10 for 157 were upstaged. The strong, accurate, medium-paced Yorkshireman, John Newstead, was having a very rewarding season and his 11 for 104 may well have contributed to his selection as one of *Wisden's* Cricketers of the Year.

The early end on Saturday afternoon led an 'old and observant townsman' to remark that for thirteen years there had not been a full day's cricket on either Wednesday or Saturday during the Cricket Week. As both days were half-holidays, gates suffered, so he suggested the possibility of starting matches on those two respective days. However, cricket's administrators were not prepared to embark upon an idea which would affect travel arrangements.

—— **1909** ——

The status quo prevailed, and twelve months later another Festival started at the end of a disastrous summer for the county, one that has often been labelled the worst season in the history of the club.

To the delight of the crowd, and the surprise, no doubt, of the visiting Australian team, Gloucestershire rose to the occasion at Cheltenham. On a dry, fast wicket, despite some overnight rain, the visitors astonishingly collapsed to 139 for 7 in an hour and forty minutes. Huggins and Dennett were causing the damage and apart from a cameo innings of 48 from Victor Trumper, the tourists looked humiliated. While spectators were enjoying their half-crown luncheon supplied by George's Ltd., dark clouds covered the ground and a heavy shower delayed the game until mid-afternoon. Bowling then became difficult and a resolute, hard-hitting, undefeated half-century by Hopkins enabled the tourists to reach 215.

A month earlier, in the third Test match at Leeds, Jessop had torn muscles in his back while fielding, putting an end to his cricket for the season. He came to the College ground to greet the visitors and watch the morning's play, but before his side went in to bat he was taken ill and had to return to his home at Shirehampton. This did not deter the county's openers, Jack Board and C. S. Barnett (father of the renowned Charles), who scored freely as 50 runs came in the same number of minutes.

Townsend, captaining the side and making a welcome return to the ground after two years' absence, joined Barnett and together they steered the county to 120 at the close of play. It was then time for visitors to the town to make their way to Montpellier Gardens to enjoy The March Hares concert company under the 'clever musical director Philip Braham'. David Burnaby and other artistes cheerfully sang their way through the show, fulfilling many requests and performing innumerable encores. Although in the past there were mutterings amongst locals about the monotony of the corporation's selection of entertainment, this time Alfred Newton's choice proved a great success.

The second day's play belonged to the brilliant Townsend who took his score to 129 in little more than two hours at the crease, making his fourth century on the ground. He was given valuable assistance by Barnett, whose brisk innings of 60 pleased the spectators as he faced the tricky bowling of Cotter; he was 'in the wars' on several occasions and caught in the ribs with a particularly lively delivery.

With over 4,500 people watching the afternoon's play, county trialist Claude Woolley, Stroud professional and elder brother of the Kent star Frank, together with the bespectacled Frank Roberts, kept the score moving freely as Cotter worked up a terrific speed. Roberts, who would be killed in action a few years later at Ypres, went on to make 80, helped by his brother and the rest of the tail-enders. When Gloucestershire reached a total of 400, heavy rain put an early end to play. Australia, 196 runs in arrears, were helped to a draw because the game did not resume until a quarter to three the following day. Left-handers Bardsley (66) and Ransford, the latter batting brilliantly for his 121, steered the Colonials to the safety of 247 for 8 as Dennett captured 6 wickets.

Rain was a spoilsport in the next two matches and no doubt there would have been a run on the raincoats (costing between 21s. to 30s.),

Gloucestershire v Australia in 1909

Jessop, having been taken ill, speaking
to Dr. Adair Dighton before leaving in a pony carriage

umbrellas and 'damp-proof socks', all available from The Famous, the well-known High Street outfitters. Batting first, Worcestershire made 292, Dennett taking five wickets, but the most exciting part of proceedings was the neat catch that Board made to dismiss Arnold. The *Looker-On* recorded his 'stentorian roar' of appeal which made spectators blink as the sound 'reverberated through the deserted halls of the College like the detonation of a cannon'. Gloucestershire reached 198, then it rained and rained.

Against Essex, only three hours of play were possible on the first day. When matters were about to resume next morning, the brothers A. W. and F. B. Roberts were nowhere to be seen. News reached the ground that they had been involved in a car crash on Shurdington Road. They had been staying in Barnwood with their brother, a vicar, and while they were being driven to the ground by his chauffeur, their Humber collided with a Siddeley whose occupants were 'out on a morning run'. Fortunately nobody was seriously hurt, F. B. Roberts landing against a signpost and injuring his back, while his brother cut his knee.

Little progress was made on the field that day, with only an hour and forty minutes of play possible, so the hosts made a big effort on the last day to try and earn themselves a win. Although both Roberts brothers were on the mend, they took no further part in the match. In reply to Gloucestershire's 162, Essex were bowled out for 88, with Dennett taking 6 for 33. In twenty-eight minutes Langdon and Brownlee made 91 and the home side declared, but Essex held out for a draw and were 47 for 5 at the close, Dennett capturing another 4 wickets.

A few weeks later, at the end of the season, E. M. Grace retired from his position as club secretary. He had taken on the job in 1873 when Gloucestershire had just started to play at Cheltenham. He had witnessed the event grow and flourish first with Lillywhite, then with Lawrence. His departure brought an end to the Graces' forty year connection with the club.

CHAPTER NINE (1910-1914)

THE 'GENTLEMAN'S PERSONAL GENTLEMAN'

—— 1910 ——

English cricket was changing as George V began his reign. With more and more professionals playing the game, the age of amateur ascendancy was coming to an end.

Gloucestershire bucked the trend and the majority of those who performed at Cheltenham at the start of the new decade played cricket just for the love of it. They would have certainly enjoyed routing Worcestershire in the first of the three Festival fixtures, thus completing the season's double over their neighbours.

The hosts secured a strong advantage on the first day due to Brownlee (25.1-6-84-6) and Dennett (28-10-36-4) bowling the visitors out for 135. At the close of play Gloucestershire were 36 runs ahead, 4 wickets still to fall and Frank Roberts on 62*. Next day the hosts scored quick runs, taking advantage of the bowlers' difficulty with the slippery ball. When rain began to fall more heavily, the impressive looking 'shields' were brought into use, consisting of canvas frames on wooden supports and wheels. They were not in use for long and Roberts batted on, making a brilliant 157, his highest score in first-class cricket, so enabling his side to reach 374. Needing 239 to avoid an innings defeat proved too much for the guests and they were bowled out in the early afternoon of the last day, 63 runs behind. To celebrate their victory, Jessop, Cornelius, Champain, Dennett and Mills, all accomplished at hitting and following the 'little white pill', went and enjoyed a game of golf on Cleeve Hill.

Singleton's hat shop in Albion Street was encouraging spectators to purchase straw hats at prices ranging from 4d. to 1s. 6d., before going to watch county champions Kent in action on the College ground. Perhaps choosing one with a wide brim might have been a wise precaution for every Gloucestershire supporter, in order to help conceal the embarrassment of being hopelessly outplayed by the visitors, who won by an innings and 242 runs.

In five hours on the first day, Kent, batting like champions, made 607 for 6 declared, setting a record which stands today as the highest innings total scored by opponents on the ground. 'Punter' Humphreys made 162, putting on 93 for the first wicket with Knott. Then, with Seymour (90), he added 140 in seventy-five minutes for the second wicket. Mason (121*) continued the assault, scoring 85 in forty minutes with Hooman, then a magnificent 134 in just under an hour with Huish.

A splendid day's entertainment on the field was followed by a first-rate performance from The March Hares concert company at the Montpellier Gardens, engaged by popular request for a second year running. This merely fuelled the fire of discontent of a *Bristol Times and Mirror* correspondent who dismissed the Festival's evening amusements as 'stereotyped'. Comparing Canterbury with Cheltenham he wrote, 'When the Cheltenham week was established its founders were confident they were going to make it a great rival of the Kent gathering.' Kent had an 'experienced manager' who made the Canterbury Festival such a success with a wide variety of entertainment and amusement for residents and those visitors to the cricket who stayed in the city for the duration of the Festival. The Old Stagers performed at the theatre, county balls took place, bands played at various venues in the city and entertainers and wandering minstrels performed nightly in the beautifully illuminated streets.

The correspondent felt that in Cheltenham during the previous twenty-five years little or nothing had been done to supplement cricket by special attractions. He pointed out that it was up to the local committee to 'use their influence to dispel the lethargy which now prevails' and if they did 'the town and the club would reap a substantial benefit'.

A few changes did follow but Cheltenham faced a particular problem. The Festival was held when many residents were away on holiday and visiting spectators tended to drive in and out by 'motor', or come on cheap daily excursions rather than stay overnight in the town. Entertainment needed to be tailored accordingly.

After overnight rain affected the pitch, Gloucestershire were bowled out for 168 and 197, with Sewell the only batsman to show any meaningful resistance to Carr, who ended with a match analysis of 26-1-110-11.

Surrey were the next visitors and on a rain-soaked pitch they gained the upper hand by bowling their hosts out for 81 and then making 213, with Ducat and Hobbs both scoring fifties. In their second innings, a

Gloucestershire revival was led by their captain. Making his only century on the College ground, Jessop scored a superb 124 in two hours, putting on 144 in eighty minutes for the fourth wicket with Sewell (46).

Surrey's new professional recruit, Bill Hitch, was an energetic all-rounder - dashing hitter, brilliant fielder and one of the fastest bowlers in the country. His 6 for 105 meant Surrey needed 208 to win and at 125 for 6 an interesting finish was brewing up. Then Hitch (48*) and Hobbs (40*) hit off the remaining 83 runs in just over half an hour, so winning a splendid contest by four wickets.

—— 1911 ——

Playing their last three games of the season, Gloucestershire earned two victories as an exceedingly long, hot spell of weather started to break up.

Alfred Dipper, now recognised as one of the most improved players in the country, arrived at Cheltenham having just made his maiden first-class century, 119 against Hampshire at Southampton. Bubbling with enthusiasm, he helped to dismiss Worcestershire for 240 with figures of 6 for 103. Dipper then made a determined 120 in Gloucestershire's total of 443, putting on 139 in a sparkling sixth wicket stand with F. B. Roberts (138). According to the *Looker-On,* Roberts 'out Jessoped Jessop' with a 'cheerful innings that greatly pleased the crowd'. Dennett, with 5 for 61, reduced the visitors to 134 and they were vanquished by an innings and 69 runs.

For the second year running Kent had an easy triumph, sweeping to a two day innings and 94 run victory. Batting first, the visitors made 334 dominated by a magnificent 148 in under three hours by Frank Woolley who drove the ball with great power. With Gloucestershire 42 for no wicket at the close of play, spectators looked forward to an interesting second day as the theatre lovers amongst them made their way to the Montpellier Gardens.

The attraction was Alfred Newton's concert company, The Mad Hatters, whose performances were described in the *Looker-On* as 'quaint and original' with a 'natural touch of Lewis Carroll humour'.

On a crumbling wicket the next day, Gloucestershire went to pieces and were bowled out for 115 and 125. Keeping a fine length and getting a good deal of vicious spin, Blythe, with figures of 18-5-45-8 and 19-7-39-6, led the rout.

Gloucestershire struggling in their second innings v Kent in 1911

Northamptonshire, who had recently joined the first-class counties, made their first visit to Cheltenham by car because of a rail strike. Starting the match on a rain-affected wicket, batsmen fared badly as twenty wickets fell on the first day. Dismissed for 134, Gloucestershire then bowled out the midlanders for 139 thanks to an excellent performance from Dennett (31-7-74-8). Further overnight rain meant that runs were just as hard to get on the second day, with 16 wickets going down for 149 runs. Thompson (35.1-14-67-7) reduced the hosts to 141 all out and at the close of play Northamptonshire were 43 for 6. Watched by a poor crowd, with many empty spaces round the ground, the visitors added just fourteen to their overnight total and thanks to Dennett (5 for 27) and Parker (4 for 28) Gloucestershire won by 79 runs.

—— **1912** ——

Twelve months after a drought and heat-wave the country was awash with rain water, with floods affecting towns as far apart as Cardiff and Norwich. Cheltenham had more than its fair share of rain and the miserable weather caused the Festival to be a financial failure. Gross receipts for the nine days amounted to a paltry £386.13s., half the normal figure and only ten pounds more than a day's takings against the Australians back in 1896. Below-average gates throughout the season meant the county's coffers were already badly depleted before the Festival, which they could usually rely on to boost the year's returns. The balance sheet was becoming an embarrassment and matters were about to become even worse.

In contrast, there was encouraging news from the committee who had taken notice of suggestions put forward two years earlier. Terms for hiring private tents on the College ground were now available on application to Mr C. O. H. Sewell at the county ground Bristol, Dr Dighton at Warwick House or Mr G. Norman in Priory Parade. An enterprising decision had been taken in a bid to create more of a sense of occasion.

The College was proving to be a happy hunting ground for Kent, who claimed their third consecutive victory as they coasted to a nine wicket win. Wickets galore fell on the first day, twenty-six of them going down for 303 runs. Gloucestershire were bowled out for 129, with Jessop, making his last Festival appearance as captain, scoring 50 out of 60 in half an hour. He then returned figures of 6.1-1-14-5 as the visitors were dismissed for 122. Gloucestershire continued their second innings the following day and with rain affecting an already sodden ground, only forty-five minutes of play were possible. Bowling unchanged, Blythe (21-5-48-5) and Carr (20-6-34-5) dismissed Jessop's men for 87, and when play started at half-past four on the final day the visitors knocked up the necessary 95 runs in under an hour.

The next match, against the Australians, was ruined by yet more rain. Warren Bardsley's 115 and Dennett's match figures of 10 for 150 provided the only sparkle on a cold, wet College ground. In reply to the tourists' 256, Gloucestershire made 150 and reduced the Australians to 67 for 7 in their second innings before further rain ended the game prematurely on Saturday afternoon.

Cricket's loss was the Opera House's gain and the celebrated Follies performed to a large audience. Numbers from the excellent advanced bookings for these talented players were swollen by the many spectators who flocked in from the sodden cricket field. The open air performances by The Mad Hatters, making their return visit to the Montpellier Gardens, were, understandably, less of a success.

The final game against Surrey was abandoned without a ball being bowled and over three wet days the gatekeepers took just £7 16s. 6d.

⸺ 1913 ⸺

At the start of the season, Sewell succeeded Jessop as club captain and the Festival proved to be an unqualified success, with the county winning all three of their matches.

Preparations took place in glorious sunshine and the event's social scene was looking brighter too. Special privileges were given to members of the county club for the first time, including providing them with their own stand and an enclosure with attractively decorated tea tables. There were more private tents than usual, where local clubs could entertain members and their guests, among them the Union Club, Cambray. None of this encroached upon the spaces used by the general public and it was generally agreed that the local committee's enterprising efforts were 'first-rate'.

In the opening match against Worcestershire, the county were without Jessop, and play on the first day was anything but 'Jessopian'. On what seemed like a favourable wicket, Gloucestershire made 237 in four and a quarter hours. Opening the innings, Barnett made a very patient 67 in

almost three and a half hours at the crease, superseding this performance in the second innings when he carried his bat to make 62* in almost three and a quarter hours.

For two days the game was a very even struggle. The visitors made 222 (Bowley 93) with new fast bowler Gange taking 5 for 95. When play started on Saturday after a delay for rain, Worcestershire needed 251 to win, but with Parker (8.5-4-10-4) and Dennett (22-10-48-4) in fine form, it proved to be too much and they lost by 129 runs.

The next game against Hampshire turned out to be the final appearance for Gilbert Jessop on the College ground; the following year he volunteered as a recruiting officer. With wickets falling around him, Jessop made 54 out of 61 in twenty-two minutes. He received twenty-four balls, scoring off seventeen of them, with 2 sixes, 7 fours, 2 threes, 2 twos and 4 singles as Gloucestershire reached 169. It is no wonder that C. B. Fry should later comment in a tribute to Jessop, 'No man has ever driven a ball so hard, so high and so often in so many different directions. No man has ever made cricket so dramatic an entertainment.'

With a first innings lead of 27, Hampshire, who went on to lose the match by 28 runs, bowled their hosts out for 152. Unceremoniously, they dismissed Jessop first ball, leaving a depressed atmosphere over the College ground. It was to remain in a somewhat doleful state as the clouds of war gathered.

Unwittingly, the last game of the Festival against Warwickshire was responsible for an enduring contribution to English literature. Amongst the spectators was P. G. Wodehouse who watched some of Gloucestershire's rising stars help the county reach 328, with Dipper (102) making his third hundred of the season. On a rain-affected wicket the next day, Warwickshire could not cope with Dennett (21.3-5-42-7) and the team was dismissed for 134. The home side knocked up a quick 172, leaving the visitors wanting 367 to win. Losing their first three wickets that evening, they slumped to 119 all out in one and a half hours on Saturday morning, as Dennett captured 6 for 29.

It was not one of the Gloucestershire players who particularly excited Wodehouse, but the Yorkshire-born, Warwickshire all-rounder, Percy Jeeves. Described in *Wisden* as 'an absolute prize', Jeeves was enjoying a successful season in the top half of the county's batting averages, and was the leading bowler with over a hundred wickets from his fast-medium deliveries.

Thirty-two-year-old Wodehouse, writing prolifically and sharing his time between London and New York, was visiting his parents who had moved from Shropshire to Cheltenham ten years earlier. From a very young age 'Plum' had both played and enthused about cricket, so a visit to the College ground was hardly surprising. Here, Jeeves' easy action caught his eye and Wodehouse was inspired as he watched him bowling. The outcome was the creation of Bertie Wooster's 'gentleman's personal gentleman', the supreme Jeeves.

Later the author wrote, 'I suppose Jeeves' bowling must have impressed me, for I remembered him in 1916, when I was in New York and starting the Jeeves and Bertie saga and it was just the name I wanted.'

From the moment Jeeves mixed Bertie's first famous hangover pick-me-up - the invigorating Worcester Sauce, raw egg and red pepper bracer - he attained that immortal status inspired by the Festival vignette. 'Leave it to Jeeves' became Bertie's motto.

Three years later, while serving in the Royal Warwickshire Regiment, Jeeves' cricketing namesake was killed in action in France. England had lost a popular cricketer of whom very high hopes had been entertained.

—— **1914** ——

In January of this fateful year, the AGM of the county cricket club was held in Cheltenham Town Hall, the first time it had ever been conducted out of Bristol. It was reported that the club was in a wretched financial position; gate receipts at headquarters had once again been poor, but as usual, solid support given by the public at Cheltenham helped to ease some of the problems. Cricket at the Festival seemed an integral part of the county's existence, but world events were about to intervene.

A week after Germany invaded Belgium on 4 August 1914, the Festival started in front of the smallest Cheltenham crowd on record. Inside two days, Nottinghamshire twice bundled Gloucestershire out cheaply to win by an innings and 69 runs. By the close of play on the first day, the visitors had bowled out their hosts for 140, with Tom Wass taking 5 for 71. Nottinghamshire then reached 147 for 2. The following morning, with reduced admission prices enticing a larger crowd, the great George Gunn made 71, batting delightfully and exhibiting a variety of perfectly-timed shots. He was ably assisted by his elder brother John (58) and Joe Hardstaff (senior) who made 53, as their side reached 322. Charlie Parker took 7 for 79, but Wass (18.3-3-56-6) then quickly led the rout in dismissing Gloucestershire for 113.

Playing better cricket in the next match, Gloucestershire might have beaten Sussex if the weather had held. The outstanding feature was the batting of Thomas Langdon, who began uncertainly then produced some hard driving and crisp cutting in his three and a half hour innings of 106. George Dennett's 6 for 51 gave his side a 122 run first innings lead, then Dipper, with 75, led his side to 256 for 8 before a declaration was made. Rain then ended proceedings with Sussex on 58 for 1, needing 379 to win.

Gloucestershire's seventeenth defeat of the season was at the hands of Surrey in the final game. In reply to the home team's 182, the visitors were given a good start by Hayward and Hobbs before Knight (58) and Ducat (74) took their team to a total of 317, despite a fine performance by Dennett (56-24-102-7). A lively knock of 48 by Sewell was the only bright spot of an otherwise poor batting display by Gloucestershire, who went down by an innings and 25 runs on the second day.

A week later, as the season was drawing to a close, W.G. expressed utter disbelief that county cricket was still being played against a backdrop of war. In a letter to the *Sportsman* he was aghast that 'able-bodied men' should be playing, while 'pleasure seekers' looked on.

His former county had experienced a disastrous season. There was great depression amongst supporters and it appeared possible that the club would founder because of the hopeless financial situation. Like everyone else, residents of Cheltenham were becoming increasingly preoccupied with the war and a combination of these circumstances presented a serious threat to the future of the Cricket Festival.

CHAPTER TEN (1919-1927)

A NEW ERA

—— 1919 ——

Cheltenham families suffered their share of tragedy in the four years of bitter fighting. The College, with its strong army tradition, was particularly affected and when the guns finally stopped firing, six hundred and seventy-five former pupils had been killed and many more seriously wounded. While those young men were falling in the fields of Flanders, present pupils cultivated parts of the Playground to grow potatoes, burying the Festival ground in mounds of soil.

A fortnight before the Festival resumed in 1919, the Bank Holiday Fete at Pittville was supported by over 30,000 people, reported in the *Chronicle* as 'all Cheltenham and his wife and their children'. Large numbers of soldiers from the battlefields paraded through the streets and the town's twelve hundred dead were remembered with a memorial shrine in the shadow of the giant trees in the Promenade.

An exceptional era had ended during the hostilities with the death of W.G., aged sixty-seven, in Kent, where he had lived since his rift with Gloucestershire. 'It is difficult to believe that a combination so remarkable of health, activity, power, eye, hand, devotion and opportunity will present itself again,' commented Lord Harris. Another link with the Lillywhite days had disappeared.

The war had caused the county cricket club to be suspended for four years. Immediately after the armistice, great efforts were made to resurrect it by a new committee consisting of former members, retired cricketers, business men and lawyers.

Under the captaincy of Foster Robinson, but minus Jessop (suffering from bad health) and Dennett (still serving with the army in India), the county's cricketers arrived in Cheltenham to play Warwickshire, Worcestershire and Leicestershire. As an experiment for the season, all matches had been limited to two days with longer hours of play. However, it proved unsatisfactory and by the time the Festival began the advisory committee had made a unanimous decision to revert to three day matches the following year, when Gloucestershire would be competing for the championship.

The glorious weather on the first morning attracted a good attendance. It was difficult to imagine the terrible events that had taken place since the last gathering and that many of those present in 1914 had since paid the price of loyalty to king and country. Having reclaimed the potato patch, Woof and his assistants had the whole ground looking magnificent, helping to quell thoughts of grief and melancholy with an atmosphere of hope and excitement for a new era.

A close-fought game with Warwickshire produced a tie on first innings. After lunch a contingent of war casualties were among the spectators who saw the hosts heading towards 177 for 7 by the close of play at half past seven, with Dipper on 99* in reply to the midlanders' total of 252. The Gloucestershire opener reached his century next day and Warwickshire's fast bowler Harry Howell, the Wolverhampton Wanderers centre forward, collected 5 wickets. The visitors collapsed in their second innings as Charlie Parker bagged a ten wicket match haul. Gloucestershire fared likewise but were saved by some sensible tail-end batting and scrambled home to victory by 2 wickets.

Beneath cloudless skies this closely-contested game was well-attended on both days. Watching cricket was one form of escapism from the traumas and changes that had affected an exhausted country, and the game had lost nothing of its attraction, despite the break and an increased entrance charge due to an entertainment tax. Admission from College Road was now 1s. 3d., reduced to 7d. after half past four; once inside the ground a place in the grandstand cost an extra 1s.1d. Reassuringly there was the familiar sight of George's caterers at work providing stand-up lunches, refreshments and teas, but due to increased labour costs the smaller stands had been dispensed with and replaced by enclosures furnished with deck chairs.

A friendly game with Worcestershire, who were not competing in the championship this season, was spoilt by rain. Similarly affected were the Festival's open air evening performances in Montpellier Gardens by The Bubble and Squeaks, a local 'Troop of Pierrots' who boasted 'novel effects'.

When cricket was possible, fine individual performances from opening batsmen helped both teams. A century from Bowley for the visitors, as Parker took 7 for 111, was matched by Dipper (99*) who carried his bat, but was ultimately let down by tail-enders.

On Wednesday, play finally started against Leicestershire at three o'clock when Robinson's men batted cautiously to reach 185. Dipper (18.2-2-46-7) and Parker (19-7-26-3) were unplayable next day and bowled out the visitors for 79. Following on, forty-three-year-old C. J. B. Wood (63) helped his side reach 200, as Dipper waded in with another seven wicket haul. The Gloucestershire opener then steered his team to an eight wicket victory with 31* to add to his first innings half century, so ending the match with an impressive all-round performance.

—— 1920 ——

For the next few years Charlie Parker was to carry the county's bowling, while Alf Dipper was to dominate the batting. Meanwhile, at the 1920 Festival, a young Cirencester Grammar School pupil, Walter Hammond, made his first-class debut. Despite his maiden appearance being a low-key performance, he would soon become an invaluable member of the team and dominate first county, then world cricket.

With the championship restored to three-day matches, high-flying Lancashire arrived in town amidst high expectations for a large attendance. The local committee, led by their capable honorary secretary Captain Allan with the assistance of Woof and his staff, ensured the ground was in excellent condition, but continuous heavy rain prevented any play on the first day.

The poor weather reduced numbers at the Festival Dance held in the Town Hall that night. Guests joined both teams to enjoy a delicious buffet produced by the Cadena Café caterers and were entertained by the Municipal Orchestra conducted by Mr Howard Shackleton, playing one-step and fox-trot 'with much spirit'. Cheltenham reflected the mood in post-war Britain as the population showed an appetite for new fashions and entertainments, and flocked to cinemas and dance halls.

On a slow pitch next day, nearly 3,500 spectators watched medium-paced Laurence Cook (37.2-7-69-7) reduce Gloucestershire to 132 all out. They also witnessed seventeen-year-old Walter Hammond, in his first innings for the county, being trapped lbw for nought by Dick Tyldesley. Lancashire's first innings lead was restricted by the bowling of Parker (21.5-6-46-6) and a draw seemed a possibility as Dipper and Robinson easily wiped out the arrears. Cook (3 for 37) and Heap (14.2-4-19-5) felt differently, for once these two were out they dismissed the next nine batsmen for 18 runs. Lancashire's openers, Harry Makepeace and

Charlie Hallows, rather typical of the new era, being dour, sturdy and efficient but somewhat lacking in carefree style, comfortably steered their team to a ten wicket victory.

Playing their final home match of the season at Cheltenham, Gloucestershire easily defeated Leicestershire in two days by an innings and 53 runs. During a chilly first day, a collection raised £21 for Dennett, who was back from six years service in India. His benefit fund totalled £62 from Festival contributions but he would need every penny of this for winter fuel if the current weather was a forerunner of what was to come over the next few months. Unbearably cold conditions had swept across the whole country, with ground frost at night in many inland districts and snow falling in the mountains of North Wales.

It was a bleak scene at Cheltenham, with only a few hardy spectators present to see Parker (17-9-22-5) and Mills (17-8-29-5) dismiss the visitors for 54. In reply, Gloucestershire made 190 with everyone chipping in except for Hammond who seemed 'unaccustomed to sheer pace' and was dismissed cheaply by fast bowler Benskin.

Monday belonged to Charlie Parker (26.1-9-35-9) as the visitors were bowled out for 83. Flighting the ball with guile, and spinning it viciously with his long fingers, he equalled the feat performed in the previous century by both W.G. and Charles Townsend who were also deprived of that last elusive wicket. For the next fifteen summers, Parker would take over 100 wickets each season. Yet the England selectors shied away from this forthright Prestbury man, one of the finest left-arm spinners of all time, only selecting him for one Test match.

— 1921 —

Lancashire provided the opening opposition, and thanks to Alf Dipper (104) making his sixth century of the season, Gloucestershire gained a first innings lead of 55. Old Cheltonian George Shelmerdine (65) and the cautious Makepeace (113), with a century opening partnership in an hour, turned the game in favour of the northerners. Tall, powerful Shelmerdine, who was more than familiar with the ground having been a member of the College XI for three years, delighted the crowd with his hard-hitting innings which included 3 sixes and 7 fours. Left with a target of 196 on the final afternoon, Gloucestershire's batting collapsed, and bowling unchanged, Dean (12.1-7-26-8) and Cook (12-6-34-2) dismissed their hosts for 70.

At the end of play the ground was littered with cast-away scorecards left by disgruntled Gloucestershire supporters, frustrated by their batsmen's capitulation, and scornful of next year's fixtures which were printed on the back. Warwickshire, Kent and Leicestershire were the proposed visitors scheduled to play at the end of August running into September; the locals could not understand why the committee had invited the two midland sides again so soon and why the Festival should be so late in the season.

Local committee members Captain Allan, Alderman Margrett, Messrs H. V. Page, F. H. Harris, H. W. Bennett, H. J. Harman and Colonel Hayward had known nothing of these arrangements and were 'indignant' at the suggestions of the central committee. Seething with anger, they issued an ultimatum stating that the proposals were impossible and unless altered they would refuse to organise the Festival.

This was not the first time, and it would certainly not be the last, that muscles were flexed between Cheltenham and Bristol, with headquarters wanting to call the tune. Cheltenham was undoubtedly the best money-making centre for the county club and could be argued to be a far more appropriate venue to host crowd-pullers like Surrey, Middlesex, Yorkshire, Lancashire and Kent, so maximising income. To arrange the Festival so late in the summer would create the risk of the ground being unavailable because of the start of the College's autumn term - but that may have been what Bristol wanted.

The organisers had certainly come up with an unusual crowd-puller for this year's Festival and it proved to be a great attraction. Housed in a large marquee was the famous 'Mars I'. The only one of its kind, the twelve cylinder, four hundred and fifty horsepower, single seat, racing biplane, designed by the Gloucestershire Aircraft Company's Henry Folland, had been made at their Sunningend works in town. Earlier in the summer, with pilot Jimmy James, the 'Bamel', as it was fondly known because of its half-bear, half-camel like appearance during construction, had won the Aerial Derby reaching a speed of 163.8 miles per hour. Entrance to the marquee cost 6d. with profits going to the hospital. Twelve months later, the pale blue fuselage and ivory-white winged 'Mars I' set the world speed record at 212 miles per hour.

Called up for the Oval Test, then not selected, Parker had been unable to play against Lancashire, so he returned to Cheltenham somewhat frustrated and ready to demonstrate his talent, which he did in both the ensuing matches.

Bad weather disrupted the first day of the Sussex fixture. Nevertheless, on a soft wicket the visitors managed to score 134 for 2, setting them up to win the game by 137 runs two days later. The popular forty-six-year-old Sussex professional, Joe Vine, reached his century next day before Wilson declared on 245 for 9. Parker (42-12-104-7) bowled well, but the Gloucestershire batting looked frail once again and they were all out for 149.

Batting again, Sussex built upon their first innings lead and although Parker (18.5-5-70-7) increased his match haul, the target was too stiff for the hosts. They ended up 137 runs short due to a fine performance from another Sussex veteran, forty-seven-year-old spinner Albert Relf (18-9-21-8).

That night, as the town prepared itself for the visit of Warwick Armstrong's 'Invincible' Australians, Leo Dawes' Band performed at the Willow Ball. As the last indefatigable guests left the Town Hall at two o'clock on Saturday morning, the College ground lay silent, preparing itself for an invasion a few hours later.

By nine o'clock next morning, spectators were beginning to assemble outside the ground in rather dull weather. When the gates opened an hour later, the numbers had swollen to around 2,000. With a huge crowd expected, safety precautions denied admittance to boys unless accompanied by their parents.

Probably no other match in the history of cricket on the College ground had been anticipated with as much enthusiasm by so many people. While on tour, the Australians had already defeated England three times and were unbeaten in all other matches. In his story *Hill Cricket*, Laurie Lee recalled bicycling down from the Cotswold Hills for a taste of the excitement and seeing 'Arthur Mailey and others in their huge cloth caps - strange bottle-faced men from the other side of the world who laughed sharply and spoke a kind of scrambled Cockney'.

Even those with only a passing interest in cricket recognised this was not a match to be missed. By midday, when the game was due to start, the ground was looking a picture in glorious sunshine, and 5,000 spectators were assembled inside, with many more still pouring in. Gloucestershire were without Dennett, who was suffering from lumbago, and the visitors left out McDonald, Oldfield and Taylor from the recent Test team. For the third time during the Festival, Robinson lost the toss and Warwick Armstrong had no hesitation in deciding to bat on a good looking wicket.

The decision was quickly justified. In under an hour, with another 1,000 people inside the ground, his side reached 100. Bardsley and Macartney were in fine form, scoring freely as the ball raced over the

A queue forming outside the ground before
play on the first day against the Australians in 1921

The grandstand later in the day

boundary rope and into the throng of spectators seated on the grass. An hour later 200 was reached. Then Bardsley (127), followed by Macartney (121), having shared a record second wicket partnership of 218, were both dismissed. This left Gregory and his captain continuing to turn the screw, by which time the ground was heaving with over 10,000 people.

Amongst the crowd was a young Cotswold choirboy, Percy Howse, together with his brother Tom, the rest of the choir and their choirmaster Revd Addrell. Bryan 'Bomber' Wells, county spinner in the 1950s, recalls Percy telling him that early in the morning his party assembled at Bourton-on-the-Water railway station, caught the train to Leckhampton and walked to the College ground. The vicar, a keen sportsman himself who played cricket for the Slaughters, gave the boys a 'never-to-be-forgotten day'. As young Percy sipped from his bottle of home-made lemonade and munched his jam sandwiches, it was the Australian fast bowler Gregory, batting without gloves, who left the largest impression, almost equalled by the perplexing fact that amateur and professional players emerged from separate entrances - a tent and the gymnasium, respectively.

On Monday morning, the Australian innings was quickly finished off by the hard working Parker (50.2-9-148-5). Then on a pitch damaged by weekend showers, Gloucestershire struggled.

The Australian team took to the field led by their captain, who was adorned in his famous huge woollen shirt. Weighing over twenty stone, this giant of a man, 'fashioned by nature' according to Neville Cardus and often likened to W.G., was completely at home in the Festival atmosphere. Perhaps he even found time to visit the tent occupied by Robertson & Co, the Colonnade Tobacconists, who sold a choice selection of cigars for which he had a strong liking.

He also had a strong liking for winning cricket matches and in front of another huge crowd his bowlers did not disappoint. Apart from Cliftonian and Cambridge blue Keigwin, a fine all-round games player who displayed defiant defence by making 47 in two hours, the hosts collapsed to 127 all out. Australia's bowlers shared the wickets, but it was Jack Gregory who looked particularly menacing. Recalling the match in his book *Cricket My Destiny,* Walter Hammond admitted that Gregory 'frightened the life' out of him when 'the ball whistled down' and one of his stumps 'cart-wheeled yards away'. Following on, Gloucestershire were soon in trouble again. With the exception of Keigwin (48*), their batsmen could not cope with the guile of Arthur Mailey and at close of play he had taken all 6 wickets to fall.

Minutes later, George's ('The Princes of Catering') were serving up a 5*s*. 6*d*. special dinner in their elegant restaurant, catering for those who were off to the Town Hall to see George Robey, 'The Prince of Mirth', in a special Festival attraction. Robey, the 'famous and popular comedian', together with a powerful company of star artistes, entertained a full-house which included members of both cricket teams. His performance, described in the *Echo* as 'an incessant crackle of fun and fancy', ended when he expressed particular delight that the Australians had come to see him, quipping, 'They have done so much for English cricket - in fact have pretty nearly done it in.' When the laughter had died away, he concluded by praising the blind heroes of St Dunstan's who were sitting in front of him in their wheel chairs, describing them as 'the dear old boys who had been smashed up'.

The following morning, as cricket got under way, Robey called in at St Dunstan's taking cigarettes and leaving signed photographs of himself, a gesture which brought much delight. Back at the College ground, Gloucestershire's spirits were sinking as Mailey (28.4-5-66-10) continued to display his magic, bowling out the hosts to give his team victory by an innings and 136 runs. The performance earned himself a place in the record books for the best bowling in an innings for an opposition team on the ground.

The story goes that in Gloucestershire's first innings, Armstrong went on early and took 2 for 53, while Mailey, given the ball when the tail-enders batted, got away with 3 for 21. In the county's second innings, the captain was hit for 54 runs without taking a wicket and threw the ball to Mailey, suggesting sarcastically, 'Here, you can have a go at the good batsmen now and I'll have a crack at the tail-enders.' The result is history and Mailey's remarkable feat provided the inspiration for the title of his subsequent book, *10 For 66 and All That*.

Three defeats on the ground had been disappointing for the county, but from a financial point of view the Festival was an unprecedented success. Close to 9,000 people paid for admission to the first two matches and total receipts reached £608 15*s*. 5*d*. A record £944 was taken on the first day's play alone against the Australians, almost trebling the previous record that had stood since the Australian visit of 1896. With an attendance of more than 15,000 over the last three days, and receipts mounting to £1,762, the county's finances along with those of the tourists had benefited, and the cut for amusement tax must have helped to broaden the smile on the face of the Chancellor of the Exchequer.

—— **1922** ——

With the town still buzzing after a visit by Queen Mary a week before the Festival, Colonel Hay succeeded the late Captain Allan as local organiser. Arrangements stayed much the same off the field, but the county's improved performance on the field was rewarded by two victories.

Bowling unchanged, Parker (21.5-10-32-4) and Mills (21-6-46-5) dismissed visitors Essex for 79 in under two hours. Robinson (71) quickly steered his team to a first innings lead of 62, despite a fine performance by Johnny Douglas (15.3-3-45-8). In the final forty-five minutes of play on the first day, Essex lost two second innings wickets, and by mid-afternoon the following day the game was over as Parker (32.1-17-44-7) proved unplayable again and Gloucestershire scored the runs required for the loss of 4 wickets.

In the next game, Gloucestershire overwhelmed Warwickshire by an innings and 163 runs. Batting first, the visitors collapsed to the bowling combination of Parker (21.2-10-29-8) and Mills (21-4-45-2) - 80 all out in the same number of minutes. Replying for the hosts, Barnett was quickly dismissed, but Dipper and the small, compact Harry Smith added 150 for the second wicket as the county went on to reach 238 for 4 by the close. A wet day followed before Gloucestershire declared on Friday having made 316, leaving Dipper unbeaten on 125. Bowling unchanged on a rain-ruined pitch, Parker (17.4-5-32-6) and Mills (17-4-39-3) destroyed Warwickshire, who were all out for 73.

Kent, one of the top flight teams in the county championship, dished out an innings and 57 runs defeat to Gloucestershire in the final match. Always welcome guests, the men from the Garden of England were popular for the exhilarating cricket they played. The hosts batted first and Foster Robinson top scored with 10 out of a total of 53, as the rest of his team crumpled in an hour and a quarter to Frank Woolley (13-5-29-4) and 'Tich' Freeman (12-4-18-6). In glorious weather, before a crowd of over 4,500 people, Kent found little difficulty in scoring runs and by the end of play had reached 248 for 9, with Woolley (82) turning in a splendid all-round performance for the day. Once again Parker and Mills shouldered the responsibility in the field, bowling eighty-one overs between them. As he grafted away for his 6 for 82, a ground collection raised nearly £50 towards Parker's benefit fund. The hard-working, popular professional was enjoying wonderful support for his benefit year and, as a way of thanking his local followers, he had taken 150 wickets at an average of just over fifteen each on the College ground, which now must have been one of his favourite haunts.

Receipts of £308 were a record for one day in an inter-county match on the ground, but the game was slipping away from Gloucestershire. The two acts of nature that followed almost saved the day. Firstly, just after ten o'clock on Sunday morning, a small earthquake shook Cheltenham causing wardrobes to tremble and buildings to shake, but with no seismic damage to the pitch. Secondly, incessant rain fell for the rest of the day and most of the next, leaving the county with a glimmer of hope for saving the match. But it was not to be. The weather picked up and Kent declared first thing on the final morning, immediately putting Gloucestershire on the spot. Barnett and Dipper opened confidently before Freeman (26.2-8-54-6) took charge as he exploited the conditions of a deteriorating wicket. Dipper carried his bat for 37 out of a total of 138, while Charles King-Turner, a member of the College XI the previous year, collected his pair for the match.

—— **1923** ——

Led by the popular and enthusiastic Old Etonian P. F. C. Williams, Gloucestershire experienced a trio of defeats at this year's Festival. Two promising recruits were in their line-up: Kent-born Walter Hammond, now fully qualified and a member of the professional staff, was joined by Tom Goddard, a useful fast bowler from Gloucester. Batting first, in perfect weather, the county made a disastrous start when Hammond was clean bowled by Douglas's first ball, giving him a run of three successive ducks. The rest of the early order batting collapsed and it was left to Smith (149) and the tail-enders to amass a total of 324. Essex also found themselves in trouble early on, before Jack O'Connor (128) and Douglas (147*) shared a record opposition sixth wicket partnership of 206. Parker's gargantuan spell of bowling (73.1-32-126-7) was not enough to prevent the visitors from taking a first innings lead of 59 and when the Cambridge captain Claude Ashton (14-1-51-7) reduced Gloucestershire to 173 all out, Essex charged home to a 6 wicket victory thanks to a cavalier 71 in an hour by F. W. H. Nicholas.

As in the previous game, none of Gloucestershire's early batsmen proved to be successful against Kent and it needed the lower order to push the total up to 139. Top scorer with twenty-six was Cheltenham's

'Bernie' Bloodworth, whose family ran a chicken and poultry food shop in Albion Street. The visitors replied with 356, largely due to England cricketer and footballer 'Wally' Hardinge making 129.

The home side started positively and were ahead of their rivals for the loss of only 3 wickets. Williams (75), Dipper (64) and Hammond (76) gave the county hope, but this time the tail did not wag. At the end of Gloucestershire's innings, the Kent wicket-keeper, Hubble, had taken nine catches and made one stumping in the match, and his team scored the 70 runs required to win by 10 wickets.

The final visitors, Middlesex, were an eye-catching team, having four of the finest cricketers in England amongst their ranks. On this occasion, Hendren, Mann and Stevens were playing in the final Test trial at Lord's and Hearne had injured his hand, so there was a glimmer of hope that Gloucestershire would avoid a Festival whitewash. Rain delayed the start until mid-afternoon when Nigel Haig won the toss and invited his hosts to bat. It looked as if his plan had backfired when Gloucestershire reached 100 for 2, with Hammond in fine form reaching a half-century. On a drying wicket, Harry Lee (19.5-5-39-8) then struck and the home team were dismissed for 154. Parker, with 7 for 78, helped to hold Middlesex's lead to 40, but by the end of play on the second day the Londoners only needed 12 runs to win. They made them in five minutes the following morning, winning comfortably by 8 wickets.

At the start of the Festival, a letter had appeared in the *Echo* asking the cricket committee if they would consider removing a portion of canvas from the perimeter fence. Many men and boys experiencing hard times could not afford the entrance fee and a gesture such as this 'would be greatly appreciated by a portion of the community who do not share very largely in the pleasures of life'. Despite interruptions for rain and the county's poor displays, attendance numbers and receipts were up on the previous year, but the canvas remained in place and kept charity at bay.

A more generous approach was displayed at the committee meeting in October when Percy Mills' benefit fund was discussed. The plan was to sell tickets at 1s each, admitting the holder to any match played in the county during the following year and also the chance to win a Bean Motor Car in a ballot. Advertised with the slogan 'A Bean for a Bob', takings would be divided equally between Percy Mills and the county, on the understanding that the maximum amount the player could receive was £1,500. Knowing Cheltenham would come up trumps, it was later agreed that the final match of the 1924 Festival against Kent would be set aside for his benefit, but an old adversary was to spoil the show.

—— 1924 ——

The new club captain, Lieut. Colonel Douglas Robinson, proved to be a most zealous leader. At a committee meeting in late July he introduced the idea of holding a Festival on the Victoria ground in Cheltenham the following summer. He had been promised the support of the Town Council and Chamber of Commerce and he realised that some ground improvements were necessary. His case was given further backing by Councillor Bates, who suggested that a Town Festival held in June or July would be a success because the schools would not have broken up and the town would be full of people. This could only be good news for the town's businesses and further discussions would take place.

Meanwhile, with the county halfway up the championship table enjoying some good results, with Dipper, Parker, Smith and Hammond in good form, neighbouring Worcestershire opened events on the College ground.

Old Cheltonian M. G. Salter took the place of the exciting new recruit Rogers who was playing army cricket, and Goddard replaced Bloodworth whose form had recently declined. On winning the toss, M. K. Foster inserted the home team. The gamble paid off, especially when Fred Root took the last 5 wickets for no runs in nine balls, a sensational feat almost equalling that of W.G. in 1877 against Nottinghamshire when he had taken 7 wickets for no runs in his last seventeen balls. No doubt there was much talk of these performances that night as guests enjoyed music by Leo Dawes' Band at the Cricket Cinderella Dance in the Town Hall.

First innings totals tied on 114. Gloucestershire's captain then steered his team to 159 by making a determined 74. This put him in such good humour that he paid the ten shilling admittance fee for a small group of people who were hovering at the gate hoping for a glimpse of the game. His generosity was rewarded when the county swept to victory by 91 runs in just two days. Bowling unchanged, Mills (13-4-29-5) and Parker (13.2-2-38-5) carried out the damage on a tricky wicket. The latter, revelling in the season's wet conditions, with a match analysis of 10 for 78, had raised his total number of wickets to 162 for the summer, with several games still to play. Despite the weather, Dipper was also having a good season, accumulating nearly 1,500 runs. He was summoned after the game and congratulated on his successful summer by the 'grand old sportsman', the Earl of Coventry, who had been watching with interest not only as patron of Worcestershire, but also because his grandson, the

Hon. J. B. Coventry, was playing. On the other hand it had been a quiet game for young Hammond who had collected a pair, an event he would never repeat on this ground.

Finishing early meant a blank day on Tuesday, so a foursome comprising match umpires Butt and Street, together with Charlie Parker and Percy Mills, made their way to the banks of the Avon at Tewkesbury for the less arduous sport of fishing. Refreshed from their break, the Gloucestershire professionals returned to work next day and immediately bowled their team into a healthy position.

Leicestershire arrived in Cheltenham feeling buoyant, having just crushed Hampshire at Southampton by 10 wickets, but they came up against Parker (33-9-65-7) and Mills (22-7-38-2) in irrepressible form, and were dismissed for 144. A lead of 35 on first innings for the hosts was due to the faultless display from opener F. J. Seabrook (73) and a brisk 40 by Rogers. The bowling performances from Parker, with 6 for 46, and Mills, 3 for 31, meant that the visiting batsmen were all back in the pavilion for 89 in their second innings, leaving Gloucestershire to coast home by 7 wickets.

Not everyone was happy with the day's events. A significant proportion of the crowd had turned up at half past eleven for the scheduled start of play only to find the match had resumed at eleven o'clock. The reason for the alteration was to give the Leicestershire team time to travel to Bradford for their game the following day, but members of the press and paying public were not impressed, particularly as wickets had fallen and the state of the game had altered. Some patrons of the club, on the receiving end of what they considered shoddy treatment, threatened to discontinue their support and it was generally agreed that in future any such changes should be given plenty of advanced publicity.

Everybody hoped that Percy Mills' benefit match against Kent would be an occasion when he would receive the just reward for his excellent services to the county. For more than twenty years, this enthusiastic town resident, the most popular professional in the team, had taken part in many match-winning situations for the county and Gilbert Jessop warmly commented, 'A cheerier fellow it would be well nigh impossible to meet, or one whom the slings and arrows of outrageous fortune so lightly affected.'

A heavy storm before the start meant only two and a half hours of play were possible on Saturday, but 2,500 people paid for admission and saw Gloucestershire bowled out for 48 by Freeman (9.5-3-20-7) and Wright (12-2-16-3), before Kent struggled to 57 for 6.

Before the game there had been a flurry of correspondence in the papers calling for Saturday's local friendly games to be cancelled so that players and supporters could go to the College ground. Leckhampton CC led the cause by putting off their game, and others followed suit. The alternative to this proposal to scratch matches, in a season when many had already been lost or abandoned due to wet weather, was to let the senior members spectate at Cheltenham, while the young could 'play while they may', making a collection for Mills' benefit on their ground.

Further heavy rain fell on Sunday night and not a ball was bowled on Monday. Nevertheless, people gathered at Montpellier Gardens that evening to watch The Spa Entertainers, who numbered among their artistes Kent cricketers Jack Hubble and Lionel Hedges, the latter also a College master and Cheltenham CC player.

Next morning, when play resumed, wicket-keeper Hubble was dismissed without adding to his score, but his team gained a lead of 28. Hammond then batted delightfully and soon after scoring his one thousandth run for the season he was bowled by Marriott for 39. Much to the appreciation of the crowd, Mills hit freely and ended top scorer with 44* when Gloucestershire declared on 179 for 9.

Kent required another 85 runs to win, with six wickets remaining when the game finished. As members of the Union Club left their special Festival tent, along with other supporters of the county, there was general agreement that further support should be given to Mills by the town club in the form of another benefit match in September. The aim was to make up for the lost income from this game and show that the townsfolk would not forget their man.

In the *Echo* next day, a Cheltenham cricket enthusiast, turned bard, summed up the Festival in the following 'effusion':

> The rain has run in rivulets and rills,
> Too much, I fear to 'benefit' our 'Mills',
> While wickets, worried by the wet, will fall,
> The bat is badly beaten by the ball,
> In order to secure our keeping dry,
> Let's play our 'Cricket on the Hearth', say I.

At the end of August, a committee was appointed consisting of Messrs E. F. Davy, W. Simmonds and A. S. F. Bruen, with W. C. Woof ex-officio, to consider the question of enlarging the Victoria ground.

—— 1925 ——

Ten months later, after a winter of planning and hard work, the county played two matches at the Victoria ground, losing to Lancashire and beating Worcestershire, before playing at Gloucester.

In early August, they were back in town playing at the College against Hampshire, Nottinghamshire and Kent. The north of the county was poking its head above the parapet and Cheltenham was becoming even more of a mainstay for Gloucestershire cricket; it remained to be seen whether there would be any repercussions from Bristol.

A Saturday crowd of over 4,000 watched Hampshire make 244, and after a day's rest on the Sunday as usual, they bowled out their hosts to gain a first innings lead of 63. Batting again, a high class innings of 94 by Philip Mead enabled his side to declare on 244 for 6, but heavy rain at lunch on the last day washed out any hopes of finishing the match, with Gloucestershire wanting 288 to win.

The ground was totally saturated the next day, delaying the start of the Nottinghamshire match until Thursday, when 31 wickets fell for 295 runs. On a very treacherous pitch, 'Tich' Richmond made the ball fizz and spin, keeping a perfect length. Almost single-handedly, he bowled Gloucestershire out twice for 66 and 89, with the remarkable figures of 15.3-4-30-7 and 15.5-4 53-7. In between, none other than Parker (4 for 50) and Mills (5 for 46) dismissed the visitors for 122, so that at the end of an extraordinary day Nottinghamshire needed only 16 runs to win with 9 wickets in hand. The following morning, for the loss of two more wickets, their victory was secured. It had been achieved without the services of the rapidly improving Harold Larwood. He had not bowled a ball and had been out for nought, but he had taken seventy-three wickets since the middle of June and was looking very much like a force for the future.

There was further embarrassment for Gloucestershire's batsmen on the first day of the match against Kent, doubtless leaving some supporters wondering whether they were getting value for money. Admission to the ground was 1s. 2d. and double this price to go into the grandstand; boys admission was half-price. For the more valiant followers, who had no fears about lost minutes of cricket due to rain or an early finish, a 12s. 6d. 'sectional' ticket gave admittance to the grandstand for all three matches, while a special concessionary ticket for 'scholars' gave the same access for five shillings.

On winning the toss, Captain Cornwallis asked his hosts to bat first. His decision was fully justified by the close of play, with his side 181 in front and 7 wickets in hand, having dismissed the opposition largely thanks to Freeman (19.2-4-34-6) for 71. On Monday, Kent piled on the agony with Woolley making a magnificent 176 before his team were all out for 418. Robinson (41), Dipper (52), Bloodworth (62) and Hammond (81) regained some credibility for their side, with Hammond showing signs that he was fast becoming one of the most exciting batsmen in the country. Freeman, with 6 for 114, ensured that Gloucestershire went down by an innings and 47 runs.

Though Kent may have won on the cricket field, it was now time to see if Gloucestershire could take the honours on the dance floor. A Festival Ball had been arranged to celebrate the re-opening of the Town Hall since its rich, colourful refurbishment. Over two hundred people attended the event, including the majority of the members of both cricket teams, with brisk, lively fox-trots and popular waltzes played by Leo Dawes' New Dance Orchestra.

During an interlude, Councillor Pates, accompanied by the captains of both teams, approached the stage. The councillor welcomed everybody to this special occasion and apologised for the absence of the mayor and his deputy, commenting that the corporation were 'playing their second eleven' - which was greeted with laughter and applause. He congratulated Kent on their victory and remarked on their popularity, illustrated by the excellent attendances on the College ground when they were playing. Captain Cornwallis responded by thanking everyone for the kind welcome given to him and his team, concluding with the words, 'Support Gloucestershire cricket; it is worth supporting.' Colonel Robinson was greeted to a rendition of 'For He's a Jolly Good Fellow' and asked all those present to thank their families and friends for all the support they had given over the past ten days, and complimented his friend on having 'one of the most attractive sides in England'. The last guests left the Town Hall at 2 a.m., reflecting wistfully that there was no cricket to enjoy next morning.

—— 1926 ——

By the start of the season, Woofie had retired as coach and groundsman at the College, and had been presented with £1,200 by past and present Cheltonians. His position was filled by George Dennett. Unfortunately,

Dennett had broken down towards the end of what had been already scheduled as his last season, but his parting with the county meant that in 1926 the captain had lost his right hand man, one reason perhaps for the trio of defeats at the Festival.

On their final visit to the College ground, the Australians, unbeaten to date on the tour, but just about to lose the Ashes for the first time in fourteen years, defeated the county in two days. A record number of over 9,500 spectators paid at the gate to watch the first day's play, but before entering the ground they were treated to a brief, but colourful, royal spectacle. With the town bathed in Saturday summer sunshine and the Promenade 'charmingly beflagged', thousands lined the streets, or filled balconies of shops and houses, to cheer the Prince of Wales as he motored through the town on an informal visit to the Public Secondary Schools' Cadet Camp at Charlton Kings.

The tourists wasted no time in taking a firm grip on the match, and by the close of play Gloucestershire had been dismissed for 144, largely due to Clarrie Grimmett's figures of 25.5-7-67-7, and his team had gained a lead of 84 with 4 wickets standing. Attention then turned to the Town Hall for the first of the Festival dances, where players from both teams joined members of the public who had paid 2s. 6d. to enjoy dancing to Leo Dawes' Band, with catering provided by the Cadena Cafe and the Sydney Arms Hotel.

Continuing with their socializing, the tourists paid a visit to Stanway House near Broadway, seat of the Earl of Wemyss. For many years during the month of August, playwright and novelist, Sir James Barrie - of Peter Pan fame - regularly took up residence in the sixteenth-century house, acting as host to his friends and other invited guests. Here in his own 'never-never land' cricket was the underlying theme, with members of the house party enjoying games on the lawn, watching village cricket and hearing tales of Barrie's own cricket team, 'the incomparable Allahakbarries'. It was Barrie's passion for the game that led him to invite the Australian team for the day and the story goes that in return for helping Macartney finish writing a long letter to his wife, 'The Governor-General', as the brilliant Australian batsman came to be known, allowed himself to be clean bowled by the persuasive playwright.

In front of a Monday crowd of 8,000, the visitors increased their lead to 143. Batting again, the hosts slipped to 119 for 7, but a two hour vigil at the crease by Dipper (42) and a flurry of runs from Robinson, shortly to retire as captain, enabled their side to stave off an innings defeat. At this time, the young broadcaster-to-be, Brian Johnston, lived with his

Top. The Australians taking the field in 1926
Middle. Gloucestershire following suit
Bottom. The encroaching crowd

family at another sixteenth-century house, Hellens, in the Herefordshire village of Much Marcle, home of Weston's cider. Remembering those childhood days, Brian Johnston recalled a visit to the nearby Festival and remembered Robinson - 'a large, imposing man', who 'frequently gave Gregory (of all people) the charge' - scoring 'an unorthodox and hurricane 32'.

Mailey (4 for 61) helped Grimmett (4 for 59) ensure that little was left for their batsmen to do and they won comfortably by 9 wickets. In just two days of play, over £1,800 had been handed over at the gate, beating the previous record takings of £1,766 gathered over three days when the Australians had visited five years earlier.

As the tourists moved on to Lord's to play the Public Schools XV, Gloucestershire started their match against Nottinghamshire. Despite lacking the services of Larwood and Whysall, the visitors were too strong for their hosts and won by 224 runs.

After their first innings, only 27 runs separated the teams. The heroes were Parker (36-9-73-8), who was charging towards his two hundredth wicket of the season at a little over seventeen runs each, and George Gunn who, according to *Wisden,* 'batted in masterly fashion', and carried his bat for 67 through the Nottinghamshire innings of 155. Dipper resisted resolutely with a stubborn 44, but before lunch on the second day his side had been dismissed by the 'cutters' of Staples (28-11-38-7) and leg-breaks of Richmond (27.3-7-74-3) who bowled unchanged. In their second innings, the visitors were able to declare on 299 for 6, thanks to 68 from Gunn, 105 from Willis Walker, making his second century of the season against Gloucestershire, and a swashbuckling 35 from their captain, Carr, which included 2 sixes and 3 fours off one over from Mills. Needing 327 to win, the home team had lost eight wickets by the close and the following day, Friday the thirteenth, proved equally unlucky, for within ten minutes of the start of play they were bowled out.

With Hobbs and Strudwick on Test duty, the last Festival match might have been in Gloucestershire's reach but for the fine all-round performance of Surrey's captain, Percy Fender. Batting first, the visitors made 198, with Fender top scorer on 53. Parker (24.4-6-107-6) and Mills (24-4-89-4) bowled unchanged as the latter, now aged forty-three, edged towards his hundredth wicket of the season, thus achieving this milestone for the first time in his long career.

At the close of play, the hosts appeared to be in a reasonably healthy position, 29 runs behind with 5 wickets in hand, so spirits were high at the Town Hall's second successful Festival dance. As the last of the late revellers finally sank into their beds, just before five o'clock on Sunday morning, residents felt an earthquake that shook the region, causing the famous landmark, Devil's Chimney, on the face of Leckhampton Quarry, to shake and crack.

The county's batting looked equally vulnerable on a quick wicket next day. Despite Dipper's 91, his side could only manage a two run lead on first innings, but when Parker (29-6-96-5) and Mills (27-4-67-3) reduced the visitors to 171, there was renewed optimism from local supporters.

Needing 170 to win, the hosts made a disastrous start with Peach dismissing Dipper and Robinson in his first over. Aftershocks and waves of uncertainty entered the Gloucestershire dressing room and on a worn pitch they were bowled out for 72 in eighty-five minutes. Fender took 4 for 25 and the whitewash was completed.

—— 1927 ——

A few days before the start of the Festival, schoolmaster and athlete Herbert Page, 'H.V.' as he was known to his friends, died in a town nursing-home. He had devoted a large part of his life to Cheltenham College, starting on entry in 1875 as a classical scholar and retiring from the teaching staff in 1923. Apart from school mastering, he had been organiser-in-chief of the College games programme for many years and was responsible for much of its cricketing success. A large number of past and present members of the College, together with many local residents, attended the funeral of this popular man who had played cricket for the county, making several appearances at the Week towards the end of the last century.

Many of the mourners were amongst the crowd who came to the ground a few days later to see the mighty Walter Hammond. Having recovered from a serious illness, Hammond had returned to the game and dominated the season with his magnificent batting. He contributed to Hampshire's defeat in the first match of the Festival, taking 3 for 91 in twenty-nine overs and scoring 56 as he charged along to his huge final total for the season of 2,969 runs, averaging just under 70 an innings.

Another player reappearing after serious illness was Harry Rowlands. On taking over the captaincy, he had little success with the bat and seemed unfortunate when tossing a coin, but he excelled in his duty as captain, successfully knitting the side together.

Having thrashed Worcestershire by an innings and 169 runs at Bristol, largely due to Dipper making 212 in a 209 run opening partnership with Sinfield (92), the Gloucestershire players arrived at Cheltenham in a confident mood and swept to a 9 wicket victory.

The visitors were bowled out for 219. In reply the hosts made 295, Dipper scoring another century, while Neale, Lyon and Hedges all made ducks, and Hampshire's long serving all-rounder John Newman, who opened both the batting and bowling, finished with figures of 40.1-9-126-7. By Monday evening the game was virtually over, with the visitors on 79 for 9. Formalities were completed next morning, by which time Parker (16-5-32-8) had bagged another twelve wicket match haul.

Wet weather spoilt the remainder of the Festival, resulting in a drawn match with New Zealand, and another against Surrey when only two and a half hours of play were possible. Outplayed by the tourists, the county were saved from defeat by heavy rain which prevented any cricket on the last day. But before the downpour, Charles Dacre had an enjoyable thirty minutes at the crease. Opening the innings for the visitors, on the ground where his father had been educated, he hit 5 sixes during his 64 out of 82. He soon announced his intention to settle in England and play for Gloucestershire and the county acquired a prize possession, a batsman of the Jessop mode, attacking, exciting, match-winning.

CHAPTER ELEVEN (1928-1934)

HATS OFF TO
HAMMOND AND LYON

—— **1928** ——

O ne of cricket's greatest ever all-round performances was witnessed at
the 1928 Festival. In five days, Wally Hammond scored three
hundred and sixty-two runs, including two centuries, took sixteen wickets
and held eleven catches, so exhibiting a rich display of talent never to be
forgotten.

For the Festival opener, Gloucestershire were without Hammond and
Rowlands. Hammond was on Test match duty at the Oval and Rowlands
had a knee injury. The captaincy was duly handed to Beverley Lyon.
Winning the toss and losing Dipper early on, the captain was soon at the
crease and after a quiet start he launched into some vigorous hitting in his
innings of 70. Then followed a run-a-minute partnership of 138 between
Harry Smith (69) and Billy Neale (96), during which a ground collection
for the former's benefit raised £36. 2s. In the middle of the afternoon,
Essex's opening bowler, R. C. Joy, caused much chortling amongst the
crowd when he bowled a maiden over including three wides, one of
which sailed high into the air going for four and finishing in the
refreshment tent. In the field for a long, tiring day as their hosts made
315, the visitors were not allowed to flounder by their wicket-keeping
captain Frank Gilligan, eldest brother of two England captains, who
inspired and enthused his team by claiming five dismissals.

Cricket on Monday was spoilt by rain, with players running on and
off the field, as the town, in sombre mood, mourned the well-respected
and much-loved Sir James Agg-Gardner whose funeral was taking place.
Described as a 'political Sir Galahad', fair and courteous throughout his
forty years of politics and service to the town, he had been a staunch
supporter of the Cricket Week from its inception. As his body was laid to
rest in the family vault of Prestbury churchyard, a friend commented that
Sir James' leading characteristics were humility, generosity and fair play,

a reminder of those same worthy qualities associated with James Lillywhite.

The late founder would have enjoyed the little cameo that took place on the ground that day while Essex were batting. A visitor on holiday from America was asked if he had seen 'that beautiful cut for four'. The American replied he had not, explaining he had been asleep, but pointed out there was also a player having a nap on the pitch. He had woken up at the precise moment that Barnett, bowling the first ball after an interruption for rain, had slipped and measured his length on the ground.

Further rain, thunder and flashes of lightening, in an otherwise hot, dry summer, meant that the match had to be abandoned as a draw, so ushering in those famous five days of cricket.

During the first three of them, magnificent performances by Hammond and Parker were largely responsible for the defeat of Surrey by 189 runs. The day before the game started, their captain Percy Fender had appeared at Marlborough Street magistrates charged with allowing his car to stay too long on a parking space at Piccadilly. It emerged that when spoken to by the constable, Fender had replied he was unable to come out earlier as he was in the middle of a game of bridge. Losing the case, he was ordered to pay a fifteen shilling fine. Fortune continued to run against him when his ring of four fielders failed to cut off the flow of Hammond's cover drives as Gloucestershire's hero cruised to 139 out of 199 in two hours and forty minutes.

In reply to the hosts' total of 304, Surrey scored 267, with Hobbs, in his forty-sixth year, making his first appearance on the ground since 1914 and treating the crowd to a magnificent innings. When Hobbs was four short of his century, the hands of the clock indicated that it was time for the lunch interval. The umpires appeared to exchange a nod of agreement that one more over should be played presumably to allow Hobbs the opportunity of reaching his hundred. Ironically, without adding to his score, he was immediately caught by Jim Seabrook, just underneath the flagstaff, off the bowling of Hammond. After lunch, bowling through the afternoon, Parker (38.4-6-117-6) treated himself to the first half of yet another large Cheltenham haul.

At the start of the final day, there was an air of expectation with the possibility of Hammond completing another century; a great battle for victory was brewing up between the sides. As he entered the nineties, a sense of excitement could be felt all round the ground, and when a 'wristy square cut for four' took him to three figures, he repeated his feat of the previous year against Surrey at the Oval. This equalled the achievement of W.G., while Jessop remained untouchable, scoring two separate centuries in a match on no fewer than four occasions.

On reaching his century, Hammond (143) hit out fearlessly, treating bowlers with little respect, so enabling his captain to declare at lunchtime, setting Surrey the almost impossible task of reaching 357 to win in just under three and a half hours.

To the bewilderment of many in the crowd, but amusement of those who knew of the wager, Bev Lyon led the team out wearing a red and white school cap. The bet with some of his players was that if he kept it on until half past two, he would be 'half a Bradbury' the richer. It is unlikely he would have speculated upon the early success gained in the second over of the innings, Parker's first from the Chapel end, when Hobbs was caught at the wicket on the third ball.

A roar of excitement from the large third day crowd greeted the early dismissal, and ten runs later, when Sandham gave Hammond the first of his six catches in the innings, Surrey's task seemed hopelessly out of reach. Like a cat hunting its prey, Parker's cunning, guile and pin-point accuracy claimed further victims, as the visitors slipped to 167 all out. Bowling without a break, returning figures of 32-10-80-7, the left-armer destroyed one of the strongest batting sides in the country as the understanding between himself and Hammond seemed to become almost telepathic. Delivering so many 'going away' balls, Parker almost wore a patch on the pitch, while Hammond seemed to know exactly which way the ball would come off the bat and positioned himself accordingly. He later admitted that towards the end of the Surrey second innings, on his way to taking five catches from the left-armer's bowling, he became quite embarrassed as the ball was steered again and again into his hands. His ten catches in the match - eight from Parker's bowling - stand to this day as a world record.

Humiliated, Surrey made their way quietly back to the Oval while Worcestershire travelled to Cheltenham for Gloucestershire's last home game of the season. Late summer dew had drenched the wicket and heavy cloud hung over the ground, holding in the humid air. In a bowler's paradise, laced with the appropriate ingredients, Hammond, the master craftsman, gorged himself to the full. Before lunch, the visitors had been dismissed for 35 by Hammond (10.2-2-23-9), who swung and cut the ball venomously, and Parker (8-7-1-1) whose one wicket, that of Quaife, was caught by the maestro who recorded the best bowling figures of his career.

By the time Dipper and Sinfield got to the wicket conditions had changed and a crowd of around 5,000, including a number of uniformed soldiers and sailors paying only 6*d* entry, basked in sunshine as the openers put on 116 for the first wicket. Hammond and Lyon then took part in another century partnership, the former making an exhilarating 80. By the close of play, the hosts led by 246 with 5 wickets in hand, no doubt leaving local supporters in high spirits as they made their way to the Town Hall to see famous London stars, Gwen Farrar and Billy Mayerl, who had been specially engaged for the Festival.

Lyon declared before lunch on Monday at 370 for 6, and having received a faint cheer from the crowd after passing their first innings score, Worcestershire gradually succumbed to the unchanged bowling of Hammond (33.3-5-105-6) and Parker (33-22-31-4), so losing in two days by an innings and 168 runs.

Gloucestershire cricket was flying high, with ten victories in the season promoting them to fifth in the championship. It was the start of a great revival, reminiscent of the best days of the Graces. Once again, Gloucestershire supporters had something to shout about, whether it was the thrilling captaincy of Bev Lyon, the sensational achievements of Hammond, or the wiliness of the unplayable Parker. The upshot of these successes on the field was an increase in support and membership, most noticeable at Cheltenham where total receipts made up from gate money, stands and car park for inter-county games reached a new high of £1,200.

However, plans were already in place for major changes the following year. These included reviving the abandoned Clifton Week in early August, which had faded away through lack of public support, and arranging further matches for the Victoria ground in Cheltenham. Naturally objections about the curtailment of the Festival were raised, but after both the manager, John Slingsby, and former manager, Major Bell Howarth, gave their support to the new proposal, recognising the advantage to the county that the change would make, it was unanimously adopted. There was a strong feeling, however, that the 1930 programme drafted for the Clifton Week should not interfere with the customary three matches at Cheltenham College.

—— 1929 ——

In 1929 the town had its fill of cricket. June's wet weather interfered with the county's game against Cambridge University on the Victoria ground, but in August four games were played in what is sometimes

A view of the ground in 1929

referred to as a 'split festival'. Two matches were staged at the College in the middle of the month, then after a disastrous trip to Trent Bridge, the county returned to play two more fixtures on the Victoria ground.

At the start of the match against Sussex, there were faint hopes that Gloucestershire might win the championship, but the talented K. S. Duleepsinhji, returning to play on his old school ground, had a hand in the visitors' exciting single-run victory, so ending any title hopes. Thwarted by ill-health, 'Duleep', or 'Mr Smith' as he was affectionately known, made 63 in a typically attractive display of free hitting in his side's first innings of 263. His strokes flowed from a light 'Harrow' bat purchased when he was a schoolboy from W. A. Woof sports outfitters shop in town. Woofie had coached the frail Duleep and recommended this size of bat 'to help his stroke making', according to his grandson, Philip Woof, who recalls that during the game his grandfather was asked to repair the bat, which was then handed to him as a momento after the sensational finish.

The hosts made a promising reply, with Dipper, Sinfield and Hammond chipping in, but the following day Lyon (62) had little support from the middle and lower order batsmen, and his side finished 49 runs behind. Enjoying his best season in a long career, Sussex and England opener, Ted Bowley, who had finished one short of a half-century in the first innings and then spun out five of the county's top batsmen with his leg-breaks, held his side together in the second innings, making 42 out of their total of 116. This meagre amount was the result of some fine bowling by Parker and Goddard, the pair ending with match analyses of 11 for 125 and 9 for 118 respectively. Goddard had proved to be the find of the season. This tall and powerful youth had begun as a fast bowler then re-emerged as an off-spinner after a spell on the staff at Lord's. It appeared that the sloping College ground had been made for this perfect spin combination of left and right-arm spinners, but sadly they were at opposite ends of their careers. Parker, now aged forty-seven, was still as good as ever after almost a quarter of a century of first-class cricket, while twenty-eight-year-old Goddard was still to reach his prime.

Wanting 166 for victory, Dipper and Sinfield put on 53 for the first wicket and victory seemed only a short step away. Wickets then fell quickly, and by stumps Gloucestershire were 97 for 5. Dipper (69) continued his three hour vigil next day, but all around him crumbled to James Langridge (5 for 72) and the hosts could only muster another 67. Recounting the game in *Cricket My Destiny*, Walter Hammond explained the defeat: 'Most of us were afflicted with that curious disease of nervousness, that occasionally attacks a team which has been doing rather better than its normal standard, and is putting everything to the venture on a thrilling game.'

Clearly the great man himself was overcome with nerves, and then shame, for he was out in both innings hitting his own wicket, although it could be argued that this may have been partly due to the higher and wider stumps that had been introduced into the game that year. There was hope of victory and the lure of that championship crown, even though wickets continued to fall on the last day. In Hammond's words, 'One player after another nervously took his guard, trembling survived an over or two, and came crawling indoors again, having cocked up a schoolboy catch or muffed a guileless ball.' In the end, matters rested with Barnett and Parker, the latter being run out on the very run that would have drawn the game, after he fell over as his legs 'gave way under him with nervousness'.

With Hammond and Hobbs playing in the final Test against South Africa at the Oval and rain restricting play on the first day to just three and a half hours, the start of the match against Surrey seemed rather an anti-climax compared to the previous day's drama. Harry Smith with 69 and 72 was the pick of the Gloucestershire batsmen, while once again Percy Fender demonstrated his all-round skills taking 5 for 52 and making 78 out of 105 in eighty minutes, before further rain brought the game to a premature end as a draw.

Lillywhite and Lawrence would have chuckled at the sight of money pouring in at the gate and the serried lines of cars parked around the College, as attendances and financial returns for these two inter-county matches passed previous records. Then four days later, with no more chance of securing championship honours, the second half of this split festival started on the Victoria ground.

Hours of hard work from Woofie and the committee members ensured the ground looked in splendid condition. Two excellent looking wickets had been prepared, encircled by enclosures, stands and Messrs George's irresistible catering tent.

A scattering of green tufts of clover then appeared, giving considerable help to the bowlers. Both teams lost an opening batsman, each retiring hurt after being struck by dangerous deliveries. In two days, on a fiery pitch, Gloucestershire defeated Warwickshire by 106 runs.

For the match against Hampshire, the bowlers were once again in the driving seat, setting up a close and exciting finish. Batting first on another lively wicket, the hosts lost 4 wickets for 48 and the organisers must have wondered if another early finish would slash their takings. Order was restored by the nimble wicket-keeper Harry Smith (66), and after several delays for rain, Gloucestershire's innings was quickly wrapped up next morning by the medium-paced in-swing of 'Alec' Kennedy (28.1-9-58-6). On a helpful wicket, Goddard (25-8-78-4) and Parker (22-5-38-5) then dismissed the visitors for 167 in under two and a half hours. Hampshire wasted no time in turning the game back to their advantage as Kennedy (22-5-52-5), helped by Newman (20-6-43-5), skittled out the home team for 117 in under two hours, so leaving themselves 163 for victory on the final day.

It was not long after play started next morning that Gloucestershire's newly-discovered spinning duo signalled their intentions on how the match would finish. Ending the season with more wickets than his superior, Goddard (21.3-5-46-7) and the seemingly ageless Parker (21-3-72-3) bowled out the visitors for 148, despite a determined, almost match-winning, tail-wagging session.

Winning by 14 runs, the county gained their fifteenth victory of the season, more than any of their rivals, earning themselves fourth place in the championship table. To a large extent this success was a result of Lyon's inspirational leadership and good teamwork. The captain had no time for stereotyped cricket; using unorthodox tactics, his simple aim was to score runs and take wickets. Players enjoyed the excitement of his type of game and crowds flocked to watch thrilling cricket. There were some who did not agree with his bold, original approach; intolerant traditionalists frowned at his methods, but they could not argue about his contribution to the ever-increasing gate receipts. These would continue to rise in subsequent years, despite the grip of the world economic crisis and the significant effect that it had on the country.

—— **1930** ——

With Gloucestershire cricket galvanised under Lyon, who was chosen later in the season as one of *Wisden's* 'Five Cricketers of the Year', the players arrived in Cheltenham full of confidence and fourth in the championship table, following two convincing victories at Clifton. Lyon was absent, attending to business commitments, so Jim Seabrook took charge for the first two games of the Festival, having been given specific instructions by the club captain to 'go all out to win' with the reminder that, 'Five points are no good to us; we want eight each time.'

The players rose to this challenge and swept to a ten wicket victory in two days against Warwickshire. In front of a Saturday crowd of 6,000 spectators, Parker (29-11-53-5) and Goddard (27-11-29-4) bowled the visitors out for 120, a total that would have been halved if Arthur Croom had not carried his bat for 58. Dipper made an unaccustomed nought; the solid reliable opener, once described by Neville Cardus as 'pale and lean, straight out of Falstaff's army', was coming towards the end of his illustrious career. Hammond and Sinfield then put their side on course for first innings lead, and a chanceless 59 by Smith gave them an 81 run advantage.

On Monday, Parker once again stirred the minds of past and present England selectors with figures of 22.5-8-44-9 as Gloucestershire went on to gather their full quota of points. Walking across the field as he went to tea, having just skittled Warwickshire, Parker chuckled when confronted by two spectators wanting to settle a heated argument that had turned into a £10 bet over whether he had ever played in a Test match.

'Of course I did,' interspersed the spinner, 'I played at Manchester in 1921 and took two wickets.'

Thereby the wager was immediately settled in the presence of the veteran left-armer, described next day in the press as 'Gloucestershire's great neglected' and still 'the most destructive bowler in the country'.

It was the opinion of a great number of people in the country, not just those in the West Country, that room should be found for Parker in the England line-up for the final Test. Top of the national bowling averages, still fit and well, it seemed impossible that the selectors could carry on ignoring him, especially after the events that unfolded over the next couple of days when he twice completely destroyed Surrey's batting.

Anyone who left Cheltenham on the morning of Wednesday 13 August on a 10s. 6d. Black and White Motorways 'Luxury Tour' to 'Cheddar Gorge and Caves, Bath and Wells' or a 7s. 6d. trip to the 'Beautiful Wye Valley, Tintern and Ross' missed one of the most conclusive days of cricket the county had ever produced at the Festival. It set them up for their second successive two-day triumph.

Displaying immaculate control of length, flight and spin, Charlie Parker (16.4-6-38-8) proved too much for the visitors, who were all back in the pavilion before lunch. After losing Dipper and Smith, Gloucestershire quickly tightened their grip on the game as Sinfield and Moore added 116 in one hundred minutes. The latter then took part in a seventy minute 123 run partnership with Charles Dacre.

Born in Tewkesbury, nineteen-year-old Denis Moore had already proved himself to be a cricketing phenomenon. A cousin of the chronicler of English country life, John Moore, of 'Brensham' trilogy fame, Denis's skills began to appear at his preparatory school, The Elms at Colwall. In his final year playing on the picturesque ground nestling beneath the Herefordshire Beacon, he took 60 wickets for 143 runs and scored 831 runs in 11 innings at an average of 166. In 1929, at Shrewsbury School, he broke all records, scoring 1038 runs at an average of 103.80. Then came his memorable first appearance for the county against Oxford early in the 1930 season, when Bev Lyon discovered Moore had not been selected to represent his university so asked him to play for Gloucestershire. Moore responded to the challenge by scoring 206. He was heralded as the 'New Gloucestershire Star', 'Another Hammond', but, sadly, severe illness the following year was to cut short his playing days. 'What promised to be a cricket career as brilliant as any in modern times was nipped in the bud,' wrote Hammond.

Moore was run out on 98, but his innings had impressed many, as had Dacre's faultless display of 92. Declaring on 349 for 8, it was over to Parker once again and he responded with figures of 32-10-53-7 as Gloucestershire won by an innings and 115 runs.

The action-packed first day had all been too much for Charles Baker, a licensed victualler from Ross-on-Wye. At around half past six that evening, he had been found lying across one of the footpaths on the ground. On attempting to lift him to his feet, policeman, Stanley Clarke, found Baker unable to stand and smelling strongly of 'alcoholic liquor'. He was taken to the police station in a taxi and charged with being drunk and incapable. Appearing before the Bench next day, he pleaded not guilty and blamed his demise on 'the excitement' of the match. Dismissing the charge, the Bench ordered Baker to pay costs of 6s. 6d., and allowed him to return to Ross and his licensed house, which he had kept 'without a stain' for thirty years.

Charlie Parker obviously did not share the same powers of persuasion. As a result of his exceptional form at Cheltenham, he was invited to the Oval for the last Test, but once again something or somebody blocked his selection. It seemed another crass decision, for here was a man who could bowl a ball which went away from the batsman, seemingly the only way in which Bradman had been troubled on tour.

Hurt and annoyed by the situation, Parker failed to appear on Saturday for the start of the final Festival match against Leicestershire. It was a pity, for his haul of 29 wickets in the first two games had given him the chance to smash his own record bag of 31 wickets in a three

Close of play 1930

match Festival. The matter came up for discussion on Monday afternoon as the county were stamping their authority on the game.

A meeting was held at the College, with Bev Lyon in the chair. He informed those present that he had requested Parker to return and play for the county against Leicestershire, if he was not selected to play for England, stating also that he had made the necessary travel arrangements for Parker to get from the Oval to Cheltenham, but the transgressor had declined to come. After a short discussion, it was decided that a special meeting of the selection committee should take place the following Saturday at half past ten at Fry's Ground, to select a side to play against the Australians.

In Parker's absence, Lyon, Smith, Seabrook and the up-and-coming Charles Barnett all made fifties, while Sinfield (5 for 50 in the first innings) and Goddard (7 for 100 in the second), took Gloucestershire to an eight wicket victory and second place in the championship table. Here they stayed for the next fortnight, ending the season runners-up by three points to Lancashire, despite having won five more games than the northerners.

Once again Cheltenham had been an enormous success. For a purely inter-county festival, another new record was established, the three victories yielding £1,158. The smooth running of the show was largely due to College master John Slingsby, who efficiently led the local committee and enthused a group of hardworking staff under his control. Efforts and dedication to duty had not changed from Lillywhite's days.

At the arranged meeting before starting play against the Australians at Bristol, Lyon informed the committee that he had recently received a most sincere apology from Parker for his behaviour and action over the Leicestershire game, and it was hoped that the harmony of the side would be restored. Indeed it was very much business as usual over the next three days. As summer drew to a close and young boys started to show more interest in fresh, juicy, red apples than old, scratched, red cricket balls, the game ended in a memorable tie. Charlie Parker played his part in a remarkable finish with ten wickets in the match, dismissing Bradman twice: vindication indeed.

—— 1931 ——

In an exceptionally wet summer, rain spoilt all three matches, each one ending in a draw. The highlight, perhaps, of nine damp days was the appearance on the ground of a weasel on the last evening of the Festival. Running wildly around the ring of spectators, squealing with fright, the destructive little animal was chased in vain by one of Woofie's terriers until he was cornered by a barrier of spectators and, as the *Chronicle* reports, 'Pop went the weasel!'

No major innings were played and the best bowling performance went to Sussex medium-pacer Bert Wensley (24.2-8-53-8). There was more cricket at Cheltenham during the week than on other grounds due to the useful slope of around fifteen feet from south to north and the sandy nature of the soil. Yet, understandably, attendances were low and deadlock on the field matched the gloomy political stalemate that existed between the Trades Union Congress and Ramsay MacDonald's government.

—— 1932 ——

'On Wednesday, August 10th, 1932, at the age of eleven, my five shilling "Scholars Ticket" clasped firmly in my hand, I made my first of hundreds of visits to a County Match, the opening match of that year's Cheltenham College Festival,' wrote W. H. Howard Lewis in an article entitled *Memories of Gloucestershire Cricket 1932-1936*. Bill Lewis, club life member and for many years a committee stalwart of the Gloucestershire Exiles, went on to recall that the day's play against Lancashire was 'intensely hot', but the 'sizzling' crowd was treated to a four hour spectacle from Hammond (164) who, although still a professional, was captaining the side in the absence of Lyon who was away on business.

The arrival of the Festival saw history repeating itself once again. After four wonderful years on the cricket field, Gloucestershire was beset with problems as some of the long-serving, loyal players reached the end of their careers. Results through the season had been disappointing, but August had brought that familiar burst of enthusiasm as varsity men, Allen and Parker, came into the side, while Dipper stood down shortly before leaving the county to become a first-class umpire.

As economic depression swept across the world and over two million Britons struggled to come to terms with unemployment, the country experienced an exceptional heat wave. Cheltenham baked in relentless sunshine and phenomenal temperatures were recorded as Hammond cruised past 2,000 runs for the season with a series of characteristic cover drives and leg glances. During his stay at the wicket, he was helped by the two brilliant and audacious stroke-making Charlies, Barnett (22) and Dacre (57), whose flashing and daring approach awakened the crowd who had been lulled into inactivity and silent meditation under the blazing sun.

In his *Chronicle* column, Chatterer, reminding his readers about 'the summers we used to have', wrote:

'Looking round the big crowd, I came to the conclusion that the only people who have retained any real faith in those summers are some of our brave old generals, admirals and colonels. They, almost alone, ventured out in panamas, although the sun was blistering hot. For they have faith in the old institutions of our country, and in spite of many trials, still believe in the "good old English summer" sufficiently to invest in a panama of a quality that shall do its wearer credit.'

Before the Festival, the mayor, Mr Taylor, had encouraged traders and residents to display flags to help 'add to the attraction of the beautiful town' and 'assist as an advertisement of the Festival'. But his words seemed to fall on deaf ears, and the town was rather colourless compared to bunting-bedecked Canterbury, where Gloucestershire's cricketers had recorded a convincing nine wicket victory ten days ago.

Test players Eddie Paynter and George Duckworth headed the powerful Lancashire team. A painstaking century from the former, together with brilliant wicket-keeping, including numerous vociferous appeals from Duckworth (who further enlivened proceedings by appearing in a trilby hat on the last day), ensured a close finish, with the hosts winning by just 44 runs.

Essex were then trounced by an innings and 12 runs in two days, as Reg Sinfield (114), Parker, with match figures of 7 for 57, and Goddard, 7 for 70, steered the county to their sixth victory of the season and a possible Cheltenham clean sweep.

The Sussex team arrived without Duleepsinhji amidst conflicting rumours about his health after he had been taken ill at Taunton a few days earlier. The famous cricketer's absence was most disappointing for Festival goers who regarded him as local talent, his skills having been developed by Woofie on the College playing fields. A bruise that had turned into neuritis was one suggestion for his non-attendance, but Woof disclosed that his former pupil had told him in a recent letter that he was very tired after playing a lot of cricket. Whatever the reasons, Gloucestershire's players would no doubt have been rather relieved about his absence from this strong, unbeaten Sussex team, who were challenging Yorkshire for the title.

Lyon returned to captain his side, glorious weather prevailed and overwhelming interest in the game meant that once again there were record receipts. Playing for the visitors were two pairs of brothers: John and James Langridge, and Jim and Henry Parks. This intrigued the young schoolboy Bill Lewis, who remembered James Langridge's first innings bowling analysis (11.5-7-8-7), describing his performance as 'absolutely incredible'.

Wickets tumbled quickly, and inside two days not one of the four innings reached 150 runs. Batting first, Sussex made 133, with top scorer Alan Melville (34) earning five of his runs when Tom Goddard stopped a ball with his cap. Langridge then reduced the hosts to 86 all out, and by close of play his side had struggled to 92 for 6, with 26 wickets having fallen in the day.

Within twenty minutes of play starting the following morning, the ground was full and bristling with excitement. Runs came quickly, and as the innings drew to a close, some huge hits from Maurice Tate enabled Sussex to reach 141, before being bowled out just before lunch. Standing in for wicket-keeper Harry Smith, who was ill, Douglas Raikes had proved to be a very capable replacement making five dismissals, but now he needed to contribute with his bat. Likewise, Denis Moore, who had played in all three Festival matches, but was still showing signs of the illness that had kept him out of the game for the whole of the previous season. Yet again, Gloucestershire struggled with the canny, slow left-arm bowling of James Langridge (22.1-3-59-6), who further justified his selection as one of *Wisden's* Five Cricketers of 1931, steering his team to victory by 56 runs.

—— **1933** ——

There was a real buzz in town at the start of the Festival. Opinions were still being strongly expressed about the recent 'Bodyline' tour, the county had started their familiar August revival and the South Western Counties Convention of Bee Keepers was about to commence, with discussion about the pedigree of honey and bees high on their agenda.

An opening stand of 90 by Worcestershire captain Cyril Walters (64) and 'Doc' Gibbons (38) was followed by a startling collapse. Losing eight wickets for 45 runs, as Goddard (26.4-8-67-6) and Parker (25-5-89-4) teased their neighbours, Worcestershire were all out for 193, then

Lyon (35) and Dacre (56), hitting boldly, steered their side to a 60 run first innings lead. On the second day, Walters (42), batting stylishly, was given solid support by Gibbons (41) and Quaife (40), but again there was no answer to the art of Goddard (23.1-3-73-6) and Parker (29-3-97-3), who paved the way for a convincing nine wicket home win as Barnett (50*) and Hammond (86*) brightly hit off the required runs in an undefeated partnership of 134.

On the opening day of the next match against Leicestershire, Winston Churchill warned the world that Germany was re-arming. Charlie Parker's career had already been interrupted by the First World War, and even though he was reaching the last phase of his playing days, he must have wondered if history was going to repeat itself. He certainly lost no time in winkling out some Leicestershire batsmen.

In the absence of Hammond and Barnett on Test duty, the county made 278, thanks largely to a sparkling 110, including 5 sixes, from Seabrook. Making his first appearance for two years, Seabrook batted in a seventh wicket 131 run partnership with Billy Neale (62*) creating a ground record which still stands. Apart from a faultless 128 by the prolific 'Jinks' Berry, the visitors, on reaching 280 for 9, seemed as if they had just shaded things in their favour on first innings, when a record last wicket partnership completely changed the face of the game. Although he was dropped three times, all-rounder William Astill (156*) and last man William Marlow (49) put on 157 together, as Parker claimed 5 for 106 from forty-six overs.

Trailing by 159 runs, Dacre (69) and Lyon (58) led a Gloucestershire comeback in which every player made a useful contribution with the bat. On 340 for 8, a sporting declaration by the fearless Bev Lyon left the visitors needing 182 to win. The gauntlet was thrown down and battle commenced. The captain led by example: fielding magnificently, he held five fine catches, and with warriors the calibre of Parker (17.4-6-46-4) and Goddard (18-7-41-6) on the front line, he was able to attack the visitors. Apart from Berry, there was little resistance and with ten minutes to spare, Gloucestershire gained a brilliant victory by 46 runs.

Buoyant with this success, along with the return of Barnett and Hammond, it seemed nothing could halt the county's dominance at Cheltenham. Derbyshire were the final visitors and Lyon's men wanted to avenge the defeat they had experienced at Chesterfield two months ago. Sinfield (35) and Barnett (52) opened confidently putting on 75 for the first wicket, so preparing the stage for Wally Hammond.

As he walked to the wicket, farmers with weathered hands and gnarled sticks, watching from their vantage points on top of wagons they had driven into the ground, joined in the rapturous applause. The magnificent, perfectly-proportioned athlete, who could have played soccer, rugby, or golf at the highest level, or perhaps even won an Olympic gold medal, was master of his art, making 231 out of a total of 431 in four and a half hours. Gone was W.G.'s record for the highest number of runs in a season by a Gloucestershire player (set by the Champion a year before Lillywhite brought the county to the College ground), along with any victorious aspirations held by the visitors.

That night, Hammond's innings must have been the talk of the Town Hall as the deputy mayor and mayoress, Alderman and Mrs P. P. Taylor, Derbyshire's non-playing, injured captain Arthur Richardson, members of both teams and 'lots of the most charming dancing girls in town' took to the dance floor and enjoyed music from Harry Jones's Premier Dance Orchestra. With the evening in full swing, numbers suddenly increased as the Cheltenham and Blackburn water polo teams arrived after their English semi-final match at Alstone Baths. The Lancastrians thoroughly enjoyed themselves amidst Cheltenham's night life, and when the party of some three hundred dancers finished at two o'clock, it was agreed that 'seldom in the summer has such a jolly dancing affair taken place in the town'.

When cricket recommenced, the visitors collapsed twice against Parker, who finished with 11 for 177. He was assisted by the smart wicket-keeping of newcomer Paul Van der Gucht, a former Radley College pupil coached by Percy Mills. Five dismissals in the match gave the tall youngster a total of ten for the Festival.

A win by an innings and 85 runs completed five consecutive victories for the county, taking them from thirteenth to ninth place in the championship table. Those farmers must have felt their journeys had been well worthwhile. With summer nearly over, they had many memories and dreams stored up for the dark months ahead, as they headed for the roads and country lanes that would take them back to their farms. Year by year, Festival crowds were growing larger as more people organised their holidays to coincide with the cricket in mid-August, knowing they would see many leading players competing against one another.

—— **1934** ——

This year, three large marquees were erected near the chapel. College master John Slingsby, superintending operations on the ground, commented the evening before play, 'The wicket is in first class condition, providing the weather holds.' It did not. Play eventually started after tea and the hosts, having been put into bat by Worcestershire, slumped to 95 for 6 by the close.

When play resumed after the weekend, Charles Dacre was not content simply to steady the ship; he was irrepressible, hitting sixes and fours as he sped along to 114. Assisted by Dallas Page (45), Gloucestershire reached 254. The visitors reply was innocuous; by tea they were 91 for 7 and not long after Sinfield (4 for 44) and Parker (4 for 45) bowled them out for 126. A faultless century from Charles Barnett (102), now fulfilling all his early promise, dominated a 115 run second wicket partnership with Hammond (57), enabling Lyon to declare at lunch on the last day, setting the visitors 363 to win.

Bowling eighty-four overs between them, Sinfield, Goddard and Parker were no better than 'all the king's horses and all the king's men' in putting Gloucestershire 'back together again'. The Worcestershire batsmen remained resolute and Gibbons defied the bowlers for over four hours as he 'stone-walled' his way to 113*, despite ironic applause from the home supporters and shouts of 'Come on Woodfull!' - a reference to Bill Woodfull, the renowned patient batsman known as 'The Rock' - every time he blocked a ball. Dogged support was given by Quaife (73*) as the game petered out to a draw, the visitors 100 runs short of their target with 7 wickets in hand.

Everything changed in the next match as records galore were set on a hard, fast wicket against Sussex. Having travelled through the night from Hastings, where they had drawn with Kent in a rain-affected match, the Sussex players were punished mercilessly in hot sunshine as Gloucestershire reached 474 for 4.

Opening the batting, Barnett (189) was the hero of the day. Setting the momentum of the whole innings, driving splendidly, he made his second hundred in two days, and in doing so reached 2,000 runs in a season for the first time in his career. Still a natural hitter of the ball, he had strengthened his defence, and the innings delighted his fellow townsfolk. An opening stand of 128 with Grahame Parker was followed by a record second wicket partnership of 251 with Hammond (137), who thrilled the crowd making his century between lunch and tea. But there was even more to come: into the driving seat stepped captain Beverley Lyon, an excellent motivator of his team. Scoring 119, he and Basil Allen (57) took Gloucestershire to 608 for 7, creating a record, which still remains, for the highest innings total ever made on the ground.

Sussex, however, were a strong team and they were fighters. For the third successive summer they would finish runners-up in the county championship and now they showed their true colours in the positive way they set about chasing this huge total. Top order batsmen John Langridge (58), Parks (42), Melville (73), Cook (66) and James Langridge (61) made Gloucestershire's bowlers toil. Then a swashbuckling 81 from Maurice Tate, in partnership with Langridge, realised 120 for the ninth wicket, setting yet another record.

Throughout the innings, Lyon kept changing his bowlers to try and unsettle the batsmen. The visitors' resilience had annoyed Hammond, and his irritation showed when he was finally persuaded to bowl a second spell. Normally bowling at a gentle pace, he suddenly let a ball fly which reared off the pitch and hit wicket-keeper Charlie Dacre on the shoulder. Hammond and Dacre were not the best of friends and the sight of the New Zealander standing up to his bowling infuriated Hammond even more. He bowled faster and faster while Dacre retreated, with an ever increasing number of balls bouncing over and wide of the keeper and racing to the boundary as byes. Eventually sanity was restored and the visitors were bowled out for 442. Parker had delivered forty-two overs and taken 3 for 157, while Goddard (28.4-6-83-5) mopped up the lower order.

As Hammond had been racing to his century on Wednesday afternoon, a ground collection was being made for his benefit fund. There could be no better time than this, and with the maestro in full swing £48 was quickly realised. The tin-shaking Gloucestershire players were assisted by club secretary Mr Tunnicliffe, who invited Councillor Horace Neate, the Mayor of Bedford, to join them. A guest for the day, the mayor, formerly of Cheltenham and an old friend of Hammond, thoroughly enjoyed himself, quickly filling his tin as he kept the crowd amused with jokes.

The following evening, when proceedings on the College ground had finished, the entire Gloucestershire team drove to Colesborne to play in a twelve-a-side game against a Cirencester and District team. Arranged by Mr Voyce for Hammond's benefit fund, permission had been given by Lieut. Colonel H. C. Elwes to use the attractive Colesborne Park ground, and the people of north Gloucestershire showed enthusiastic support for the event. Special coaches were laid on from Cheltenham and Gloucester and a crowd of over 2,000 gathered to enjoy the informal cricket, showing their appreciation by contributing £30 to a ground collection. The *Echo* reported that it was 'cricket with a laugh in almost every stroke', with the game played 'in a spirit of fun'; the County were obviously 'intent on having a bright knock and a short one'. When bad light stopped play, Cirencester and District had made 184 for 6 (J. Hitch 127*) in reply to the county's 250 for 10 declared, and all eyes focused back on the College ground for the impending day's play.

Cricket author and lecturer G. D. Martineau recalled the following incident midway through Sussex's second innings: 'I entered the ground in time to hear excited applause on the dismissal of a Sussex batsman. I forget who it was, but I took the liberty of glancing over the shoulder of a rather severe looking parson, and observed him entering on his scorecard : ". . . c Sin b God 7." ' Apocryphal or not, the official scorecard actually read: 'W. Cornford c Sinfield b Goddard 8'.

Sussex fought bravely, but apart from Thomas Cook's 93 and an elegant 52 by Alan Melville, little could be done to stop Goddard who returned figures of 21.5-4-71-6, and Gloucestershire quickly knocked off the runs required to win by 7 wickets. The match had realised 1,319 runs for 30 wickets and as soon as it finished, George Cox, the Sussex all-rounder, sped back to London. As a member of the Arsenal playing staff, he had been released to play at Cheltenham only after urgent talks with the club. It was now time for him to put his bat away, carry on his football training and prepare for Arsenal's practice match next day.

As the local aircraft industry grew and Dowty's continued to expand in its small Lansdown mews workshop, employment in the town, the population of which now neared 50,000, received a boost. This gave the council good reason to continue its programme of slum clearance, concentrating on the area behind St Paul's. Here they were clearing away some of the worst eyesores of the 'Garden Town' and building new houses, but visitors to the Festival would be largely unaware of these improvements as they arrived on the plush College ground for the match against Surrey. An earlier encounter in the season had resulted in the Londoners giving Gloucestershire a good thrashing by an innings and 75 runs, but matters were reversed over the next three days with the hosts demonstrating all round superiority and winning by 279 runs.

Struggling on 49 for 4, a middle order revival followed as Page, Allen, Sinfield, Neale and Cranfield took the total to 305. Surrey then laboured against Sinfield (21-4-93-5) and the fifty-year-old Parker (33-7-77-4), the only bit of fight being shown by Errol Holmes who made a stirring 42 including 5 sixes in half an hour.

Reg Sinfield was having a useful Festival, part of a productive season in which he became the first Gloucestershire professional to achieve the double of 1,000 runs and 100 wickets, a feat that had not been accomplished for the county since C.L. Townsend in 1898. He was not required to bat in the second innings. Lyon made a brilliant 189, his highest score for the county, and Barnett scored 76. Together they featured in a partnership of 201, enabling the captain to declare on 353 for 6, setting Surrey 398 to win. They collapsed miserably for 118, largely due to Parker's 5 for 36, with help from his namesake, Grahame, and the ever effective Goddard.

CHAPTER TWELVE (1935-1939)

UNDERTONES OF WAR

—— 1935 ——

Another end-of-summer heatwave greeted spectators at the start of the Festival, but the fiery pitch was not so welcoming for the players, and batsmen trooped in and out of the pavilion as 22 wickets fell for 409 runs on the first day. Worcestershire were the visitors and apart from Hammond (69) and Stephens (48), who added 100 for the second wicket, the hosts could do little against the penetrating Perks (20.2-7-57-6). Batting at number ten, the tall left-hander followed his bowling with some fearless hitting, eventually being run out for 48 as his team was dismissed for 200. In the final hour of this eventful first day, the hosts went nine runs ahead, after losing both openers, Sinfield and Stephens.

Worcestershire quickly turned the screw next day. Dick Howorth (8.1-2-15-6), with some cunningly flighted slow left-armers, was helped by Reg Perks (10-1-33-4), who completed a great all-round performance. Scoring the 42 runs needed for victory, the guests lost two wickets. One of them was Charles Bull whose dismissal was particularly memorable, snicking the cagey old veteran Parker into Hammond's waiting hands and giving him his two hundred and twenty ninth - and last - catch off the great bowler.

Deputising for H. F. Wade, Horace Cameron led the impressive South African side on their first visit to the ground. The result against Gloucestershire appeared a foregone conclusion, for South Africa were undefeated on the tour with fourteen victories to their name, including a 157 run defeat of England at Lord's. The hosts, meanwhile, had lost their last seven games and were hovering around the bottom of the championship table.

Gloucestershire's new captain was Dallas Page. Tragically, both he and his opposite number would be dead just over a year after spinning the coin together, a toss which Page won, electing to bat.

Sinfield provided the backbone to the innings with an attractive knock

167

of 102, consisting of well-timed drives and strong leg-hitting, as he and Billy Neale (61) added 102 in just over an hour for the sixth wicket. All out for 279, the county's total was topped by ten, thanks to a fine three hour innings of 122 by Ken Viljoen, with Hammond, Goddard, Parker and Sinfield sharing the wickets.

Amongst the large crowd was a small boy in a blue aertex shirt. Standing by his father's side, Nico Craven watched the game with great interest, explaining later, 'It was the crouching wicket-keeper who took the eye and fired my imagination.' This was to be the first of a lifetime of annual visits for Nico. Few people have watched as many hours of cricket at Cheltenham, or talked so loyally and enthusiastically about it. None have written so regularly and warmly about it as this Festival wordsmith.

The game suddenly took off at the start of Gloucestershire's second innings. Opening with Reg Sinfield, Charlie Barnett, who had batted at number seven first time round, launched a fierce onslaught on the bowling, making 46 out of 52 in half an hour. Hammond capitalized on this flying start, driving and late-cutting magnificently, scoring 123 out of 209 at a run-a-minute on a wicket that was becoming increasingly helpful to bowlers. At the end of the second day, having taken a firm grip on the game, Gloucestershire were all out for 298.

If the visitors repeated their first innings total they would win the match, and at 150 for 3 they looked set for victory. During the morning's play, Reg Sinfield had spotted a ladybird on his shirt and mentioned to his captain that it might just be his lucky day. With two wickets to his name before lunch, including that of captain Cameron under the new lbw rule, he skipped the meal and waited eagerly for play to resume. By tea, he had steered his side to an historic 87 run victory with a cunning spell of bowling, taking 5 for 31 as the tourists' last 7 wickets fell for 51 runs. Bill Lewis recalls, 'It was a wonderful occasion and for hours after the game, many of us crowded outside the pavilion shouting for a sight of our heroes.'

Lyon and Page eventually came out to the great delight of the supporters, and with drinks in their hands toasted 'the very good health' of the crowd. While the players enjoyed praise and adoration, the mayor, Mr E. L. Ward, addressed a happy throng saying that it was one of the most historic games ever played on the ground. News of the South Africans' defeat spread quickly, gaining larger national recognition when Roy Ullyett, celebrated cartoonist of *The Star,* suggested that England's Test selectors, who had been keeping the Essex fast bowler 'Nipper'

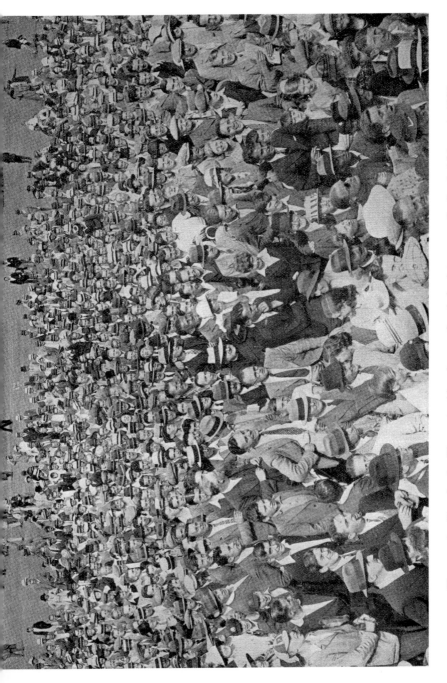

The crowd calling for the Gloucestershire players after their victory over the South Africans in 1935

Read out of sight from the tourists, should change their plans and select the entire Gloucestershire team to represent their country for the final Test at the Oval. In the event, Read did indeed make his England debut and took six wickets.

A fortnight before the start of the Festival, a meeting had been called to consider the question of insuring gate receipts. After detailed discussion, it was agreed that the matches would be insured with Eagle Star and British Dominion Insurance Company at a premium cost of £140. 8s. This would cover a sum of £1,200 net divided between the three matches to be played, £250 for the Worcestershire fixture, £700 for South Africa and £250 for Middlesex. So far, the premium had been money down the drain as the South Africa match alone had been a huge financial success yielding £1,600 in receipts, entrance to the ground on this occasion having been increased to two shillings.

Back in June, on hearing the College had 'a most promising player in the school eleven named Eagar', enquiries were made by the county as to his availability for the two inter-county fixtures at the Festival. He could only make the last match, against Middlesex, so the eighteen-year-old represented his county for the first time and took to the field with fifty-three-year-old Charlie Parker who was making his last Festival appearance.

In the *Echo*, further praise was bestowed on John Slingsby for his 'skill and enterprise', along with his 'customary body of willing and loyal helpers', ensuring the 'general arrangements for the public and others were in every way pleasing'. Having witnessed Eagar's success at school, Slingsby must have been particularly pleased with the boy's first innings score of 23. The *Chronicle* commented: 'He literally lived up to his name in the field . . . he has plenty of strokes, knows how to hit the ball and possesses sound discrimination.'

Batting first, Gloucestershire, in elated mood, made 344 thanks largely to Hammond (124) and Barnett (78), who featured in a 175 run two and a quarter hour second wicket partnership. Another oldie, forty-six-year-old 'Patsy' Hendren, with an undefeated 71, and Owen-Smith (70) kept Middlesex in the game as Goddard (34.4-6-139-8) and Parker (31-6-108-2) bowled the visitors out for 300. Without Sinfield, who had injured his thumb, the county could only muster 180, and Hendren, with 70* in the second innings, guided his team to a 4 wicket victory.

After eight days of cricket, which had been watched by 23,231 spectators, with gate receipts of £2,165, it was time to say goodbye to two old professionals after long, distinguished careers. 'Young Jack'

Hearne, who had started with Middlesex in 1909 and played 24 Test matches for England, was about to retire, along with Charlie Parker, cornerstone of Gloucestershire cricket, who, for the sixteenth season in succession, had taken over a hundred wickets, and by December would be appointed to the list of first-class umpires.

Over the next four years, during the build up to the war, Gloucestershire enjoyed one of their most successful spells on the College ground, losing only once in twelve matches.

—— 1936 ——

In March, while Hitler was building his military might, Golden Miller made racing history at Cheltenham's 'other festival', by winning the Gold Cup for the fifth consecutive time.

Growing in popularity and importance, Race Week at Prestbury, one of the major events of the National Hunt season, was part of Cheltenham's 'new look', with the town now advertising itself as 'England's Favourite Winter Resort'. When summer arrived, the cricket season would be one of triumph and tragedy, with the Festival once again the turning point of the season, bringing a trio of victories.

In front of a Saturday crowd of over 7,000, George Emmett and Andy Wilson, both completing a two-year qualification period, made their debut for the county against India. In glorious weather, the kind that might have come straight from the sub-continent, the tourists were baffled by the spin of Reg Sinfield (27.2-13-38-4), who dismissed the last four batsmen without a run being added to their total of 154. In reply, Barnett and Moore started briskly, followed by a fine 81 from Hammond, so when people started to gather at the Town Hall for the municipal dance, prospects for the county were looking good.

Expressing his regret at interrupting the dance, the mayor, Councillor D. L. Lipson, gave 'a hearty welcome' to both teams, and to guests from the New Education Fellowship Conference, which was being held in town. Even though, as usual, many inhabitants were away at the seaside, Cheltenham was awash with cricket lovers and forward-looking educationalists. Expressing his delight at being able to watch the tourists play, the mayor then handed over to Dallas Page who extended further warm greetings to the All India team before Mr Harvi, for the visitors, 'thanked the mayor and citizens of Cheltenham for the welcome they had been afforded'. He concluded by thanking Gloucestershire's captain, going on to say that it had been the first time while on tour that they had been able to play under their own conditions, but their success had been limited. The *Chronicle* reported: 'There was a very good attendance at the dance, at which the Ambassadors dance band, directed by Hector Davies, provided the music with skill and verve. It was a cosmopolitan gathering - Americans, Germans, Frenchmen and Indians - educationalists and cricketers, all entering into the spirit of the dance with enthusiasm.'

Another large crowd of just over 5,000 watched Monday's intriguing play. Everyone chipped in to give the county a first innings lead of 159 runs and with 8 wickets down in their second innings the tourists were still behind. Once again it was Sinfield (35.5-11-79-5) who was causing the problem, ably assisted by Monty Cranfield (19-4-43-4) who was standing in for the injured Goddard. A forceful ninth wicket partnership of 100 between Baqa Jilani (59) and Amir Elahi (45) saved the follow-on, but undefeated innings from a back-on-form Denis Moore (44) and Wally Hammond (35) gave their side victory by 8 wickets.

Schoolboy Arthur Hemmings, later to become captain, then secretary and treasurer of Redmarley CC, was typical of many youngsters keen to share in the excitement of the day. He was dropped off at the ground and told to meet up with his mother by the railings at the end of play. If he did but know it he was in distinguished company, for also on the College ground was seven-year-old David Sheppard, destined to captain Sussex and England, and later to become Bishop of Liverpool. 'My grandparents lived at Woodmancote and we came to stay for the cricket week at Cheltenham each summer when I was a boy,' recalls Lord Sheppard. Standing by his father's side, along with the villagers of Dumbleton who had come to see their champion Vic Hopkins, he watched Hammond almost single-handedly earn his team a five wicket win against Surrey.

Batting first on a difficult wicket, the visitors were bowled out for 210. Apart from Hammond (108), who batted faultlessly, Gloucestershire's batsmen struggled against Brown (31-6-83-6) and Gover (3 for 37), finishing 17 runs in arrears. Some hard hitting from Brown (60) and Barling (78) left the hosts needing 288 for victory. Charles Barnett, one of *Wisden's* Five Cricketers of the Year, loved a challenge and he sped to 70 out of 89 in an hour. Moore (43), Hammond (62), Sinfield and newcomer Jack Crapp saw their side home with half an hour to spare.

Coming from behind again on first innings, Gloucestershire completed their trio of victories when beating Sussex by 3 wickets. Without Barnett and Hammond, the latter busy cracking 217 against India at the Oval, Sussex reached 266 thanks to Parks (78) and an undefeated 88 from James Langridge. Cranfield, who had retained his place in the side despite Goddard's recovery from a strain, took 5 for 70 in twenty-eight overs. Billy Neale, with 52, led the reply and honours were pretty even at the end of day one.

It was very much an ordinary Sunday in Cheltenham next day, with church bells ringing, families walking and cricketers enjoying their day off. Meanwhile in Berlin, the Olympic Games ended, with an angry Hitler hurrying away from the stadium as the crowd cheered United States sprinter, Jesse Owens, winner of four gold medals.

Matters were altogether more sporting than in Berlin when play resumed on the College ground and some vigorous hitting by George Cox (52) formed the only resistance to Goddard's accuracy and spin (27-5-66-7). James Langridge (26-7-49-5) made things difficult for Gloucestershire, but a steady 21* by Eagar, at a crucial time, tipped the balance in favour of the hosts.

In an otherwise wet summer, rain did not cause a solitary interruption in nine days of play. Over 21,000 people attended, including more women spectators, who, according to the *Echo* attended purely for social reasons in the past, but were now 'genuinely interested in the game'. The three Festival victories were followed by three more wins out of four games with the county rushing up to fourth place in the championship.

Delight became tragedy. Only a few hours after winning the final match of the season at Gloucester, Dallas Page, driving home in his sports car, collided with a motor cycle and crashed into a stone wall near Cirencester. Managing to climb from the car, he was taken to Cirencester Memorial Hospital but died from his injuries early next morning. Two months later, South African, Horace Cameron, opposing captain the previous year, died of enteric fever.

There was more sadness the following April when William Woof, who had been in poor health for some time, died at his home in Suffolk Road. For over twenty years he had bowled his slow left-armers for the county and for twice that length of time he had been coach at the College. He had founded a sports business in town, was a keen follower of all types of sport and was a well-known breeder and exhibitor of fox terriers. Working with the pupils, he was not only a good cricket coach but, as the *Chronicle* reported, 'a factor for good' in the forming of many a boy's character.

—— **1937** ——

The county retained fourth position in the championship under their new captain Basil Allen, who led by example at the Festival. Worcestershire were the opponents in the first match and their openers Bull and Buller got them off to a good start before Kimpton (92) carried their total to 310, despite the cleverly flighted off-spin from Goddard (18-4-68-6). In reply, Gloucestershire could only muster 196, leaving their guests in a strong position. For the hosts, something extraordinary needed to happen and it did. Like Cotswold stone, Tom Goddard seemed to mellow with age, but despite this he was now enjoying, arguably, his greatest season. His figures of 28.4-4-113-10 in Worcestershire's second innings created an unbeaten record to date for the county on the ground, and the towering spinner was on his way to passing Parker's record number of wickets in a summer.

Set to make 317 on a wearing wicket, at 15 for 2 Gloucestershire's hopes seemed dashed. However, coming together on Monday evening, Hammond made 178, his thirteenth century of the season, while Allen made 78. They created a record third wicket partnership of 269 and the hosts went on to win by 3 wickets.

Derbyshire were the next visitors and suffered in the same way as they had done four years earlier, although their innings and 84 run defeat was one run better than last time. The hosts scored 392, with the captain, once again in fine form, making 128, while Hammond made 63 and Crapp, 57. On the second day, Derbyshire were bowled out twice for 228 and 80 in four hours. All 20 wickets were taken by Goddard and Sinfield, who ended with match analyses of 12 for 145 and 8 for 129 respectively.

Rain prevented any play on the opening day of the match against Sussex. There were further breaks for rain on the second day which belonged to Grahame Parker (102) and Reg Sinfield (72), who put on 162 for the first wicket. Next morning James Langridge, with 5 for 32, finished off the innings on 276. In the short time remaining, the visitors just managed to nose in front reaching 278 for 4, thanks to brilliant batting by Parks (127) who was assisted for a while by H. E. Hammond (52), later to become coach and groundsman at the College.

A month later, George Dennett, former county cricketer and successor to Woof as College coach, died at his home in Old Bath Road after a lengthy illness. He had enjoyed a long and successful career with Gloucestershire and had been a popular member of the College staff. In

Spectator Herbert Champney is prepared for
any weather at the 1937 Festival

his warm, personal tribute, colleague John Slingsby wrote, 'George has passed on – a great man, but, still more, a great gentleman . . . It can safely be said that everyone, master or boy, who came in contact with him felt they had found a real friend; his chief attributes were patience and optimism.'

—— **1938** ——

This year, patience and optimism were both required by Gloucestershire supporters. The county's cricket was under a cloud, recording many more defeats than victories. This was largely due to the disorganisation of the team through injury, illness and the loss of Hammond, now an amateur and captain of England, along with Barnett, Goddard and Sinfield who were called away on Test match duty. The unsettled atmosphere in the team was reflected in the weather, when a violent thunderstorm broke out the night before the opening match against Hampshire.

Next morning, under clear skies, Basil Allen won the toss and faced a hard decision. His choice to bat first on a wet pitch seemed rather foolhardy, and this was confirmed when the county were dismissed for 134. Rain caused further interruptions and despite good bowling from Goddard (27-6-61-5), Hampshire nosed ahead by 38 runs. At the close of play Gloucestershire were 132 for 8, having lost 6 wickets for 23 runs at one stage of their innings, and the scene was set for the final day's play.

Overnight, westerly winds blew fresh rain clouds along the Bristol Channel and up the Severn estuary, causing the start of play to be delayed until just before one o'clock. The hosts were quickly bowled out, leaving their opponents 103 to win. Not too difficult thought some; but now there was hot sunshine and Tom Goddard.

On a drying wicket he was almost unplayable, and the sparse crowd, who had paid only 6d. entrance due to a threat of further rain, witnessed the master at work. Bowling to his trap of three short-legs and a silly mid-on, with the ball spinning sharply and 'popping', Hampshire lost their first 6 wickets for 38. Helped by Sinfield (17.3-3-30-3) and some good fielding, Goddard (17-4-26-7) swept his side to an unexpected victory by 44 runs.

After play, drizzle was followed by steady rain and then an overnight deluge. A sodden pitch greeted Nottinghamshire in the morning and the match was abandoned without a ball being bowled for the second time only in sixty-six years of cricket on the ground.

As Hitler strutted round making threats and demands in Europe, gradual 'prepare for war' activities were going on all over Cheltenham, but it was business as usual for the final match of the Festival.

Worcestershire were the opponents, going down by 2 wickets as the hosts came from 66 behind on their first innings. Needing 247 for victory, everyone in the Gloucestershire team reached double figures, but it was thanks to particularly careful batting by Crapp (44), Allen (31) and Emmett (30) that the target was reached.

Mr Pite, headmaster of Cheltenham College, was told in a top secret communication that in the event of war the College buildings would be commandeered. Day by day, life in the town was changing with industries starting to make products essential for combat. Later, residents would witness some of the town's Regency wrought iron work being pillaged by the Ministry.

The tranquil scene depicted in John Betjeman's poem *Cheltenham* was under threat. Although it describes a school game, it conjures up an ambience similar to that of the Festival, along with the atmosphere and traditions of the town in an era soon to be lost forever:

> Floruit, floret, floreat!
> Cheltonia's children cry.
> I composed those lines when a summer wind
> Was blowing the elm leaves dry,
> And we were seventy-six for seven
> And they had C.B.Fry.
>
> Shall I forget the warm marquee
> And the general's wife so soon,
> When my son's colleger [1] acted as tray
> For an ice and a macaroon,
> And distant carriages jingled through
> The stuccoed afternoon?
>
> Floruit. Yes, the Empire Map
> Cheltonia's sons have starred.
> Floret. Still the stream goes on
> Of soldier, brusher [2] and bard.
> Floreat. While behind the limes
> Lengthens the Promenade.

[1] Mortar board.   [2] Schoolmaster.

—— **1939** ——

The lime-lined Promenade was a route that some of the 8,766 spectators would have taken to the ground for the first day of the match against the West Indies. A large shadow had hung over many cricket grounds throughout the summer, but just for a moment thoughts of the impending, inevitable horrors were brushed aside and the townsfolk gave a warm welcome to Rolph Grant and his touring team. In anticipation of a big crowd, the organisers had increased seating by 500 in the stands and another innovation was the creation of an entrance at the far end of the ground to benefit the people using the new car park in Old Bath Road, which could hold 1,000 cars. This replaced the former car park in College Road which had been converted into tennis courts.

At lunch, after a morning where raincoats and umbrellas were a necessary addition to summer attire, Gloucestershire had taken 9 wickets for 110 runs, including 'The Black Bradman' George Headley, whose cheap dismissal caused considerable disappointment to the crowd. Amongst them, watching his first first-class match, was twelve-year-old Tom Graveney along with his brother Ken and two school friends.

'We caught a train from Temple Meads that morning,' recalls Tom Graveney. 'We sat on the grass, clutching our sandwiches. I had heard so much about George Headley. George Lambert bowled him a bouncer and it went to the boundary like a bullet. Moments later he rocked back and his foot tipped the bail off.'

As the players left the field and made their way to one of the large marquees where the mayoral lunch was going to be held, Graveney wandered round the ground, past the flagpole where the maroon flag of the West Indian team fluttered, watched the rope going up round the wicket and savoured 'the wonderful atmosphere'.

Meanwhile some 120 guests were received by the mayor and mayoress, Mr John Howell and Mrs Stewart Billings. The *Chronicle* reported the mayor's words of welcome in which he described the tourists as 'a good sporting side who played bright and attractive cricket'. He said the citizens of Cheltenham were behind him 'in giving every assistance towards making the Festival a happy one and they were particularly fortunate in being able to watch two such great cricketers as Hammond and Headley'. He concluded by insisting that 'a fine county like Gloucestershire' should not have to 'depend on the vagaries of the weather for its financial support', and he urged those present 'to try and

At the mayor's lunch. Major Henson, Walter Hammond, the Mayor and Mayoress of Cheltenham, R. S. Grant the West Indies captain and their team manager Mr J. M. Kidney

A last glimpse of the Festival before the break for war in 1939

increase the present membership of the county club'. Thanking the mayor, club president, Sir Stanley Tubbs, commenting upon the weather, suggested that 'St Swithin . . . should be made a member of the club and even ordained as its saint!' as this might 'compel him to show favour'. Before leaving the rest of the guests to finish their lunch, the two team captains gave their thanks and Hammond wished the visitors 'a happy time in Cheltenham and for the rest of their tour'. These celebrations were mentioned by the former Sussex player, A. E. R. Gilligan, in his Empire wavelength broadcast from the ground that evening.

Play resumed with an exciting last wicket stand of 52 in half an hour between Stollmeyer and Clarke, then Gloucestershire made a most promising start, reaching 100 for 3 against a varied attack which was supported by some brilliant fielding. David Sheppard, on another summer holiday visit to his grandparents, remembered 'Learie Constantine's electric movements and throwing in the field'. His next visit to the ground would be after the war - this time as a player rather than a spectator.

Suddenly, thirty-seven-year-old 'Connie' struck with the ball, taking 4 wickets in three overs for 6 runs. Now more of a medium-pace bowler, he finished with 5 for 40 from thirteen overs as the hosts lost their last 6 wickets for just 36 runs, ending their innings 10 runs in arrears.

On a pitch kept moist by heavy morning dew, batting remained difficult, but patient displays from Headley (40), Gomez (50) and the Stollmeyer brothers helped their team reach 220. The challenge was now on for Gloucestershire.

Openers, Barnett and Emmett, put on 59, then Neale (70) joined Emmett (84) and together they added 132 for the second wicket. Within five minutes of each other they were back in the pavilion, but had come out on top at the crucial stage of the game and it was now up to Hammond and the young 'Podge' Brodhurst to finish the job. Predictably, England's captain made a speedy 33, hitting a six and 4 fours.

At the other end, Brodhurst, a recent Cambridge blue, had been asked in July by the county secretary, Colonel Hugh Henson, if he would be available to play if required. Old Malvernian Brodhurst had been a long-time opponent of Old Cheltonian Desmond Eagar in fixtures between their schools and later in the varsity match. Now the 'two young fancy cap amateurs', as Brodhurst described himself and Eager, were rubbing shoulders with the country's leading players. 'The old pros were very friendly,' recalls Brodhurst, 'especially Reg Sinfield, Billy Neale and Andy Wilson.' In the West Indies' second innings, he recollected that when he was fielding at forward short-leg to Goddard's bowling, 'before every over there came from Tom Goddard a gruff "A bit closer please Mr Brodust" '. He described the time when George Headley was batting and had made about 26 when 'he popped up' a catch to him. 'I dropped it: not a word and I felt ghastly! Fortunately he was out for 40. We beat them by 7 wickets . . . I was not out, watching Wally at the other end!'

During Gloucestershire's successful run-chase, Hammond passed his 2,000 and Barnett and Emmett their 1,000 runs for the season. These fruitful proceedings on the field were matched by lucrative receipts of £1,077, a record for the Festival for a 1s. 3d. gate, contributed by a crowd of 16,446.

The match against Derbyshire started with Gloucestershire third in the table and in with a real chance of winning the championship at last. Batting first, the visitors made 193, with Scott and Lambert taking 4 wickets each, then the hosts were routed for 81 by Copson (13-1-45-5) and Pope (13.3-4-25-5). A hard, fast pitch was proving to be a quick bowler's paradise as Derbyshire lost 3 more wickets before play ended on the first day.

Slumping to 48 for 6 the following morning, the visitors were rescued from further embarrassment by George Pope (57) who helped his side reach 148, as Scott (17-2-52-4) and Lambert (14.2-1-69-6) again enjoyed exploiting the precarious pitch. Needing 261 to win on an unreliable wicket was a tall order for the county, but the players and loyal supporters knew victory was paramount if that elusive title was going to be secured.

The game fluctuated throughout the afternoon as runs and wickets were added to the scoreboard. Batting superbly, Hammond led the way with 87, followed by Emmett (58) and Crapp (40), and just before half past six, when play was scheduled to finish, the county needed 39 more runs with 5 wickets in hand. With the light fading it was obviously in the interest of the batsmen to continue next morning, so it seemed totally absurd when Hammond suddenly claimed the extra half hour's play during which two more wickets fell.

The final morning was packed with thrills. Two of the remaining three wickets went down for the addition of 10 runs, so four were needed for a Gloucestershire victory. Last man, Lambert, joined the resilient Billy Neale (27). Each batsman scored a single, then going for a big hit to finish things, Neale skied a catch to Denis Smith. The game was over and spinner Tommy Mitchell had taken 5 for 75. The Sussex ghost of ten years before had been resurrected and it could be argued that the captain's inexplicable decision to play on in poor light the night before had lost the match and subsequently the championship.

The third Test at the Oval took away Hammond, Goddard and Compton from the match with Middlesex. Gloucestershire were dismissed for 214 as the tall, lean leg-break and googly bowler Jim Sims returned figures of 23.4-3-109-7. His team then took a first innings lead of 33, thanks to Robertson's solid 87.

Behind the boundary ropes, within the rooms and corridors of the College, plans were being finalised for the evacuation to Shrewsbury School, while, in town, officials were preparing for the arrival of 2,500 young evacuees from Birmingham.

Matters improved enormously in the county's second innings. Making his only century of the summer, Crapp (101), assisted by Neale (76), Barnett (45) and Lyon with his enterprising 44, enabled the hosts to declare on 327 for 7. Middlesex never looked like getting the runs and when the score reached 65 for 7, some carefree slogging started. Runs came quickly, but at 108 their final wicket fell. Sinfield had impressive figures of 7-0-48-6 and the hosts were home by 186 runs.

While concern over runs and wickets occupied some minds, the Cheltenham Civil Defence Committee was discussing the more pressing matter of the construction of public air raid shelters. Plans were made to dig trenches in the centre of town capable of holding 10,000 people for those who were away from home at the time of an air raid. Two 3.7 inch anti-aircraft guns, each weighing ten tons, arrived from Bristol and thousands of gas masks were ready for distribution.

After the Festival, cricket continued throughout the country, albeit somewhat half-heartedly, with Gloucestershire finishing third in the championship. Farmers reported a good start to the harvest, but their green and pleasant land was now at war. Germany had invaded Poland and Europe was trembling. Winston Churchill spoke of fortitude and freedom as everyone became aware of an era slipping away. Six years were to pass before another Cheltenham Cricket Festival would take place.

CHAPTER THIRTEEN (1946-1949)

IN A FESTIVAL SPIRIT

—— 1946 ——

A year after an atomic bomb had been dropped on Hiroshima, preparations were in hand on the College ground for the Festival's resurrection.

It had been a wet summer and the torrential downpour of a fierce thunderstorm flooded the pitch, damaged tents and delayed the start of the game against India until after lunch on the second day. Sheets of wind-driven rain swept across the ground, quickly blowing down two marquees, flooding nearby roads causing vehicles to be marooned, and flattening the ripening corn in the surrounding countryside. Rushing across the hills, the angry gale uprooted the exhibits tent at the Andoversford and District Horticultural Society's annual show, overturning tables, scattering cakes and other produce on the ground and smashing eggs and vases containing flower exhibits. It was as if the chaos of war was still directing operations, especially as the tourists had left a divided country, where thousands were dying in inter-communal rioting during the countdown to independence.

After the storm, the Nawab of Pataudi inserted Gloucestershire on a wicket suited to ducks. Watching from the repaired press tent, John Arlott later recalled in his autobiography, *Basingstoke Boy*, 'Charlie Barnett gave a flourish, Andy Wilson jogged along and Hammond made 30* in a vignette of his craftsmanship, before he declared at 132 for 3 in an attempt to make a match of it.'

Pataudi rose to the challenge, promoted himself to opener and in making 71 was the only batsman to master Tom Goddard, who, despite a fractured little finger on his right hand, spun the ball viciously on a slow, drying wicket. India's captain made a sporting declaration when they were three runs ahead with eight wickets down, Goddard having taken 7 for 81. Barnett, Neale, Crapp, Allen and Emmett all made useful runs, but Mankad, with 5 for 72, and Sarwate, 4 for 43, called the tune, bowling the hosts out for 187.

Requiring 185 to win in just under three hours, the tourists lost their captain for a duck, before Cook (3 for 83) and Goddard (4 for 66) battled out the innings with Amarnath, who made a quick 48, and Hazare, a steadier 56. As the afternoon progressed, a crowd of over 5,500 were treated to an exciting finish, something that they would have thought hardly possible given the late start to the game.

In true Festival spirit, the contest had been kept alive by the enterprise of the two captains and although the result was a draw, either side could have won. Describing the climax in the *Chronicle*, 'Extra Cover' wrote: 'With two wickets in hand, India, whose batsmen had indulged in a hurricane of hitting in the last twenty minutes, wanted eight runs to win, with two or three minutes to go. Sarwate crouched ready for Cook's slow leg-spinner – walked down the wicket to meet it – missed – and Wilson, behind the stumps, made no mistake. The umpires ruled that there was no time for another over, and the game had ended with India requiring eight runs with one wicket in hand, for victory.'

In his first season of county cricket, Cecil 'Sam' Cook had taken his hundredth wicket. The promising, slow left-armer from Tetbury was the only newcomer in a side which, in contrast to much of the postwar world, had changed very little. There had been no player casualties resulting from the conflict, the only loss being Reg Sinfield who had retired to take up a post as coach at Clifton College. But one fundamental change was about to take place, for as the county's captain left the field, unbeknown to all, he had made his last appearance on the ground. Walter Hammond, one of the most complete cricketers of all times, was off to captain his country at the Oval and would then prepare to set sail for Australia.

Sent in by Surrey in the next match, the county ended eight runs down on first innings with Cook (23-6-63-6), who was quickly becoming a popular successor to Charlie Parker, proving to be the perfect foil for Goddard (22-8-45-4). Barnett (101) and Wilson (59) opened the second innings with a century stand, and supported by Basil Allen (47), set Surrey the target of 292 to win in just over four hours. A solid stand between Bob Gregory (87) and T. H. Barling (49) put the visitors in a strong position, but despite his fractured finger, Goddard would have none of this and his remarkable figures of 33.3-11-82-9 saw Gloucestershire home by 55 runs.

Top score in the next match was a meagre 38, made by Worcestershire's Dick Howorth. The hosts were twice bowled out cheaply by the magnificent Reg Perks, with his 'tireless sort-of agricultural-balletic action' as Frank Keating described it. Call it what you will, Perks' fast-medium pace left Gloucestershire reeling as he took 5 for 54 in the first innings along with 5 for 40 by Redmarley-born Peter Jackson. Then bowling unchanged, Perks returned figures of 21-6-42-9 and, but for a dropped catch, would have taken all ten wickets to follow in the footsteps of Arthur Mailey. Singleton (54*) and Yarnold quickly knocked off the runs required and Worcestershire cantered home by ten wickets.

—— 1947 ——

Large oaks from little acorns grow and James Lillywhite would have been overwhelmed by the fever pitch atmosphere in Cheltenham for the 1947 Festival. Some 60,000 people watched seven days of cricket and many of them are still around with a story to tell.

Under normal circumstances, the match against the South Africans would have been a feast of cricket, a Festival highlight; on this occasion it was merely the curtain raiser, a prologue to the main act that was to follow. Expecting lots of cars, the police allowed parking on the College side of Sandford Road, College Lawn and Thirlestaine Road. Bath Road was kept a forbidden parking area, although, for 2s., cars could be left at Sandford Mill Farm on the Old Bath Road.

In brilliant sunshine, the tourists batted first on a pitch that favoured bowlers. Dennis Dyer (74), making his highest score of the tour, steered his side to 225 and by the close of play, with Barnett and Crapp at the crease, the county seemed well set on 89 for 2. Throughout the day, an unfamiliar voice had wafted across the ground as Dana Niehaus gave his commentary in Africaans, alongside the gentle tones of Raymond Robertson-Glasgow's radio broadcast.

Gloucestershire collapsed quickly next morning to 185 all out. Perhaps it was because their energy had been used up the previous night at the first of four dances held in the Town Hall during the Festival; or maybe it was simply the spin and bite of Athol Rowan (18-3-40-4) on a dusty wicket. Together with Vivian Smith (12-2-33-3) he removed the county's last 6 wickets for just 37 runs, and the visitors greatly enjoyed themselves that afternoon building a substantial lead. Promoted to open the innings, Fullerton made 70 and Mann a whirlwind 63 in three quarters of an hour, but 28 of their 288 run lead had been struck off in the last quarter of an hour of play by Charlie Barnett and Grahame Parker, in what the *Chronicle* described as 'an atmosphere of village cricket'.

As the scorching weather continued, Gloucestershire started the last day needing 260 for victory with all their wickets in hand. Temperatures in the nineties had been recorded earlier in the week and the hot, dusty pitch produced familiar conditions for the tourists. Improvised newspaper hats, straw hats and umbrellas helped to give spectators a little shade and sales of ice cream and lemonade rocketed, but the hosts wilted under the heat as Rowan (29.5-12-47-7) bowled his team to victory by 133 runs.

After the tourists' departure for the fifth Test at the Oval, all eyes focused on Cheltenham when Gloucestershire took on Middlesex over whom they had a four point lead at the top of the table. Blessed with glorious weather, harvesting was in full swing; but for a couple of days, the gathering of corn slowed down as parties of supporters were bussed to the ground from all the surrounding areas to watch 'the game of the season'.

Middlesex had led the championship from the start of the season, after walloping Gloucestershire by an innings and 178 runs at Lord's, reigning supreme until early July when Basil Allen's men had overhauled them. For the next month they remained neck and neck and now the Cheltenham confrontation was billed as 'the championship decider'.

Saturday 16 August was one of those post-war days still relatively free of the many alternative attractions that would soon emerge as prosperity increased and motor cars allowed greater mobility. Fifty coach loads of Middlesex supporters made their way down from the capital; one was sighted in Charlton Kings shortly before eight o'clock in the morning with the driver asking the way to the College ground. Aware of the scale of the forthcoming invasion, Lieut-Colonel Henson, the county secretary, now responsible for all the Festival arrangements, had squeezed in as many seats and stands as possible. For this was the place to be and not even the Test match could compete. Creating a record for a county fixture on the ground, 14,500 spectators watched the day's play behind closed gates.

At half past six, five hours before the teams took to the field, residents of Fairfield Avenue, Mrs Lea and Mrs Voysey, arrived outside the ground and sat down on the low wall near the Thirlestaine Road entrance. Twenty minutes later, Mr Rolfe of Priors Farm arrived at the Sandford Road gate and so the queues began to grow. The *Echo* reported that 'the waiting crowd whiled away the time in various ways. Some had brought books and newspapers as well as lunch baskets; women had their knitting, boys their favourite magazines.' But the biggest treat of all for the patient crowd came from local Bach Choir member Jim Walkley, who was 'running through some of the great master's motets'.

By a quarter past nine, so many people were waiting for admission that it was decided to open the gates an hour earlier than advertised. Gloucestershire supporter John Mace joined the queue with his grandfather, as it slowly progressed towards the gate. He remembers 'the good humour, respect and exemplary behaviour' of those around him.

Just after eleven o'clock, the rival captains inspected the wicket. A sigh of disappointment could be heard from the home supporters as Walter Robins chose to bat first. Commenting after the game, the Middlesex skipper said, 'We were fortunate in winning the toss, which on a wicket made for spin meant winning the match and, as it turned out, the championship as well.'

In hot sunshine, the battle between ball and bat commenced. Nico Craven describes in *That Darn'd Elusive Championship*, how 'the first trick' went to Middlesex. Deprived of Compton and Robertson on Test duty, Brown and Edrich put on 50 for the first wicket, but by lunch the visitors had slumped to 125 for 7, Tom Goddard causing the damage. Roars of delight from the home supporters greeted each Middlesex dismissal, the largest cheer coming when Cook removed Bill Edrich for 50, which turned out to be the top score of the match. The Middlesex and England batsman was not playing for his country. An injury had left him fit to bat but unable to bowl and throw, so the selectors had left him out of the team. For Middlesex, it was simply marvellous to have their man on board - one half of the Compton and Edrich sun-baked summer fairy tale of 1947, when each scored over 3,500 runs.

On the brink of collapse, the visiting tail-enders started swinging their bats and much to the annoyance of Tom Goddard (20.3-4-70-7), Sims (32), Sharp (14*) and Young (27) dominated what was, arguably, the decisive phase of the match. By mid-afternoon, when the final wicket fell, they had steered their team to 180.

Allen and Barnett started brightly, putting on 37 for the first wicket, but then tension took over as wickets fell every few runs and supported by some very keen fielding, Sims (22-4-65-6) and Young (25.1-8-55-4), of whom Gloucestershire players had now seen more than enough, bowled out their hosts for 153. In the remaining ten minutes of play, Middlesex did little to increase their 27 run lead, yet received a sharp reminder that the competition was far from over when Goddard produced what Craven describes as 'a weekend special' to remove Edrich for five.

There were plenty of attractions for locals and those staying in town

to keep their minds away from the tense uncertainties of what might follow. A Tea Dance was held in the Town Hall, followed by a two shilling hop till midnight, while the Spa Orchestra, conducted by Arthur Cole, gave a concert on Sunday evening. Swimming at Sandford Park open air pool; tennis and putting at Montpellier Gardens; boating at Pittville Park and golf on Cleeve Hill and at Lilleybrook were well supported attractions due largely to the continuing fine weather. The town was experiencing a record-breaking heatwave, with an average of over eleven hours of sunshine a day.

Monday brought another huge crowd happy to endure temperatures in the eighties, and with equally high degrees of expectation. For the second time in the match, Middlesex batsmen wrestled with Gloucestershire's bowlers and pulled the initiative their way when Robins joined night watchman, Harry Sharp, and they added 70 together. Sharp (46) dealt skilfully with Goddard, hitting eight leg-side fours, while his captain made 45 before swinging at Goddard and hitting what promised to be a huge six - but was not. The Middlesex skipper fell, arguably, to Cheltenham's greatest catch, certainly the most talked about. It must have resembled the ball in *The Catch* written by local Hartpury-born poet F. W. (Will) Harvey: 'whizzing, fierce, it came . . . burning like a flame'.

Aged nine, Frank Keating witnessed the event and recalled this magnificent catch, which was made by Cliff Monks, in an article written for *Punch* almost forty years on:

'That morning, as Middlesex slogged to set some sort of target on a broken biscuit of a heatwave wicket, the metropolitan captain, R. W. V. Robins, had launched himself into a spectacular, steepling on-side hoik. The only fieldsman remotely near it was our first-team makeweight, the chunky, blond stonemason and Sunday organist from Coalpit Heath, Cliff Monks. He had to make about 50 yards at full pelt. As the whirring thing curled down, Monks took off like Banks going for the top, far corner. He held it, and by way of celebration came down in a series - I can still see it as plain as yesterday - of almost slow-motion somersaults. Memory also insists that, had he not caught it, the ball would have split my own youthful head open as I sat on the grass with the throng.'

Goddard (22-4-86-8) and Cook (18.5-8-35-2) then resumed command as the visitors' last 6 wickets fell for 16 runs, and Gloucestershire were left needing 169 to win on a worn pitch. Barnett, who had just received news that his record-breaking benefit fund totalled almost £3,000, immediately set about the Middlesex bowlers, hitting a six and 2 fours before falling lbw to Young for 17. After a scratchy start, Jack Crapp chiselled his way to 40, but the remaining batsmen made little impact on the game. In his nostalgic book *Vintage Summer: 1947*, John Arlott describes their doom: 'Goddard, swinging, edged Young's orthodox spinner to Edrich at slip. Sims, back in place of Sharp, had Scott - still attacking - stumped, and it was all over - innings, match and - as everyone felt, and the event proved - Championship.'

Middlesex were victorious by 68 runs and Young had impressive figures of 19-9-27-5. The two day game of 'ifs' and 'buts' was typical of Arlott's 1947 season which he described as 'a summer of joys which, it had sometimes seemed during the war years, could never return'.

Both captains were interviewed after the match, Basil Allen commenting, 'I am certain that the type of cricket shown in this match is what the public wants. Cricket is a much better game on a wicket where the bowler has a fair chance than on a pitch on which the bowler's only hope is for the batsman to make a mistake.'

Test selector, Walter Robins, spoke of wanting to develop and encourage spin bowlers, saying, 'This was just the type of wicket needed . . . It was in every way a wonderful game and much closer than the margin of 68 runs indicates.'

With time the great healer, having the following day off must have rejuvenated Gloucestershire's players who bounced back to just beat Glamorgan by 29 runs. On 11 for 4, the county looked washed up all over again, but a plucky 56 by Andy Wilson and 36 from George Lambert enabled their side to reach 172. Cook (23.5-9-56-6) caused Glamorgan's collapse, giving Gloucestershire a first innings lead of 16. Barnett (62) and Allen (46) put on 95 for the first wicket and the hosts started to take control of the match, but it was quickly dragged back by Muncer's off-breaks and his career best bowling figures (14.5-4-36-8). Capturing his one hundredth wicket of the season, Gloucestershire's last nine wickets fell for 43 runs in an hour.

The visitors found the 155 needed just too much, especially as Goddard had another field day, capturing his two hundredth wicket of the season in his spell of 12.3-0-61-8. By a quarter past four on the second day, the match was over. A total of 48,012 people had paid to see seven days of Festival cricket, gate money was just over £5,000 and the rental paid to the College amounted to £280.

—— **1948** ——

On the brink of bankruptcy, the country was still exhausted from the effects of war, and rationing was biting hard. There was a chronic shortage of petrol and even black market spivs found supplies scarce. Ironically, these grim circumstances gave a welcome boost to Cheltenham's tourist industry. Seaside holiday resorts were suffering from empty rooms and cancelled bookings, while the town's hotels and boarding houses were doing brisk business. With the petrol shortage, Cheltenham was more accessible than distant coastal resorts for large numbers of people from the Midlands and Wales. In addition, the town's reputation was growing as an important centre for a wide variety of sporting and cultural activities.

The Cricket Festival was one such attraction, steeped in history and still holding vivid memories of the previous year's excitements. Many lovers of the game had arranged their summer holiday in order to be able to watch all three matches, so it was unfortunate that rain should spoil the first two. The county's disappointing performances on the field also meant reduced takings.

Twenty-one-year-old Tom Graveney was making his first appearance at the Festival. He remembers losing to bottom-of-the-table Northamptonshire and being 'done by a beamer, from Clarkie' (Bob Clarke) in the second innings, when he was 'propping' for Charlie Barnett. In the visitors' first innings, Oldfield and Nutter batted stubbornly, helped by some poor fielding. Geoffrey Need, a long-standing Gloucestershire supporter, reminisces, 'Three times in three overs the ball lobbed gently from Nutter's bat into Colin Scott's hands - and out again; for such a brilliant fielder, I found this laughable - though few of the crowd did!' At last, Goddard trapped Oldfield lbw and Need recalls, 'I never heard such a mighty shout, even from Goddard!' endorsing Frank Keating's description of the huge-handed spinner: 'His appeal appealed. HOWAZEE! would reverberate round the fringe of hills above us from Cleeve to Birdlip. Even the Malverns shuddered.'

Despite half centuries from left-handers Crapp and Wilson, Gloucestershire ended up 9 runs behind on first innings. Dennis Brookes (75), supported largely by Oldfield (42*), with minor contributions from Webster, Barron and Davis, took the visitors to 208 for 4 when a declaration was made, leaving the hosts 218 to win in just two and a half hours.

From the start, Barnett chased the target. Hitting powerfully and cleanly, one of county cricket's most punishing opening batsmen entertained the crowd with a run-a-minute century, but apart from Crapp and Graveney's contribution, he was given little support. Brookes recounts the final stages of the match: 'Charlie Barnett played a splendid innings and from our point of view got out just at the right time. He was on 107 when he cut a ball to the left hand of Vince Broderick fielding in the gully. Reaching back, Broderick collected the ball and with one movement threw the wicket down. Barnett thought it was going for runs and had set off and was consequently run out.'

Last men Goddard and Cook were together at the start of the final over. It seemed as if a draw was inevitable as Sam Cook blocked the first two balls. Then, remembers Brookes, 'he had a rush of blood and slogged the next ball to deep mid-off and Northants won an improbable victory'.

Playing against Nottinghamshire in the next match, Gloucestershire gained their most impressive win of the whole summer. Rain spoilt proceedings on the first day, but the hosts, helped by some faulty fielding, began to build a good total. Emmett (88) and Graveney (64*) assisted Crapp (124), who heard of his selection for the final Test and the forthcoming MCC tour to South Africa while making his century, and Gloucestershire moved to 354 for 5 declared. Apart from Keeton and Winrow, their openers in both innings, Nottinghamshire collapsed twice and were bowled out for 168 and 88. Making the ball fizz awkwardly in the second innings, Goddard (11.4-5-16-6) passed one hundred wickets for the season and certainly had no reason to listen to the advice of cheeky spectators who, according to Frank Keating, enjoyed suggesting field placings to him, by calling out, 'Eh, Ta-am whadabout a bloke atop o' Leckhampton, or on the roof o' that College chapel!'

Jack Crapp left for the Oval Test and proceeded to make a duck on the same day that Don Bradman, making his last appearance for his country, was so unceremoniously dismissed for nought, second ball, by Eric Hollies. Meanwhile at Cheltenham, Surrey started to gain the upper hand. A splendid innings of 127* by Jack Parker helped his team to reach 260, as Goddard took 5 for 84 from forty-one overs. A flurry of flowing drives from Barnett (54) ended when he was caught and bowled by Jim Laker, with Gloucestershire only mustering 145. A bruised finger prevented Goddard from bowling in the second innings, but Monty Cranfield stepped in with 5 for 60 and the hosts were left needing 291 to win. With the target seeming unobtainable for Gloucestershire, the county was helped by rain, reducing play on the last day, and at the close they had limped to 124 for 9.

As the rain fell, people gathered in the toy department of Cavendish House to meet 'Coco', the famous clown from Bertram Mills Circus, who was signing copies of his autobiography *Coco the Clown* during a break between performances at Sandford Park. Next day, as Festival matters were being tidied away for another year, a large crowd gathered at the College to watch international stars Fred Perry, Dan Maskell and Yvon Petra, along with other professional lawn tennis players, compete in a series of tennis matches.

—— 1949 ——

Opening opponents this year were Essex, and Tom Graveney clearly remembers the mayor's lunch and his rather eccentric speech at the end of the morning's play:

'We all put on our blazers and walked across to a marquee on the hospital side of the ground. The mayor stood up and welcomed "the men from Exeter", and went on to say it was a pity that neither side was very good, but at least in Gloucestershire we do have very high hopes of two young men, "the brothers Gravity" . . . From that time on D. J. Insole has never ever called me anything else but Gravity!'

When the mayor finished, it was well past the start of play time, but the crowd were not too bothered as they were still licking their lips over the bright, pre-lunch, record opening-partnership of 169 between George Emmett (95) and Basil Allen (99). Jack Crapp made a dogged 85 and the Smith cousins helped themselves to 4 wickets each before Goddard (4 for 51) and Cook (5 for 26) bowled the visitors out for 148 on what Graveney describes as 'a spin bowler's paradise'. He then took charge, making an attractive 78, and *Wisden* reported that 'his elegant stroke-play' marked him out as 'one of the best young batsmen in the country'. Needing 452 to win, Essex seemed to be grinding out a draw on 181 for 5, when it was time for elder brother, Ken, to stamp his mark on the game. In thirteen balls, he took 4 for 6 with his fast-medium in-swingers, and finished with figures of 16.1-3-45-6 as his side swept to victory by 253 runs.

Dickie Dodds made little impression on the scorecard, but a personal misfortune meant he never forgot the game. 'Cheltenham will always be remembered by me as the place where I lost the wristwatch I had carried all the way through the war - including much time in Burma. What a

193

watch. What adventures we went through together.'

Winning the toss in the next match, Surrey took advantage of batting first and forged their way to 374. Everyone made runs, but it was Jack Parker (102), driving powerfully, who led the assault, making his second consecutive century on the ground. Overnight rain flawed Gloucestershire's chances. On a drying pitch, six of their wickets fell for 76 before Wilson and Lambert added 58 together, but Laker (18-7-30-5) finished off the innings and the county followed on 206 runs behind. They made a dreadful start, Alec Bedser dismissing Allen and Graveney in his second over. Crapp, Emmett and Wilson batted stubbornly, but at the close of play Gloucestershire were still 62 behind with 5 wickets remaining. Matters were quickly concluded next day, as Surrey gained an innings and 10 runs victory.

Final visitors Glamorgan, champions the previous year, were not repeating their achievements and the game ended as a mid-table 'bore' draw. On the first day, accurate bowling and excellent fielding by the visitors meant that Gloucestershire could only proceed slowly to their total of 340. A fifth wicket partnership of 151 between careful Crapp (132) and hard-working Wilson (73) provided the backbone of the innings.

The visitors replied with conviction. Davies and Clift featured in a 93 run first wicket partnership, but the innings fell away as Sam Cook (30-11-64-7) and Tom Goddard (34-19-31-2), bowling unchanged for almost three hours, dismissed their opponents for 170. The follow-on was not enforced and Gloucestershire pottered to 180 for 8 before Allen declared, leaving Glamorgan four hours to score 351 to win.

On the final day, with half an hour of play lost to rain after lunch, the visitors made no effort to chase the target and Shentons had little to do on their pedal printing machine at the Chapel end of the ground from where they sold up-to-date scorecards. As the game slowly petered out, the crowd began to barrack Wilf Wooller who showed his objection by staging a 'go slow', and the county *Yearbook* sadly records, 'The match ended on a note of futility.'

CHAPTER FOURTEEN (1950-1954)

'BORE' DRAWS

—— 1950 ——

By now Cheltenham had become widely recognised for its varied and popular festivals. In addition to cricket and National Hunt Racing, the arts world was represented by the Festival of British Contemporary Music and the Festival of Literature, the inaugural event of which had taken place the previous autumn as a result of the enthusiasm of John Moore, cousin of cricketer Denis.

On the county cricket circuit, attendances were starting to fall and there seemed to be an alarming lack of direction and sense of urgency about the game. The great appeal of cricket appeared to be waning. Slow play was catching on as teams placed an ever increasing amount of emphasis on not losing, resulting in more and more drawn matches. Cheltenham reflected this national trend and from 1950 to 1954, of the fifteen matches played, nine were draws. The mood on the cricket field could even have been compared to the impasse in world politics at that time with the Cold War stand-off between the USA and Russia. Moreover, life in Britain was changing, with greater opportunity to enjoy a variety of leisure activities, leaving less time to watch cricket. At the same time a growing interest in football was starting to kick in.

Rain interfered so much with the opening match that Gloucestershire and Middlesex were able to complete only one innings each. In his final year of captaincy, Basil Allen (131) led his team to a total of 440. He was helped by the ever-improving Martin Young (98), who just missed out on making his fourth century of the season, and the free-hitting Andy Wilson (70), who recalled many happy days at the Festival. The county's keeper explained how, with ingenuity, he overcame a particular problem:

'Before the College authorities modernised the pavilion, we changed in dressing rooms on benches and the coat hooks were far too high for me to reach. By the time August arrived, I was too tired to climb up on the bench to hang up my clothes . . . I found a solution. I brought six four-inch nails with me at the start of the Festival, borrowed a hammer from the groundsman and nailed them in at a convenient height. But I was careful not to do any damage when I took them out at the end!'

In reply to Gloucestershire's innings, Middlesex made 296, due to a brilliant 130 by Brown, but the hosts took first innings points thanks to George Lambert (27-3-116-5) and Ken Graveney (16-4-57-4). At the age of forty-eight, veteran G. O. Allen made a rare appearance for the visitors and led his team in the absence of Walter Robins. He was also one of the panel at the Festival Brains Trust held in the Town Hall, along with Tom Goddard and Basil Allen, his Gloucestershire namesake. On this occasion, one of the most experienced players in the game, Gubby Allen, insisted that the standard of English cricket could be raised by playing less: 'If cricket were played three days a week the standard would unquestionably be raised and a lot more people would take up the first-class game. Players would be able to have another occupation.' But Goddard disagreed, commenting, 'I never see any harm in cricket six days a week. You cannot have too much of it.'

The three panelists were quizzed on first innings points allocation, fast and spin bowling, the West Indies touring team and time-limitless Test matches. The lively debate was seasoned with music by the Spa Quartette and songs by the Audrey Sheather Girl Harmonists of Churchdown.

Worcestershire crawled to 162 for 6 on the first day of the second match before rain interrupted play at tea. George Chesterton, former Worcestershire player and county president, recalls that an old bull-nosed Morris, the property of Cambridge blue Tom Wells, was conspicuous by its absence in the car park that day. The New Zealand-born amateur had been asked to make his county debut at the expense of one of the professionals, a decision that was justifiably unpopular amongst the regular players. Perhaps Wells did not want to cause trouble, or maybe the old car failed to make it through the floods; either way he lost his place at the eleventh hour and after this was only picked once more for his county.

Heavy rain fell during the night and the game did not resume until half past five that afternoon. In forty-five minutes of play, Don Kenyon's patient innings of 81 came to an end and at the close the visitors had reached 181 for 8.

A flurry of activity saw three declarations made on the last day and suddenly a result seemed possible. Gloucestershire were set 207 to win in one hundred and forty minutes on a spiteful wicket. With the ball lifting head high and wickets tumbling, the visitors seemed to be edging towards victory, but a gallant 54 in just over an hour by Sir Derrick Bailey saved his side from defeat. This was a true hero's stance in the face of humiliation by the neighbours, for which the big-hearted Bailey was rewarded with the county captaincy the following season.

The game proved to be Goddard's farewell appearance at the Festival, for the following July he was forced to retire following a debilitating bout of pneumonia and pleurisy. The magnificent off-spinner 'played his cricket with an uncomplicated passion', according to David Foot who describes him as 'an illusionist at Cheltenham, where batsmen were apt to spar at what seemed like a mythical ball'. It was sad that the lion with the dogmatic roar of a shout should leave the Festival for the last time more like a lamb, with the unusual figures of 28-12-54-1.

'In the summer of 1950 West Indies cricket firmly established itself,' records *Wisden*. The team had obviously made their impression on eleven-year-old Ian Harrison who, according to the *Echo*, arrived outside the College ground at a quarter to seven, starting a queue hours before the county took on the talented tourists. Rain was falling and continued to do so as the crowd on the pavement began to grow, reliably kept informed of the state of the ground and the likelihood of play by Colonel Henson as he toured the roads in a police patrol car. At noon, Basil Allen issued a statement saying that no play would be possible before lunch, but half an hour later the gates were opened and a crowd of 5,000 people streamed into the ground. Once settled, they were encouraged by the appearance for a pitch inspection of Allen, Stollmeyer (standing in as the tourist's captain in place of John Goddard) and Jim Hammond, the College coach and groundsman. To the crowd's delight, it was soon announced that play would start at a quarter to three, by which time numbers had swollen to around 7,000 and Stollmeyer, on winning the toss, predictably inserted his hosts.

After forty-five minutes of play, with the county on 39 for 2, Sonny Ramadhin was introduced into the attack. Spectator Joe Miles remembers 'the small man, with sleeves buttoned down and wearing his cap'. 'The batsmen were at once in doubt, difficulty and despair,' reported the *Echo*. Thirty-five minutes later, Gloucestershire were all out for 69 and Ramadhin's figures read 6.4-2-15-8. According to *Wisden*, 'In one spell of eleven balls he took four wickets without conceding a run, and wound up with four wickets in ten balls for four runs . . . He did not bowl a loose ball, and by cleverly disguised finger spin he turned his deliveries sharply either way.'

Tom Graveney wryly recalls the start of the West Indies innings: 'We were a bit unlucky. Clive Walcott came in after we had taken a couple of wickets early on and he went to hook George Lambert, got an edge and Andy caught him behind the stumps. He was on about three or four and the umpire gave him not out.' Putting this behind him, Walcott continued to hook powerfully and supported by the artistic, attacking Everton Weekes, the tourists began to take charge.

Bubbling with enthusiasm from their recent Test match victory at the Oval and securing the upper hand in this game, the West Indies cricket team went dancing the hula hula at the Opera House that night. Furthermore, according to the *Echo*, Stollmeyer had accepted an invitation from Felix Mendelssohn to attend the second performance of his show, and the players had been invited to join 'the South Sea Lovelies in their traditional native dances' which would come as a climax to the evening.

On Sunday morning, while the players rested, a Sportsman's Service was held at Bethesda Methodist Church. The mayor and mayoress, Alderman and Mrs P. T. Smith, Cheltenham's M.P., Major W. W. Hicks Beach, other civic dignitaries and many well-known local sporting personalities were among those present who listened to the preacher, Revd Reginald Palmer Barnes, a minister from Barbados and secretary of the West Indies touring team. In his address, he likened cricket's qualities to those of Christianity, in both cases having to play 'with a straight bat', and went on to speak about his missionary work in Barbados. The Revd Maurice Jelbert, minister at Bethesda, paid tribute to the West Indies team and congratulated them on their fine performances throughout the tour, commenting, 'We all know of the prowess of such great bowlers as Ramadhin and Valentine.' Next day their skills would sweep the tourists to an overwhelming victory.

Prior to this, a Monday crowd of over 12,000 watched Walcott 'pound and thump' his way to 126 and Weekes complete an attractive 57. Derrick Bailey remembers his part in Weekes' dismissal, recalling, 'Martin Young winded himself, fielding at cover. The two St John ambulance men had difficulty dragging him off the field and I took his place.' Jack Crapp fielded as substitute and Sir Derrick concludes, 'Weekes made such a correct stroke, cutting smartly to the off, and I was able to be in position to catch him!'

To the spectators glee, they then witnessed Tom Goddard's replacement, seventeen-year-old John Mortimore, who was making his first-class debut for the county, help to bring about a batting collapse with a sensational session of bowling. The *Echo* reported, 'In a spell of four overs after lunch, he dismissed Walcott, Christiani and Williams for only 11 runs.' With Cook's figures, 24.4-8-60-5, the visitors were dismissed for 271.

If it had not been for a fourth wicket stand of 50 between Tom Graveney and Martin Young, Gloucestershire's second innings total would have been most embarrassing. The county's batsmen did not middle very much as Ramadhin continued where he had left off on Saturday afternoon. 'Tom played him well,' recalls Arthur Milton. 'It was a sunny day and he could actually see the ball spinning in the air, coming down to him and could tell which way it was going to turn.'

Not wanting to miss out on the fun, Alf Valentine (17.2-6-31-4) helped Sonny Ramadhin (19-6-36-5) bowl their side to victory by an innings and 105 runs and Gloucestershire's chirpy wicket-keeper had collected a pair. Both times, Andy Wilson was clean bowled by Ramadhin; Milton and Graveney both chuckle with laughter as they remember the moment.

'Andy watched Ramadhin from behind his arm early in the second innings and was convinced he could now pick him,' recalls Milton. Later, as he walked to the wicket to join Tom Graveney, he quietly, yet confidently, told him, 'I've got him worked out now.'

Graveney watching from the non-striker's end remembers, 'The ball pitched six inches outside Andy's off stump, he padded up and it knocked his middle out!' There is consolation for Wilson because after a pause Graveney confessed, 'At this early stage in his career, nobody could pick him.'

The loss of a day's play against the tourists accounted for a drop in attendance figures of 5,000 for the 1950 Festival, while a combination of uncertain weather, lack of popular appeal of matches and slow play were responsible for a more worrying drop of 10,000 the next year.

—— **1951** ——

Showers restricted the opening day against Kent to two and a half hours of play, so there was much catching up to be done when the game resumed on Monday. At lunch, Gloucestershire were 200 for 3 with fifties from Graveney and Allen, but by mid-afternoon they had slumped to 279 all out, due largely to an impressive spell of bowling from Doug Wright who took 5 for 23 in nine overs, ending with figures of 26.5-4-82-6.

Arthur Fagg proceeded to make a patient century for the visitors, putting into practice everything he had taught the boys when he had coached cricket at the College five years earlier. Then, just as Kent seemed to be heading towards Gloucestershire's total, Colin Scott (24-7-42-6) was given the second new ball and took 5 for 24, as the last 7 wickets fell for 55 runs. With time slipping away, the game finally fizzled out to a draw, after a declaration by Bailey left the visitors 165 to win in just over an hour and they turned down the challenge.

For the next match, Wilf Wooller led Glamorgan up to Cheltenham from the Festival atmosphere of Weston-super-Mare and the result was another unexciting stalemate. On what Arthur Milton would describe as 'definitely a wicket to bat first on', Gloucestershire were bowled out for 195 by spinners McConnon and Muncer and the left-arm, medium-pace of Watkins, with five dismissals from wicket-keeper Haydn Davies.

A moment of drama arose in the middle of the afternoon's play when eighty-year-old Robert Leach, former principal of Gloucester Technical College, collapsed in the members enclosure and was attended to by two St John ambulance men. Meanwhile, a gateman cycled the short distance to the hospital, summoned an ambulance, which arrived and took him across the road, but Mr Leach, a regular attender at the Festival for a number of years, died twenty minutes after being admitted to hospital. While this sombre turn of events was unfolding off the field, Gloucestershire's spinners, Sam Cook (56-26-69-3) and Bomber Wells (55-26-98-3), were toiling away, but as the game moved on the visitors gained a first innings lead of 94 thanks to Clift (53) and Jones (65).

In a stand of 101, Milton (61) and Graveney (54) knocked off the deficit, and at six o'clock on Thursday evening, with a fierce hit to leg for 4 off Muncer, Tom Graveney completed his 2,000 runs in a season for the first time. Plodding on to 243 for 9, Gloucestershire then declared, leaving the visitors twenty-six overs to make 150. They declined the challenge and finished on 63 for 2.

Former Gloucestershire CCC president Norman Walters has attended over fifty Festivals at Cheltenham, but admits he has probably seen 'less cricket than anyone else'. His association with the Festival started in the early 1950s when on Saturdays he became a *Bristol Evening Post* reporter.

There was plenty for him to do on the first day of the final match of the 1951 Festival, with Kenyon (120) and Wyatt (61) featuring in a third wicket stand of 152 and Worcestershire reaching a total of 318. However the *Evening Post* reporter was not working alone and recalls, 'There were no telephones on the ground, so Janet (Mrs Walters) was my copy runner, taking my scribbled notes to Mr W. A. Woof's shop, where they allowed her to make a reverse charge call to the newspaper office. She made six journeys throughout the day, stopping at tea time.' This was the start of their long and dedicated stint of work for the county, with Bristol as their base and the Cheltenham Festival an ever-increasing, yet enjoyable, challenge to their entrepreneurial skills.

The Walters missed Monday's 'firework display' by George Emmett. Arthur Milton recalls, 'Once he got going, he was unstoppable. You couldn't set a field to him.' This was certainly the case as he hit 100 out of 150 in one hundred and thirty minutes before lunch. According to the *Echo*, 'The cloud of fear-ridden batsmanship and solemn defence which has hung over the Cheltenham Cricket Festival was today swept aside by George Emmett . . . his glorious innings was full of the gay shots of a natural stroke player.'

Enjoying the scene was the cast of the new radio serial, *The Archers*, which was in its first year of being broadcast. Bomber Wells can picture them all roaring with laughter after a little episode on the square. He recalls, 'George never bothered to play a ball on the off-side, he just swept, mainly against the spin. In one over he hit Roly Jenkins for three successive fours, and before bowling again Roly walked down the pitch towards Emmett, looked all round the ground, then with his hands on his hips roared out in a deep, loud voice, "Stemmett, if you don't like me, tell me to my face, but don't keep taking it out on the bloody ball".' Apparently the crowd erupted and the cast of *The Archers* was, recalls Bomber, 'in tucks!'

Basil Allen made 75 and Derrick Bailey scored a captain's innings of 77* in a partnership of 138 with Emmett, and he was able to declare 99 runs ahead on 417 for 8. Before play ended that night, Worcestershire lost their first innings centurian for nought, giving rise to an uneasy night's rest for the remainder of the team, knowing they faced an uphill task on a deteriorating wicket. The following morning, John Mortimore (12.2-3-35-5) spun out the opposition for 74 to give his side victory by an innings and 25 runs.

—— **1952** ——

The *Chronicle*, in a pre-event editorial, was most eloquent and upbeat about this year's Festival:

'Of all Cheltenham's festivals, none has more popular appeal than that

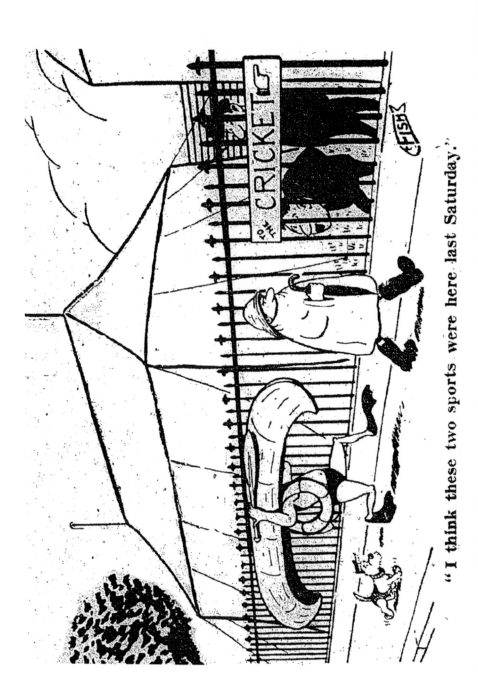

"I think these two sports were here last Saturday."

devoted to cricket, which opens on the College Ground today (Saturday) with the visit of the Indian tourists, their last game before the Test match at the Oval. Cricket will be almost the sole topic of conversation next week in hotel lounge and public house bar, at factory bench and behind office desk. There will be a thirsting after news of the latest position at the College Ground. At such times as this, when the very trees and the bricks and mortar that shut in the streets of the town seem to breathe cricket, it behoves all to brush up their knowledge of the sport. Those who can discourse with a seemingly authoritative air on the finer points of the game find a new popularity.'

Going on to describe the 'greats' who had played on the ground in former years, the passage ended by making reference to the 'young players of today', with the reassuring words, 'The glorious traditions of the past are being worthily maintained in the firm grip of their wrists.'

Geoffrey Need remembers 1952 as 'a somewhat rain-spoiled Festival'. Colonel Henson went a few stages further: 'It is the worst Cheltenham Festival I have experienced.'

No matter how much preparation and hard work had been carried out beforehand by the local committee members and willing volunteers, the rain could not be kept at bay. Two and a half inches fell in Cheltenham during the first eight days of August and there was only one day in the whole month when it did not rain. It was hardly surprising that the overall attendance, excluding members, plummeted to just over 21,000 and both matches were drawn.

Arrangements had been made for several events linked to George Emmett's benefit fund to take place while the county's cricketers were based in Cheltenham. Johnny Moss and his orchestra would provide the music at a Town Hall dance to which the Gloucestershire and Indian players were invited and there were benefit matches, featuring the full county XI, sheduled against Cheltenham Police at the Victoria Ground, and against Mr L. T. Vowles's XI on the Woodpeckers' picturesque ground in Ashleworth.

Unfortunately a soggy ground and shortened first day welcomed the Indian tourists, but an attractive innings of 63 by Emmett, helped by 48 from Young, meant Gloucestershire reached 106 before the first wicket fell on Monday. Graveney (56*) batted carefully but received little support, and the county were all out for 198. Apart from Adhikari (80), India were all at sea to the bowling of Wells (32-9-67-4) and Lambert (14-6-17-3) on a slowly drying wicket. Then a sporting declaration by Bailey, who had already announced that he would be unable to continue as captain the following season, set the tourists 108 to win in one hundred minutes. Adhikari propped up the innings again, while some hefty whacking by Umrigar (35) saw them home by 6 wickets, with nine minutes to spare.

On a pitch that was always going to wear badly, rain on the last day of the second match may well have saved Leicestershire from defeat. Enjoying another fine season, Jack Crapp made 110, his highest innings of the summer, in his usual entertaining way. Together with Arthur Milton (61) who was continuing to improve and, according to *Wisden*, 'adding concentration to his already excellent technique', the two of them scored 123 at just over a run-a-minute for the third wicket. In contrast to Crapp, Milton took time to accumulate his runs, doggedly staying at the crease for almost three hours. But his patience proved to be important, for once he had been dismissed, the last six wickets fell for 46 runs to Walsh and Jackson.

Leicestershire's openers Lester (32) and Smithson (57) put on 92 together, then a remarkable collapse took place. Making his first appearance of the season, John Mortimore, on army leave, dismissed Lester in his first over and carried on to finish with the impressive figures of 28-7-58-7.

Enjoying a first innings lead of 70, Gloucestershire immediately got themselves into trouble against some fine spin bowling by Walsh (9.3-2-17-3) and Jackson (13-6-25-5), eventually losing their last seven wickets for 42, leaving the visitors 167 to win. After a delayed start of almost two hours on the final day, a fiery spell of bowling from George Lambert (23-4-41-5) ripped the heart out of Leicestershire's batting and they still had a long way to go, needing 83 more runs with only four wickets remaining, when bad weather washed out the rest of play.

The rain clouds that put paid to this match were to be the cause of the unforgettable disaster in North Devon the next day. Excessive rainfall turned Exmoor's streams and rivers into a raging torrent resulting in the deaths of thirty-six people and devastation to the town of Lynmouth. It was in the shadow of this tragedy that George Emmett's benefit match against Warwickshire got under way.

On an unpredictable wicket, with the ball lifting sharply, 20 wickets fell for 199 runs in the day's play. The visitors were quickly back in the pavilion as Lambert (19-4-37-5) and Scott (18.3-4-39-4) made use of the conditions, but the Gloucestershire batsmen fared no better and were dismissed for 91 by Bannister (13.3-4-36-5) and Hollies (19-11-18-5). No play was possible on Monday, but events moved quickly on the final day as Gardner (54) and Ord (46*) took Warwickshire to 164 for 6 when Dollery declared, leaving the hosts needing 178 to win in one hundred and fifty minutes. A flurry of runs came from the beneficiary, but as wickets fell, it was Milton (63), records the *Yearbook*, who 'showed his usual nerve in a crisis' and stuck in there for over two hours as Gloucestershire edged nervously to 132 for 6, so ensuring a draw.

—— **1953** ——

By now Norman Walters was the club's unofficial public relations and press officer, giving thought, along with others, to the formation of a Supporters' Club. Despite the rather wobbly financial position of the club, this idea was deemed unnecessary by the committee, a decision that would be reversed the following year. There was always plenty for Norman to do at Cheltenham as an ambassador for the club away from headquarters, gathering information and talking to members. He continued with his newspaper work, but this was about to come to an end and his role at the Festival would change significantly.

With the Coronation celebrations still echoing in people's ears, commemorative mugs sitting on mantelpieces and Cheltenham residents, like millions of Britons, sampling the newly-created 'simple, yet delicious' Coronation Chicken, the opening match against Sussex produced a tense and contentious climax.

The visitors, who were to finish the season as championship runners-up, were flying high under the inspirational leadership of David Sheppard, soon to be starting his career in the Church. Winning the toss, Gloucestershire made hay against some mediocre bowling, reaching 385 for 7 before Jack Crapp, the county's first ever professional captain, declared. George Emmett got the county off to a brisk start and went on to make 116, while Graveney (65), Lambert (68*) and the captain himself (64) all batted well. Sussex began encouragingly, but suddenly slumped to 209 all out as their last 5 wickets fell for 59 runs. Asked to bat again, they soon lost Langridge, and Gloucestershire looked to be in a strong position at the end of play.

Gloucestershire Exile John Light, describing himself as 'a keen but impecunious thirteen-year-old', hitch-hiked to the ground from Rendcomb. He remembers the 'dramatic' final day's play when 'a Suttle-inspired Sussex recovered, the wicket held up better than was expected and eventually Gloucestershire, having bowled Sussex out, had to chase a

205

target of 169 to win'. Suttle (108) and Cox (95) featured in a fourth wicket stand of 180, while Doggart's 50* and Sheppard's 44 helped to give the visitors what seemed to be a defendable, or possibly even victorious, total. Light continued, 'Some vigorous batting saw Gloucestershire ahead of the clock and although wickets had fallen, victory seemed assured.' Then something happened that he had never seen before or since.

Aware that the game was slipping away, the Sussex captain suddenly introduced some very unsporting tactics. John Light recalled, 'Sussex were blessed with a battery of accurate, medium-pace bowlers, led by Ian Thomson who was called into the attack at the College end joining Jim Wood from the College Lawn end. With the majority of fielders placed on the leg-side, each ball pitched about two feet outside leg stump. As a result the game became ridiculous. John Mortimore took guard eighteen inches outside the leg stump, to illustrate exactly what was going on, and the crowd became restive.'

Having been happily relaxing on an August afternoon, the spectators' mood suddenly changed, recollected Light: 'First there were boos and then jeers. Then came the cushions, thrown onto the outfield by irate spectators, from the College end right round to the gymnasium.'

Gloucestershire had already claimed the extra half hour in search of victory and Tom Graveney takes up the story, recalling how Jack Crapp, 'a wonderful man, the salt of the earth', responded to the situation. 'Jack was absolutely marvellous. He never said a word, watched it for three overs, suddenly got up, went through the gate and walked out to the middle. "Could I have a word with you?" he said, as he approached David Sheppard, continuing, "If you don't want to play cricket, I'll take my men off." This shattered David. He went white and suddenly everything went back to normal and they nearly beat us!'

Indeed, this was so, for once the cushions had been cleared, John Light remembers, 'The game continued with a properly set field and proper bowling. Common sense seemed to have prevailed. Thomson took three wickets in four balls and the match ended with Andy Wilson safely playing out the last over with the young David Allen at the other end.'

Gloucestershire finished on 154 for 9 and when recently asked of his memories of playing at the Festival, David Sheppard admitted, 'Playing at Cheltenham brings back one uncomfortable memory . . . I decided to use the tactics that had saved England in the Headingley Test the previous month. Trevor Bailey had bowled down the leg-side, making it almost impossible for the Australian batsmen to play their normal strokes. Like all cricketers, we discussed the rights and wrongs of this and I instructed our bowlers to bowl down the leg-side, with most of the fielders placed there.'

Wisden described the game as having 'a thrilling finish' but Sussex's captain conceded, 'I was ashamed at the tactics I had employed. We played Gloucestershire again ten days later and I went into their dressing-room before the match and apologised to Jack Crapp.'

The *Echo* reported, 'Much will be said and thought about Sussex's ten minutes of defensive leg-side tactics - they may have cost them the game - but it should also be remembered that they had earlier fought themselves out of an apparently hopeless position by scoring 315 runs at the rate of eighty-two an hour. It was magnificent cricket.'

The game had a devastating effect on Andy Wilson. After blocking out those final few balls, he returned to the pavilion where, according to Arthur Milton, 'We all got onto him for being so cautious, but he replied in that characteristic whisper, that he was not going to give them the match after what they had done.' Still boiling with rage from his dressing room ragging, the next day Gloucestershire's keeper vented his anger on Worcestershire's bowlers.

Milton recalls, 'We had lost a few wickets and when Andy came in, I had made 43. He'd still got the needle about him and I'll never forget how after forty-five minutes he had scored 76, all his runs coming in fours - nineteen of them!' Milton (nicknamed 'Steve' by Wilson because of his bandy legs which he joked were similar to those of the jockey Steve Donaghue) made 73 and recalls that Wilson 'hit everybody, including Reg Perks, all round the ground, and in our partnership of 101 in just under an hour he had made 82 of them!'

Bowling his usual immaculate line and length, George Chesterton picked up 5 wickets as the hosts reached 321 for 9 before declaring. Worcestershire then faltered on a damp wicket as Cook (24-13-34-5) and Mortimore (14.5-6-31-3) made full use of the conditions to bowl them out for 140. Following on, the two spinners continued to cause problems and at tea time on the final day it looked as if the visitors, on 174 for 7, were fighting a lost cause. Devereux and Perks had other ideas and added 78 in fifty minutes, before their side were eventually all out for 259, Mortimore finishing with figures of 29-11-63-5 and Cook 26.1-11-29-4. Needing 79 to win in half an hour, the hosts tried hard, but the accurate bowling of Perks and Chesterton kept the runs down, claimed wickets and Gloucestershire ended up on 44 for 5.

In the final match of the Festival, Gloucestershire twice batted ineptly against Lancashire, who charged to victory in two days by an innings and 19 runs.

The home side were missing Tom Graveney, one of *Wisden's* Cricketers of the Year, who was on Test duty. Meanwhile for the visitors, Geoff Edrich, who nine years later would start working at the College and, amongst other duties, prepare Festival wickets, was prevented from playing through injury. The previous day at Old Trafford, during his dogged three hour innings of 81* against Northamptonshire, he had suffered an unremitting onslaught from Frank Tyson, including several blows to the hand. Edrich recalls, 'I drove down from Manchester that night in my Austin Eight and stayed at the Queen's Hotel with the rest of the team. Next morning I could not grip my bat, so went across the road to the hospital where an X-ray revealed a broken bone in my hand. It was plastered and I drove back home, so missing the opportunity to play on this lovely ground.'

There was no need for the visitors' captain Nigel Howard to worry about losing a player or the toss, as a fast and fiery Brian Statham unsettled Gloucestershire's batsmen after Emmett and Young had added 72 for the first wicket. Tattersall (25.3-8-48-5) took the largest haul of wickets as the hosts last nine wickets fell for 82 and although Lancashire found making runs difficult, they ended up enjoying a first innings lead of 68. On a damp, awkward pitch, Gloucestershire quickly threw in the towel, being bowled out for 49 in just over an hour and a quarter, with the left-arm spinner Bob Berry returning impressive figures of 7-5-17-5.

It had been an unobtrusive last game on the ground for Andy Wilson, the quiet, effective wicket-keeper and batsman, who was similar in many ways to his predecessors, Harry Smith and Jack Board. Being run out without scoring seems rather a sad finale for the man who eventually settled at Keeper's Cottage, in the village of Redmarley, and was eulogized by John Arlott in *The Guardian*: 'I do not believe you will find one cricketer who does not like Andy Wilson with a fraternal fondness.'

—— 1954 ——

As final preparations were being made on the day before the start of the Festival, a horrific air crash stunned the county. All four members of the American crew of a B47 six-engine jet atom bomber were killed when their aircraft crashed in a corn field, a mile from the United States Air Force base at Fairford. With this disaster very much on people's minds and under unwelcoming grey skies, Pakistan, making their first tour of this country, arrived at the College ground.

'The match was utterly ruined by rain,' reported the *Yearbook*. Despite only forty minutes of play being possible before lunch on the first day and only eight hours of cricket being played in the entire match, there were fond memories of the occasion for eighteen-year-old Malvern College captain Richard Whiley. He modestly explained, 'My selection was in no way a matter of merit. Colonel Henson, himself an Old Malvernian and highly autocratic secretary of the county club, decided that young Whiley, having been in the XI for five years, must be some good.' He had been asked earlier in the season to play for the county against Oxford University, but the school had refused permission. This was to be his one and only game for the county and he felt awkward about 'poor David Carpenter, who had been doing moderately well as opening bat' being dropped to twelfth man, and nervous when 'entering the dressing-room and meeting as team-mates men whom I had hitherto regarded as gods'. He sat down quietly and unpacked his bag. The gods were human, for at that stage, he recalls, 'Jack Crapp shook hands with me, apologising for the fact that he was wearing gloves (because of the severe eczema on his hands) and warned me that professional cricketers sometimes used language that I might not approve of, but they were nice chaps really - as indeed they were.'

Then Test star Tom Graveney introduced himself to the youngster, gave him a bat and a pair of batting gloves and said, 'Let's go outside and I'll bowl you a few.' His nerves began to settle as the growing crowd looked on.

Scoring 84 in one hundred minutes, Graveney (50) and Milton (42) steered their side to a respectable score on a difficult pitch. Wickets tumbled, but according to the *Yearbook*, Whiley 'defended stubbornly for over an hour' and when Crapp declared at 143 for 9 he was 7*. Batting with Bomber Wells, Whiley recalled, 'The entertainment value was great . . . At one point the ball lodged in the top of Bomber's pads, whereupon he shook it out on to the ground. Imtiaz, the wicket-keeper, went to pick it up but Bomber dribbled the ball off in the direction of gully pursued by Imtiaz.' A. H. Kardar, the captain, who had wished Whiley well as he came out to bat, did not find this amusing and appealed twice to umpire Syd Buller for 'obstructing the field', but the umpire affected not to hear the first one and Whiley recalls how the umpire called 'Not out!' in 'a contemptuous voice' when Kardar repeated his appeal.

Nineteen-year-old Hanif Mohammad, partnered by Alim-ud-Din, added 50 at a run-a-minute before bad light and rain ended play. Next day, in Pakistan's innings of 176, Arthur Milton, already top of the national catching list, held five catches and in the final half hour of play, opening the batting with Martin Young, Whiley remembers Hanif Mohammed bowling to him and 'sending down alternate left and right arm deliveries'.

With fresh Cotswold air in their lungs, the tourists travelled to the Oval and produced an inspired performance for the fourth Test to beat England by 24 runs. Derbyshire took their place on the College ground and Bomber Wells chuckles when recalling the match, despite his team being beaten by an innings and 52 runs.

The teams had met only a week before at Chesterfield, when Graveney's innings of 222 had played a large part in the county's 60 run victory; but for this encounter he was away on Test duty and their batting collapsed.

Wisden reported: 'On a drying pitch, Jackson, Gladwin and Morgan routed Gloucestershire in seventy minutes.' All out for 43, Jackson (6-1-8-4), Gladwin (9-4-24-4) and Morgan (3.1-0-11-2) sat down in the pavilion and watched their side gain a first innings lead before lunch.

Wells explained, 'The mayor was standing outside a large marquee waiting to greet the players as they came in for lunch. It was quite obvious that he had just arrived at the ground because as I walked in with Les Jackson, he remarked, "Typical Derbyshire, forty six without loss; it's no wonder that nobody bothers to watch cricket much nowadays." I smiled and explained the situation!'

The visitors reached 216, thanks largely to Hamer (87), then Gloucestershire lost Carpenter before the close of play. Apart from George Emmett (77), who showed stubborn resistance, the county's batsmen folded to Gladwin (26-14-24-5) and Morgan ((21-9-32-4) and Derbyshire swept to a two-day victory.

In the final match, Yorkshire-born Frank McHugh made use of a green wicket against champions Surrey, who quickly lost 6 wickets for 53. Eric Bedser and Roy Swetman improved matters, adding 49, before they were dismissed for 143.

McHugh (29-10-41-6) recalled bowling with Bomber Wells: 'He was notorious for his short run and during his over I certainly knew about it first hand. I had just finished my over and having collected my sweater from the umpire, strolled wearily back to the long leg boundary. About halfway there, having just adjusted my sweater, I heard a shout of

"Mac!". I casually turned around and saw the ball travelling past me to the boundary. In that short time, Bomber had bowled three balls!'

It had been a memorable day for McHugh; together with John Mortimore he was awarded his county cap by Jack Crapp in the dressing room at lunchtime and the two of them then led the team onto the field. When Gloucestershire went out to bat, Alec Bedser struck with his first ball.

Geoffrey Need, who was standing near the sightscreen at the Chapel end, describes what happened. 'Alec Bedser took off on his slightly "rhinoceros-charge" run-up to bowl the first ball of our innings; it swerved out on a perfect length and then suddenly cut back to trim the bails of poor old George Emmett.'

Milton buckled down and made 76 in three and three quarter hours. Crapp declared 10 runs ahead, and with the visitors on 75 for 4 in their second innings, the contest looked evenly balanced. Then a fifth wicket stand of 142 between Barrington (103) and Subba Row (47) swung the match, and Gloucestershire were left to make 269 at a run-a-minute to win. The contest never materialised as Bedser (20-3-51-4) and Surridge (16-6-31-6) bowled Surrey to victory by 156 runs, helping them edge ever closer towards their third successive county title.

CHAPTER FIFTEEN (1955-1959)

MACKINTOSH AND SANDWICHES

—— 1955 ——

'The boys haven't arrived to run the tuck shop. Would you run it?' committee member Peter Legge asked Norman and Janet Walters one morning.

'So we did,' recalls Norman. 'It was a little six-foot-square tent at the Chapel end. There was a pile of chocolate, a queue of customers, no change, no price list - it was a nightmare!'

An hour and a half later the boys turned up and Norman, who was by now quite ensconced in his trading activities, told them to 'push off' and go and see Mr Legge. This was the birth of the club shop which soon began to prosper.

County cricket, however, was not flourishing and money from Test matches had to be given to counties to help them survive. Televising cricket encouraged people to stay at home rather than go to a county ground. There was also the suggestion that broadcasting pictures of the extensive debris left behind after a day's play led to copy-cat behaviour at the Festival. The *Echo* reported, 'The quantity of paper, cartons and bottles left at the end of a day is appalling and no appeals can seem to persuade any but a few people to take away their wrappings and return their bottles.'

An element of unruliness and vandalism was concerning the Festival organisers and it was reported that the behaviour of boys round the main stand and the dressing-rooms would no longer be tolerated; they would be barred from the enclosure unless accompanied by adults. Police were asked to keep firmer order on the ground, while Colonel Henson appealed to grown-ups to keep boys under control and to stop them playing with bottles, as broken glass was 'a constant danger'.

There was no shortage of spectators on the first day of the match against the South Africans. Long before the gates opened at half past nine, queues began to form, with the people waiting by the Sandford

212

Road gate able to enjoy the sound of organ music wafting from the College Chapel. Motorists had to contend with the first day of the town's new traffic plan, with diversions and one-way systems up and running to try and ease congestion.

Although the sun had to battle with a fair number of clouds, the ground looked in fine condition, thanks to the hard work of Jim Hammond and his assistants, and around 11,000 watched proceedings during the day. For many, Festival cricket still had its appeal, illustrated by the fact that over 40,000 spectators watched the three games.

One of those enthusiasts was Jean Ough who was making her first visit to the ground. 'I arrived by train,' she recalls. 'Walking through Cheltenham, I reckoned if I saw someone with a rolled up mackintosh and a packet of sandwiches, they were going to the cricket.' She followed them . . .

Young and Milton gave their side a good start, then Vivian Smith dismissed Young and Graveney with successive deliveries, and ended with 5 for 75 when Gloucestershire were all out for 184. Despite scoring 58, Arthur Milton was most concerned about losing his wedding ring which had fallen down a drain inside the changing-room, but it gave non-playing Jackie McGlew a challenge to which he responded, finding the ring and tickling it out of the drain with a long piece of wire.

In reply, Murray (51) and Goddard (93) put on over a hundred for the visitors, but once they had been removed on Monday, possibly the most dramatic collapse in the history of the Festival followed, caused by one bad ball. Eight wickets fell in nineteen minutes for 21 runs. Those responsible were Mortimore (18-5-42-4), together with Wells (15-5-39-4) who recalls the event:

'They were in no difficulty at all, needing a mere handful of runs to go in front. It was then that I produced the "magical ball", my seamer, which pitched a foot outside the leg stump. It was swept hard and hit George Emmett on the ankle. The air was blue as our skipper was carried off for treatment, telling me in no uncertain terms exactly what he thought of me and that "bloody seamer". Acting captain George Lambert immediately switched ends for Morty and myself and the wickets suddenly began to fall. We were bowling out a Test side! Eventually, South Africa took a very narrow lead and that lovely old BBC commentator, Rex Alston, came up to me afterwards and said that for the first time in his life he had been lost for words. The wickets were going down so quickly that he had to tell the controller in the studio to come back to him later on when he could make sense of what had happened!'

Graveney made amends for his earlier failure by making a splendid 98 on what had become a difficult wicket, *Wisden* reporting that he curbed 'his natural desire to attack'. By midday on the last day, the visitors started their task of making 213 to win, but on 108 for 3 rain closed in and deprived spectators of witnessing an interesting finish, possibly even a repeat of that Gloucestershire victory twenty years earlier.

There was plenty of banter flying round during the next match against Glamorgan, who never recovered from their disastrous start of 32 for 5 on a green, moist pitch. Wilf Wooller with 46* stopped the rot, but by mid-afternoon Gloucestershire were in pursuit of the Welshmen's total of 135.

Wooller was keen to unsettle Milton and Young, who were struggling to score runs, and Hugh Davies, who had just completed an over, remembers his frustrated captain's antics. Apparently he called out, 'Stop the game! Looking at you two, I'll pay for you to go to Monte Carlo and with all your luck you could make a fortune in the casinos!' Hugh Davies recalled, 'There was laughter all round, then Syd Buller said, "Mr Wooller, will you please get on with the game!" - and we did.'

Milton, Graveney and Emmett played fluently, but the *Yearbook* describes the highlight of the Gloucestershire innings being 'a knock of 42* by Bomber Wells, his highest in first-class cricket, scored in 23 minutes'. The hero remembers, 'Haydn Davies was keeping wicket for Glamorgan and Wilf Wooller was bowling. Before he bowled, he called down the pitch to Haydn, "With all the luck we've had today, we only want this big fat one to plonk me for six on top of the pavilion. I'll eat my hat if he does." Haydn laughed. The first ball he bowled me, I hit him onto the pavilion roof and Haydn shouted out, "Where's your hat, skipper?" rocking with laughter.'

With Parkhouse injured, it was a tall order for the visitors to score the 190 runs needed to avoid an innings defeat. Before lunch on the third day Gloucestershire had won by an innings and 9 runs. This was great news for Arthur Milton and Tom Graveney who rushed up to Cleeve Hill for an afternoon's golf, a little treat they always gave themselves if a game finished early at Cheltenham.

An array of stars was missing from the final match. May, Laker, Lock and Graveney were all playing for England and despite winning in two days, Surrey were stretched on a difficult pitch. After a devastating morning spell of 5 for 19 by George Lambert, the champions recovered to make 180, thanks to some hard hitting by Dennis Cox who was particularly carefree against Wells during his innings of 57. Apart from Young (42), who batted steadily, and Wells (37), who slogged merrily, Gloucestershire fared even worse, slumping to 135 for 9 at the close with Alec Bedser and Peter Loader taking four wickets each.

A wet weekend prompted Emmett to declare first thing on Monday morning, a decision that proved wholly justified as Wells (13.4-4-29-5) and Mortimore (7-0-19-3) skittled the visitors out for 77. Needing 123 to win, the county were 8 for 2 at lunch, both Milton and Crapp having given tame catches to Micky Stewart at short-leg off rising balls from Alec Bedser. Emmett plodded on, but was given little support, and Surrey won this absorbing contest by 43 runs.

—— 1956 ——

With the Suez crisis bubbling and corn crops on the Cotswolds showing promise of a good harvest, Gloucestershire's cricketers arrived in Cheltenham. Their recent run of success had put them in a strong challenging position to upset either Surrey or Lancashire at the top of the table. Everyone was in agreement that the side's success was due to the large amount of effort from all the players and the imaginative leadership of George Emmett.

His decision to insert Sussex in the first game was questioned by some at the start, and by many more on the third day when the visitors swept to a ten wicket victory. Matters could so easily have gone the other way, but with nine wickets down for 212, Parks dug in to make 102 and edged his side up to 264. Cook (34.2-13-58-5) bowled splendidly, but Wells had an off-day just like the batsmen in his side. The county could only muster 103 runs, and following on they fared only a little better, making 174 as Marlar (39.3-14-87-7) made full use of a drying wicket.

Batting first against Glamorgan, Milton (74) and Young (62) got the county off to an excellent start. Graveney and Knightley-Smith carried on the good work, but rain then washed out the second day and a draw seemed the only possible result. The game needed a boost and the two captains, with some inspirational decisions, provided spectators with an enthralling final day.

Wilfred Wooller recalled that Cheltenham had always been a pleasant venue for both Welsh players and spectators alike. A South African tourist had written a glowing tribute on the appearance of the town's magnificent floral displays, including flower-beds around lamp-standards, hoping Cape Town could achieve a similar effect. Wooller remembered 'the playing fields of the ancient school enclosed to the west by graceful buildings . . . and the knowledge that sporting history has been made on the playing area'. He liked Cheltenham because he could 'always make a game with George Emmett. I could agree with him a fair rate, giving both sides a chance'.

Their calculations for a close finish were pretty accurate. Emmett declared immediately at 235 for 3. Wooller instructed his batsmen to go for runs and having avoided the follow-on, he declared at 87 for 3. Gloucestershire then batted for just over half an hour, with Tom Graveney becoming the first player to reach 2,000 runs in the season. Another declaration set the visitors 195 to win in a possible three hours. The challenge was there: 65 runs an hour on a sluggish pitch, with a wet, slow outfield. Wooller (46) scored briskly, but as *Wisden* records, 'The Welsh county found their task too great against the clever spin bowling of Cook and Wells.' By a quarter to six, the clouds had rolled away and thanks to the enterprise of both captains the Festival spirit was alive, spectators satisfied and Gloucestershire had won by 68 runs.

On the eve of the match against Kent, high winds blew down one of the large refreshment marquees and overturned sightscreens and ice-cream kiosks. The marquee, situated on the hospital side of the ground, belonged to Ron Sills' local catering firm and was used to prepare lunches and teas for the players, and to provide sit down meals for the public. It looked a sorry sight when play eventually started after the wind had helped to dry out the playing area.

Only two days were needed to beat Kent, thanks to the spin bowling of Cook and Wells. Memories came flooding back as veterans Crapp (87) and Emmett (95) featured in a magnificent fifth wicket partnership of 180, enabling a declaration at 289 for 6 to be made just before lunch on the second day.

On a 'square turner', Kent struggled against Wells (15-9-13-4) and Cook (14.1-8-11-6) who bowled out the visitors in an hour and a half for 45. Following on, only Cowdrey showed resolve, steadfastly carrying his bat (65*), although he was dropped early in his innings by Emmett, and Wells (29-6-65-5) insists, 'I had him lbw several times.'

With the game fast slipping away from the visitors, Tom Graveney reminded Godfrey Evans that any catches he might give should be directed towards Arthur Milton who, for the second time in three years, was leading the Brylcreem competition for the most catches in first-class cricket. Graveney recalls, 'Having scored a few, Godfrey, who had itchy feet and seemed to be wanting to get away, told Arthur to move a bit straighter and the next ball pinged into his hands!'

By a quarter to seven, Gloucestershire had won by an innings and 75 runs and moved up to second place in the championship table, providing a fitting Festival farewell to the retiring Colonel Henson, who had been county secretary for the last twenty-one years.

—— 1957 ——

Overnight showers prevented any play until the early afternoon of the first day in the match against Sussex. Two highlights followed: the first was the start of a faultless, skilful innings by Revd David Sheppard on a difficult pitch, and the second, a devastating spell of fast bowling from Tony Brown, who took five wickets in eighteen balls. When the rain returned, play ended early and the players and officials of both teams retired to the mayor's reception.

Breaking with tradition, Councillor Irving had arranged an evening reception in place of the longstanding official luncheon. He greeted each of the guests and soon there was a happy atmosphere, with cricketers, councillors, policemen, scorers and umpires all chatting together. Added to this, the players wives had been invited, a gesture much appreciated by Jean Milton, who recalls, 'We felt cherished.'

Sunday was no day of rest for David Sheppard, nor was there time to ponder how to continue his innings if the rain ceased on Monday. Instead, he gave sermons at two local churches. In the morning, the congregation overflowed at St. Barnabas and the service was relayed into the adjoining hall, while in the evening, at St. Mark's, the church was so full that many people had to sit on the floor.

There was very little cricket the following day; Sheppard finished with 72 out of 169 and Gloucestershire struggled to 19 for 4 before bad light halted proceedings, rain completely washing out the final day.

The wet weather continued and overnight the River Severn rose almost three feet to cause flooding on the low lying land at the Mythe, Tewkesbury, for the first time in August for twenty years. Inevitably the match against Hampshire had a delayed start, but within two days the hosts had won by seven wickets.

Desmond Eagar was making a welcome return to the ground. Having left the county in 1939, he had been part of the great revival of Hampshire cricket and was now in his last season as captain. Earlier in the year, his father, Colonel Eagar, a long serving Gloucestershire CCC committee and council member and chairman of the Cheltenham committee, had died. He had worked hard to further interests in the club in Cheltenham and the surrounding northern part of the county. It would have pleased him to see that the gate money from three matches on the College ground this year was just half of that raised from nine at Bristol.

Winning the toss, and knowing how quickly a wet Cheltenham wicket would deteriorate, Eagar elected to bat first. John Mortimore rubbed his hands with glee when he was called up to bowl, wrapped his fingers round the ball and proceeded to take 7 for 37 in seventeen overs as the visitors were dismissed for 125. Some attractive and powerful shots from Emmett (41) helped Gloucestershire secure a first innings lead of 52, and having lost their first 2 wickets without scoring, the spin of Cook (14-10-12-4) and Mortimore (16-4-41-3) proved too much for Hampshire's batsmen who collapsed to 66 all out. Needing only fifteen to win, there was a minor panic in the home dressing-room as Sainsbury removed Emmett, Young and Graveney for one run, showing that only a slightly larger target would have led to a very interesting finish.

Forty-nine years had passed since Yorkshire last appeared at the Festival. Now, in a low scoring game dominated by bowlers, Gloucestershire narrowly won by 2 wickets in two days. It was Sam Cook's benefit match and a Saturday crowd of over 8,000 helped to swell his fund, with a ground collection raising £175 and a bat competition making £100.

Yorkshire were bowled out in two and a half hours, with Smith, Brown, Cook and Wells sharing the wickets. Stubborn resistance from Illingworth (70) prevented their total of 133 looking silly, and when it came to Gloucestershire's reply, it was Emmett who was the anchor, making 62 out of 183. The hosts capitalized on their valuable lead and, as in the first innings, made short work of skittling their guests, this time for 118, thanks to Cook (17-8-28-4) and Wells (21.5-8-43-6).

The *Yearbook* reports: 'Gloucestershire were left with a day and a half in which to score 69 runs for victory. No batting task is easy at Cheltenham in the fourth innings and this occasion proved no exception. In one and a half hours, 8 wickets fell for 56 runs and defeat for the home county seemed imminent.' Arthur Milton remembers cutting Wardle, the ball bouncing off Close's head into Trueman's hands, and then the dramatic ending when the players were recalled onto the pitch after stumps had been drawn.

There was drama within drama, for as the *Echo* explained, it was 'a game of two endings':

'When the scores were level, the players and umpires, misled by the repeat scoreboard and thinking the match was over, left the field only to be called back by the scorers. By this time, children had run all over the pitch and the ground was swarming with people.'

Bomber Wells recalls, 'We had started to celebrate; you didn't beat Yorkshire many times in those days. We were half way through our drinks when there was a tap on the door and the umpires appeared to tell us they'd checked the scorebooks and found that we still needed one run to win. Sam Cook nervously strapped on his pads again and out went the Tykes, closely followed by Bobby Etheridge and David Smith our batsmen. All the rest of us had our fingers crossed and poor old George Emmett had already started on his second cigarette within five minutes.'

Silence descended upon the ground. Illingworth bowled the remaining three balls of his over - no score, no wicket. The first ball of Wardle's next over fizzed past wicket-keeper Binks for a bye and much to the beneficiary's relief, Gloucestershire were home and dry.

Wardle (16.2-8-25-6) had bowled magnificently, but looking back on the game, Wells reflected, 'We should never really have won; the great Johnny Wardle was unplayable and if only he'd let Jimmy Binks stand back to him, I feel sure we would have lost. The ball turned and lifted so much, even from a length, that no keeper in the world stood a chance when it did that.'

—— **1958** ——

Wisden records, 'Cricket in England suffered cruelly from rain in 1958.' It was the wettest season on record, turnstile numbers dropped and counties struggled financially due to lost revenue. A couple of draws, an innings defeat and a fair bit of rain were the Festival momentos in a year when the county finished fourteenth in the championship table.

On the first day's play against New Zealand, twenty-two wickets fell for 254 runs, with bowlers enjoying themselves on a damp pitch. Cave took 5 for 39 as the hosts were bowled out for 106, after which Cook (22.2-12-41-6) and Wells (15-4-41-4) dismissed the visitors for 127. At the start of Gloucestershire's second innings, Young and Milton were dismissed before the close of play. During an interrupted second day, the county edged their way to 160, leaving the tourists 140 to win. Ten for no wicket overnight remained untouched the following day - not a ball being

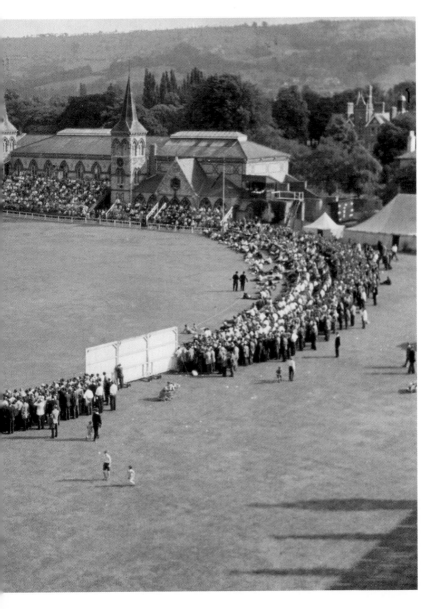

Gloucestershire v New Zealand, 1958

bowled - but twenty-five people turned up to watch, yielding gate receipts of £2 16s. By late afternoon the rain stopped, but the new county secretary, Harold Thomas, announced over the loudspeaker that due to a hole in the covers, water had seeped onto the wicket. In response to this, a few angry spectators gathered round the players entrance to demand their money back and the police had to be called to quieten them.

Ron Nicholls and Barrie Meyer were also in trouble. The two Bristol Rovers footballers had been placed on the transfer-list by their club for preferring to play cricket rather than start training for the forthcoming soccer season. As rain limited play on the first day against Glamorgan, they must have wondered if they had made the right choice, especially when the visitors reached 256 on the second day, and bowled Gloucestershire out for 67. A defiant 77 from Martin Young held up the visitors momentarily on the last day, but they won by an innings and 41 runs before lunch.

Rain ruined the chance of a result in the fixture against Warwickshire, although both captains tried their best to produce a finish. A full, first day's play saw Mortimore (73) lead the charge against some crafty, accurate, slow left-arm bowling by Hill (54.3-29-70-8). After a blank second day, M. J. K. Smith declared on 143 for 5, 122 runs behind Gloucestershire, who added a quick 71, setting the visitors 194 in two and a half hours. As soon as they had reached double figures, the heavens opened and everyone went home early.

—— 1959 ——

The sun blazed incessantly throughout the summer - exhausting for gardens but perfect for cricket. For Gloucestershire, who finished second in the championship, it was regarded as one of the most successful seasons in the county's history.

On the eve of the Festival, an official announcement was issued from Buckingham Palace stating that the Queen, 'in good health', was expecting a baby early next year, the future birth being the first to a reigning British sovereign for more than 102 years.

To welcome the news, a clear sky embraced the lush green grass on the square, which contrasted with a rather parched looking outfield, as the crowd gathered for the start of the game against Glamorgan. The visitors treated Festival goers to a feast of runs with a number of fielding errors helping the batsmen. Peter Walker, dropped early on, proceeded to score 113, while Bernard Hedges, who also 'received a life', made 76, as they helped to steer their side to a total of 371. Walker recalls, 'I always enjoyed playing at the College ground where the close proximity of the crowd helped the Festival atmosphere.'

On this occasion, the atmosphere was rudely interrupted by the weather. Throughout Sunday evening violent thunderstorms and torrential rain hit the region, and according to Wilf Wooller 'a captain's prayer was answered'. Cranham Feast was awash and the heavy Bank Holiday traffic on the county's roads had to heed the 'Beware of rain' warnings from the AA. After the long, hot summer, the resistance on some road surfaces had been greatly reduced and the increased risk of skidding in the rain made roads highly dangerous.

On Monday, with the wicket suiting seam bowling, Milton batted for four hours and made his first Festival hundred as the hosts were bowled out for 213. Wooller recollects, 'I pulled a hamstring muscle, but kept on bowling in my turn as I interchanged my bowlers.' Following on, Milton and Young gave the county a glimmer of hope, putting on 55 before bad light stopped play.

Further overnight rain helped Glamorgan's bowlers, and in just over two hours they bowled Gloucestershire out for 120; but by now Wooller (17-9-31-4) was suffering. Adding to his hamstring injury, he had pulled a muscle in his arm, remembering, 'At the fall of a wicket, I rushed off for pain injections. Then the other arm went, more injections. I was in a parlous state . . .'

For Gloucestershire, who had been doing so well, defeat by an innings and 38 runs was not part of the script, although to a certain extent they had only themselves to blame, with some fairly inept batting. Fortunately their pain was short-lived and they were soon back on winning ways, whereas Wooller's discomfort after leaving Cheltenham would grow even worse. He recalls, 'As I could not play the next game, I climbed in a small Ford which I had borrowed as my car was in dock and set off for Saundersfoot where my family were holidaying. As I laboriously covered the 160 or so miles, I began to seize up and arrived at my destination set solid. I blew the horn to attract attention and had to be levered out of the small car in agony. I lay in the sea for three days recovering.'

After the Glamorgan defeat, a Tom Graveney benefit game was held at the Victoria Ground, ending in an honourable draw, and the next fixture, against Middlesex, was his benefit match. Still suffering from a broken finger that had plagued him since early July, county captain Graveney won the toss for his team and watched from the pavilion as they raced to an innings and 60 runs victory in two and a half days. This was largely due to another maiden Cheltenham century, this time from Milton's fellow opener, Martin Young, whose 140 out of 290 for 9 declared gave his side just the right start. Before the close of play on the second day, Middlesex, following on, were 28 for 1, Cook (21-8-42-5) having earlier prised them out for 127.

That night Young was hurt in a car crash, cutting his chin when his car skidded off the greasy road and collided with a tree as he was returning from a Supporters Club social evening at the Star Hotel. Although not badly injured, Gloucestershire took to the field without him next day, with Middlesex's Bob White deputising, and he watched on from close quarters as Cook (15.2-6-33-5) and Mortimore (13-7-31-4) bowled out his team mates for 103 before lunch.

While Arthur Milton spent the afternoon playing golf, others made their way to the Town Hall for the Ideal Home Exhibition. A couple of days earlier, the mayor, Councillor A. G. Dye, had opened the event. Describing Cheltenham as 'a trading centre of the West of England', he envisaged the exhibition 'would stimulate trade in the town and district', and hoped that the labour saving devices would 'remove some of the drudgery for the poor husbands!'

Well over 40,000 people were expected to visit the exhibition, while another excitement in town came in the form of comedian, Bernard Bresslaw, who appeared at the Regal cinema. To the delight of his fans, he wandered on stage between films, rolled his eyes, dropped his jaw and bellowed out, 'Hello, Cheltenham, It's me - Twinkletoes!' before giving a hearty plug for his forthcoming film *The Ugly Duckling*.

Meanwhile, on the College ground final preparations were being made for the match against India as Arthur Milton, returning to The Star from his round of golf, sat down to eat the eggs and bacon that Harry Williams had cooked for him.

Wanting the opportunity to play more first-class cricket, Bomber Wells announced before the start of the final game that he would be leaving the county at the end of the season. He had become a firm Festival favourite, but would soon be back at Cheltenham playing for his new county, Nottinghamshire. Since his retirement from the game, this endearing raconteur has spent many hours watching, commenting and reminiscing on the ground where he once starred.

Roy invited Gloucestershire to bat on a damp wicket, but his bowlers made little impression as Milton (77) and Meyer (63), the latter standing in as opener for Young, added over a hundred for the first wicket. The stage was now set for the county's forty-six-year-old master batsman, George Emmett, who according to the *Echo,* 'bowed gracefully out of big-time cricket . . . with the cheers of a delighted Cheltenham Festival crowd ringing in his ears'. 'The side's experienced artist', as David Foot referred to him, made his last appearance on the ground and punished the bowling, making 85 in seventy-seven minutes.

Describing the scene when he was out, the *Echo* reported, 'It was an emotional moment as - smiling broadly - Emmett began the long walk back to the pavilion. The applause began as soon as he started his triumphant march. As he moved nearer, he waved his bat in the air, acknowledging the thunderous ovation. Then the crowd near the players' entrance rose and started cheering. Emmett doffed his cap in a final gesture of appreciation and disappeared.'

On Monday, despite 'Polly' Umrigar's 80, India were soon in trouble against Cook (21.2-13-27-5). They were bowled out for 179, and by half past eleven on the last day Gloucestershire had declared on 186 for 4, leaving the visitors 326 to win. Without Umrigar, who had damaged his finger, the Indian batsmen buckled after lunch, apart from some stubborn resistance by the left-handed opener, Contractor (48). Up against some hostile bowling by David Smith, who in six overs took 4 for 14 and ended with figures of 17-4-32-5, the tourists were dismissed for 133 and the county won by 192 runs.

CHAPTER SIXTEEN (1960-1969)

THE SWINGING SIXTIES

—— 1960 ——

Despite arriving at Cheltenham without a championship win for over a month, the county's players put this behind them and beat Hampshire by six wickets in the opening match. A decision had been made to start the Festival a week later than usual in an attempt to escape the rain which had affected play and attendances in recent years. The plan worked: cricket was played on all nine days and gate receipts topped £2,000.

Hampshire began impressively. Building on an opening partnership of 103 by Marshall and Gray, Horton and Ingleby-Mackenzie made half centuries, before declaring on 315 for 5. The visitors seemed to take control as they dismissed Gloucestershire 60 runs in arrears, due largely to a characteristic spell of bowling from Derek Shackleton (34.4-14-61-5).

Amongst the spectators was keen Hampshire supporter Cliff Michelmore, presenter of the BBC programme *Tonight*. Enjoying a six-week holiday away from the glare of television cameras, he watched seventeen-year-old Anthony Windows, the Clifton College captain, make his county debut. The young player helped his skipper keep the visitors' attack at bay as they threatened to run through Gloucestershire's batting. Forty years later, his son, Matthew would be a prominent member of the Gloucestershire side.

With Hampshire now batting, the game suddenly swung dramatically. Some clever off-spin bowling by David Allen (15.2-5-31-5) gave the county a scent of victory as the visitors were bowled out for 116. After only eight overs, Shackleton bruised his finger and was unable to bowl. The depleted Hampshire attack could not contain Martin Young (114*) and the hosts reached their target of 182 for the loss of 4 wickets.

During the early and middle part of the season, Tom Graveney had made few runs, having been troubled by an injury to his shoulder muscle, so it was particularly pleasing for the Festival crowd to witness 'vintage

Graveney' in the game against Middlesex.

'The bowlers were very good - they kept hitting the middle of the bat!' recalls Graveney modestly, who made his highest score of the season, 142*, as wickets tumbled around him. Batting for nearly four and a half hours, this flawless innings, his only century on the College ground, was described as 'a masterly display of faultless technique' in the *Echo*:

'The longer he stayed the larger he seemed to grow in strength and stature until his beautiful, flowing cover-drives completely dominated the scene. By mid-afternoon he was bestriding the scene like a Colossus, and the fielders, in the covers and elsewhere, were wringing their hands painfully and inspecting their fingers for damage.'

In what turned out to be his last season for the county, but not his final appearance on the ground, Graveney certainly gave the crowd a memory to treasure.

Replying to Gloucestershire's total of 221, Middlesex batted with steady, solid determination, for fresh in their minds was the twenty-nine run defeat Gloucestershire had dealt them at Lord's only a week earlier. The Russells put on 124 together and the visitors declared on 320 for 6. With rain interrupting play on the second day, the game became a stalemate on a damp pitch, the hosts reaching 280 for 9 as Peter Parfitt, finding lots of turn, finished with figures of 32-21-39-4.

Coinciding with the first day of the match against Kent was the start of the football season. High-flying Wolves were at home to West Ham and doubtless some locals made the journey to Molineux rather than to the College ground, especially as the Oval Test had already deprived the visitors of Colin Cowdrey.

The football fans missed some interesting cricket. Kent's acting captain, Arthur Phebey (61), steered his side to a total of 246 before the hosts struggled against some accurate bowling by Halfyard and Dixon. *Wisden* reported that Graveney (54) was the only batsman to offer 'protracted resistance'. After play that evening, Sir George and Lady Dowty hosted a reception for the players and officials of both clubs, along with members of other local sporting organisations. The informal gathering proved to be a great success, partly because in previous years the last team at the Festival had always been neglected socially.

Partying was over and rain fell on Monday. With Gloucestershire all out for 140, the visitors extended their lead of 106 and by the final afternoon, Phebey's declaration on 177 for 4 left the hosts needing to make 284 in two hundred and twenty minutes. On a tricky wicket, Young,

Carpenter, Windows and Hawkins were the only batsmen to reach double figures. Wickets fell and the writing was on the wall, but the county's lower order put up stubborn resistance and at one stage batted out twelve successive maiden overs, without a single run being scored for thirty-five minutes. When Sayer removed Mortimore with a mean, lifting, good-length ball, the end was in sight and David Halfyard's mixture of medium-paced swing bowling and off-spin (30.3-16-61-6) gave Kent victory by 156 runs with half an hour to spare.

Four months later, just before Christmas, Tom Graveney parted company with Gloucestershire. Elegant and stylish, this great batsman had scored almost 20,000 runs for the county in twelve years. David Green, in *The History of Gloucestershire County Cricket Club,* remarked how sad it was that 'mismanagement, pure and simple, should have caused the County to lose such a rich talent'.

—— **1961** ——

One Tom replaced another as county captain. The new incumbent, Old Etonian and amateur player, Tom Pugh, led his team to victory over Kent at the festive Canterbury Week seven days before the Festival at Cheltenham. The cathedral city no longer displayed the colourful bunting and illuminations that had decorated the streets in the time of Lord Harris, but it could still boast a large semi-circle of lively tents and marquees, far outnumbering the small collection erected each year on the College ground.

Back in Gloucestershire county secretary Harold Thomas was quoted in the *Echo* as saying, 'We look to this festival, to save the ship from sinking . . . County cricket, if not yet at the financial crossroads, certainly seems to be approaching it.'

Financially, the Stroud Week had been reasonably successful, but Gloucester had not reached its target and there were rumblings that this fixture was in jeopardy for the following year. So, through the passage of time, little had changed and Lillywhite's legacy needed to stump up once again. From nine days of cricket the county pot needed to amass £3,000, which would give a profit margin of £1,500 after costs.

In the end the target was not reached and it was suggested that the reduced gates, which resulted in takings of just over £1,500, were the result of cold, showery weather, the lure of television coverage of the final Test and a certain amount of repetition in fixtures. Glamorgan were becoming rather familiar visitors to Cheltenham, having appeared four times in the last six years. Gloucestershire supporters wanted to see some new blood and this would come the following year with a visit from the Pakistanis.

Football was flexing its muscles again on the first day of the Festival, with over a thousand people attending Cheltenham Town FC for its public trial game. They did not miss much at the College ground: by mid-afternoon, Glamorgan had bowled out their hosts for 166 with Don Shepherd (24-10-44-5) enjoying the benefits of a damp wicket. In reply, the visitors collapsed to 123 all out, with off-spinners Allen (28.3-13-59-6) and Mortimore (22-10-46-3) causing the damage.

The longer the game continued, the harder it was to score runs and the familiar Cheltenham saying of this era - 'Win the toss, bat first, then spin them out' - was once again proving itself correct. Gloucestershire made 177 as Shepherd helped himself to another four wickets, while Walker (38.2-12-68-6) grabbed the larger haul. Scoring the 221 needed to win was always going to be a tall order for the visitors, and the mere thought of their task probably contributed to their rapid collapse. With Allen (21-9-25-6) and Mortimore (19-10-28-3) dictating matters, Glamorgan's batsmen caved in, and on the final morning when their last 5 wickets fell for only 9 runs, their total of 80 left the hosts victorious by 140 runs.

A splendid all-round performance by Lancashire's Roy Collins with a century in the first innings, 46 in the second and match-bowling figures of 9 for 135, helped his side win a close contest by 55 runs. Both teams were without a key player as Statham and Allen were representing their country in Peter May's sixty-sixth and final Test match. Gaining a first innings lead of 91, Lancashire steadily built up a strong position when they batted again, despite good bowling by Brown (23-5-45-4) and Mortimore (26-6-82-5). Gloucestershire were left needing 311 to win. A watchful, fighting innings by Ron Nicholls, making his highest score on the ground (99), led the reply, while Pugh and Windows made useful contributions. However, the target was just too much and they were dismissed for 255.

In cold, unsettled conditions, a century, coloured with characteristic drives from Kent's left-handed Peter Richardson, was the difference between the two sides after the first innings of the last match. Gloucestershire collapsed to the bowling of Jones (9-6-12-5) and were all out for 165. Richardson's 111 was the major contribution to the visitors' total of 276, during which all-rounder Derek Hawkins returned his career-best bowling figures of 20-1-81-6. Batting again, Nicholls made a half-century and Young was left on 49* when his team were dismissed for 178, before Kent quickly cruised to a 7 wicket victory.

—— 1962 ——

The summer was abnormally cold and unseasonable, and wet conditions spoiled the opening match of the Festival, with only ten hours of cricket possible against Pakistan. Even so, it was a blessing that the event had been moved away from the Bank Holiday weekend when two and three quarter inches of rain had fallen on the Monday, believed to be the highest rainfall for any single day since records were first kept in the town in 1878.

As a small thank you to those people who had responded to the county's cry for financial help by becoming new members, several changes had been made on the ground, so improving spectator facilities. Harold Thomas was away ill, so arrangements had been carried out by Richard McCrudden, with help from local committee members, especially Messrs Moore, Woof and Lewis. In response to criticism about the inadequate seating, a new stand in the members' enclosure had been erected which provided five hundred tiered seats, helping to accommodate the large increase in membership from the north of the county. In addition, throughout the ground more refreshment tents and lavatories were provided, with details of their location shown on a map printed on the scorecard.

In between the showers on the first day, the tourists reached 180 for 7, Mushtaq Mohammad's commanding 48 helping to relieve some of the gloom. Even less cricket was played on the second day as Gloucestershire, in reply to Pakistan's total of 233, were reduced to 88 for 5 by the accurate bowling of Fazal and D'Souza. In order to try and find some purpose in playing the last day, Pugh declared 58 behind, but further rain ruined the chance of anything but a draw.

There was little change next day as the depression prevented play from starting until half past four, when Gloucestershire proceeded to bowl out Lancashire for 90. This was John Mortimore's match: already having taken 3 for 13 from eleven overs, he now made a solid 72 which helped to give his side a first innings lead of 137. On the last day, Cook (11.4-8-15-4), who would finish the season at the top of the national bowling averages, and Mortimore (13-9-9-5) put on a formidable display.

Wisden reported: 'After some delay through rain the last eight Lancashire wickets went down for 28 runs.' Gloucestershire were home by an innings and 73 runs.

This heralded the start of a hugely successful climax to the season which brought the county five wins out of the last six games. The only defeat came after the Festival at the hands of Worcestershire on their way to becoming champions, while Gloucestershire raced to fourth place in the table.

The match against Nottinghamshire saw the welcome return to the ground of Bomber Wells. 'It was wonderful to be back at Cheltenham,' he recalls. 'It was a funny feeling, seeing hundreds of people I knew and wondering if they would want to see me hit all over the ground or whether they would be sympathetic.'

He need not have worried for he walked off to warm applause at the end of Gloucestershire's first innings of 205, with figures of 32.3-17-55-5. Nottinghamshire were then bowled out for 104, largely thanks to David Smith (19-9-45-6).

Next followed the innings of the summer, one of Cheltenham's finest displays of belligerent batting. Earlier in the season, Cambridge blue, Tony Windows, had 'tipped off' the county about his South African colleague, Johannesburg-born R. C. (Ray) White. His accurate judgement had been quickly confirmed in early July when the light blues played Gloucestershire at Bristol, and in making 59 and 74, White, according to the *Yearbook,* 'gave the spectators a foretaste of his skill'.

On the second day, the visitors having been on and off the field because of rain, White strode out to bat. Despite the wicket not being in the most perfect of conditions for a major batting performance, facing sixty-balls in sixty-eight minutes, the South African produced an electrifying innings of 102*, consisting of 13 fours and 4 sixes. It was the fastest century of the season and would have been even quicker if he had not had to spend time changing his pads when a buckle broke. This whirlwind display was similar to Jessop's performances on so many occasions. The *Yearbook* described it as 'an exhibition of controlled hitting and of cold-blooded slaughter of good-class bowling . . . it was reminiscent of the hey-day of Gloucestershire cricket'. Wells, who was on the receiving end, remembers, 'It was a beautiful knock. We thought we'd bounce a few round the ears of this university chap, but he hammered us all over the ground!'

The rest of the game was a formality. Needing 334 to win, the visitors struggled on the final day. Between the showers, Cook (16-7-34-5) turned the ball viciously, bowling his side to victory by 184 runs. At the end of the Festival, Richard McCrudden praised the 'heroic' people of north Gloucestershire for their loyal support in such adverse conditions, and promised better protection for the wickets next year. In turn, the *Echo* congratulated Mr McCrudden for his announcements over the public address system, including his 'prompt information to spectators after wicket inspections, providing bowling analyses at the ends of innings and, when it was possible, reading out the scores in other matches'.

—— 1963 ——

A few days before the start of the Festival, the biggest robbery in British history took place when the Glasgow to London mail train was held up and thieves made off with £2.5 million. A small slice of the takings from the Great Train Robbery would have been most handy to help Gloucestershire solve some of their financial problems. Things had been getting steadily worse in recent years, merely reflecting the country at large which itself was facing a huge balance of payments crisis.

With Martin Young's car breaking down on the way to the ground, Arthur Milton joined Ron Nicholls to open the innings against Nottinghamshire, and the two of them provided a tasty start to the Festival. Nicholls, who went on to make 91, just missed a century before lunch, as their sparkling partnership realised 130. Added spice was given to the morning's play when square-leg umpire Syd Buller 'called' the Nottinghamshire slow left-arm bowler, Keith Gillhouley, four times for throwing. White then made a characteristic 65 and the county were dismissed for 291 when Bomber Wells captured the wicket of his former colleague, Sam Cook.

The visitors did a little better, with Bolus and Hill featuring in another century-opening partnership, the latter going on to hit 20 fours and a six during his attractive innings of 129. Gaining a first innings lead for the loss of only 5 wickets, the visitors declared, thus leaving the game wide open for an exciting finish.

After quickly losing their first innings hero, Gloucestershire's batsmen responded positively in true Festival spirit, with Milton (49), Young (103) and White (61) enabling a declaration to be made, leaving the visitors to score 252 to win in three hours. In only two and a half hours, John Mortimore's guile had guided Gloucestershire to victory by 104 runs. Gaining his best figures of the season (18-9-44-6), he and his

Ken Graveney, standing on the left, watches his Gloucestershire batsmen in action against Nottinghamshire in 1963

colleagues found a few spare minutes for celebration before their night out at the Everyman Theatre, where they were entertained in the Long Bar by members of the Cheltenham Everyman Theatre Association before watching a performance of *Doctor at Sea*.

Having met the cast and some of the audience at the end of the evening, the players were clearly still at sea the following morning at the start of Martin Young's benefit match against Worcestershire. Asked to bat first by Don Kenyon, the hosts floundered on a damp wicket against the accurate bowling of Jack Flavell (16.3-3-51-5) and Bob Carter (16-4-30-3) and were quickly dismissed for 104. After a shaky start by the visitors, Tom Graveney (58) helped to halt the rot and Worcestershire went on to reach 217.

'It was very odd going out to play against Gloucestershire. I didn't like it,' recalls Graveney.

Moving to 126 for 3, due largely to Ron Nicholls 54* (one of 18 half-centuries he scored on the ground), the county pulled the game back, so setting up the possibility of an interesting final day's play, only to see it washed out by rain.

To complete the Festival, Sussex won a see-saw match by 21 runs. Batting first, despite Oakman's resolute 77, the visitors struggled against the spin of Cook (28-12-40-4) and Mortimore (30-9-78-4) and were dismissed for 196. Gloucestershire replied with 231 and when Mortimore swept Sussex aside with figures of 25.2-13-35-7, the hosts were left needing only 90 for victory. A poor start, with the loss of three quick wickets, led to an embarrassing finish, with lively bowling from Thomson (18-12-22-5) and Buss (13.2-8-19-5) routing the county for 68.

—— **1964** ——

While the youth revolution of the sixties was getting into full swing, county cricket continued to falter and gates further diminished as the game seemed to be losing its excitement. Its traditions and disciplines began to appear out of place in a world where rules and the old order were being challenged. Gloucestershire crumpled simultaneously, three defeats at Cheltenham contributing to a dismal season. They finished bottom of the championship for the first time since 1914, which was a disappointing end to Sam Cook's career.

Midland rivals, Warwickshire and Worcestershire, were battling things out at the top of the championship table and both feasted on the points they gathered at the College ground. Warwickshire came first, winning an exciting match by 5 wickets, having been 115 behind on first innings.

On a green wicket, the hosts found runs difficult to make, eventually reaching 216 on the second day. On the Sunday in between the first two days of the match, Festival umpire Ron Lay had been injured in a benefit match for Sam Cook on the Victoria ground. During a sparkling innings of 117 by Ted Dexter, Lay's ankle had been on the receiving end of a straight drive from the England captain, but he had bravely soldiered on to the end of the game. With Lay hospitalised for X-rays, Geoff Edrich, the College cricket coach, was appointed from Lord's as official umpire for the rest of the match. Warwickshire wickets fell quickly before his eyes as they were bowled out for 101, with Windows taking 5 for 36. On the final day, the visitors pulled themselves together after being set a target of 298 to win in four hours. Ibadulla, Smith and Hitchcock all chipped in towards the run-chase, but the victory was brought about by splendid batting from Bob Barber (82) and Jim Stewart (91*) who saw his side home with two minutes to spare.

Glamorgan inflicted further pain on Gloucestershire, winning what might have been a close match by 110 runs. If little was happening for the county on the field, there was certainly great activity off it, with various fund-raising activities being staged to boost the unsatisfactory bank balance. In the forefront was Cheltenham Corporation, inspired by the efforts and ideas of Councillor Aimbury Dodwell.

Gloucestershire trailed the visitors by 46 runs on first innings, and after play on the second day, Dodwell had organised the first of his Festival 'fringe' events - 'Meet the Cricketers at a Wine, Beer and Cheese Party' - at the Pittville Pump Room. The event raised £30 for county funds and put a bit of spirit into the players. Glamorgan were bowled out for 119, Tony Brown taking 5 for 42, leaving the county needing 166 to win. On a wearing wicket, disaster struck and in three quarters of an hour Gloucestershire were reduced to jelly at 16 for 5. Don Shepherd (2.5-2-5-4) was virtually unplayable and the hosts were all out for 55 after John Mortimore had enjoyed slogging 23.

With top versus bottom of the table, there was a distinct possibility of a whitewashing for Gloucestershire as they took on Worcestershire. The visitors, who were enjoying their steady run-in to winning the championship, recovered from a poor start of 56 for 6, to reach 143. The hosts also found runs difficult to make, but thanks to Martin Young's 55 they managed to tie on first innings. Kenyon (91), Headley (66) and

Graveney (45*) led Worcestershire's charge in the second innings and they were able to declare at 281 for 4, leaving their opponents four and a half hours batting. From the offset, Gloucestershire never really looked in charge of a run-chase and were bowled out for 174 three minutes before the end, with Jack Flavell swinging and seaming his way to match anaysis of 51.2-16-110-10.

—— 1965 ——

This year's Festival brochure included listings of all the fringe events in the town and surrounding area. Any enquiries could be directed to the information caravan on the College ground, and for pavement-bound shoppers, it had been arranged that scoreboards giving the latest 'state of the game' details should be displayed in the shop windows of Cavendish House and The Famous.

As chairman of the Cheltenham Cricket Festival Committee, Aimbury Dodwell was determined to see the county reap some benefits from their various fund-raising activities. He showed his commitment by sacrificing two days of his Cornish holiday, returning from St Ives during John Mortimore's benefit match against Worcestershire for a Wine, Beer and Cheese Party and entertainment he had arranged at the Pittville Pump Room. It was the kind of dedication Lillywhite would have applauded, especially set against a background of renewed murmurings about the practicality of staging the Festival in Cheltenham and a suggestion that the matches should be played in Bristol.

At five shillings a ticket, the evening was a huge success with people turned away from the door and drinks running out long before it was time to go home. The party goers enjoyed listening to the Cheltenham Playhouse Company and the Operatic and Dramatic Society giving excerpts from their recent *Old Time Music Hall* production. It was reminiscent of the old days at the Cricket Week; Cheltenham was swinging with the rest of Britain, albeit in a different way, into the mid-sixties.

A month after the death of Walter Hammond, the arrival of Kent heralded a nine-day, sun-baked Festival, with the first day belonging to their opener Mike Denness who made an attractive 112. On reaching 284 for 6, the visitors declared. Tony Brown returned figures of 29-3-93-5 and Gloucestershire replied positively. Arthur Milton (110) scored his first century on the ground, while Mike Bissex made a stylish 92 and together they featured in a fourth wicket stand of 153 which steered their side to a first innings lead of 21.

While the mayor, Councillor Bertram Taylor, welcomed guests to his reception in the Town Hall on Monday evening, anticipating the pleasure of seeing 'a gracious game, in a gracious setting, in a town of gracious living', the Moody Blues were in town, thumping out numbers for younger cricket enthusiasts at the Big Beat Dance.

On the morning of the final day, Mortimore (15.4-4-31-3) and Allen (20-5-45-5) proved to be a handful and bowled the visitors out for 158, leaving the county the seemingly straightforward task of making 138 to win. In two hours the game was over, Kent having bowled Gloucestershire out for 82, with Dixon (20-7-38-6) and Underwood (17.3-5-37-4) inflicting the damage.

Worcestershire, heading for their second successive championship title, were the next visitors. A vigilant innings of almost seven hours from Ron Nicholls (99) helped Gloucestershire reach 210, which the visitors then topped by 43, thanks to an exciting century partnership by Tom Graveney (47) and Basil D'Oliveira (81), the latter making his first appearance on the ground. The new recruit then demonstrated his all-round skills by capturing four Gloucestershire wickets and taking two catches off Norman Gifford's bowling, as the hosts were bowled out for 173.

Needing 131 to win, the champions were suddenly 19 for 3, with Mortimore and Allen enjoying the benefits of a worn wicket. Tom Graveney, already at the crease, recalled the moment when D'Oliveira came out to join him. Graveney walked down the wicket and said to him, 'The ball is turning square: I can't play this - I'm charging everything.' He knew if he stayed where he was, he'd be caught at short-leg. 'I decided to eliminate the three short-legs and kept pushing it, shoving it and nicking it past slip,' he recalled. 'We were lucky that Cooky wasn't playing, making the ball leave the bat.'

However, Graveney still finds the manner in which D'Oliveira played that day 'absolutely astonishing', saying, 'The outstanding thing was that Basil was in his first season, playing first-class cricket against two England spinners. He did exactly the opposite to me, going back to everything, until they pitched the ball right up, when he would hit it over mid-off!'

Graveney (59*) and D'Oliveira (55*) took their side to victory. The great all-rounder's best remembered innings, he admits, was not the Test match or county centuries, but this occasion, when he helped his side win on 'a wicked Cheltenham turner'.

Local supporters paid their four shillings admission charge to the ground for the first day's play against Sussex, hoping for better fortune. Fittingly, The Beatles' record *Help* was topping the national charts and their film of the same name had been showing all week at the Odeon.

Assistance came in the form of the unflappable Arthur Milton, who made the highest score of his career, 170, in just under seven hours. 'We batted on,' he recalls. 'It was unusual, but we wanted to have the best of a deteriorating wicket.' His fine knock formed the backbone of Gloucestershire's total of 370, one of the highlights being a 99 run fifth wicket partnership with Gloucester-born David Bevan, who hit 2 sixes and 7 fours in his innings of 63.

Sussex just managed to save the follow-on, making 231, and the hosts consolidated their lead as half-centuries from Nicholls and Russell enabled Mortimore to declare at 146 for 5. Never looking like reaching their target of 286, the visitors were dismissed for 108 by the clever spin bowling of Allen (21-3-50-4) and his captain (17.2-7-21-5), who was pleased, no doubt, that under his leadership the receipts had reached an all time best of £3,268.

—— 1966 ——

Kicking off the Cheltenham gathering, a fortnight after England's football team had won the World Cup and a toothless Nobby Stiles had danced round Wembley Stadium, Sussex trounced Gloucestershire by ten wickets.

This match was Bert Avery's first experience of the Festival. As Second XI scorer, he was asked to help out Sussex when their scorer was suddenly taken ill. He jumped at the offer of earning a pound a day and was driven from Bristol to the ground by Mike Bissex, where he joined Gloucestershire's scorer, Fred Dudderidge. Bert, later to become the club scorer and archivist, chuckled when recalling the 'do' at the Town Hall, when Sussex's captain, the Nawab of Pataudi, delivered his speech in Indian, with Les Lenham standing by his side acting as interpreter. 'Suddenly,' recalled Bert, 'Pataudi broke into English and there was a lot of laughter!'

For Ron Nicholls, this was an important fixture. Having chosen it for his benefit match, he was anxious to see three full days of play, as he had been plagued by bad weather at other recent benefit games. The weather held, but Gloucestershire's batting did not. With his team on 58 for 3, the beneficiary found himself walking to the wicket to face England pace bowler, John Snow, on a hat-trick. The generous Sussex fielders gave Nicholls a run off his first ball, and having overcome the crisis, he went on to make the top score (35) out of a total of 149. Despite Mortimore and Allen taking four wickets each, Sussex gained a useful lead of 53 and from then on the game quickly slipped away from the hosts.

Batting again, Gloucestershire were soon reduced to 39 for 7 and an innings victory for the visitors seemed on the cards, but some stubborn tail-end resistance prevented this and Sussex were left needing 44 to win, which they reached without loss. Devastating bowling by Snow (18.2-3-37-5) and Tony Buss (21-10-31-5) had caused the rout, earning their side a two day victory, which was not good news for the Nicholls benefit fund.

Sunday, however, had been an occasion for two contrasting fringe events, one of which raised £370 for the beneficiary. At Smith's ground, The Newlands, Gloucestershire had taken on the International Cavaliers in a televised, forty-over spectacle. In reply to the county's seemingly inadequate total of 161, Pakistan captain, Hanif Mohammad, had opened the innings for the Cavaliers who ended up fifteen runs short of victory, despite an elegant half-century by Tom Graveney.

Apart from the BBC television viewers, over 4,000 people had attended the game, some of whom had been present earlier in the day at Cheltenham Parish Church for the Festival service. Addressing the large congregation, Canon Hanson spoke of the importance of the Cricket Festival as a high-spot in people's working lives. He reminded those present of the close connection between the Church and 'the grandest of all games', and the fact that many of the best-known cricketing families in the county - the Graces, Champains, Jessops, Townsends and Barnetts - had produced one or more parsons and urged that in the future this alliance should be encouraged and continued.

In true Christian spirit, Sussex's players sacrificed the day's holiday they had earned and played a sixty-over challenge match against the county. It was a sporting gesture that helped to keep the Festival alive until the arrival of Surrey, hotfoot from Bradford, where they had beaten Yorkshire, the championship leaders.

The game against the Londoners was one of the season's experiments, limited to sixty-five overs in the first innings. Changes were made to the Gloucestershire team in order to strengthen the batting, but to no avail, for in forty-four overs they were dismissed for 119.

It was clear to Festival goers that the county's batting lacked class.

Low finances had led to a shortage of quality players and replacements for those who were injured or out-of-form, and the club seemed to be stagnating, rather like British industry which was losing trade to foreign competitors.

Surrey made 200 in their allocated overs, largely due to an entertaining third wicket partnership of 115 between Ken Barrington (76) and Micky Stewart (55), while David Smith took all 6 wickets to fall for 44. Gloucestershire's batting showed some improvement next time round, but when wickets started falling once again, John Mortimore put himself in as night-watchman and on the morning of the second day he made 75 in forty-five minutes, hitting 6 sixes and 5 fours in the county's total of 189. However, the rally was not enough and Surrey won easily by 7 wickets before the close of play.

Another day off was good for Arthur Milton's golf, but bad news for the county's coffers. Golf was booming and the Cotswold Hills, Cirencester and Lilley Brook clubs were thriving.

Meanwhile, after losing the third day's gate money for the Surrey match, the county's takings were £1,200 down, when compared with the equivalent stage of the Festival the previous year. The secretary reported the matter as being 'very serious', so it was a good thing that over seven hundred people gathered at the Town Hall for the third Wine, Beer and Cheese Party, proceeds of £100 later being handed over to the ailing club.

Surrey departed and Middlesex came to the Festival, as Tom Graveney was thumping 165 off the West Indies attack back at the Oval. The capital was vibrant, but not just with cricket, for according to *Time Magazine,* the 'swinging city' had 'burst into bloom' and Carnaby Street and King's Road were the hub of the fashion capital of the world.

Fashion was such at Cheltenham that Gloucestershire in the previous two fixtures had won the toss, batted first and lost the match. The trend was not broken. Middlesex gained a first innings lead of 158, largely due to Peter Parfitt making 96, with Smith taking 6 for 91. Then, for the first time in the Festival, the hosts topped 200 as West Indian Richard Stewart, a trialist with Gloucestershire at the start of the season, took 5 for 63. The damage had been done and the visitors reached their target of 75 in under an hour, for the loss of one wicket.

—— **1967** ——

At the start of its new season, on the back of the World Cup success, football was enjoying waves of enthusiasm. The county, suffering from indeterminate batting and financial gloom, was low in the championship table and about to receive another whitewashing at Cheltenham.

This was the 'the summer of love'. 'Flower people' danced and recited poems about peace as the county's supporters made their way to the College ground hoping to savour success. For the first time in the Festival's history four matches had been arranged, Richard McCrudden describing it as 'an experiment, purely for financial reasons'. There was no extra cost in putting on the fourth match, so receipt records stood a chance of being broken. It all hinged on two factors: good weather and absorbing cricket.

On the opening morning, the band of the 1st Battalion, The Gloucestershire Regiment marched from the Promenade to the ground, but it was evident soon after the start of play, that the hosts' batting lacked the bandsmen's discipline. On a damp wicket, Worcestershire's opening bowlers, Bob Carter and Jack Flavell, caused havoc, quickly reducing the home side to 43 for 6. A little flurry of runs from the tail-enders held matters up until mid-afternoon when Gloucestershire were all out for 123, partly due to the brilliant fielding at short-leg by Ron Headley who took five catches.

The visitors batted steadily and despite Allen's figures (36-13-75-5), gained a first innings lead of 124. By close of play on the second day Gloucestershire, on 72 for 1, had started to fight back. The revival was led by Ron Nicholls (58), but bad weather prevented play until after lunch on the final day. Then Norman Gifford (34-23-53-5) struck, taking the last 4 wickets for 2 runs, as the hosts slumped to 155 all out before the visitors went on to win by 10 wickets.

Next day, a monsoon-like downpour brought a sudden end to the afternoon's play against Pakistan, who had recently suffered a ten wicket defeat in the Test match at Trent Bridge. A large crowd had been expected because it was early closing day, but play and takings were washed away and the tourists returned early to the Hotel Majestic.

When the game continued, bowlers from both sides enjoyed the conditions. Bissex (28.5-12-84-5) and Mortimore (19-5-60-5) dismissed the tourists for 176, then Intikhab Alam (30.1-8-52-7) caused problems as Milton and Brown made fifties in Gloucestershire's total of 208. That

" Of course cricket isn't the same. Why, only yesterday as I went in, I was searched for empty bottles and toilet rolls."

Festival fun in the *Gloucestershire Echo*, 1967

evening players from both teams mingled amongst the six hundred guests at a party in the Town Hall, where entertainment was provided by Peter Tilley's Showband, Shurdington's Gaiety Girls, the Singing Waiters and the Can Can girls from the Newman School of Dancing.

Pakistan made quick progress next day, reaching 214 after some lively hitting by Ghulam Abbas (64) who cracked 3 sixes and 6 fours, while Bissex (20-4-73-5) and Mortimore (10-1-42-4) gave the county a sight of victory. But the Pakistani bowlers would have none of this and left-armer Pervez (13.3-5-21-6), with Intikhab (22-6-51-4), bowled out their opponents for 133, which was 49 runs short of their target.

Lancashire, low in the table like their hosts, very nearly achieved victory in the next close-fought contest. Batting first, the visitors recovered from a poor start to make 284, with Shuttleworth, Pullar and Higgs the main contributors. With his successful England career behind him, Brian Statham was now captain of his county, and with Ken Higgs he made early inroads into Gloucestershire's batting, reducing them to 66 for 5. History then repeated itself as all the tail-enders chipped in towards the final total of 264. Reducing Lancashire to 81 for 6 in the second innings put Gloucestershire into a strong position, but Lloyd (41*) and Shuttleworth (50*) enabled Statham to declare, leaving the hosts to make 190 in one hundred and forty minutes. They struggled to reach 132 for 9 against a penetrating attack, the *Yearbook* recording: 'Gloucestershire made heavy weather of their task, but just managed to avert defeat.'

On the first day of the match against third-placed Leicestershire, 'wasps in waves like attacking aircraft continually assaulted the press tent' according to A. A. Thomson, writing in the *Times*. 'But none was so waspish,' he remarked 'as the spin attack of Lock and Birkenshaw which disposed of Gloucestershire early in the afternoon for a woefully modest total.' Jack Birkenshaw (16.3-2-34-6) and Tony Lock (19-7-37-4) bowled out their hosts for 106, then both featured the next day in an eighth wicket partnership of 119 in ninety minutes as the visitors built up a first innings lead of 248.

It was about time Gloucestershire's batsmen dug in and eked out some runs, for there had been a run-famine in recent years and this was not good news for the Festival organisers; above all, spectators like to see batsmen scoring. They rose to the challenge and made 402, their highest Festival total for sixteen years.

One person on the ground not impressed was Mrs Evelyn Gough, the 'ladies' tent attendant, whose view of the cricket was 'conveniently' blocked by the sightscreen. The seventy-three-year-old told the *Echo* that cricket meant nothing to her, commenting, 'I do more knitting here than I do the rest of the year put together.'

Despite Gloucestershire's efforts, Leicestershire had no difficulty in scoring 158, to win by 6 wickets. Finishing the season at the bottom of the championship table now seemed inevitable for Gloucestershire. Local supporters went home chewing over the words of the club's chairman, Jack Clarke, who had mentioned the possibility of Sunday play on the College ground in the near future when he was speaking at the Rotary Club's weekly luncheon.

'We have to be progressive,' Mr Clarke told the *Echo*. 'The College Council have been approached and we await their decision on the matter.'

—— **1968** ——

Boasting its new status as an Area of Outstanding Natural Beauty the Cotswolds experienced a delayed harvest; the week before the Festival, Cheltenham's meteorological office recorded just over five hours of sunshine. This threatened to make a difficult start for the county's new secretary Grahame Parker, who had recently taken up the post following Richard McCrudden's death at the end of the previous year. There were other changes too: Arthur Milton was captain, David Green had arrived from Lancashire and was to have a splendid Festival, while Mike Procter had exploded onto the scene, although knee trouble was preventing him from bowling at this stage in the season.

The Festival commenced with David Smith's benefit match against Worcestershire, during which the beneficiary himself took his one thousandth wicket for Gloucestershire. A swashbuckling 79 by Ron Headley led the visitors to 224, then Basil D'Oliveira (27-11-51-6) bowled his side to a first innings lead of 45. Headley, with a half-century, thwarted the hosts again, as Brown (17-4-28-5) helped to keep the game within Gloucestershire's reach, the visitors being dismissed for 166. Needing to score 212 in three and a quarter hours, David Green led the way with 72, but everyone else struggled against Carter (20-3-59-5) and D'Oliveira (14.2-2-29-4) and the visitors won by 53 runs.

Given the go-ahead, Jack Clarke's idea had been a resounding success, with over 6,000 people, the largest crowd seen on the ground for many years, watching Festival cricket on a Sunday for the first time. There was seating on the ground for 2,500, but missing from the arena was the familiar steep stand that had stood in front of the gymnasium every year since the early days of the Cricket Week. Recently, it had lost its popularity because of young boys causing a nuisance running up and down the steps. Stands, tents and the small scoreboard had all been shuffled round, and in a tent in front of the science block a small collection of Gloucestershire cricket memorabilia was on display, including the bat with which W. G. Grace hit his hundredth hundred.

Writing in the *Echo,* Andy Wilson, describing Cheltenham as 'one of the most pleasant grounds in the country', reckoned that Gloucestershire needed to win two out of the three games in order to finish midway in the championship table. They narrowly missed out in both the remaining fixtures.

Stormy weather limited play against Sussex to less than eight hours, and rain finally brought the game to an abrupt end at lunch on the last day. It was a most unfortunate outcome for the county who had worked themselves into an unassailable position, thanks to some watchful batting by Ron Nicholls (91) and hard hitting by David Shepherd (59). In reply, Sussex struggled from the offset and on a difficult wicket they declared on 44 for 9, having saved the follow-on. Bissex finished with very impressive figures (4-2-2-4) before the rain arrived.

David Green opened the innings against Surrey, making a brisk 92, reminiscent of the way in which Charlie Barnett used to set about the opposition. At the opposite end of the innings, Mortimore (46*) hitting 3 sixes, and Smith (21) hitting 2 sixes, featured in a last wicket stand of 64 in half an hour, thus enabling their side to reach 242. The visitors were in disarray against Mortimore, Allen and Bissex and were bowled out for 176, whereafter Gloucestershire made 104 for 4 declared, leaving Surrey ninety-five minutes to make 171 - a tall order on a spinner's wicket. In the absence of Arthur Milton, David Allen was captaining the team and he must have wished that he had given his side more time to bowl at the opposition, for at the close they were 43 for 6, finding life at the crease most uncomfortable.

According to the cricket writer and broadcaster Alan Gibson, discomfort was also being experienced on the ground every time anyone visited the 'ladies' or 'gents'. Gateman Richard Sharp remembers the 'gents' as 'a hole in the ground, with two planks to stand on, surrounded by canvas'. Gibson wrote at length about the improvised facilities and how out-of-keeping they were with Cheltenham's regency splendour, and when a woman had the misfortune to fall into the 'ladies pit', he likened the incident to the relief of Mafeking.

Ablutions apart, Andy Wilson, writing in the *Echo,* raised the age-old debate about fans in the north of the county being convinced that Cheltenham, rather than Bristol, was the best centre for county cricket. He was happy to admit that 'there is more atmosphere about cricket at Cheltenham than at Bristol . . . it's a Festival after all - and we have the tents and the splendid academic setting', but he was aware that 'administratively, it would not be practical'.

Author and poet Kit Wright recalls an event involving his father, a 'steadfast visitor', who savoured the atmosphere during the sixties:

'He used to go every year with another old prep school master, the only one to be able to drive. But only just; and so difficult did my father's friend find the one-way system that he broke down in tears.'

Fortunately, his father found a policeman who 'sat in the back of the car and tutored the driver in the intricacies of the network' and accepted a pint of beer after guiding them safely to the ground.

Kit Wright's own poignant poem about the 'Festival Fringe', *Understudies,* must strike a chord with would-be cricket stars of all ages:

> The Cheltenham Cricket Festival Fringe
> Unravelled on a long green lawn
> Under a house of weathered brick
> That rose in the year my father was born.
>
> The Henry brothers in Fifties summers
> That memory vows had never a cloud
> Were batsman, bowler, fieldsman, umpire,
> Scorer, commentator and crowd.
>
> The Henry brothers, Michael and John,
> Were the whole alternative Gloucestershire side
> And all of the loyal opposition
> From early May till the Summer died.
>
> Enormous poppies as dark as peonies
> Softly split in the tall green light
> Of the chestnut tree with its candles glowing
> At close of play and the birth of night.
>
> And still it guards, that herbaceous boundary,
> Festival games as true as then.
> The Fringe is on with defiant cricketers,
> Boys disguised as middle-aged men . . .

—— 1969 ——

In fields and on lawns throughout the county, many of these 'alternative' matches would have been played in the summer of 1969. No doubt in most of them Gloucestershire would have won, for that was what was happening under the captaincy of Tony Brown. His positive approach to the game was reminiscent of former glorious years and when they arrived in Cheltenham, the county had been top of the championship table since June. Morale was high.

Heavy overnight thunderstorms prevented play from starting promptly on the first day. This brought disappointment for the crowd and Festival organisers, but while the players sat and waited for action to commence, they heard some very pleasing news from club chairman, Michael Jarrett, when he announced that it had been decided by the club to give the players £1,000 if they won the championship.

Spirits rose even higher when the sun appeared, a breeze got up and play started. To the delight of the supporters, Tony Brown (18.4-7-18-5) and Mike Procter (17-8-23-4) proceeded to skittle Worcestershire out for 98.

The following day saw the first John Player Sunday League game on the ground, bringing in takings of over £1,000. On a hot, sunny afternoon, Tom Graveney won the toss, elected to bat and Rodney Cass and Ron Headley gave the visitors an excellent start, making 56 in eleven overs. The crowd of around 8,000 then witnessed the dismissal of Graveney with a catch by Tony Brown, 'one of the greatest ever seen on the College ground' according to the *Echo*, adding 'even Graveney joined in the applause as he walked off'. Chasing a total of 152, after a poor start, Mike Bissex (46*) and his captain steered their side to a four wicket victory.

With the sound of Sunday's cheering crowd still filling their ears, Gloucestershire's batsmen took the upper hand on Monday in a hard fought day's play led by David Green (82) making his one thousandth run of the season for the county. Milton made 67 in just over three hours while newly-acquired 'Noddy' Pullar (62) had to retire with a bruised wrist as the hosts went on to declare at 258 for 4. By the close of play, Worcestershire had lost three wickets all to Procter, who was now at the top of the national bowling averages. They were still trailing by 126 runs and it seemed that the next day would be a mere formality.

'It was a cliff-hanger after all,' wrote Denzil Batchelor in *The Times*.

More thundery rain prevented play from beginning until twenty to four, when, under dark skies, 7 wickets fell for 33 runs. Mortimore (13.3-4-20-5) bowled the last man, Brain, as the rain returned and Gloucestershire snatched victory in the nick of time.

Worcestershire headed home and Tom Graveney, in his benefit year, had played his last game on the College ground. In a tribute to Graveney, Sir Neville Cardus wrote:

'If you add up all the notes of a Mozart symphony you'll know next to nothing of the style and rarity of the music. So with an innings by Tom. His batsmanship would still hold our attention and give delight to the eye, and to our appreciation of the meaning and appeal of cricket, if the scoreboard were taken away and abolished . . . Graveney, in fact, is one of the few batsmen of today you can call an artist, one who stimulates our aesthetic reactions.'

These were glowing words about the man who, when remembering playing on the ground, commented, 'It was always the beginning of the end of the season, it was cricket to be enjoyed . . . You had your fun cricket at Cheltenham.'

Never underestimate the Welsh dragon! In mid-July, Glamorgan had given Gloucestershire a good hiding at Cardiff, and on the eve of the return fixture on the College ground, the Welshmen were twenty-four points behind their hosts, with two matches in hand.

In *Gloucestershire Road*, Grahame Parker writes, 'The Gloucestershire innings opened shakily and the game was lost before lunch on the first day. A psychological paralysis had gripped the leading batsmen . . . For too long they had been looking over their shoulders at Glamorgan on the charge behind them.'

Writing in *The Times*, John Woodcock saw the opening encounter as 'Glamorgan's day to an overwhelming degree. In bowling, batting and fielding they gave Gloucestershire a lesson which could, when the season ends, be seen to have decided the championship'. To home supporters, these wounding words brought back waves of memories of that encounter on the ground against Middlesex in 1947, when similarly everything had gone horribly wrong.

Without Shepherd, Meyer or the injured Pullar, the hosts quickly found themselves 9 for 3 and by lunch they were 53 for 7. After the interval the nightmare continued in front of a large crowd, the local element of which was by now rather despondent, with Nash (15.2-6-37-6) making full use of the damp pitch as the hosts were all out for 73.

The not-out batsman was replacement wicket-keeper, Lancashire-born

Stuart Westley, enjoying the excitement of his county debut. Suddenly, there seemed to be nothing in the wicket for Gloucestershire's bowlers, although Westley remembers 'the difficulty keeping wicket to Mike Procter, who bowled from the edge of the crease and swung the ball in to the right handers'. But all this made little impression on Glamorgan's batsmen; furthermore, there was only slow turn for Allen and Mortimore.

After a steady start from Jones and Davis, Majid Khan came to the wicket and quickly showed everyone who was in charge. According to Nico Craven in *That Darn'd Elusive Championship,* 'Majid Khan waved his magic wand and wafted eleven boundaries - 3 sixes and 8 fours - in a jewel of an innings worth many more than the 69 runs recorded in cricket's domesday book of noughts 'n' crosses.'

At the close of play, the visitors were 198 for 4, pressing on next day to reach 283. Despite a defiant 52 by David Allen, the game was over by a quarter to seven that night and Glamorgan had won by an innings and 50 runs. They had raced to within eight points of Gloucestershire and were now on their way to winning the crown. A month earlier, many had come to Cheltenham for the funeral of the Rolling Stones' guitarist, Brian Jones, and since then a steady stream of mourners had visited his grave at the cemetery; Gloucestershire's defeat brought a further melancholy atmosphere to the town that night.

The gloom was cast aside the following evening at the Festival dance and discotheque in the Town Hall. Nothing could stop Alderman Dodwell and his committee from coming up with novel ideas to raise money, and this year he had organised a twenty minute, six-a-side indoor cricket match between county players and a 'W. G. Grace' team. Mike Procter, Ron Nicholls, Wycliffe Phillips, Ken Graveney and Don Perry were amongst those who cavorted round the ballroom floor as Aimbury Dodwell led his 'Grace' team to victory by twenty-two runs.

Another innovative idea was the scrapping of dress code. Anything cool, comfortable or casual was allowed and among the six hundred guests, mainly teenagers, dress ranged from young men in their sports clothes to girls in bikinis. Former England cricketer, Colin Milburn, who had recently lost the sight in one eye after a car crash, helped Cheltenham disc jockey Alan Pitman spin the records for the discotheque and the night proved to be a great success.

Rain ruined the final match against fourth-placed Warwickshire. Green and Milton gave their side a good start, but Tom Cartwright (33-17-44-5) and Lance Gibbs (30.1-8-58-4) bowled out their hosts for 189. By the end of a rain-interrupted second day, the visitors were 17 runs behind with 2 wickets left to fall; but all that fell from then on was rain, and the match was abandoned.

CHAPTER SEVENTEEN (1970-1975)

GLORIOUS GLOSTERS

—— 1970 ——

By the time they arrived in Cheltenham, Gloucestershire had nose-dived from top to bottom of the table in twelve months. Although it was centenary year, the club was in a quandary. The appeal had been a failure and support and morale in the club was at a low ebb. A good Festival was needed to re-charge the batteries.

Sunshine greeted the first day and the College ground looked in good shape as a result of the hard work put in by Geoff Edrich and the ground staff, still using the old school roller affectionately known as 'Genevieve'.

Hampshire were the first opponents and there was great pre-match excitement surrounding the possibility of fellow South Africans, Mike Procter and Barry Richards, opposing each other, dependent on the latter recovering from a back injury. Richards played and on the third day he set the Festival alight.

Tony Brown won the toss, elected to bat and his team was soon 38 for 4. They were rescued by the two Mikes, Bissex (50) and Procter (61), before the last 5 wickets fell for 51 runs and they were all out for 190. Gaining a first innings lead of 17, largely due to Mortimore's bowling (20-2-58-5), and helped by another half-century from Bissex, the hosts plodded to to 139 for 8 by the close of play on the second day.

Gloucestershire's tail wagged productively the following morning, a last-wicket stand between Meyer and Smith realising 76, leaving Hampshire to make 247 in just over four hours. After lunch, in forty-five phenomenal minutes, Barry Richards punished everything that was bowled at him during a glorious innings of 94, which included 2 sixes and 9 fours. Going for the big hit to reach his century, he was stumped by Meyer, but the damage had been done and the visitors went on to win by 4 wickets.

In *Gloster's Centenary Cricket*, Nico Craven writes, 'The day had given us weather and a setting worthy of great cricket. Richards had provided all that was needed to complete the perfect picture.'

The next visitors were champions Glamorgan, who proudly flew the pennant on the College flagpole. Once again, Tony Brown won the toss and chose to bat first and it seemed to have been a wise decision when the county were dismissed before lunch on the second day for 324. Local supporters were smiling even more when the visitors were 15 for 2 after eight overs. Before play was resumed after lunch, players and spectators observed a minute's silence in memory of the late Syd Buller who had played and umpired several times on the ground and whose funeral was taking place in nearby Worcester that afternoon.

Meanwhile, Majid Khan had obviously heard what Barry Richards had done earlier in the week. Throughout the afternoon Majid (157) batted magnificently, balls banging over the boundary like supersonic Concorde which was flying once again from Fairford, after four months on the ground while being fitted with more powerful engines. He featured in two delightfully entertaining partnerships, firstly putting on 176 in two hours with Tony Lewis (87), then 119 with Bryan Davis (63). Bad light brought an early end to an enthralling day's play, with Glamorgan 32 runs ahead and everything set up for the final day.

The start was promising with Green and Nicholls knocking off the deficit and pushing on to 64 before the first wicket fell. As had happened so often earlier in the season, the county's batting then fell apart as Don Shepherd (41.4-18-46-5) and Peter Walker (41-20-66-5) bowled them out for 152. Needing 121, the visitors cruised to victory by 5 wickets, so completing two successive crushing defeats. Nico Craven wrote, 'Perhaps I may be forgiven for having given a sigh of relief when I heard that Glamorgan would be by-passing Cheltenham in '71.'

The final opponents were old rivals Kent, also celebrating their centenary year. Six weeks earlier they had been alongside Gloucestershire at the bottom of the table, but their fortunes had improved, while others faltered, and on arriving in Cheltenham they were charging towards winning the championship.

For the third time, the hosts batted first and made the familiar poor start. It was 33 for 3 when Mike Bissex came to the wicket, but he soon scored his one thousandth run of the season and then made his way to a maiden championship century (104), featuring in a 128 run partnership with David Shepherd (52). Derek Underwood (34.2-16-68-6) took full advantage of the slope by bowling from the College end, and the county were eventually dismissed just before the close of play for 289.

That night strong winds and heavy rain swept through the Forest of Dean and across the Cotswolds, damaging fruit, vegetable and corn crops. In Cheltenham, trees blocked roads, while on the College ground a tent was flattened and the main scoreboard overturned; but it did not stop Kent from winning Sunday's JPL match by 6 wickets.

On Monday morning Kent were soon 13 for 2, and by early afternoon they were all out for 140, so missing the follow-on by one run. Mortimore had taken 5 for 43. Batting again, Gloucestershire scored at a good rate, making 190 at under a run-a-minute, leaving the visitors to score 340 in six and a half hours.

The final day began with Kent needing 320 runs with 9 wickets standing. It was a tall order indeed, but Mike Denness (97) and Asif Iqbal (109) rose to the challenge and featured in a fourth wicket stand of 105 in ninety-five minutes, steering their side towards 'mission impossible'. At tea, with Asif on 106*, the visitors needed 11 runs to win with 4 wickets standing and many local spectators packed their bags and left for home.

It was a foolish move, for while the tea cups were being washed up, there was drama, as described in the next day's *Echo:*

'It is one of the fascinations of cricket that it can provide those prolonged periods of tenseness which no other sport can quite match; those naive enough to refer to it as a dull game should have been forced to watch those remarkably tense final overs at the College last night.'

During these final overs, Asif added three more runs before being caught by Meyer. Then Underwood, attempting a mighty six, was caught on the mid-wicket boundary by Green. More runs were scored before Bissex bowled Graham. With two still needed for victory, last man Dye survived the final ball of the over, then a pull to leg from Leary, followed by the same shot from Dye, gave the visitors thirteen points and they were a step nearer their title.

From a Gloucestershire viewpoint, the Festival star was Mike Bissex, who was awarded his county cap. Despite the disappointing results, a profit of almost £1,000 had been made, but possibly most important of all were the memories that many spectators would take home. Over the winter months they could reminisce about those golden performances by a number of gifted batsmen, which contributed to a centenary special.

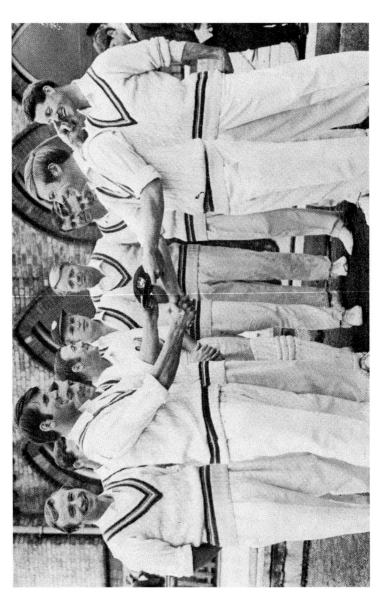

Tony Brown presents Mike Bissex with his county cap in 1970

—— **1971** ——

After a poor start to the season the county rallied, and by Festival time they were within striking distance of the top of the championship table. Their progress faltered on the College ground, and due to rain and inconsistent batting all three matches were drawn.

The Festival opened with a presentation. Nico Craven had been so impressed with the contributions made by Mike Bissex in 1970, that over the winter he had come up with the idea of awarding 'Glorious Glosters', the equivalent of 'Oscars', for the best Gloucestershire performance in each match and for the player adjudged to be 'Man of the Festival'. Craven sought, and gained, support for his idea from Michael Jarrett, Grahame Parker and the local committee, and when given the nod he persuaded the famous sculptress, Josephina de Vasconcellos, to design the award which was then cast in Surrey by Victor Tozer.

On the Saturday morning before play started, Mike Bissex was awarded the first bronze casting for his outstanding contributions the previous year. It was in the form of a hand holding a miniature flagpole from which hung a flag made of a cravat in the county's colours. There were four more 'Glosters' to be won over the next ten days with the county providing adjudicators and the county chairman giving his full approval, convinced the awards would enhance the whole Festival.

The beautiful copperplate handwriting of Bert Avery, now the county scorer, recorded Gloucestershire on 64 without loss at lunch against Worcestershire, with Nicholls and Lanchbury matching each other for runs. At the start of August, Evesham-born Robert Lanchbury, a former Cheltenham Grammar School boy, had replaced the injured, forty-three-year-old Arthur Milton, and the morning's play had been a dream start for the Lord's ground staff youngster. Wickets fell throughout the afternoon and by the close of play the visitors were 18 for 2, having lost Glenn Turner for nought, in reply to Gloucestershire's total of 213.

On Sunday, the county entertained Warwickshire in a JPL match, and a classy 74 from Ron Nicholls steered his team to a 30 run victory in front of a crowd of over 6,000. The good news continued on Monday, with Worcestershire being quickly spun out for 87. The damage was done by the economical Mortimore (22.2-15-18-3) together with Bissex (21-7-50-7) who, in returning his career best figures, also earned himself another 'Gloster' award, presented to him at the end of the match. Meanwhile, there followed some brisk run scoring by the hosts, with

255

David Shepherd's unbeaten 51 enabling a declaration to be made. The visitors were left needing 337 to win the match.

It was a tall order on a wicket that was taking spin, but rain ruined the last day, reducing the proceeds for Barrie Meyer's benefit match. With only fifty minutes of play possible, Worcestershire were spared defeat, finishing on 74 for 4.

Funds were still low, and in order to reduce outlay costs the players' and members' large marquee had been dispensed with. For the first time, players ate in the College tuck shop while members made do with an extension to the main public tent. Northamptonshire arrived and David Allen returned to the Gloucestershire side having been out of action since May, so he and Mortimore were in harness again. A difficult pitch and interruptions from rain were the main features of a low-scoring game which was abandoned, with Gloucestershire on 90 for 3 chasing 266 for victory.

Although Mortimore and Bissex both claimed five wickets in an innings, it was David Allen's five in the match that won the judges vote for the 'Gloster'. Reporting in *The Times,* Alan Gibson wrote, 'A Gloucestershire member gives a trophy to the best Gloucestershire player in each match of the Festival. It is, to be sure, a rather alarming trophy, a replica of a large fist, just the thing to coax baby to sleep. Henry Blofeld, the adjudicator, wisely awarded the honour to Allen.'

Rain prevented Bert Avery's pen from writing anything in the scorebook on the first day of the match against Hampshire. The atrocious weather meant that despite the huge efforts that were being made, the club was now looking at a loss at Cheltenham of around £1,000. It was grim news, alongside the report that a thousand diseased elm trees in the town needed to be cut down and the news that unemployment in the area was higher now than at any time since the war.

Richards and Greenidge got the visitors off to a brisk start when play eventually began just after midday on Monday. At about the same time, the mayor, Charles Irving, was giving his assurance that the town council would give financial support to the county if it felt unable to afford to play in Cheltenham. After ninety-nine years of cricket in the town, the idea of using Bristol and its permanent facilities as an alternative to Cheltenham was being banded around again. This would save the county some £3,000. But if the town could subsidise the Music Festival, the mayor could see no reason why money could not be put aside to support the Cricket Festival: 'Everyone should have a slice of the cake.'

Back on the field of play, Mortimore, Allen and Bissex had their guests in a spin, dismissing them for 130. However, by the close of play, Sainsbury and Cottam had dished out some similar treatment, having reduced their hosts to 77 for 6. The sun shone on the final day as Hampshire nearly pocketed the points for victory. Building on their first innings lead of 33, the visitors declared at 150 for 5, leaving their opponents just over two and a half hours to reach the target. A poor start led to the early arrival of Procter and Knight, whose 71 run partnership in an hour placed their side in an encouraging position at tea. However, the interval proved to be their downfall and the county plunged from being likely winners to embarrassed losers as 6 wickets fell for 10 runs. Once again, the destroyers were Sainsbury (23-10-42-5) and Cottam (27-10-64-4), but they could not winkle out the last pair, Meyer and Davey, before the end, with Gloucestershire still 52 runs short of their target.

Mike Procter won the 'Gloster' award for the match, while David Shepherd, top scorer in three of the innings, picked up the man of the Festival 'Gloster'. Optimism was in the air as Harold Bishop, the county treasurer, confirmed that preparations were underway for the following year's visitors to the College ground - Lancashire, Warwickshire, Derbyshire and Middlesex. The treasurer reminded everyone that given good weather, money could be made at the Festival. It was reassuring to know that one hundred years of cricket at Cheltenham would be celebrated in twelve months' time.

—— 1972 ——

The curtain rose with wining, dining and dancing. This year, yet again, Gloucestershire had a chance of clinching the title if they won all three matches. An extra stand had been erected at the Chapel end, between the scoreboard and the sightscreen, and there was feverish activity on the ground as the BBC cameras were installed in preparation for televising the JPL match against Warwickshire. David Allen, Barrie Meyer and Mike Bissex had all made their final Festival appearances the previous year, but into the fold had come one of *Wisden's* Five Cricketers of the Year, Zaheer Abbas, along with fellow Pakistan Test batsman, Sadiq Mohammad. At long last the batting had been strengthened, and all the ingredients were on hand for a very special centenary celebration.

With Tony Brown unfit, Mike Procter won the toss and chose to bat first against Lancashire. Controversy was in the air, for this was David Allen's benefit match and it had been expected that he would play, despite the fact that on the few occasions he had played throughout the summer his wickets had been rather expensive. He was not chosen and instead his place went to David Graveney who was no stranger to the ground. He had watched both his father (Ken) and uncle (Tom) playing for Gloucestershire, and remembers the occasion in 1964 'when my father was caught by my uncle off the bowling of Jack Flavell to give Worcestershire victory'.

Opening up the Festival for the last time, Arthur Milton (63), timing his sweet drives and glances to perfection, gave the county just the start they needed. Three runs short of a century-opening partnership with Ron Nicholls, Milton - later the worthy winner of the 'Gloster' - was bowled, prompting the entry of the gold-rimmed bespectacled Zaheer Abbas. Since joining the club, he had played little county cricket and his Cheltenham debut was inauspicious as he promptly trudged back to the pavilion without scoring. The middle order rallied, but wickets continued to fall and the county were bowled out for 218; by the close of play Lancashire, on 74 for 1, were chasing confidently.

There was great excitement on Sunday with the arrival of cameramen and commentators for the historic, first-ever televising of cricket on the College ground. Play started and before viewers had settled into their chairs at home, Gloucestershire had lost 2 wickets without scoring a run. The rest of the afternoon belonged to Mike Procter, who made 109* in 23 overs and kept those self same viewers perched on the edge of their chairs, absorbing his brisk batting display amidst the Gothic setting. This was a television spectacular befitting any centenary celebration, until rain rudely intruded onto the screen leaving the pundits to recount the innings and debate the 'what might have beens'.

Championship cricket returned next morning, with Gloucestershire faithfuls hoping the heavy rain would have affected the wicket to make life difficult for Lancashire. Instead, their batsmen became more watchful and resolute and David Lloyd (104), Harry Pilling (94) and Clive Lloyd (72) steered their side to 354 for 7 before a declaration was made, leaving the hosts a lot to do on the final day. It was too much, and in the end rain was their saviour as they tottered to 174 for 9 by the close, 38 runs ahead and only a hair's breadth away from defeat.

That night, as Lancashire departed and Derbyshire arrived, the band of the Royal Gloucestershire Hussars gave a concert at the Town Hall. It was the forerunner of a series of celebrations arranged by the Festival committee, and the music must have been playing in the Gloucestershire's players ears all next day as they started to overhaul their guests. By the close of play, thanks to the determination of Ron Nicholls, the hosts had made 88 for 2, half the visitors' total.

In advance of the centenary buffet supper to be held in the College dining hall, MCC president Freddie Brown arrived on the ground next day and was treated to a feast of runs by Nicholls (82) and Procter (95). Gloucestershire reached 303 and this was followed by a mini-revival from the visitors. It was steadfast county cricket, the likes of which had taken place on the ground for a hundred years.

The MCC president was joined by Gloucestershire's patron, the Duke of Beaufort; their president, Jack Clarke; chairman, Mike Jarrett; the mayor, Alderman Terry Joyner and his wife, along with the players from both sides and many other guests. The theme of the evening was to ensure that cricket survived for another hundred years and everyone present was asked to write their name on one pound notes and hand them in for a draw, the proceeds of which would go towards financing the county's efforts to find and nurture young players from within its boundaries. There were several speeches before Mr Brown's congratulationary address when he spoke of 'the delightful ground', emphasising how the College 'lends itself to attractive cricket where the batsman has a chance to make his strokes all day'.

In his final year with Derbyshire, South African batsman Chris Wilkins pushed on to an attractive century next day, as newcomer David Graveney (26-14-63-5) and seasoned professional John Mortimore (38-15-73-4) winkled out the visitors for 232 just before lunch. This left bags of time for Gloucestershire to make the 106 runs needed for victory, but they made heavy weather of their task. On 90 for 5 anything could have happened, but a few more runs and a whack from Shepherd secured 18 points and Ron Nicholls cheerfully collected the 'Gloster' award.

The championship was still within the county's grasp and the chatter was all about this at the Sportsmen's Dance in the Town Hall that night. Year by year, the event was becoming more popular and the Town Hall dress rule was waived as usual, in order to attract a wide variety of outfits from the members of the various sporting clubs in town. Still masterminding the occasion was Alderman Dodwell who told the *Echo,* 'I am always disappointed that the swimming and water polo clubs do not take us literally. I would love to see them attending the sportsmen's dance in the gear applicable to their particular sport!' Another indoor cricket match took place and there was a 'yard of ale' competition, with the evening's proceeds being shared between the club and David Allen's benefit fund.

Just as they had done twenty-five years ago, Middlesex spoilt the party. The swaggering city boys showed no compassion for the title chasers, stuffed the bulk of the points into their pockets on the final day of the Festival and ensured Gloucestershire would finish the season third in the table.

Winning the toss, Gloucestershire batted first and Zaheer's delightful 75 was his highest county championship score of the season. The hosts reached 260, despite some excellent pace-bowling from John Price (16.2-5-40-7), before the visitors took a first innings lead of 28. By close of play on the second day Gloucestershire were 50 runs ahead with 6 wickets remaining, and matters looked decidedly dicey for the final day. Zaheer top-scored with 58, his two stylish innings earning him the 'Gloster' award, while Edmonds (31-12-64-4) and Titmus (23.4-9-56-5) bowled their hosts out for 177. Middlesex effortlessly scored the 150 runs needed to win and Gloucestershire's two month unbeaten run, during which they had amassed 130 points, had come to an end.

It was also the end of an era: Arthur Milton's Festival playing days had finished. 'Happy times,' he recalls, 'in beautiful surroundings, where the cricket was always entertaining.'

—— **1973** ——

On the recommendation of the Test and County Cricket Board's Pitches Committee, the Festival wickets were prepared by David Bridle, groundsman at the county ground, Bristol. During each of the previous two years, inspector of pitches Bert Locke had been called in and it had been agreed that there was room for improvement. With the West Indies coming to town, it was important to have matters right on the field. The visitors were without a scorer, so Mrs Poulton, Gloucester City's scorer, took on the job with Bert Avery and together they had great fun trying to work out who the tourists were.

'I bought her a souvenir tour book,' said Bert, 'but it was impossible to match the names with the pictures, they just didn't correspond. Faces had changed, beards had been grown and others had been shaved off!'

They had plenty of time to make their minds up, as the tourists over rate was a deplorable thirteen per hour. At the close of play, Gloucestershire had reached 213 for 9, Zaheer's stylish 81 being the highlight of the day's play. After a wet weekend, the College ground quickly filled up when play commenced after lunch on Monday and

John Mortimore inspects the pitch in 1973

onlookers were entertained by Headley (62) and Boyce, who followed up his 5 for 45 with an innings of 87. Clinging to a slender first innings advantage, the hosts lost further play on the final morning, but during the afternoon they extended their lead, declaring soon after tea. This left the visitors twenty-one overs in which to make 110 to win.

In *Best Out of Five,* Nico Craven describes the game's conclusion: 'The weather had the last word. Eleven balls remained to be bowled when a sudden short sharp shower sent the players in search of shelter from the storm. West Indies needed six runs and Gloucestershire two wickets. Both were denied the fruits of victory.'

The next match, against Worcestershire, provided an opportunity for a little bit of neighbourly sparring in a rehearsal for the following week's Gillette Cup semi-final at New Road. Winning the toss, the hosts chose to bat, and by the close they were rubbing their hands with delight, having made 270 before pinning their guests down on 25 for 4.

It was Mike Procter's match. After his first innings score of 40, he stamped his authority on the game by catching out Worcestershire's opener, Parker, then taking the wickets of Ormrod, Khan and Cass in four balls. The visitors never recovered and were bowled out for 135. Procter, now firing on all cylinders, exchanged the ball for the bat and when stumps were drawn on the second day he had made 106* in just under two and a half hours. This enabled Tony Brown to declare on 218 for 8, leaving his opponents to make 354 in six hours during the last day. On a wearing pitch, the visitors started well, but during the afternoon, after Glenn Turner had been dismissed for 70, John Mortimore (37-12-101-6) took charge of matters. However, control was momentarily wrestled away from him just before the end of Worcestershire's innings when last man in, John Inchmore, clubbed him for 30 runs in an over. He hit 3 sixes followed by 3 fours, before being caught on the boundary by Mortimore off the bowling of Graveney on the seventh ball he received. Victory went to Gloucestershire by 138 runs and unsurprisingly the 'Gloster' went to Mike Procter.

Over the next four days, Gloucestershire outplayed Warwickshire to win the JPL by 146 runs and the championship match by 228 runs. The visitors were somewhat depleted, having lost Kanhai, Kallicharran, Murray and Gibbs to the West Indies touring team, while Amiss was playing for England. When Procter (118) cracked his second successive century and guided his team to a first innings total of 325, the midlanders had a steep hill to climb.

They fought hard and avoided the follow-on, but Gloucestershire were soon building on their first innings lead of 123 and Procter's 28 runs from ten balls sent the locals home feeling very happy. Their delight continued next day when the visitors were bowled out before lunch for 100, allowing ample time for Gillette Cup thoughts and dreams in advance of their journey to Worcester the following day.

—— 1974 ——

Gloucestershire's victory by five runs beside the Severn, followed by triumph in the final at Lord's against Sussex, all seemed a distant memory when champions Worcestershire opened the 1974 Festival in great style, as the two old enemies - economics and rain - tried their best to wreck proceedings once again.

There was yet another obstacle that the county had to overcome, that of injured players. The *Echo* reported, 'Never in the history of Gloucestershire cricket has it been more pertinent to mention that the Cheltenham Festival is played on a ground opposite a hospital.' There were seven players on the injured list, and Grahame Parker quipped that they should all be put in hospital for the night and wheeled out across the road and on to the ground in the morning!

On the opening day, Worcestershire declared on 390 for 5, making full use of the excellent batting strip produced by David Bridle. Backbone of the total was Glenn Turner's four and a half hour innings of 181, consisting of a six and 28 fours - 'a sparkling exhibition', according to *Wisden*, which 'laid the foundation of Worcestershire's easy win'. By the close of play, Gloucestershire had reached 57 for no wicket, but the rain clouds moved in and the potential money-spinning JPL match had to be abandoned the next day.

With the weekend deluge over, play began after lunch on Monday with Worcestershire's bowlers impossible to cope with on a wicked, drying wicket. It was nearly all over that night, but Gloucestershire, who had already been dismissed for 142, hung on until the next morning before being bowled out a second time for 122. Gifford and D'Oliveira caused the county's downfall with match analysis of 40.5-13-67-9 and 33-13-64-8 respectively.

Then the bickering started and yet again civil war raged in the county, bringing north against south: Cheltenham was doomed, Bristol would take all. Sunday's JPL wash-out had deprived the county of around £1,000, adding fuel to the fire and weight to the argument of the Bristol members who had put forward a plan some weeks earlier to take all the following year's fixtures for themselves. The wound had burst wide open again and when Grahame Parker commented, 'It is a wonderful festival, but Gloucestershire CCC have serious economic problems and must look at them overall,' the locals decided it was time for action.

The mayor, Councillor David Martin-Jones, led the way by announcing the formation of the Society of Friends of the Cheltenham Cricket Festival. Talks were immediately held between officers of the newly-formed society and Frank Twiselton, the county chairman, resulting in the society making a pledge to guarantee raising £3,500 to stage the Festival in 1975.

The news was announced over the public address system at lunch-time on the first day of the game against Derbyshire. Gloucestershire supporters were already in high spirits for the weather was good, play had started on time after Tony Brown had won the toss with his lucky Winston Churchill memorial coin, and youthful Andy Stovold (42), along with the mature Ron Nicholls (53), had played attractively during the morning. Hearing that the short-term future of the Festival was safe, everyone enjoyed their lunch even more than usual, particularly Church of Scotland minister, Douglas Craig. As a former admirer of Wally Hammond and a Gloucestershire follower ever since, he was making his fifth successive six hundred-mile round-trip from Galloway, devoting his entire holiday to cricket at Cheltenham. He told the *Echo* that he liked 'the atmosphere' of the Festival and would not contemplate watching cricket at Bristol or Gloucester, where 'there is no atmosphere'.

During the afternoon, Indian spinner Venkataraghaven reminded spectators that bowlers also played a part in the Festival, as he worked his way through Gloucestershire's batsmen to return his season-best figures 37.3-8-102-7. On a slow-turner next day, David Graveney (36.5-13-70-7), despite being hampered by a split spinning finger, maintained the bowlers' grip on the match by collecting the best bowling figures of his short career, so giving his side a first innings lead of 108.

As a celebration of the Festival's safekeeping, openers Nicholls and Stovold put on 140 for the first wicket at the start of the county's second innings. It had been reported that forged banknotes were circulating round Cheltenham and a number of local traders had suffered. There was nothing counterfeit about the way in which these two set about their business. Right from the start, Andy Stovold was in charge, dispatching Alan Ward's first ball over the mid-wicket boundary for six. His style was reminiscent of Charlie Barnett, and Stovold smiles as he recalls the bowler's retort, 'If this little fellow can hit me out of the ground, I'm packing up.'

Twenty minutes after play had started the following morning, Stovold reached his century. It was an outstanding innings by the young player and was the first hundred by a Gloucestershire wicket-keeper since Andy Wilson's at Dudley twenty-one years earlier. Nico Craven remarked that 'The applause lasted longer than usual . . . I was delighted. It indicated to me that it wasn't just what you did, but also the way you did it, that still counted for something in the first class world of cricket.' Declaring on 238 for 2, the visitors were left five hours to make 347, but rain significantly curtailed play and they finished on 133 for 3.

Staffordshire-born Andy Brassington made his Cheltenham debut in the next match against Nottinghamshire. 'I was really nervous', he recalls, 'but Roger Knight looked after me.' The first morning was lost to rain along with the whole of the last day, resulting in a draw. But when play was possible, Ron Nicholls made an elegant 68 in Gloucestershire's 282 and the visitors were dismissed for 172.

'On a drying wicket, the ball turned square,' recalls wicket-keeper Brassington, whose two catches off David Graveney (21-5-85-8), along with three by the agile Alastair Hignell, helped the left-armer improve on his career-best figures from the previous game, and brought back memories of Charlie Parker's huge hauls.

David Graveney recalls: 'The last Gloucestershire bowler to take ten wickets in an innings was my father against Derbyshire at Chesterfield, in 1949. It would have been nice to have followed in his footsteps, but when Bill Taylor middled one, hitting me for six, it wasn't to be.' Reflecting on Alastair Hignell's catches, the Gloucestershire spinner remarks, 'He was the bravest of fielders, standing close in for the bat pad catch, never wearing any body protection.'

Looking likely winners, Gloucestershire's cricketers were not the only frustrated people in town when further rain arrived. Outside G.C.H.Q., Benhall, civil servants had angrily stuck their umbrellas into the sodden grass on the roundabout, while demonstrating in support of their pay claim.

—— **1975** ——

When preparations were already well under way for the Festival, David Graveney and Andy Stovold received their 1974 'Glosters' at a Cheese and Wine party organised by the Gloucestershire Exiles at Lord's.

Four years earlier, at a small meeting in London, the Gloucestershire Exiles had been formed with Vincent Coronel as chairman, his wife Laura as treasurer, and Ken Daniels as secretary. Their aim was 'to promote the affairs of Gloucestershire CCC' among Gloucestershire followers living outside the county. Social events were organised and membership had grown rapidly, with the most popular gathering being the annual pilgrimage to Cheltenham.

For the first time, both Sundays were used for JPL matches, making the Festival eleven consecutive days. Fringe events consisted of a players' reception at the Victory Club and the unveiling of a plaque at Gilbert Jessop's birthplace - 30, Cambray. Above all, though, there was no shortage of hot sunshine, attracting large crowds and leading to record receipts.

Fifties by Luckhurst, Denness, Cowdrey and Woolmer enabled Kent to reach 257, but in the final session of play on the first day, a Gloucestershire charge, led by Zaheer, made the total look rather small.

Next day was everything that the 'Society of Friends' could have wished for. It emphasised the popularity of the event and the county cricket club treasurer could not believe his eyes. The fact that Kent won the JPL by 41 runs was immaterial as a crowd of 10,000 brought in a record income of £3,750 for the day. 'We are absolutely thrilled,' commented Grahame Parker. 'It provides proof of the great support we get in this end of the county, if proof is needed.' Saturday's crowd of over 5,000 had realised over £1,600, so after only two days of cricket, the county was already well in credit.

It was hard to imagine that things could get better, but they did. On Monday, 441 runs were scored in blazing sunshine and there were boundaries galore as Zaheer (111), Asif (67) and Cowdrey (94*) pasted the bowling. Next day when the visitors declared, Colin Cowdrey, still the supreme master of batsmanship, was left undefeated on 119. For Andy Wilson, Cowdrey's century was the highlight of the Festival and it left the hosts needing 343 runs to win in just over five hours.

At tea, they were charging along on 245 for 2, with Knight and Procter in complete command. After the interval, the tall, powerful, left-handed Knight, who had carefully built his innings before accelerating, continued on his way to a splendid 120, while Procter (58) took on the challenge in characteristic fashion. After their departure, Kent began to take a firm grip on the match. Gloucestershire ended up on 332 for 9, with *Wisden* reporting, 'It was an absorbing match full of entertaining cricket with changing fortunes and played under delightful conditions.'

Beating Warwickshire by 4 wickets in the next fixture gave the county their second championship victory of the season. The visitors' total of 263 was dominated by Kallicharran, who was run out on 98 going for a second run, so missing a well-deserved century. Gloucestershire's reply of 387 was made up of attractive contributions by Zaheer (91), Stovold (77) and Procter (63), and when Warwickshire were dismissed for 234, a mere 111 looked an easy target for the hosts. There followed some anxious moments in the home dressing-room as 3 for 3 became 57 for 6, but Shepherd (39*) and Graveney (16*) saw their side home. Looking as fit and lean as ever, John Mortimore had been coaxed out of retirement for this and the following game and the wily spinner finished with match figures of 58.5-26-84-5.

For the second year running, Worcestershire trounced their hosts, this time by an innings and 39 runs. Struggling at 138 for 7, the visitors were rescued by Basil D'Oliveira (80) and the tail-enders, who took the score to 297, and by the close Gloucestershire were wobbling on 50 for 3.

Next day, another bumper attendance justified what had been a controversial decision in switching the JPL game against Essex from Bristol. Receipts of almost £2,000 from a crowd of around 4,000 appeared to represent a clear endorsement of the judgement and meant that over £10,000 had now been taken at the Festival, amounting to £7,000 profit.

As the money was being paid into the bank, an astonishing collapse was in progress on the College ground, with six Gloucestershire wickets falling for 18 runs; all out for 68 in twenty-eight overs was a poor show as Imran Khan finished with the impressive figures of 11.3-2-36-6. Following on, 229 behind, the county batted with more confidence. Sadiq reached his fifty with a glorious cover drive, before Gifford dismissed both him and Shepherd in successive balls. Eight fielders clustered round the bat for the hat-trick ball, which Hignell attempted to play but missed. With Brown (71) playing a spirited captain's innings, but without the services of Zaheer and Procter, Gloucestershire looked frail and were finally dismissed for 190. So ended John Mortimore's final appearance on the ground, where he had played in a record seventy-one matches over a quarter of a century.

CHAPTER EIGHTEEN (1976-1979)

RECORDS, RAIN
AND THE CORPORATE GAME

—— 1976 ——

By the time the Festival arrived, Zaheer Abbas (fondly known as 'Zed') had established himself as one of the world's leading batsmen; he provided a thrilling start to proceedings by scoring 78 in seventy-five minutes against Glamorgan.

There was a fair bit of tut-tutting around the ground for the Festival was starting on a Wednesday, rather than the usual Saturday, and with just two championship matches and a JPL there was less than a week of cricket. But if quantity was lacking, the quality of play on the first day was definitely up to standard, for after Zaheer left the scene Procter (84) took over, helped by Shepherd and Graveney. With Gloucestershire dismissed for 339, Glamorgan made a brisk start to their reply, ending the day on 75 for 1.

On Thursday the visitors' captain, Alan Jones, led the way with 71 and everyone else chipped in to reach a total of 292. After tea Gloucestershire moved swiftly into a position of authority as Sadiq and Zaheer added 74 together, the latter plundering his way to a second match fifty. Next morning, Sadiq had reached 134* when Tony Brown declared, leaving the visitors just under four and a half hours to make 301. Another spirited innings from Jones (63) held Glamorgan together for a while, but when he was out, wickets fell regularly to Procter, Graveney and Childs, and their final total of 168 gave the hosts victory by 132 runs.

This win was the start of Gloucestershire's late push towards the top of the championship, for only two weeks earlier they had been lounging third from bottom in the table. In the next game, they beat Essex in two days by an innings and 64 runs, and when Cheltenham was over they won the remaining four out of five championship matches. But they had left themselves too much to do and finished up a very creditable third in Tony Brown's last season as captain.

Winning the toss, Keith Fletcher chose to bat first and must have regretted the decision when his side was suddenly 14 for 3. At this stage he joined Graham Gooch (79) and they steadied the ship adding 52 together, but by mid-afternoon their last wicket fell at a total of 160 and John Childs ended with figures of 5.4-1-19-4. Over the next three and a half hours Gloucestershire lost no time in overtaking the visitors' total, ending the day on 211 for 4. Tormentor-in-chief was Zaheer, who dispatched the ball to all parts of the ground as he and Hignell (50) added 102 for the third wicket. Then new batsman Procter simply watched on as Zaheer continued to punish the bowling.

Although Gloucestershire were bottom of the JPL table, a large crowd gathered the next day to enjoy an exciting game which Leicestershire won by 4 runs. Roger Tolchard, nipping up and down the wicket, and Brian Davison, hooking and driving, each scored 65 for the visitors in a partnership of 108. Chasing 207, Sadiq, Hignell and Shepherd struck the ball soundly, while Cheltenham CC all-rounder David Partridge, making his first team debut, batted gallantly as the game was drawing to its conclusion.

After the day of fun and high spirits, it took Zaheer just over an hour to reach his 150 and a couple of minutes later he was caught at deep mid-wicket for 153. Brown scored 43, but it was Brian Brain who created the headlines by making his career best score of 57, including two boundaries in which the ball ended up in a tent. Lever kept bowling (44.2-10-127-8), and Gloucestershire were eventually all out for 391 after Brain and Childs had put on 55 for the last wicket. Four wickets each for Procter and Childs helped dismiss Essex for 167. This total would have been far smaller had it not been for a defiant 66* by Ray East. During his innings East was struck on the chest several times by the hostile bowling of Procter, who was spoken to in the heat of the moment by umpire Dickie Bird.

Six days of cricket had realised thirty-six points for the county, a fine ending to Tony Brown's Cheltenham playing days; but takings were down. Balancing such factors would be one of his many responsibilities on taking up the post of secretary and manager on the retirement of Grahame Parker.

—— **1977** ——

This year the old order was almost restored with eleven days of cricket scheduled, starting on a Saturday against Surrey. There was a buoyant atmosphere, with Gloucestershire supporters basking in their team's current success which was largely attributable to the inspirational leadership of Mike Procter. Fresh in everyone's mind was the memory of the previous week's victory in the Benson and Hedges Cup at Lord's, when they had beaten firm favourites Kent. Now, on the first day of the Festival, they were to resume their serious challenge for the championship.

Gloucestershire made a dreadful start and if Graveney and Shackleton had not put on 51 for the eighth wicket, their team would never have reached the total of 197. Highlight of the day for Surrey was some fine swing-bowling by Geoff Arnold (21-8-24-6) and for Gloucestershire the brilliant fielding of Jim Foat to run out John Edrich, a prime scalp before the end of play.

The attendance had been smaller than usual for the first day of a championship match because the town's Silver Jubilee Festival was in full swing at Pittville Park, where a crowd of around 17,000 joined in the fun. Amongst the revellers were two hundred visitors from Cheltenham's German twin town, Gottingen, some of whom manned a stall selling schnapps and frankfurters. Later that night it was almost like the Festival evenings of old, with a magnificent firework display staged at Pittville lakeside by the committee members of the Midlands Electricity Sports and Social Club.

On Sunday, half-centuries by Stovold and Zaheer, along with a five-wicket haul for Julian Shackleton, steered Gloucestershire to their first JPL win at Cheltenham for four years. In the same competition a week later, in front of a large crowd, the hosts hammered Kent by 9 wickets with ten balls to spare, as Birdlip's David Partridge took 5 for 47 and Sadiq (73) and Stovold (98*) starred in an opening partnership of 151.

Rain washed out the second day's play against Surrey, so ruining the chances of an interesting finish. Despite a wet wicket, the final day was surprisingly good for batsmen, with the visitors taking a first innings lead of 48, followed by Stovold (64*) and Zaheer (79*) enjoying an entertaining, unbeaten partnership of 140, before the game ended in the inevitable draw.

Worcestershire were the next opponents and Mike Procter produced an all-round performance reminiscent of the days of W. G. Grace. Facilities on the ground had changed considerably since W.G's days. A hundred years on there were more stands and marquees with a variety of businesses and organisations represented: Whitbread, Cheltenham Saracens, St Stephens, the Victory Club and the Old Patesians' Association.

In addition, Cotswold Hospital Radio was broadcasting live to patients from the ground for the first time. But out in the middle little had changed; wickets had to be taken and runs scored and just like W.G., 'Proc' was good at both.

The visitors batted first and at lunch they had lost 2 wickets, but by tea they were all out for 167. During the second session, Procter (18.5-5-35-7) had found extra energy to make the ball rear up and unsettle the batsmen, while the spin and accuracy of John Childs from the other end was the perfect contrast. At the close of play, the hosts were 109 for 4 and the game seemed evenly balanced, but at a fund-raising party that night Nico Craven reminded Mike Procter that Gloucestershire expected him to do his duty next day and score a century.

The captain no doubt slept on this remark, for when he came in soon after the start of play, with his team on 112 for 5, he grabbed the situation by the scruff of the neck and scored 108 before lunch, much to the appreciation of Thursday's large crowd. Towards the end of his swashbuckling innings, he had been joined by nineteen-year-old Philip Bainbridge, making his county debut, who watched in awe until his captain departed, then proceeded to make a useful 40.

By the time Gloucestershire were all out for 338 and Vanburn Holder had taken 7 for 117, Procter had enjoyed a short rest and it was not long before he had fired himself up again to reduce the visitors to 124 for 8 at the close. Next morning, in a quarter of an hour, the game was over and Procter (20-6-38-6), with a little help from his friends, had defeated Worcestershire by an innings and 35 runs.

When play started in the last match against Sussex, Gloucestershire were third in the table, twenty-four points behind leaders Middlesex, with a game in hand. Four days later, having won by eight wickets, they were still third, twelve points behind new leaders Kent, having played the same number of games. Things were hotting up at the top; it was glorious weather and there was an atmosphere of intense expectancy.

According to *Wisden,* 'Everything else in this match was dwarfed by the batting of Zaheer, who set a world record when he became the first player to score a double and a single century for the third time.' Furthermore, he was 'not out' in each of his innings.

Until the stroke-making maestro had picked up his bat and played a classic cover-drive late on Saturday afternoon, the day had belonged to John Barclay (105) who only a week earlier had made his maiden championship century. Together with his captain, Peter Graves (56), Barclay put on 119 for Sussex's opening partnership and during the afternoon of blistering hot sunshine, he gave Gloucestershire's bowlers little hope of a breakthrough, while Javed Miandad (48) entertained the sun-hatted crowd with some fetching wristy shots.

Watching his son from the shade of the New Club tent, Kit Barclay was unaware of the movements of Jack Venn. Earlier in the afternoon, the New Club's honorary secretary had walked back to their headquarters in Montpellier Parade and returned to the marquee half an hour later, clutching a bottle of champagne. In the eighty-eighth over of the day, John Barclay reached his century, the cork popped and a glass of cool sparkling champagne appeared as if by magic over his father's shoulder for the celebration toast.

Sussex reached 309 for 7 in their first innings allocation of one hundred overs; bowling a third of them, David Graveney had taken 4 for 90. Almost immediately the visitors pounced by removing Sadiq for nought, bringing Zaheer to the wicket to join Stovold. By the close, the pair had stroked their way handsomely to 97 without further loss. It had been one of those wonderful Festival days, full of sunshine and boundaries, while Norman Walters in the supporter's shop had done a roaring trade selling Gloucestershire sun-hats to ill-prepared Sussex supporters.

By now, Mary Parker's club merchandise marquee had been replaced by an ex-AA demonstration caravan, which had been purchased for £35. Based at Bristol, it was towed up to the College ground each year. With Janet Walters in charge and Norman at her side, together with stalwarts Jack Britton and Stan Brookes, trade prospered.

On Monday it looked as if Zaheer could go on for ever. He reached his century well before lunch, and just before four o'clock he became the fourth Gloucestershire player to reach a double century for the county at Cheltenham. Joining Grace, Townsend and Hammond, he was in distinguished company.

With a first innings lead of 44, the hosts then worked themselves into a strong position as their guests ended the day on 142 for 5. But next morning, John Snow (56), helped by his fellow tail-enders, ensured that Gloucestershire were left a challenging target to win the game; 219 runs in just under four hours would keep them in the title race.

Sadiq and Stovold gave the county just the start they needed, before Zaheer took command. 'All eyes were on the tall sinewy figure of Zaheer Abbas,' wrote John Mason in the *Daily Telegraph*. 'He was supreme.' In the last over before tea, one more sun-kissed cover-drive brought up his hundred and took him into the record books. Soon after the interval, he guided Gloucestershire to an eight wicket victory, finishing undefeated on 108.

Making his first visit to the Festival, umpire Don Oslear had witnessed the remarkable innings from the middle. 'When I am asked who are the best batsmen I have seen in my career, it is a difficult question to answer as I have seen many, but no matter how much I endeavour to whittle down my list it always contains the final letter of the alphabet, Z.'

For the third year running, Zaheer had been the outstanding player of the Festival and he was presented with the 'Gloster' award, while the county pocketed a profit of around £9,000 for the event. Gloucestershire continued in the race for the Schweppes sponsored county championship, a contest which held its sparkle for a further month, resulting in a fight to the finish of the season when they were pipped to the post by Middlesex and Kent, who tied in first place.

—— **1978** ——

Writing in the *Gloucestershire and Avon Life*, Charlie Barnett considered the Festival to be 'the pivot of the county's season':

'In the beautiful setting of the College ground and with the enormous loyalty that the festival enjoys in the north of the county, there could not be a more enjoyable place in which to play cricket. The families are all at home, the children from their schools, it is holiday time and that is the kind of atmosphere that pervades the entire festival. It does not matter how the county has fared in the previous months, if the sun is shining the crowds will flock to Cheltenham.'

Sadly the sun was not shining this year. Due to rain, there was only half a Festival and the centenary of 'The Week' celebrations were a miserable wash-out. Not only was the start delayed, but six of the eleven days of cricket were lost. Writing in the *Yearbook,* club chairman Ken Graveney made the point that it allowed 'the press and pessimists' to suggest that the event would be discontinued, but he concluded, 'I personally could not imagine a cricket season without a Cheltenham Festival.'

Derek Randall made 54 in three hours on the first day as Nottinghamshire struggled to reach 221 for 8 on a slow pitch, and after play had finished, Mrs Rosemary Truscott's Festival opening party took place in the College dining hall. Then it rained for five days.

On the sixth day the waters subsided, allowing the county to beat Glamorgan by seven wickets in a single innings match. The arrival of Hampshire was greeted with further rain and after the visitors were victorious in the JPL game, a dull, unimaginative stalemate was the conclusion to the championship match. There were go-slow, delaying tactics from both teams and the players were greeted by shouts of 'rubbish' as they left the field for tea on the last day. Cricket, crowds and caterers had all suffered, but the good news was that event sponsors, the Dowty Group, had generously covered the costs and everyone was left hoping that the following year, with cricket starting a week later, the rain clouds would not be reappearing.

—— 1979 ——

Three months after Margaret Thatcher came to power, Chris Coley organised and ran his first Cheltenham Festival. 'My job,' he recalls, 'was to link and provide lines of communication between the county cricket club, the Cheltenham committee and the College' - a challenging assignment for the College old boy, still performing the role a quarter of a century later. Earlier in the year, he had also taken on responsibility for the club's sponsorship and advertising on Grahame Parker's retirement to Devon, and there were instant signs of his marketing skills.

As marketing manager, Chris Coley immediately started to capitalise on what he calls 'the boom of commercialisation', establishing corporate hospitality on the ground in the form of business marquees which joined the arc of club tents. Instant praise came from Mike Wynn, of Rea Publicity, who witnessed the 'marvellous time' enjoyed by the Walker Crosweller management and their 'customer-guests':

'The surprising feature of the day was the amount of business that went on. Though the cricket was entertaining, the general atmosphere was so relaxed that the marquee very quickly became the centre of discussions that had nothing to do with cricket.' The marquee was booked for the following year and Festival corporate entertainment had taken off.

Opening opponents were Yorkshire, making their first appearance for twenty-two years since being beaten in Sam Cook's memorable benefit match. Batting first, Gloucestershire made 288 for 8 in their hundred overs. The Stovold brothers featured in a short partnership, while Alastair Hignell, after chopping a ball onto his stumps without removing a bail, went on to make his first championship century (102).

Just after six o'clock, when Saturday night revellers were about to get going, the game took off. Geoffrey Boycott, making his first appearance on the ground, was rapped on the pads by Brain and Procter, and on both occasions everyone on the ground - except for the Yorkshire supporters - appealed loudly. But Boycott stood firm, so Procter worked on the other batsmen with devastating results. Pounding in from the College Lawn end, he claimed the second lbw hat-trick of his career - only a week after his first - removing Lumb, Athey and Hampshire with wicket-keeper Andy Brassington recalling every ball being 'plumb'. Gloucestershire supporters left the ground in party mood, with the visitors ending the day on 42 for 4.

Everything was going well for the hosts. Next day they beat Yorkshire by six wickets in the JPL; Sadiq Mohammad top scored with 78 and there were record receipts of £6,338. Something had to go wrong and it did in the form of bad weather. Play resumed after lunch on the final day and Boycott (95) and Carrick (128*) helped Yorkshire to reach 303 for 8 at the close, while Mike Procter finished with figures of 36-11-107-6.

The following match, with Worcestershire, was also bedevilled by rain and no play was possible after mid-afternoon on the second day. The first morning belonged to Zaheer (61) and to Sadiq, who went on to make his sixth century of the season (102). By late afternoon, after Hignell's 65*, Gloucestershire reached 308 for 8 in their allocated hundred overs. Procter immediately ripped into the visitors, leaving them on 36 for 3 at the close, and when rain stopped play next day they had reached 142 for 9, still needing 17 to avoid the follow-on. Brain (24.2-5-53-4) and Procter (21-5-53-5) had done the damage and would no doubt have enjoyed the opportunity of bowling at the visitors again, in pursuit of an innings victory.

After a blank first day in the match against Surrey, Gloucestershire beat the Londoners by six wickets in the JPL, which was followed by two days of the most exciting championship cricket. Another century from Sadiq (124), who ended the season with a batting average of over 60, along with contributions from Zaheer (64) and Procter (50*), enabled the hosts to declare on 250 for 3. Surrey then responded in true Festival spirit, declaring 50 runs behind, thanks to positive batting from Clinton (82) and former county player Knight (58). The contest was set up for an interesting final day.

Next morning, Roger Knight, with two wickets in two balls, made Gloucestershire's batsmen feel very uneasy, before the flamboyant Procter took charge and hit a seventy-six minute century, the fastest of the season in the championship. Just before lunch, he hit three successive fours and after the break made 72 in twenty-six minutes, before being bowled by Knight (16-5-44-5) for 102.

Gloucestershire's declaration left Surrey needing 267 to win in three hours. This they achieved off the last ball of the match, with one wicket remaining. Graham Roope (84) had held the Surrey innings together, before being stumped by Brassington off Graveney, and in the end it was left to the last pair, Pocock and Wilson, to steer their side home with a scrambled bye. It was breathtaking stuff and although, as *Wisden* wrote, 'a tie might have been a more just result', it was the kind of finish that must have delighted Chris Coley.

CHAPTER NINETEEN (1980-1986)

THE WINNER TAKES IT ALL

—— 1980 ——

In his book *Playing a Supporting Role*, Nico Craven writes of the season, 'Nobody (that I met) could remember Gloucestershire arriving at Cheltenham without a single win in the County Championship.' It had indeed been a most disappointing season, but the Hitachi Skydivers who landed on the ground on the opening day must have brought some lucky manna from heaven, for the county proceeded to win all three championship matches, something that had not been done at Cheltenham for almost fifty years.

Chris Broad, a former Colston's School boy in his first full season for the county, upstaged Geoffrey Boycott's performance of the previous year by making a century (116) in his Festival debut. Hampshire were the opponents and the lofty left-hander gave guests in the marquees something else to talk about at lunch other than the weather. As the food arrived on the tables at the end of the morning session, Gloucestershire were 151 for no wicket, with Broad and Sadiq firmly in control. Then, while much of the population were relaxing on an August Saturday afternoon, the visitors worked away, taking all ten wickets as the hosts doubled their score.

On Monday, Hampshire found it difficult to cope with Alan Wilkins (20-6-50-5) and were bowled out for 178; by tea time on the final day, Gloucestershire had won the match by 197 runs. A winning roll was underway as they pocketed the first twenty of their fifty-three point Festival haul. Hampshire had narrowly avoided the follow-on and when the hosts batted again, Sadiq (90*) had given his captain the opportunity to declare, leaving Pocock's men four hours to score 300 runs to win. On a worn pitch, it was not surprising that spinners David Graveney (15-8-24-5) and John Childs (8.2-0-38-3) caused the batsmen too many problems and wrapped up the game, leaving plenty of time for ground preparations in readiness for the next visitors, Worcestershire.

Two days earlier, the legendary 'Voice of Cricket', John Arlott, had made his final broadcast from the College ground during the JPL match. Much had happened since his description of Gloucestershire throwing away their hopes of winning the championship in 1947, when he had explained to radio listeners in his familiar voice, one busy Saturday, that the ground was filling up 'as the farmers came down from the hills'. It was appropriate that his beloved Hampshire were playing during his last commentary on the ground, but disappointing for him that they lost in a rain-affected contest. On the other hand, it was just another match and as Nico Craven says of Arlott, 'He has never made the mistake of taking the game too seriously. He has always known that there's more - much more - to life than cricket.'

After a somewhat quiet season by his standards, Mike Procter awoke and dominated the next match. Inchmore (20-3-62-5) and Holder struck early on for Worcestershire during the first morning as the hosts, having been put in, slumped to 27 for 3. Procter emerged in fighting spirit, immediately hitting an explosive 73, enabling his side to reach 178. Then as a gale began to blow, the guests cruised to 84 for 1, with Turner reaching his fifty before rain stopped play.

The storm that hit Cheltenham that night was nothing compared to the one that surged across the College ground next day as Mike Procter ripped through Worcestershire's batting, taking 7 for 9. The visitors slumped to 111 all out, and by the close the hosts had a lead nearing 200. On the final day, apart from a defiant half-century from Alan Ormrod, the honours belonged to Procter, his mixture of seam and off-spin earning him another seven wicket haul and a match analysis of 43.2-16-76-14, the best championship bowling performance of the season. Dismissed for 148, Worcestershire lost by 96 runs, part of their second innings downfall being caused by the agile Brassington who claimed four dismissals.

'Everyone wants to play at Cheltenham,' said Brassington. 'They are great cricket wickets, giving a bit to everybody; for bowlers there is little margin for error and, because of the bounce, spinners do well and close fielders get catches.'

Middlesex, the champions elect, arrived at the Festival having just been beaten for the first time in the season. Leicestershire had been the victors at Lord's by an innings with a day to spare. The Londoners, without Mike Gatting and John Emburey on Test duty, were keen to get back to winning ways.

Procter inserted the visitors on a damp pitch and by the end of the first day, in reply to Middlesex's 220, Gloucestershire, on 37 for 5, were staring the follow-on in the face. Next day, a superb innings from Zaheer (81*) helped to give his side a 55 run victory over Mike Brearley's men in the JPL and all too quickly Monday arrived, with Gloucestershire in a bit of a pickle. Sneaking their way to 109, the county made Middlesex bat again and midway through the morning session on the last day, having lost time due to rain, the visitors declared, setting their hosts 270 to win, but more to the point, leaving themselves almost five hours to bowl them out.

At half past two, Gloucestershire's captain took guard with his side precariously positioned on 65 for 3. Local supporters were mumbling that he should never have let Middlesex bat first. Within three hours the game was over, Gloucestershire having won by 6 wickets, with *Wisden* describing Procter's innings of 134* as 'one of the best ever seen on the College ground'.

Middlesex's Bill Merry recalls, 'We outplayed Gloucestershire for two and a half days and thought we'd done the hard work getting Zaheer out.' Uncharacteristically, Brearley had miscalculated and there was nothing that the thoughtful captain could do to remove his opposite number, with matters made worse by Procter being dropped at slip when in his fifties.

By tea, Gloucestershire needed 105 to win in one hour and twenty overs. Frank Keating and David Foot hurried through their cakes in the New Club tent, eager not to miss a ball when play resumed; they could just sense a glorious victory. When it came, their host Nico Craven was - for once - almost lost for words as he attempted to describe the South African's only century of the season.

Later he wrote, 'Procter played all the classics and gave many an encore. There were flowing drives and delicate cuts; there were vicious hooks and powerful pulls. There were shots timed to such perfection that they easily pierced Brearley's astutely placed fields.'

The Festival was over; Gloucestershire had beaten the weather and all their opponents, echoing the title of the current chart-topping song by Abba, *The Winner Takes It All*. Mike Procter, one of the world's great all-rounders, like Grace and Hammond, had used the College field to demonstrate his huge talent. Sadly, those final six days of the Festival, when spectators witnessed this virtuoso display, proved to be his Cheltenham swan-song, for by the following August the knee injury that had plagued his career compelled him to retire from playing for the county.

—— **1981** ——

Under the captaincy of David Graveney, Gloucestershire staged a come-back at Cheltenham after an ailing season. Three out of the five matches were won, one lost and the other drawn.

Over thirty years on, Graveney, now chairman of England selectors, reflected on the Festival: 'What always amazed me was that we were playing on very natural wickets; ground that had other uses for the rest of the year. In 1981, John Childs, Sadiq and I were fortunate to take wickets because the pitches were still conducive to spin.'

On the opening day against Surrey, after four hours of play had been washed out, *Wisden* reported that time was 'quickly made up as the spin bowlers of both sides enjoyed themselves'. Honours were even after first innings. Surrey made 160, bowled out by Childs (19-5-69-6) and Graveney (11.3-5-18-4). The hosts topped this total by 6 runs as Pocock (29-12-59-3) and Intikhab (27-7-69-4) spun their web. In Surrey's second innings, apart from Butcher (90), nobody could cope with Graveney (27.1-7-54-6) who was ably assisted by Childs and Sadiq taking two wickets each, as the visitors were dismissed for 170. There was then a minor panic in the home dressing-room as Pocock removed Sadiq for nought in his first over, but youngsters Broad (76*) and Bainbridge (75), both of whom reached 1,000 runs in the season, swept their team to an eight wicket victory with a splendid partnership of 142.

The defeat seriously affected Surrey's title hopes, but there was some consolation, for over the weekend they had taken the points in a low scoring JPL fixture, with match winner Monte Lynch (69) striking 3 sixes and 6 fours to see his side home by 3 wickets.

Marketing matters were changing. Chris Coley had spread his wings and was now applying his entrepreneurial nous to running his own corporate hospitality company 'Sporting Concepts'. Helping him on a freelance basis at the Festival was Marie Journeaux. Since the Benson and Hedges victory in 1977, she had been using her marketing skills successfully to promote the club's membership campaign and now she was involved with the corporate side of Cheltenham. She remembers affectionately those prominent Festival landmarks on the corner of Sandford Road and Thirlstaine Road, the poster boards, handiwork of designer David Griffiths, which announce Festival dates, visiting teams and hours of play.

Involved with the project for a number of years, Marie Journeaux recalls, 'Once the posters were finished, it was time for me to contact Peter Legge, the regional committee chairman, who would arrange for the boards to be brought out of storage at the College and put firmly in place for their annual pasting.'

She remembers how their DIY team of two would set to work: 'Armed with a bucket, pasting brush and posters, I used to meet Mr Legge at the College and he, in turn, would be carrying a packet of paste.'

They knew where to find an outside tap and used fallen twigs to stir up the gluey mixture and were then ready for action. With Peter Legge holding a chair, Marie Journeaux was responsible for pasting the boards and positioning the posters.

'We really did make a good comedy duo,' she reflects. 'Passing motorists must have laughed themselves silly whilst waiting at the traffic lights. And the lorry drivers - well! I lost count of how many blew their horns and shouted various comments!'

Over the years, their DIY skills have proved to be of a high standard, for the posters have never peeled off, matching the quality of Gloucestershire's cricket against Hampshire, their second opponents in 1981, whom they pasted by an innings and 86 runs.

Umpire Don Oslear had just been shown the nominated sides before the match started, when Gloucestershire's plans were suddenly turned upside down because their young Australian fast bowler, Mike Whitney, was summoned for Test duty.

'It was not unusual for me to have a nominated side changed,' recalls Oslear. 'What caused comment was the fact that the player had played so little first-class cricket.'

As the bowler made haste to Old Trafford, Sadiq stepped into Whitney's shoes and was one of the Gloucestershire players to make full use of batting on a good pitch, enabling David Graveney to declare on 381 for 7 after ninety-nine overs. Bainbridge (61), Zaheer (68), Sadiq (43) and Windaybank (46*) were all disappointed to see Alastair Hignell (97) caught on the boundary going for a six to reach his century. But a good day's work had been done and not just by Gloucestershire players, for Hampshire's Cheltenham-born Michael Bailey had taken four of the wickets to fall in twenty-nine overs.

Nico Craven wrote in *Tea for Twenty Two,* 'The Gloucestershire spinners were the toast of Cheltenham Town at closing time on Thursday.' Fifteen Hampshire wickets fell on the second day and had it not been for a fighting 84 by Trevor Jesty, the visitors would have been heading back to the New Forest that night. In destroying their opponents,

Graveney and Childs had repeated what generations of Gloucestershire spinners had done at Cheltenham and finished with match figures of 8 for 71 and 7 for 107 respectively. Ironically, it was Sadiq who took the final wicket next morning, when victory was secured after just fourteen balls.

Without the services of Procter and Brain, the likes of Bainbridge, Broad, Hignell, Graveney and Childs had risen to the challenge and were all shouldering the increased responsibility admirably, but no doubt they were frustrated by the rain-delayed start to the next match against Kent. The break in play gave spectators an opportunity to attend a signing session by author and illustrator Aylwin Sampson, whose acclaimed book *Grounds of Appeal* had recently been published, and included two views of the College ground. Once the game started, the pitch on the ground today proved to be a placid one, and the batsmen thrived with the match ending in a draw.

Batting on into Monday morning, having lost the JPL the day before by 5 wickets, Kent finally declared on 310 for 6, the highlight being an attractive 93 from their captain Asif Iqbal. The pleasantly-paced pitch enabled the hosts to get off to a good start and was tailor-made for Bainbridge (81) and Zaheer (136*) to feature in a third wicket partnership of 188. Having sped off the mark with five runs on his first ball - a single and four overthrows - 'Zed' never looked back, passed 2,000 runs for the season and gave the normally 'deadly' Derek Underwood little respect. After tea, his stroke-making continued and once he had peppered the College gymnasium, a declaration was made on 336 for 3.

Craven felt this was when the Festival should have ended, 'with Zaheer at the height of his powers . . . Tuesday couldn't be expected to "follow that" '.

The sage was right. The hosts managed to take 6 wickets the next day, and Kent reached 276 before setting their opponents 251 to make in just over two hours. *Wisden* recorded that 'with five wickets going for 71, Gloucestershire called off the chase'.

Joking that Zaheer 'certainly did fail' when being dismissed for 2 in this innings, Don Oslear continues, 'In my two Festivals, I had seen "Zed" play seven innings - four of them were "not out" - and he had scored 552 runs, at an average of 184 . . . I think it could be said that he would settle for me "standing" when he took guard in any match.'

A view of the Cheltenham Cricket Festival by Aylwin Sampson

—— **1982** ——

There were various changes amongst the administrative posts within the club this year. In particular, Don Perry was appointed chairman in place of Ken Graveney. Perry was a former captain of cricket at Cheltenham Grammar School who might well have played for the county but for the war. Referred to by Grahame Parker as 'one of the leading sports authorities in the north of the county', he had a challenge on his hands: money was short, Zaheer was representing Pakistan and there were changes within the playing staff.

Despite Gloucestershire's disappointing results leading up to the Festival, it was again proved beyond doubt that here in August the season's attendance figures and gate receipts were made to look respectable. In three championship matches over £10,000 was taken, compared to just over £5,000 from Bristol's eight fixtures. Meanwhile, companies were becoming ever keener to support the event as Thatcherite entrepreneurs could see the value of sponsorship, ranging from a match day ball to an entire three-day game.

Nottinghamshire enjoyed their visit to Cheltenham, winning the championship match by 106 runs and the JPL by 47, thanks to Richard Hadlee (100*) making his first century - spiced with 3 sixes - in the competition.

Since Procter's departure, Gloucestershire's cricket had inevitably lost some of its cutting edge, and in response to the visitors' 197, the hosts could only muster a reply of 111. Eddie Hemmings (21.3-8-31-5) was their downfall, and after the visitors declared their second innings at 284 for 6, the hosts were left with over a day to make 371 to win. Andy Stovold reached fifty, wearing one boot that was larger than the other to protect a badly bruised toe, while Hemmings (32.5-14-73-4) and Such (30-6-112-5) were dismissing his team mates.

With the championship in sight, Middlesex arrived in town enjoying a forty-five point lead in the table. But without the injured Mike Brearley and Test-bound Mike Gatting, they found themselves in dire trouble at the end of the first day's play, having slumped to 30 for 5 in reply to Gloucestershire's 247. Making the first of his many appearances for the county on the ground was the England Young Cricketers' wicket-keeper, Robert 'Jack' Russell of Stroud, who, despite making nought in his debut innings, secured his first Festival dismissal by catching Wilf Slack.

The match twisted and turned next day, and after being dropped on 19,

Middlesex's Roland Butcher was missed twice more, rode his luck and went on to score 173 out of a total of 277. On reaching his century, the hard-hitting Barbadian made his last 71 runs, which included 2 sixes and 9 fours in just forty-one minutes, inspiring Nico Craven to write in *Summer and Sunshine* of 'an afternoon when a Gloucestershire attack without the injured Graveney was put to the butcher's blade and simply slaughtered'.

It was former Kent and West Indies all-rounder, veteran John Shepherd, who finally captured the elusive scalp of Butcher and claimed his one thousandth first-class wicket, while another new recruit, Franklyn Stephenson, eased his way to the top of the county's bowling averages with figures of 26-9-69-5. The last day, Friday the thirteenth, was unlucky both for spectators, who were deprived of play before lunch due to rain, and for Middlesex, who had their guests firmly in the noose on 141 for 7 at the end of a further rain-interrupted afternoon and had to settle for a draw.

Essex were the final visitors and only 19 runs separated the two sides after first innings. Stovold (83), Sadiq (75) and Shepherd (67*) were the main contributors to the county's total of 322, as John Lever took 5 for 78, while McEwan (91), Pont (50) and Turner (64*) responded for the visitors.

After the hosts had won a closely contested JPL by five runs, the championship game fizzled out to a draw. There was some light relief on the last night of the Festival, when Phillips, the auctioneers, conducted a 'Sale of Cricketana' in the Hardy Room to raise money for club funds. A wide selection of items came under the hammer, ranging from nineteenth century books to modern scorecards and autographs, with particular interest focussed on a bone-handled walking-stick presented to W. J. Kent by W. G. Grace, with a decorated and inscribed silver band.

On the final day, rain halted Essex's brave two hour chase towards the demanding target of 256 runs set by David Graveney.

—— 1983 ——

Former club president and life-long Gloucestershire supporter Mervyn Moore died just before the start of the Festival. As chairman of the Cheltenham regional committee for over twenty years, the highly respected Old Cheltonian had been at the heart of organising many Festivals. The county's cricketers produced a fitting tribute by beating

Glamorgan twice in the first four days by an innings and 9 runs in the championship match, and by 5 wickets in the JPL.

In the three day game, the Welshmen were unlucky in having to bat second and third on a pitch that dealt out 'shooters' and 'lifters' and which was consequently reported to Lord's for its misbehaviour. It spelt out the end for the faithful 'Genevieve', a College favourite, described by David Bridle as 'an old cocoa tin of a roller' with no weight, rendering her 'useless for preparing a wicket'.

Winning the toss and batting first, the hosts reached 376, with Shepherd (98*) and Stovold (83) the main contributors. Apart from Rodney Ontong, who top-scored in both innings with 81 and 46, Glamorgan fell foul firstly to Childs (30.2-10-77-5) and then to Shepherd, who took full advantage of the unpredictable pitch and ended with second innings figures of 32-10-64-7.

A heavy roller was borrowed to help prepare the wicket for the next match against Warwickshire. From then on, there were more runs than grumbles from the batsmen of both sides and hundreds galore for the remainder of the Festival. A third wicket partnership of 190 between Andy Stovold (164*) and Zaheer Abbas (109) was the feature of the day. Stovold's five and a half hour stay at the crease contrasted with Zaheer's graceful fiftieth century for the county, and at the close the home supporters had no worries, with the visitors on 29 for 2 in reply to Gloucestershire's 356 for 5 declared.

At the beginning of the season, the popular and talented keeper, Andy Brassington, plagued by injuries, had been replaced by the highly gifted Jack Russell. The youngster was enjoying an excellent summer, riding high in the national wicket-keeper's table and attracting the attention of Test selectors. When he caught Warwickshire's run-maker Alvin Kallicharran on Thursday morning, one of his fourteen dismissals at the Festival, it seemed as if Gloucestershire had matters firmly under control. However, it was not to be, for quietly, in front of the sun-baked, golden College buildings, David Smith (109) and Denis Amiss (52) enabled Norman Gifford to declare at 303 for 9.

The final day went right to the wire. Gloucestershire's batsmen moved the score along smoothly and they finally set their guests the target of 271 in just over three hours. The challenge was taken up led by Smith (66) and Kallicharran (48), with contributions from the rest of their team, and Warwickshire won by scampering a bye off the last ball. It was Festival cricket at its very best and there was more to come over the next four days with the visit of Yorkshire.

In a rather strange way, the milk floats of Cheltenham played a part in what is often referred to as one of the most controversial periods in the history of Yorkshire cricket. As the employees of the dairy in Imperial Lane went about their early morning business, Geoffrey Boycott was awoken, then tossed and turned as every float passed his hotel bedroom window, finally emerging rather wearily in the morning. He was not in the best of moods on arriving at the ground and the situation was aggravated further when he was told he needed his blazer for a team photograph, which meant a walk back to the hotel. Richard Sharp, who had been on duty at the Chapel Gate since half past seven, had been spoken to sharply by Boycott as he marched out, and was now given another blast on the cricketer's return.

The prolific former England opener then proceeded to express himself, albeit rather slowly, with his bat. With him at the crease was Kevin Sharp, who was ultimately run out for 121 after playing a positive, entertaining innings. He recalls, 'I was out of form at the time and it was lovely to score a hundred on such a beautiful ground.' Boycott and Sharp featured together in a 224 run record third wicket partnership for opponents on the ground. The hot sunshine was being enjoyed by spectators, but the heat, along with Boycott's slow progress, made his captain and manager, Ray Illingworth, boil. The temperature rose even higher when the batsman ignored signals to get a move on. At the close of play, on a good wicket, Boycott had made 140* in over six hours, on a ground with a lightening fast outfield and relatively small boundary; the controversy was up and running.

Recalling the events in his book *The Tempestuous Years 1979-1983*, Ray Illingworth writes, 'It was, in a nutshell, the day that broke the camel's back - that particular camel being me.' Over the following months, reprimands and recriminations flew in all directions up and down the corridors of power at Headingley, with blame bouncing from one party to another as long-standing resentment, wounded pride and subtle jealousies were aired.

Yorkshire had arrived at the Festival near the bottom of the championship, but top of the JPL table, a position their supporters would have willingly swapped round. Eager to maintain their lead, there were whoops of delight as they won the high-scoring Sunday match by 4 wickets and there were further smiles for the northerners who declared on 344 for 5, then grabbed the initiative as Gloucestershire crashed to 76 for 5 on Monday morning. There followed a fighting matinee performance from Paul Romaines (100*) and John Shepherd (93), who added 171 and enabled David Graveney, having collected maximum batting points, to declare 37 runs behind.

When the visitors went to the crease again, Boycott was a different man. According to *Wisden,* he was 'in far more sprightly mood' and 'carried the Yorkshire second innings'. It was a surprise when Graveney 'prised him out 3 short of a second century'. Illingworth declared early in the afternoon, leaving his hosts to score 277 in just over three hours. Chris Broad (100), making his last appearance on the ground as a Gloucestershire player, and Zaheer Abbas (75) led the charge, which, like some of the latter's cover drives, was timed to perfection as the county raced home to win by five wickets with eleven balls to spare.

Reporting in *The Guardian* next day, David Foot wrote, 'Ears were burning and some motors spluttered with indignation as the large North Country contingent went home last night . . . This was the home county's third championship win of the season and a jaunty finale to the festival.'

—— **1984** ——

The following poem, *Cheltenham Cricket Festival,* appeared in the August edition of *Cotswold Life.* Written by Vincent Keyte, one of the triumvirate of headmasters who 'reigned' at Beaudesert School near Stroud for over thirty years, it sets the familiar scene as the curtain rises on the College ground:

> The College buildings, viewed from Members' stand,
> With close green turf between,
> Provide a setting for the Festival,
> That gracious cricket scene.
> In every year, as fitful August comes,
> With rain or warming sun,
> True followers of the game arrive
> To join the fickle fun.
>
> In spite of grumbles when the weather damps
> The ardour of the crowd,
> Or when they wheel the clumsy covers out
> Against the threatening cloud,
> The sport endures, an English heritage
> On this enticing square.
> Is there a fairer field in all the land
> Which cricket lovers share?

Sensing the unsettled atmosphere surrounding the White Rose county, Bill Athey made his way south to join Gloucestershire for the summer. Helped by some useful scores at the Festival, he finished the season top of the county's batting averages.

The Gloucestershire team arrived in Cheltenham without 'Zed'. After thirteen seasons, during which he had scored thousands of runs, many gracefully gathered in front of the golden Gothic buildings of the College, this 'prince of batsmen' had retired from county cricket. Festival-goers mourned his absence and with three drawn matches, everything seemed rather dull.

In the opening fixture against the Sri Lankan touring team, the hosts made 278 for 4 declared. Paul Romaines led off with 83 and was well supported by former Warwickshire player Wootton who was run out for 97, and the youngster Cunningham (61*). The tourists raced ahead to 286 for the loss of only one wicket, as Wettimuny (123*) and Silva (91) featured in an opening partnership of 190. On a rain-interrupted final day, Gloucestershire then faltered against the medium-pace of John (14.2-2-58-6), reaching 116 for 6 before further bad weather ended the game.

Struggling at 70 for 5, Glamorgan were rescued by the promising Hugh Morris (81) helping them to reach 258, then fifties from Tony Wright and Andy Stovold enabled Graveney to declare on 252 for 8. The visitors sped on in their second innings and a declaration left Gloucestershire needing 250 to win at five runs an over. While Athey (72) and Shepherd (37) were still together at the crease, a victory was in their grasp, but when both batsmen were dismissed in the space of three balls, the tail shut up shop for the last six overs and they finished on 207 for 8.

Against Surrey, with Andy Stovold keeping wicket in place of the injured Jack Russell, Tony Wright volunteered to open the innings and proceeded to score his maiden first-class century (139). It was a Boycott-like vigil, lasting just over six and a half hours, during which he received little prolonged support apart from Bill Athey (65). The visitors gained a first innings lead of 87, as old friend, now rival, Roger Knight made 142 in another six hour stay at the crease, with a fiery spell of bowling by David Lawrence earning him a five wicket haul. Then the game quietly petered out with the hosts on 225 for 6 in their second innings. The only clear result at the Festival had been when Gloucestershire had beaten Surrey by 6 wickets in the JPL; it had been a year rather lacking in Vincent Keyte's 'fickle fun'.

— **1985** —

This year, twenty-three and a half hours of playing time were lost due to rain. Put in by Leicestershire on a seamer's wicket, the county struggled against the excellent fast-medium bowling of Les Taylor (17.4-3-45-5), who later in the day was selected to play for England in the next Test match. Gloucestershire would never have reached their total of 134 had it not been for a courageous effort by Philip Bainbridge (33), one of *Wisden's* Five Cricketers of the Year, who batted on with a broken index finger. The visitors then struggled, until Peter Willey denied Gloucestershire's fast bowlers the final breakthrough they wanted and his stubborn 52 earned his side a lead of 115. Rain and a dogged 47* by Tony Wright on the final day saved the county, who were only six runs ahead with five wickets in hand at the close.

Bad weather had spoilt the start of the Festival and the normally well-attended JPL match was a virtual wash-out in more ways than one. It was pouring with rain when the players and umpires arrived at the ground on Sunday morning and having spent a couple of hours staring out of the pavilion window at the bleak situation, England and Leicestershire captain, David Gower, made noises that his team might as well return to their hotel. Hearing of this, Roger Moore, managing director of the first major Festival sponsors, Duraflex, already entertaining friends and players wives in his marquee, invited the cricketers to lunch. Taking up the offer, they entered his marquee, and saw before them a large table full of fine food and drinks.

Over a long lunch, which stretched into the afternoon, salmon and fillet steaks were washed down with an abundance of wine and Pimms. Meanwhile, unbeknown to the partying players, the rain had stopped and the sun was shining. The strong wind that had earlier blown over the scoreboard, together with the exceptional draining qualities of the ground, were beginning to make the umpires, Roy Palmer and Mervyn Kitchen, think that a short game might be possible after all.

Roy Palmer remembers the look of astonishment on David Gower's face when he entered the marquee to tell him that play would start soon after five o'clock. Almost bowled over by the news, Gower brushed aside concerns over his being in a fit state to play, downed his Pimms and spluttered, 'If you can umpire, Merv, I can play.'

Meanwhile, Andy Brassington recalls the scene in the dressing-room - 'where lots of black coffee was quickly being swilled back' - when a player from each side 'suddenly had to be replaced'. Apparently Leicestershire's opener, Ian Butcher, had poked his head round the Gloucestershire dressing-room door 'just as Paul Romaines was practising his golf swing with a cricket bat', and Butcher's nose took the full force of the blow. This left him in no fit state to play cricket, while Romaines, burdened with guilt and the after-effects of his lunch, also withdrew from the contest.

In his autobiography, David Gower writes, 'I went in No 4, gave Graveney the charge first ball, and although I never saw it I somehow hit it over long on.'

Although Gower was caught having scored eleven, Roy Palmer suggests, 'Gloucestershire didn't want to get David out, because the wind kept blowing him over! . . . and it seemed that Bill Athey was seeing more than one ball, judging from his long barrier positioning!'

The slog-out ended with the visitors winning by seven runs and Gower concludes, 'In honour of our triumph, I duly led the troops straight back into the tent.'

It was obviously good Test match preparation for England's captain, for on leaving Cheltenham he made the short journey up to Edgbaston and proceeded to score a scintillating 215 against the Australians. Meanwhile, the Festival match against Nottinghamshire was being seriously hampered by rain. In the short time possible for play, the visitors reached 216, with the former Gloucestershire player, Chris Broad, just missing out on a fifty, and the county's new off-spinner, Jeremy Lloyds, taking 5 for 37 before the hosts reached 15 for no wicket.

Although rain had spoilt action on the field, there was no dampening of spirits at Suzee Moore's Festival fashion show. For a number of years, Roger Moore's wife had organised a glamorous fund-raising evening in Cheltenham, when players and professional models held hands as they paraded down the catwalk. On this occasion, amidst howls of delight, the highlight was David 'Syd' Lawrence's break-dancing, which clearly loosened up his limbs for the next match.

Warwickshire chose to bat first and according to *Wisden* were 'swept aside by Walsh and Lawrence in under two and a half hours'. With these two pacemen in full cry, the Gloucestershire team was one of the most feared bowling sides on the circuit, and over the next decade their star bowlers would enjoy great success on the hard, fast Cheltenham wicket.

In pursuit of the visitors' 127, the hosts looked vulnerable on 19 for 4. Then a fifth wicket partnership of 133 between Jeremy Lloyds (54) and Kevin Curran (63) was followed by some hefty hitting from Courtney

Walsh (31) who, Geoffrey Need remembered, 'carved 2 sixes over deep third man'. At the close of a rip-roaring day's play, Gloucestershire were all out for 253 and Gladstone Small (21-3-80-5) had also made use of a 'flying track'. Summarizing the events in *One Good Season Deserved Another,* Nico Craven recalled 'a summer and sunshine day when the ball always seemed to end up either in the hands of the fielders or at the feet of the spectators.'

After a rain-ruined JPL, which Gloucestershire won by thirteen runs, only eight overs of play were possible on Monday. But on the last day the county's fast bowlers brushed Warwickshire's resistance aside, dismissing them for 211. Courtney Walsh ended with career-best match figures of 39.5-9-128-13, while Lawrence captured 6 for 129. The hosts knocked off the required runs to win by seven wickets. On a day when hardly any other play in the country was possible, their twenty-three points took them back to the top of the championship table.

By the end of the season, the county had slipped to third position, but nevertheless earned praise from their new patron, HRH The Princess of Wales, in a message which read, 'Having viewed the Club's meteoric rise up the county league, I wanted to send my warmest congratulations on such skilful cricket.'

—— 1986 ——

As both mayor of Cheltenham and chairman of Gloucestershire CCC in 1986, Don Perry recalls, with a twinkle in his eye, a bizarre scene at the civic reception: 'I welcomed myself and replied, thanking myself for coming!'

He had witnessed the Festival open on a pitch that was tailor-made for fast bowling and Hampshire's Malcolm Marshall, taking the new ball, quickly put the county's batsmen on the hop. As so often happens under these circumstances, however, it was the bowlers at the other end who quietly picked up wickets, so when Gloucestershire were dismissed for 201, Marshall had shared the prey with Connor, Tremlett and James.

By the end of the second day, the hosts, batting again, were only 27 ahead with 8 wickets in hand. Hampshire had taken a first innings lead of 69, due largely to a 112 run ninth wicket partnership between the plucky Chris Smith (72*), batting virtually one-handed with a broken finger caused by a 'Lawrence-lifter', helped by toothache-troubled Tim Tremlett (52).

The final day fluctuated even more than the first two. Andy Stovold (48), also batting with an injured finger, bravely held Gloucestershire's innings together, but Marshall (22-6-44-4) and James, with his championship-best figures (16-4-34-5), bowled their hosts out for 184 soon after lunch, leaving the visitors the simple target of needing 116 to win.

Walsh and Lawrence opened the bowling and David Graveney recalls: 'Hampshire were cruising along at 39 without loss, looking well-set for victory. I couldn't decide whether to make a bowling change or not; the fielders were starting to mutter. I gave them another over and Gordon Greenidge was caught at slip. If he'd middled it, the ball would have sailed into the town centre . . . The game suddenly changed.'

Bill Athey, who caught Greenidge, recalls the moment and describes the wicket as 'the best in England at the time - there was so much pace and bounce'.

Everything that came Athey's way he held, including two more slip-catches, as Hampshire wickets began to tumble. Curran, Graveney and Romaines were holding on to their chances as well and Romaines caught Hampshire's captain, Mark Nicholas, off a skyer at deep third man right in front of the New Club marquee where those inside were about to take afternoon tea. Their chairs were perched on a raised platform, a tradition which goes back to watching cricket in India when everybody could sit inside the marquee out of the hot sun, yet have a clear view from their tiered seats.

There was a buzz of excitement around the ground at tea time, and whoops of delight straight after the interval when another wicket fell and Hampshire were 83 for 6. Not long afterwards the contest was all over; Gloucestershire had won by 17 runs. Courtney Walsh (16.5-5-34-6) and David Lawrence (16-2-64-4) had bowled unchanged, Walsh collecting his second six-wicket haul of the match.

Gloucestershire supporters like Chris Bentall were jubilant. As the game finished he said to John Woodcock, *The Times* cricket correspondent who was standing next to him, 'Now we will win the championship.'

Woodcock calmly replied, 'We'll see.'

Next morning, at the end of his match report, Woodcock wrote, 'Fancy having to go and watch yet another Test match when the championship is producing days like this!'

Gloucestershire were fifty-four points ahead at the top of the table and could hardly wait for the Nottinghamshire match to start. In the event, rain held them up and it was to end in a draw. When they eventually got going, Philip Bainbridge (105), making his only century of the season, and Andy Stovold (81) helped their side reach 345. Bainbridge was captaining the team in the absence of Graveney, who had left himself out in the belief that the pitch would favour pace bowlers. The stand-in skipper must have felt helpless as the Nottinghamshire openers, Broad (105) and Robinson (108), put on 221 for the first wicket, a record partnership for opponents on the ground. Walsh and Lawrence had been tamed, and on 300 for 3 Clive Rice declared. In the remaining five hours of play, the hosts slumped to 58 for 5, before being rescued by an unbroken stand of 191 between Kevin Curran (117*) and Andy Stovold (74*).

Making his first appearance on the ground had been nineteen-year-old Mark Alleyne, a product of the Haringey Cricket School in London. According to the *Yearbook,* the youngster was 'one of the most exciting prospects the club has encountered in recent years'. Later in the year, he would be awarded the Cricket Society's Most Promising Young Cricketer Award, but while playing for these three days at the Festival he had witnessed the making of four centuries. Acquiring a taste for runs at Cheltenham, over the next decade he would be thrilling the crowds as Gloucestershire's foremost centurion of his era on the ground.

Test duty deprived the final visitors, Middlesex, of Mike Gatting, Phil Edmonds and John Emburey and the hosts of Bill Athey. On winning the toss, David Graveney inserted the Londoners, who took advantage of dropped catches and batted on after a weekend storm. They were bowled out on Monday for 349, with Walsh (35-9-95-5) becoming the first bowler to take one hundred wickets in the season.

There had been no play because of rain in both of the Sunday JPL matches, and to ensure there was no repetition of the previous year's antics, players had been banned from the Duraflex tent. Further rain interfered with the championship game, so Gloucestershire declared on 61 for 3 and Middlesex followed suit at 68 for 1, leaving their hosts to make 357 in a minimum of ninety overs.

Gloucestershire were bowled out for 252, with Jeremy Lloyds making 94. This marked the beginning of the demise of the county's championship challenge. It was compounded by victory for Essex, their nearest rivals, who also had a game in hand. The champagne celebration in the dressing-room after the victory against Hampshire had been premature, for after Cheltenham there followed a series of defeats and draws which saw the county finally finish runners-up to Essex. Agonisingly, they had missed out again.

CHAPTER TWENTY (1987-1997)

SALUTE WALSH AND ALLEYNE

—— 1987 ——

Norman Walters and his team of helpers were now operating the shop from a hired portakabin, for the caravan that had been towed up annually from Bristol was now on the scrap heap. On its 20 m.p.h. return journey down the A38, in a precariously unroadworthy state, Norman's convoy had narrowly missed being stopped by the police on Berkeley Hill as they attended to another vehicle. The gypsies' warning was heeded.

Attached to the front of the replacement cabin was a large awning under which Jack Britton sold books. Norman recalls, 'Inside, we were open from half past nine until after close of play and were never quiet. It was now quite big business, for on a good day we would be taking over £2,000.'

At the end of the day, Norman and Janet would retire to their hotel room, tired and in need of refreshment, laden with their day's takings. Norman reflects that 'keeping large sums of money in the bedroom was not a clever habit, but it was the only possible course if we were to balance up every night, which was essential'. It was hardly top-level security, but they did take precautions with the cash.

'We carried it into the hotel in shopping bags along with the paraphernalia of the day, and when we went to eat, it was always locked in a suitcase and hidden away. Anyway, fortune favoured the brave, or the foolish, for we never lost a penny through theft.'

Making its ground debut, perched alongside the club shop, was Wisteria Books, the author's small, family-run business, selling antiquarian and second-hand cricket books and ephemera. Indulging in eleven days of cricket quickly appealed to other entrepreneurs, and over the following years the caravan was joined by a wide variety of trade stands, some more long-lasting than others, all of which provided an interest for spectators throughout the day and added to the atmosphere on the ground.

Within the first half hour of the Festival, Lawrence clean bowled Leicestershire batsmen Cobb and Willey, but this did not prevent the visitors from amassing 367, with Briers (91), Gower (56), Whitaker (62) and Whitticase (59) the main contributors. The hosts replied with 288, led by Paul Romaines scoring 99, his highest championship score for three seasons, which was followed by a classical David Gower century (105*) in his last appearance on the ground. Set 315 to win, Gloucestershire were reeling at 107 for 6, although a rearguard action from Vibert Greene (62*) and Jack Russell (50) temporarily held up the inevitable. But with DeFreitas taking 6 for 94, Leicestershire won by 63 runs adding to their Sunday Refuge Assurance League success.

'I can still picture our disastrous start against Surrey (0 for 2),' recalls Geoffrey Need. 'Stovold chopped Sylvester Clarke's first ball straight to second slip and Athey was lbw.' Their saviour was Philip Bainbridge who was dropped in the slips early on, but then, according to *Wisden,* 'went on to dominate century stands with Wright and Curran, hitting 21 fours in his 151'.

In reply to Gloucestershire's 353 for 9 declared, Surrey belted 189 runs in the morning session next day, their hero being the swashbuckling Monte Lynch (114) who reached his hundred before lunch from ninety-nine balls. Switching roles, Bainbridge (25.1-8-70-5) took charge of the match again and the visitors were dismissed for 330. With Clarke injured, Gloucestershire quickly rattled up 292 and declared, setting their opponents 316 to win in sixty-six overs.

As worthy Festival cricketers, Surrey immediately took up the challenge and 100 for 1 almost became 200 for 3, but for a brilliant caught-and-bowled by David Graveney to remove the formidable Monte Lynch. The captain's handiwork cost him ten stitches in his right hand, but he had set the standard for further fine fielding. While he was across the road in hospital, Surrey continued to chase their target, but Gloucestershire held on to their catches and won by 52 runs.

Referring to the final match against Kent, *Wisden* records, 'With Curran hitting two sixes and fifteen fours in his third hundred of the season, and Athey (seventeen fours) returning to form, Gloucestershire delighted their supporters by dashing to 436 for 7 on the opening day.' Added to this came a stylish 82 from Mark Alleyne, the first of his many Festival contributions; then after a topsy-turvy Kent innings the visitors finished 113 runs in arrears.

Having won the RAL game by five wickets over the weekend, the hosts seemed to be cruising towards making a declaration on the last day, when Igglesden (18-1-53-5) and Underwood (12-2-28-2) suddenly had other ideas. As lunch approached, the two bowlers dismissed five Gloucestershire batsmen for 23 runs, leaving the county 243 ahead with three wickets in hand, but the possibility of an interesting finish to the Festival was washed away by rain which fell for the rest of the day.

—— 1988 ——

Festival gate receipts reached a record £35,000 in 1988. The opening game against fourth-placed Surrey was a fascinating contest throughout, and started off with the visitors making 312, as Clinton (102) batted for nearly six hours with a leg strain. Australian Terry Alderman, replacing Courtney Walsh who was on Test duty, took 4 for 81, but his most meaningful contributions to the match would come later with his bat. By the close of play on Saturday evening, the hosts were an embarrassing 12 for 3; and, to rub salt into the wound, Surrey beat them next day in the RAL.

Sylvester Clarke (21.1-5-44-5), bowling very fast and gaining tremendous lift, was warned for persistent short-pitched bowling, having already broken two knuckles on Bill Athey's right hand. Gloucestershire wickets continued to fall, and with nine of them down the brave Yorkshireman returned to the action to help Alderman, who scored the vital run to save the follow-on.

Anything Clarke could do, Lawrence could do better, and the Gloucester-born paceman, who was having an outstanding season, earned himself career-best figures (14.5-0-47-7) as the visitors were skittled out for 115. The hosts needed 265 to win and Stovold and Wright hammered on to 55, before a large, bright, sinking sun dazzled them as it started to slide behind the College classrooms - and 'sun stopped play'.

The following morning, the openers carried on together until Clarke struck with the total on 74, and by lunch time the county had collapsed to 132 for 8. Home supporters were already starting to look forward to the visit of Warwickshire next day, and in the absence of Athey, a gallant last wicket stand by Curran (101) and Alderman (43*) transfixed the crowd and transformed the game. Eventually, in the last over before tea, Clarke (32.1-14-63-6) became the Festival spoilsport when he had Curran caught in the gully. The spectacular entertainment was over; the two heroes had added 111 together and Surrey scrambled home by 21 runs.

With the Festival alight, Gloucestershire were invited to bat first by

Warwickshire, and Stovold stoked the embers with a quick-fire 52. The hosts declared on 356 for 8, helped by Romaines (99) and Bainbridge (119) who featured in a partnership of 160. After a fluent 84 from Asif Din, the visitors declared 49 runs behind.

Batting again, Bainbridge (70) and Romaines (50) continued their own party for two in the middle before Graveney declared, setting his opponents 284 to win in sixty-one overs. With Lawrence taking 4 for 71, the visitors edged their way nervously to 191 for 8 and time ran out.

There are many occasions when playing conditions come under the scrutiny of those feared men, the 'pitch inspectors'. Groundsmen lose sleep and counties lose points if the wrong boxes are ticked in their report. There were no such worries at that time for the groundstaff, for under the guidance of John Taylor they had produced excellent 'tracks'. In his final report on the match that had just ended, Paul Fitzpatrick wrote in *The Guardian:* 'John Taylor is a well-respected groundsman, and he produced a pitch that was approaching the ideal sought by the TCCB; it was dry, had some pace and bounce in it and yet encouraged the batsmen to play shots, of which there has been a glut since Wednesday. There was something for everybody, in fact.'

There was more praise to follow at the end of the final match of the Festival, with over 1,000 runs being scored. Graveney's gamble in putting Yorkshire in on an excellent batting-pitch came badly unstuck, as did Carrick's decision to impose the follow-on.

Fine weather greeted the start of what Nico Craven described as 'The Real McCoy'. In *Waiting For Cheltenham,* he wrote, 'There was some justified excitement on the home front when Terry Alderman, an out-and-out swinger, took three quick wickets during snifter time in the tent. The lunchtime scoreboard made good reading - 103 for 4 in 32 overs - and led to happy talk during the interval and between mouthfuls of Norma's smoked mackerel and fruit salad. It was a score that flattered to deceive, however, and turned out to be nothing more than "fool's gold".'

By the close, a maiden century from Byas (112), along with Blakey (40) and Carrick (81), had put Yorkshire back on course, enabling them to declare on 367 for 8, while the hosts had reached 21 without loss.

Next day David Green wrote in the *Sunday Telegraph,* 'Festival cricket has an enduring appeal. The grounds are almost without exception attractive and the pitches interesting. Players, I am sure, react positively to being in surroundings totally different from their staple diet of headquarters grounds . . . Cheltenham, once a spinner's paradise, is nowadays one of the quickest and bounciest pitches in the country.'

Indeed, there was plenty of bounce about the ground that day as a huge crowd, producing £10,000 in gate receipts, watched Gloucestershire record their only victory of this year's Festival. Beating Yorkshire by three wickets in the RAL, they kept themselves on course to finish the season second in the table.

One of the Festival highlights took place the following day, on the eighth day of the eighth month in 1988, with a special gathering of the unique '88 Club. The *Yearbook* records the club's formation a few years earlier: 'When Fred Dyke enquired of Shaun Mullan the score, and the reply came back "Eighty Eight" in that singular Northern Irish accent, echoed by that redoubtable Shirehampton supporter, Dave Cook, little did they know what they had inaugurated.'

With some forty members, including several players, one of whom was Courtney Walsh who had taken 88 wickets in 1986, the club had its own tent on the ground, courtesy of Dennis Deacon, where members proudly wore their '88 club tie with its distinctive eight shamrocks motif.

Whatever was happening in the cricket, and there was plenty of excitement to come, it was always going to be a special day for members, and having used various modes of transport to reach the ground, they gathered in the 'infamous tent', where at exactly 8 seconds past 08.08 on 8.8.88, a champagne toast was proposed to their club and Gloucestershire cricket. Photographs in front of the scoreboard followed and throughout the day there were guest appearances from playing members including David Graveney and Jack Russell, and the 1988 beneficiary Andy Brassington. Finally, in the evening, at 8 minutes past 8, Andy Stovold was presented with a tie.

On the field, the county, all out for 214, had performed poorly as Sidebottom (17-4-34-5) plugged away on a baking hot day to give his side the upper hand. By the close, Yorkshire were still five runs ahead having taken two of Gloucestershire's second innings wickets, but Bainbridge and Curran were together and looking on good form. In the first session next day they added 154, and when Curran (98) was out soon after lunch, he and Bainbridge, who went on to make his highest first-class score (169), had added 213. It was to be Graveney's last appearance on the ground as captain; that winter there would be upheavals at the club and controversial changes would follow. But now, at 404 for 6, he declared, leaving his opponents to make 252 in just over two and a half hours. It was tempting to go for the runs on such a fast-scoring ground, but in grabbing three early wickets, Alderman gave Yorkshire little choice but to let matters close quietly at 104 for 4.

John Woodcock reported in *The Times* next day, 'It was, extraordinarily enough, the best pitch I have seen this season - extraordinary for being on the sloping outfield of a school ground. The normal square is 50 yards from where the counties are accommodated. But since the boys went home, the roller has been at work most days, preparing the way for some entertaining, well-attended, eagerly-sponsored cricket.'

—— 1989 ——

Against opening opponents, Lancashire, eleven wickets fell before lunch on the first day. On a pitch oozing pace and bounce, a formidable spell of bowling by Courtney Walsh (12.5-2-40-6), ably assisted by Kevin Jarvis (9-1-37-4), routed the northerners for 93. Gloucestershire's first five batsmen found conditions equally difficult before Bainbridge (128) and Alleyne (111), making his first century for three years, featured in a ground record sixth wicket partnership of 245.

Batting again, 301 behind, Lancashire were soon in trouble as Walsh sent Mendis across the road to hospital with a damaged finger. Although Atherton, Jesty and Watkinson fought hard, Walsh picked up 4 for 64 and Graveney's spin earned him figures of 4 for 51. Mendis then reappeared for the last eight balls of the day and managed to see them out with Fitton before play closed with the visitors on 278 for 9.

Heeding medical advice, Mendis did not bat on the final morning. Don Oslear recalls, 'A three day match therefore ended as a win on the third day with no play having taken place on that day, although a wicket had not been taken. The result had not been achieved on the second day as both batsmen were "not out" and remained so on the third day. If it had rained on the third day and no play had been possible, even though one batsman would not have been able to bat, the result would have been a draw.'

An innings victory for the county was followed by a somewhat controversial 188 run defeat at the hands of Middlesex. With England's first choice wicket-keeper, Russell, away on Test duty, getting a better view than most of Marsh and Taylor's record-breaking opening partnership, Mike Gatting and John Emburey were both playing for the visitors, having been left out of the England team because of their membership of the forthcoming 'rebel' tour of South Africa.

Gatting and Graveney were tour captain and manager respectively, and this was the cause of what was probably the only demonstration ever to have taken place outside the ground. A noisy mob walked along Sandford Road past the hospital, turned into Bath Road and round into Thirlestaine Road, before pausing near the pavilion gate entrance for a rowdy harangue. It was most 'un-Cheltenham like' and to show his contempt, Gatting (110*), batting at the Chapel end, struck his tour manager for a huge six which sailed over the marquees and into the car park.

Martyn Ball, a member of the Young England team, was Gloucestershire's twelfth man and remembers being called into action after Middlesex paceman, Ricardo Ellcock, had bowled his first over. In pursuit of the visitors' 222, Wright and Butcher were opening for the county on a lightning fast wicket when, recalls Ball, 'at the end of the over, Tony Wright signalled to me to bring out a box!'

Torrential rain fell overnight causing water from the pavilion side of the ground to seep under the tarpaulin sheets and covers and onto the pitch. As a result, the umpires had a difficult decision to make the following morning.

'The start was delayed for some time,' recalls Don Oslear, 'but when my colleague and I decided to get going, our decision was not met with universal approval.'

Gloucestershire skipper Bill Athey was unhappy and the umpire comments, 'I bet it would have been different if the roles had been reversed and David Graveney was about to bowl on the damp pitch instead of John Emburey.'

Making full use of the conditions, Emburey recalls it was 'a most enjoyable morning' as he returned his career best figures of 14.3-2-27-7.

Meanwhile, Oslear had been at the centre of another controversy, namely the dismissal of Mark Alleyne, which added to his already rather uncomfortable morning: 'Alleyne hit a ball from Emburey high to deep, straight, long-on, where Simon Hughes caught the ball, crashed backwards against the boundary boards, slid down them and sat on the grass.'

Gatting appealed and Oslear gave Alleyne 'out'. As the batsman walked towards the pavilion, the umpire remembers, 'All hell broke loose, with boos and jeers coming from all around the ground. Then I was abused as we left the field for the lunch interval, and my colleague Alan Whitehead was so incensed that he took over the public address system and stated, in no uncertain terms, that I was correct.'

Batting again, Middlesex rattled on and by the close had reached 206 for 7. Next morning, declaring on this total, they left their hosts needing

Courtney Walsh in action against Lancashire 1989 (*The Times* London)

307 for victory. Emburey (26-8-39-5) continued where he had left off in the first innings and, assisted by Williams and Hughes, Middlesex bowled out Gloucestershire for 118.

Returning home after the match, Martyn Ball had a night out with friends in Chipping Sodbury. The following morning he was still sleeping off the effects of the previous night's ale when his father woke him at a quarter past nine to say that Bill Athey had telephoned, wanting him to play in the match against Derbyshire. Arriving just in time for the start, Ball found himself fielding on a fast outfield, where he and his team mates took a pasting from Bowler (57), Morris (121), Sharma (77) and O'Gorman (124).

'I remember dropping an easy caught-and-bowled chance from Tim O'Gorman when he was on 10,' reflects Ball. It was not the only missed opportunity and by Saturday evening the visitors had reached 422 for 6.

On Sunday, in their second match of the Festival, the county lost the RAL fixture against Derbyshire, which did not help their position at the bottom of the league table.

Next day the visitors declared on 448 for 9 and Gloucestershire reached 111 for 3 before rain moved in. Just before lunch on the final day, when the hosts had crept along to 175 for 6, a fierce storm broke out over the ground and the final afternoon was washed away.

Club committee member Michael Simpson maintains, 'The worst possible moment is when it rains on the last day of the Festival.' Perhaps on this occasion it was for the best, for it was difficult to see how anything else but a dull draw could have resulted.

—— 1990 ——

At the beginning of a new decade, educational matters such as examination timetables and school term dates made it necessary to start the Festival in July, rather than early August. As they had done ten years earlier, Gloucestershire arrived at Cheltenham without a championship win, but once again playing at the College resuscitated their flagging fortunes.

A parched outfield produced an aggregate of 1,244 runs in the drawn game with Yorkshire which started on 21 July. Being a Saturday, only three business marquees had been taken, but the guests of the county's main sponsors, Apple Centres West, along with spectators in the Barclay's Bank and Cheltenham College tents, enjoyed watching

Ashley Metcalfe. Launching the Festival with a sparkling 108 ball century before lunch, he went on to make 162 and his opening partnership of 204 with Martin Moxon (66) helped Yorkshire to reach 451 for 6, before a declaration was made.

The hosts also enjoyed the conditions, as Dean Hodgson (65) and his captain Tony Wright (78) put on 126 for the first wicket. Then the consistent Philip Bainbridge, in his last Festival, made his sixth century (152) on the ground, so joining Alf Dipper and Zaheer Abbas in the record books, in second place behind Hammond who had a total of nine. With Athey making 68 and Walsh slogging 63* in forty-two balls, including 4 sixes and 6 fours, Gloucestershire were eventually bowled out for 574. The run spree continued as Blakey (94) and Robinson (70*) reduced the deficit and the game ended with the visitors on 219 for 3.

That elusive first championship win of the summer came in the next match, when the county convincingly beat Northamptonshire by an innings and 128 runs. On the first morning, a fiery spell of 3 for 11 in twenty-five balls by Courtney Walsh rocked the visitors who never seemed to recover. Curran and Lawrence joined in the wicket-taking and by the close of play the county had edged 31 ahead with eight wickets in hand. The following day, Wright reached his century (112), Curran made 86 and with everyone else chipping in the declaration was made on 455 for 9.

According to *Wisden,* 'Walsh knocked the heart out of the Northamptonshire second innings by the sheer pace and variety of his attack, capturing 5 wickets for 9 runs in 27 balls.' By the close the visitors had slumped to 113 for 6, and on the last day a resilient 82* from Felton, along with hold-ups for rain, frustrated Gloucestershire. Then Walsh, producing the best championship bowling figures of the season (19.2-6-58-8), finally struck.

The match against Surrey provided a thrilling finish to the Festival with four results possible off the final ball. It was the kind of finale that made Marie Journeaux smile. Now working for Chris Coley's company, it was her job to market marquees. A conclusion like this, in the last scene of the final act of the play, was sure to sell spaces for next year.

Winning the toss, Ian Greig asked his hosts to bat first and at 27 for 2, with Bainbridge retired hurt, it seemed a good decision. Mark Alleyne recalls, 'I was pleased to be in the side, having played very few first team games in the season as I was out of favour with Eddie Barlow. The first ball I faced, I was dropped at fourth slip.' Putting this behind him, Alleyne went on to bat for five hours, making his highest first-class score to date (118). At the close of play, in reply to Gloucestershire's 301, Surrey were nine without loss.

By Sunday morning, the construction of a large gantry had been completed at the Chapel end to house the television cameras and commentators for coverage of the RAL match. The cameras may have reminded some of the home crowd with longer memories of the time the film *If* had been shot at the College - and perhaps had them wishing 'if only' they could win in a televised match . . . Their wishes came true, for despite their loss to Yorkshire the previous Sunday, the county swept to a five wicket victory, thanks largely to a dazzling 113 by Bill Athey. It was good television.

Back on the championship trail, Surrey declared their first innings 101 runs behind their hosts. Gloucestershire, helped by Athey with 86*, also declared, leaving the visitors to make 304 in fifty-nine overs and just as they had done three years earlier, they rose to the challenge. Darren Bicknell followed his first innings (83*) with 81, as Monte Lynch, revelling in the pace and bounce of the wicket, made a speedy 77. Surrey looked in command, but Lawrence (15-3-54-5), bowling very fast, brought Gloucestershire back into the game. Off the penultimate ball, wicket-keeper Richard Williams held a fine catch to bring the downfall of the ninth wicket. With three runs required for victory, last man Waqar Younis swiped at the last ball from Lawrence, was almost caught by Williams off a desperately hard chance, but scrambled a single. At 302 for 9 the match was drawn, but those present would never forget the spirit and tense atmosphere created by that narrow margin on the last ball of play. Three days later, when the Festival would normally have been starting, Cheltenham experienced the highest-ever recorded temperature to date in the United Kingdom: 37.1 degrees centigrade.

—— **1991** ——

Australian pace bowler David Gilbert, referred to in *Wisden* as 'more a workhorse than a match-winner', and lively left-armer Mike Smith both made their ground debuts in the first match. Tony Wright won the toss and on a damp pitch inserted Glamorgan and was quickly rewarded when David Lawrence took 3 wickets in four overs and their score slipped to 57 for 5. Matthew Maynard came to the crease and in three hours he made 129, including 23 fours and a six, scoring particularly freely off Lawrence, pulling and hooking the paceman fiercely if anything was dropped short.

By the end of the day, the hosts were struggling on 114 for 7 in pursuit of Glamorgan's 247. As everyone went home to relax and relive the day's events, Gerry Wolstenholme and his family set to work on creating the first edition of his two page journal, *The Cheltenham Spectator and Festival News.* Working late into the night and early next morning, Gerry completed his copy, visited the printer and brought Volume One, Number One, to the ground the next day.

As spectators were reading the review, Gloucestershire's batsmen were being bowled out for 140 by Watkin (17.4-3-49-5) and Frost (15-4-44-4), before Maynard proceeded to entertain Saturday's spectators with another sparkling century. To the delight of the considerable Glamorgan contingent in the crowd, he reached three figures in an hour and a half from eighty-three balls, so equalling the previous fastest hundreds of the season by Ian Botham and John Morris. Mike Smith recalls, 'He hit me for six and the ball ended up inside one of the cone-shaped loudspeakers, so the game was held up for five minutes while someone got a ladder and pulled the ball out!'

A third wicket partnership of 173 between Maynard and Hugh Morris (84) enabled Butcher to declare on 294 for 7. Facing the daunting task of needing to make 402 to win, disaster struck immediately for the hosts when they lost Hodgson and Romaines in the first over. When Jack Russell joined Richard Scott on the last morning, with the score on 123 for 5, nobody would have predicted what was to follow. Reviewing the season, Chris Hewitt wrote in the *Yearbook:* 'Pride of place goes to Jack Russell's match-saving innings against Glamorgan . . . an object lesson in sheer bloody-mindedness. Few things are certain in this world, but you can always back Jack not to roll over and die.'

When Scott departed, having made a forceful 122, Russell was joined by Lloyds (61) and together they added 110, giving the optimistic guests in the corporate tents a hint of a Gloucestershire victory. Wickets fell as Frost (29-7-99-7) returned his career best figures, but Russell (79*) stood firm and forced the draw, having been at the crease for over five hours.

New signing, Andy Babington, played for the county in the next match against his former club, Sussex. On the first day, according to Judith Halliday in the *Echo,* 'At least five cricket matches began at Cheltenham College on that same morning.'

She certainly chose the right morning to visit the ground for the following day's play was completely washed out and the game failed to get underway until a quarter to two on the final day. Walking round, while Hodgson and Wright were adding 117 runs, she focused on 'life the other side of the boundary'. Those other 'cricket matches' she mentioned were being played by children with tennis balls and Mark Alleyne joined in one of these contests as he strolled round the ground. He found it considerably easier to score runs here than he would later out in the middle, when he picked up one of his seven ducks of the season. Judith watched Wisteria Books 'doing a roaring trade as cricket magazines and books old and new, including that fountain of all knowledge Wisden', passed into 'enthusiastic hands'.

By lunch time, she had made it round to the corporate hospitality tents, where she suddenly heard 'the traditional thwack of cold beef against bone china'. She commented, 'The finely decorated tables are more reminiscent of a wedding buffet than a sports ground . . . Champagne glasses clink and the fresh cream flows and a few business deals are sorted out under the warm Gloucestershire sun while another few of those runs, or overs, or whatever, go up on the scoreboard.'

Some of those mysterious 'whatevers' were five runs picked up by Bill Athey, when the ball struck a fielder's helmet which had been placed behind the wicket-keeper. More runs mounted from the blade of Babington's bat as he smashed 58 from thirty balls, including 5 sixes and 3 fours, but by the end of an eventful day's play, Jones (23-3-84-5) and Dodemaide (33-3-130-5) had bowled the county out for 283. Rain then fell for a day and a half, both sides forfeited an innings and the game ended with Sussex on 199 for 7, chasing 284 to win.

A large first-day crowd turned up for the match against Worcestershire, hoping to see a display from the legendary Ian Botham, making his first appearance on the College ground. After a solid 65 from Tim Curtis and a brisk 79 by Damien D'Oliveira, spectators waited in awe as the bronze colossus Botham strode confidently to the wicket. He did not disappoint, for as *Wisden* reports, 'After some early miscues, he located the middle of the bat and struck twelve fours and a six in his 74 from 83 balls.' After the letdown of his departure, spectators settled to watch Newport smash some late runs, enabling Worcestershire to reach 333. In his *Daily Telegraph* report next day, Jeremy Allerton commented of Botham, 'In Barnum and Bailey terms he is a marketing man's delight and was probably responsible for a high percentage of the excellent crowd of 4,000 . . . it will be interesting to see whether "Falstaff" in bowling mode, can delight the exchequer to the same extent today.'

In front of Saturday's audience he took 3 wickets, while the lively

Graham Dilley (15.3-7-45-4) shook up Gloucestershire's batsmen. The exception, however, was Wright who played a captain's innings (120) and was given sound support by Alleyne (44) as the county avoided the follow-on, by reaching 241. The afternoon session then belonged to Worcestershire's tall Australian, Tom Moody, whose 80, containing 12 fours, was 'rich in aggressive strokes' according to *Wisden*.

Sunday heralded a return to one day cricket. Essex were the visitors, and just as Derbyshire had done a week earlier, they comfortably defeated their hosts. The final morning of the championship game saw Worcestershire score quickly. Lawrence, who was making his final first-class appearance on the ground, and Gilbert picked up four wickets each before a declaration was made, setting Tony Wright's men a target of 317 in eighty-five overs. At tea they were well placed on 146 for 2 and Gloucestershire supporters were beginning to realise they might just outplay their neighbours and grab the points. But sixteen overs later, Dilley (16-1-39-4) and left-arm spinner Stemp (28-6-85-4) had exposed the frailty of their hosts' batting, having bowled them out for 208.

—— 1992 ——

Club president Don Perry had much to reflect upon when he returned home to Charlton Kings at the end of the thirteen day Festival. The county had won three out of their five scheduled games and lost the surprise bonus NatWest quarter-final fixture.

It is often remarked that one of the blissful things about Cheltenham is that nothing ever seems to change. This year something did, for the press were no longer in their tent at the Chapel end of the ground. They had been moved to a writer's paradise, the balcony above the racquets courts with its panoramic outlook over the ground, previously the sacrosanct viewpoint for College masters.

Gathered in their gallery, the journalists wrestled with words and studied statistics as Yorkshire's captain Martin Moxon confidently made his way to 183 during a seven hour innings, recording the highest score for a Yorkshire player on the ground. At one stage, he was partnered by the nineteen-year-old Indian Test star Sachin Tendulkar, who excited spectators with his attractive 45.

In reply to the visitors' 364, on 103 for 8, Gloucestershire's tail wagged. Justin Vaughan (80), a New Zealand doctor born in Hereford, playing in only his second championship match, along with Courtney Walsh, who whacked 44, and last man Mark Davies (32*) together took their side to a respectable 257. Yorkshire's wicket-keeper, Richard Blakey, made six dismissals and Peter Hartley took 5 for 66. By the close of play, the hosts were back in the hunt having taken two early wickets as Yorkshire batted again. Then rain washed out Monday's play.

With a large crowd assembled for the Sunday League game, Jack Russell surprised onlookers by arriving at the ground in a helicopter. Having just been left out of the England team, the impressive entrance, although uncharacteristically ostentatious, was typical of Russell's fighting spirit. He would not be put down. Training with his team mates was followed by a couple of catches in Yorkshire's innings of 200, then a point was made again, right at the end of the match. With the hosts needing twelve to win off the last over, *Wisden* reports, 'Russell despatched the first three balls for a six and two fours to reach 41 in 21 balls.'

As the game ended, Jack Russell's agent Jim Ruston smiled. He was standing just in front of the 'Jack Russell Arts' marquee, a new addition to the trade stands on the ground. Having met the previous autumn, Jack had told Jim about the Festival and Jim immediately saw a business opportunity. Norman Walters had always displayed some of the artist's pictures in the club shop, but now with their own base on the ground, there was more room to exhibit the artwork. Jim Ruston recalls, 'We had a small tent with a pole in the middle and on sale was the colour print "The Moment of Victory" and several black and white pictures, the one of Gloucester Cathedral being very popular. We had a good Festival, so I ordered a larger tent for the following year.'

Many spectators had already made their way home when cavalier captaincy by Hampshire's Mark Nicholas suddenly rejuvenated the next match. It provided the kind of Festival action that Lillywhite would have applauded. Before Nicholas' flash of inspiration, the contest had pottered along rather quietly after Walsh (22-8-33-6), in his benefit year, had bowled out the visitors for 167. At the end of the second day, Gloucestershire had reached 339 for 8, the highlight being Alleyne (86) and Russell (75) adding 158 for the fifth wicket.

Hampshire had made a good start in the championship, but of late had rather lost their way. With the aim of securing some much needed points, Nicholas suddenly declared on 274 for 8, setting his hosts 103 to win in nine overs. Scott hit 5 sixes in a rapid 42 against his old county and Gloucestershire, despite losing wickets, were almost on course. Malcolm Marshall was then brought back for the final over, runs dried up and they finished on 95 for 7.

Making his first visit to the ground was Ken Faulkner who had been invited to come along by the jovial and popular John Flint. John's book business was flourishing, selling items at the Festival using the county shop as a base. Ken recalls, 'John had an agreement with Norman Walters that he wouldn't sell new books and at the same time, with his contacts in the trade, including Foyles, he was able to supply the shop with new and remaindered copies.' It was a good working arrangement, but sadly, one that would not last much longer.

Customers browsed at his bookstall as Sussex batsmen Smith (61), Lenham (83) and captain Alan Wells (63) took the visitors to 300 for 5, but a quick collapse suddenly found them 324 all out. Only Hodgson (82) and Russell (41) coped with the Sussex spinners, Donelan (36.2-13-77-6) and Salisbury (30-9-64-2), as the county finished up 103 behind on first innings.

By the close of play on the second day, the game looked evenly balanced with the visitors on 169 for 6. Having noted the success of spinners Martyn Ball (25-2-101-5) and Mark Davies (20.3-1-84-3), Wells declared, leaving the hosts to make 346 to win, confident that his spinners would bowl them out. Hodgson retired hurt without scoring, but fellow-opener Bill Athey followed his century (105) in the Sunday League victory against Sussex with a magnificent 181, his highest score for the county. Mastering the spinners, he was helped by Alleyne (46) and Russell (57) and the target was reached. Recalling the match, Athey, who was to join Sussex the following season, smiles and remembers 'a good win, on a difficult wicket against Donelan and Salisbury'.

The Festival organisers were purring. The event had been well attended; just under fifty firms had entertained in the marquees and the club tents had bulged. There were a further two new trade stands: artist David Byrne was selling his cricket prints and portraits, and the large Calor Gas display stand handed out a constant supply of tasty barbequed sausages to passing spectators. Under normal circumstances, it was now time for Attwoolls to take their marquees down, the cigarette ends to be picked up and the College groundstaff to start transforming the brown, trampled grass into rugby pitches for the autumn term. All this had to wait, for there was more cricket to come on Wednesday 29 July.

Gloucestershire were in the quarter-finals of the NatWest trophy and with major refurbishment still taking place at Bristol, the match was moved to Cheltenham. As soon as the Sussex game was over, the ground was a hive of activity. An extra stand was erected, more seating was brought in and final arrangements were made to cater for the large numbers expected in the corporate hospitality marquees.

The morning arrived, cloudless and sunny, and an early queue formed outside the ground, reminiscent of the old days. From half past seven, hungry early risers were tucking in to a full English breakfast, with a roll and coffee for £2.50; half an hour later Wisteria Books was bustling with customers.

The ground filled up; players arrived and savoured the scene. Winning the toss, Tony Wright chose to bat first. Some accurate bowling pegged the hosts back and despite fifties from Athey and Vaughan, their total of 236 never really looked enough.

It had always been Norman Walters' policy to keep the shop open from half an hour before start of play, until 'doors shut' thirty minutes after close of play, but that rule was about to go out of the window:

'From the moment we opened, it was like the tide coming in and just before 3 p.m., with morning cups of coffee untouched and no hope of anyone having time to eat, I shut the doors and posted a notice that we would re-open in twenty minutes. By the time the last of the inside customers had been shooed out, a difficult job with a queue forming outside, five minutes had gone, but at least we were able to draw breath, mop brows and relax. Then we suddenly realised how fish must feel in an aquarium! There were windows down the side of the cabin and each one was filled by eager faces pressed to the glass. Before our break had expired, there was tapping on the windows and doors and when we eventually did re-open, it was like an avalanche.'

Gloucestershire supporters were hoping for a quick avalanche of Essex wickets, and with hefty beefburgers lining the stomachs of those crowded into the bulging beer tents, the moment of drama that everyone had waited for was about to unfold: Courtney Walsh, top of the national bowling averages, was bowling to Graham Gooch, captain of England.

Walsh's first delivery lifted, came off Gooch's glove and the ball fell just short of the close fielder. But even if it had carried he would have been 'not out' - it was a no-ball. Having survived the rest of the pace bowler's salvo, Gooch sailed serenely on, helped by Prichard (58) and Hussain (30). His century came up with a huge on-drive off Walsh which headed high towards the classroom block, and on hitting Smith through the covers he reached 105*. Essex had won the game with seventeen balls to spare. Derek Goddard wrote in the *Echo*, 'The great man Gooch, batting like a latter-day W. G. Grace, did it in the grand manner.'

In *Benson and Hedges Cricket Year* David Lemmon commented, 'Gooch became the first man to win nine awards in the sixty-over competition, but an award should also go to Cheltenham and the Gloucestershire club for the excellent facilities provided for the paying customers. Would that all grounds showed such concern for those who watch.'

Less than a month after the Festival had finished, the Test and County Cricket Board announced their decision to play all county matches over four days from 1993. The idea sent ripples of anxiety through the minds of festival followers and organisers, who were concerned that the inflexibility of the new scheme would further threaten these age-old gatherings. Gloucestershire's secretary, Philip August, could see the difficulties that might arise. He maintained, 'We must continue with Cheltenham. It has a unique place in the English summer and, apart from anything else, we normally take sixty per cent of our season's gate money there.'

—— 1993 ——

An innocent bystander would not have known what all the fuss had been about when the 1993 Festival began. Nothing had changed: Gloucestershire were once again searching for that elusive championship victory, lovers of the game had twelve days of cricket ahead of them and the Wisteria Books caravan was rolling up for its seventh visit to the ground. As usual, setting out the stall early every morning required a team effort from the whole family, including all four children - George, Edward, Barnaby and Emily then aged fifteen, twelve, seven and five respectively. In the June edition of *Cotswold Life,* Amanda Simons described the scene:

'While the vast, ride-on mowers are making their stately circuits of the field we are busy erecting the caravan's awning, putting up bookshelves and trestle tables and setting out books, magazines, commemorative plates, photographs and prints . . . On busy days it is not unusual for customers to arrive before books are even out on the shelves. Some buyers are *Wisden* enthusiasts seeking elusive editions to complete a "run". Others seek reminiscences of eminent players and writers of the past such as Lord Hawke or Lord Harris, P. F. (Plum) Warner, H. S. Altham or Herbert Farjeon. Statistics appeal to some browsers while Brian Johnston's humour, Arthur Mailey's cartoons and the many varied publications by Christopher Martin-Jenkins all attract their respective buyers.'

This year, Derbyshire yearbooks were in demand for they were the opening opponents setting up an interesting bottom of the table clash. Courtney Walsh had taken over the captaincy from the out-of-form Tony Wright, and he must have wondered what he had let himself in for as the visitors piled up runs on the first day. Despite having been 58 for 4 and losing thirty overs for rain, by the close they were 408 for 5.

The day belonged to John Morris and Dominic Cork who shared a record partnership of 302 for Derbyshire's fifth wicket. Morris could not stop hitting boundaries and there were 32 fours and 3 sixes in his first ever double century. His final score of 229 stands as the highest ever made by an opponent on the ground. Saving the best till last, he scored his second hundred in seventy balls during the last session of the day. Cork was also a hero, for while making his maiden championship hundred (104) he was suffering badly from a hamstring injury which prevented him from bowling in the match. Mike Smith recalls, 'I had a shocker, nought for 108 in eighteen overs!'

Derbyshire carried on batting next day, and just before lunch they were all out for 521. Gloucestershire were then bowled out for 139 in thirty overs. Nothing had gone right all season and now it seemed even their usual Cheltenham fortune had deserted them. However, following on 382 behind, the county looked a different team. Broad (120), Russell (99*), Hodgson (64) and Hancock (56) were the main contributors to their total of 520, as Allan Warner finished with match figures of 10 for 120. On Saturday evening, Derbyshire had made 42 of the 139 needed and after a break for the one day game, they reached their target before lunch on the last day to win by seven wickets.

Until Sunday 1 August 1993, pyjamas at Cheltenham College had been confined to school trunks, clothes lists and boys dormitories. This was now no longer the case as Gloucestershire played Derbyshire, albeit for not very long, in the recently formed Axa Equity & Law League, sporting the new coloured clothing.

By the normal half-way stage of a Sunday game, this one was over. Derbyshire had won by eight wickets. Perhaps the guardian angels that watch over the Gothic chapel objected to the coloured clothes, white ball and black sightscreen and wanted it over and done with, but it did not hurry the spectators home. Next day in *The Daily Telegraph* Clive Ellis wrote, 'The festival crowd continued munching their sandwiches and absent-mindedly sipping their cups of tea as if they were convinced they had just watched a trailer to the main feature.'

Gone were the days of impromptu games, such as eleven county players batting with a broomstick against a 'town eighteen'. Instead there were two friendly games which took place over the next two days. The first was for David Lawrence's benefit, with his XI taking on a Rest of the World XI. Still suffering the effects of his horrendous shattered knee injury, the ever popular and much loved 'Syd' drew a crowd of around 3,000 to the ground, where to the relief of all he bowled at nearly full pace off his normal run, throwing in a bouncer or two and receiving huge applause.

The following day Gloucestershire took on Somerset in a Challenge Cup match to commemorate W. H. Brain's hat-trick of stumpings on the ground one hundred years earlier. The cup and a cash prize was donated by the wicket-keeper's grandson, Christopher Brain, chairman of the Cardiff based brewery S. A. Brain and Co. Ltd. and the day proved to be an entertaining interlude before the reappearance of county cricket on the eighth day of the Festival.

The first two days of the match against Lancashire moved slowly. After all, there were four days to complete it, but in the end only three were needed. Lancashire took the whole of the first day to reach 294, during which a student carrying out a GCSE Geography fieldwork project made some interesting observations. Top mark for ground facilities went to the spacious, convenient car parking area, while 'bottom' marks went to the ever-controversial public lavatories.

By the end of the second day, having at one stage been 131 for 4, the county had moved into the lead. The following morning, Alleyne (142*) put on 105 with Kevin Cooper (52) who made his maiden fifty. Just before lunch the hosts were all out for 450 and Philip DeFreitas had taken 5 for 104.

Gloucestershire's captain then took charge. Bowling brilliantly and helped by Cooper, Alleyne and Babington, Lancashire were 69 for 6 within twenty-three overs. A wagging tail helped to prevent an innings defeat, but it did not take the county long to score the fifty-eight runs required to give them victory by nine wickets. The tide had turned and Gloucestershire looked a different team for the rest of the season.

On 8 August, the 88 Club assembled and Shaun Mullan organised tie presentations. With the final over about to start in the AXA Equity & Law combat, the noise level rose in the Montpellier Wine Bar marquee. Enjoying its first year on the ground, throughout the Festival the marquee had proved to be a popular place for players to gather for a post-match drink. With Lancashire needing three runs for victory, and with three wickets in hand, Mark Alleyne was getting full support from the wine bar vocalists. The all-rounder conceded two runs, took two wickets and the last ball brought a run out. The match ended as a tie.

—— 1994 ——

The 1994 Festival must be remembered as one long triumph for Mark Alleyne. He helped himself to wickets, including one haul of five in an innings, made two hundreds and almost scored two more. Just as Britain's economy was awash with money, so Alleyne's bat was full of runs and as Nico Craven recorded in *A Watching Brief,* 'He provided the deserving Gloucestershire supporters with both classical stroke play and some razzle-dazzle entertainment.'

It all coincided with the arrival at the College of a new head groundsman, Geoff Swift. Formerly a works engineer at Dowty's, he had gained pitch-preparation experience when caring for the grounds at Arle Court. Walking over the College ground with the estates bursar, Jesse Gibbins, in February 1994, just before taking up his post, Geoff recalls, 'I'd never seen so many daisies in my life . . . I started with a huge challenge, but during my first week the weather was favourable and we managed to get lots of work done.' By the time the Festival arrived the outfield was already in better shape, and by the end of the season the square had improved so much that Geoff and his staff were awarded a TCCB pitch commendation.

Play started in shimmering heat and visitors Yorkshire had the best of the first day. A third wicket partnership of 134 featuring Matthew Windows (73) and Bobby Dawson (71) was the highlight of the county's innings of 291, and by the close of play, replying for the visitors, openers Martyn Moxon and Michael Vaughan wasted no time in knocking up 126.

Everything changed next day as Walsh (4 for 75), helped by Cooper and Alleyne each taking three wickets, bowled the visitors out for 247. Then followed a fine century by Alleyne (109), with Tony Wright (85) and all the other batsmen contributing towards a second innings total of 484. Needing 529 to win, Yorkshire, already somewhat demoralised by the exhausted Richie Richardson's announcement of his imminent departure home to the West Indies, along with a knee injury to Moxon, caved in to Gloucestershire's hostile captain. Martyn Ball recalls, 'Courtney was flying in and I was standing thirty yards back at first slip. It was superb bowling - Yorkshire's batsmen seemed to have fear in their eyes . . . I think they wished they weren't there.' Ball held on to five catches in the innings, four of them off Walsh's bowling (18-4-85-6), and after an hour of play on the final day, the hosts had raced to a 324 run victory. They had completed a double over the northerners, for the day before the county had won the AXA game by three wickets largely due to 102* from Mark Alleyne, his second hundred in two days. It had been a splendid start to the Festival for sponsors Astec Communications.

Although disappointed about being left out of the England team, Jack Russell was enjoying a busy benefit year. Arrangements had been made for his Gloucester Greats XI to take on a Rest of the World XI in between the championship matches, and it was a tribute to the popular, hard-working club vice-captain that hospitality tents were full and the ground had an air of excitement on the day.

In the souvenir programme Russell wrote, 'The Cheltenham Cricket Festival has been tremendously popular for more years than most of us can remember. Each year I look forward eagerly to playing on the famous College ground. The atmosphere is something special, and expectations always high.'

For the crowd, expectations were certainly high as 'Zed' was back in town, having been flown across the world courtesy of the Jack Russell Fine Art Gallery. He did not disappoint them.

It was proving to be a hectic Festival for Jim Ruston who recalls, 'We had a bigger tent than before, half of which had Jack's pictures on display, incuding the new print of the Cheltenham College pavilion. The other half displayed benefit items, such as ties and brochures . . . We were negotiating the purchase of the building next to the gallery in Chipping Sodbury at the time but finalising the deal was taking longer than we'd hoped. Eventually the solicitor rang me to confirm that the transaction had gone through when Gloucestershire were fielding, so I gave Jack the thumbs up as he looked my way at the end of an over!'

Kent somewhat spoilt the second half of the Festival for Gloucestershire supporters, because they caused it to end a day early, winning both the championship and AXA games by the same margin of 50 runs. But there was great entertainment as the four day match see-sawed towards its climax on the evening of the third day.

It all started with a flurry of runs from Mark Benson (159) and Trevor Ward (98) notching up an opening-partnership of 209. With the score on 287 for 2, the Kent players sipped their tea with smiles on their faces, but they had not noticed the warning in their tea leaves, for just over an hour later they were all out, having lost their last eight wickets for 64 runs. Hero of the hour was Mark Alleyne. He returned his career-best figures of

'THE PAVILION,
CHELTENHAM COLLEGE'.

14.2-2-78-5, twice on a hat-trick, before leading Gloucestershire's reply of 271 with a fine 96, batting 'with skill, composure and a pleasing variety of attacking strokes', according to Christopher Martin-Jenkins in *The Daily Telegraph.*

The visitors started the last day on 117 for 6 and were quickly finished off, leaving their hosts needing 285 for victory. In the middle of the afternoon, with Gloucestershire on 94 for 7, the game seemed as good as over, but the Festival's two 'men of the era' had other ideas. Mark Alleyne scored 80 and Courtney Walsh 66, his championship-best innings. Together they added 127 and just for a moment the seemingly impossible seemed possible. But when both batsmen were dismissed, the innings folded on 234.

In *Wisden Cricket Monthly,* David Foot wrote of Mark Alleyne, 'The Cheltenham festival often seemed to belong to him. He occupied the crease for a great deal of the time, with two hundreds and a 96. And a borderline bat-pad went against him when he might well have won the match against Kent.'

—— **1995** ——

Courtney Walsh was touring the country with his fellow West Indians, so Jack Russell took on the county captaincy. He led by example, keeping wicket as efficiently as ever and having an excellent season with the bat. His determination was rewarded at the College ground when a recall to the England side was announced, bringing a warm response from a large supportive crowd.

Three of the season's newcomers were on show for the first game against Lancashire. On his arrival from Surrey, Monte Lynch immediately strengthened the batting and Javagal Srinath was also proving to be a very useful replacement having stepped into Courtney Walsh's shoes. Perhaps most exciting of all was Birmingham-born and Australian-raised Andrew Symonds - the sensational sort of player perfectly suited to Festival cricket.

Winning the toss, the visitors' captain Mike Watkinson, who was also about to get a Test call-up, chose to bat first and must have rued the decision when his side were 92 for 7 at lunch. But a run-a-minute century partnership between Ian Austin (43) and Warren Hegg (61) gave Lancashire fresh hope and they were finally dismissed for 231. Gloucestershire's bowlers had shared their prey, although the honours for wicket-taking went to Andrew Symonds, whose brilliant fielding led to the run-outs of Fairbrother, Wasim Akram and Chapple. Everything had changed by the end of the day with the hosts restricted to 44 for 5. Monte Lynch had failed to score and when Symonds was out first ball next day, the county seemed to be staring at the follow-on.

As fifteen wickets had fallen during the first day, umpire Ray Julian had no option other than to report the pitch to Lord's, at the same time expressing his opinion that bad batting was the cause of the collapse and the pitch was definitely not to blame. Knowing this was the case anyway, Geoff Swift nevertheless breathed a sigh of relief when he saw Jack Russell at the wicket taking on Lancashire's bowlers. A partnership of 125 followed between the ever-improving Rob Cunliffe (92*) and his captain, who made a determined 83. It was enough to impress the England captain, Mike Atherton, who was fielding at slip, along with the onlooking chairman of selectors, Ray Illingworth, who commented, 'Russell made it look easy enough.' When the selectors met next day at the Queen's Hotel, Gloucestershire's wicket-keeper was picked for the forthcoming Test.

The hosts were bowled out for 265 by Wasim Akram (23.5-6-58-5) and Ian Austin (26-10-50-4), giving them a first innings lead of 34. As evening approached, Gloucestershire supporters revelled in an incredible spell of match-winning bowling and watched the visitors slump to 87 for 8.

In *The Times* next day, Alan Lee enthused: 'There are a handful of championship games each summer that live in the memory and this, for all its brevity, will be one of them. On the first morning, Lancashire were in disarray, and on the second, Gloucestershire were close to despair. Both rallied manfully, but it is Gloucestershire who have consolidated their recovery and, after two days of somersaulting fortunes, they are in sight of a famous victory. In a torrid final session yesterday, Lancashire were torn apart by Javagal Srinath and Mike Smith, as underrated a new-ball pair as there is in England. Bowling unchanged for more than two hours, they shared eight wickets, improved their combined championship aggregate to 97, and severely deflated Lancashire's title aspirations.'

On Saturday morning, as readers were flicking through their newspapers checking that the previous evening's astonishing events had really taken place, journalists were swirling round under the caravan awning at Wisteria Books, eager to find statistics and biographical material on Harold Larwood that would help them complete their daily columns. For the great bowler had died overnight in a Sydney hospital and after a minute's silence on the ground, play got underway.

Warren Hegg was caught behind off the second ball, then Mike Smith took the final wicket to give him figures of 22.3-6-60-5, while Srinath's 22-4-53-5 was equally impressive. Tony Wright (30*) and Matt Windows (51*) scored freely, with the winning run coming just after lunch to give the county victory by ten wickets. Next day, the Red Rose suffered another defeat. In front of a crowd of over 4,500 for the AXA match, with the gates closed before the start and several hundred people turned away, a final few hefty whacks from Andrew Symonds, who hit 2 sixes in his 47 from thirty-four balls, sealed the game.

Alan Lee had concluded his report by saying, 'The cricket has been so enthralling that the customary Cheltenham diversions, the browsing at bookstalls and promenading around the marquees, have had to be postponed. Big crowds have sat, absorbed, through the drama.' It meant that Ken Faulkner was having a gentle introduction to running John Flint's bookstall, a business he has since successfully developed. Having already prepared for the Festival, but with his health in a serious state, John had asked Ken to manage the stall for him. Sadly, following an operation, John died the following month.

There was no cricket on Monday, but in the evening a 125th anniversary dinner took place at the Town Hall. After the meal an auction was held which raised over £3,500 and this, together with the proceeds from the dinner, was split between the county and The Lord's Taverners. Gloucestershire's chairman, Dickie Rossiter, welcomed the four hundred and eighty guests and Sir Colin Cowdrey, president of the Taverners, responded by saying, 'It is lovely for the whole of cricket to see Gloucestershire, under that wonderful cricketer Jack Russell, alive and up there in the top six of the county championship.' The climax of the evening came with an hour-long show from impressionist Rory Bremner whose 'tongue was in good form', according to the *Echo,* as he progressed from politicians to sporting personalities and others in the world of entertainment. Next day, as Lord Vestey's International Sportsmen's XI were defeating The Lord's Taverners, Bremner, unable to play because of a broken finger, gave a thirty minute rip-roaringly hilarious commentary from the balcony, running relentlessly through a line-up of impersonations.

A mixture of first and second team players represented Gloucestershire the following day against the touring Young Australians. The visitors' side, bulging with talent, was managed by former county player David Gilbert, and although Hayden, Elliott, Law and Ponting all displayed their ability, Gilbert must have been particularly impressed with Mark Alleyne's match winning 102*.

Money was swirling into the county's coffers and as the championship game against Essex commenced, the previous year's record takings of £36,000 was about to be smashed. With Jack Russell resuming his Test career at Old Trafford, Mark Alleyne was handed the captaincy and on winning the toss invited the visitors to bat first. Nasser Hussain made 85 and Ronnie Irani 54, but no one could master the in-swing of left-armer Mike Smith who returned career best figures of 23.4-7-70-7. By the evening, the hosts were in hot pursuit on 115 for 3, with Monte Lynch and his captain together in the middle.

Nico Craven, our modern day diarist, celebrated his sixty years of watching county cricket at Cheltenham with a champagne toast and lunch party in his Festival headquarters, the New Club tent. Norma Hall, described by Keith Wheatley in the *Financial Times* as 'the bustling blonde manageress, who runs the tent like a combination of officers' mess and day centre for the elderly', was toasted as she fed the guests, while Lynch (111), Alleyne (77) and Symonds (123*) made hay in the sunshine.

Symonds was in full flow when the last wicket fell. Having hit 18 fours and 4 sixes, he reminded the visitors how to bat and Gloucestershire sped on before the close, continuing into much of the third day. In scorching sunshine, Darren Robinson made his career best score (123), while Mark Waugh (80), Nasser Hussain (65) and Ronnie Irani (68) helped their side reach 437. By the close of play on Saturday evening Gloucestershire were on 62 for 4. With Cunliffe absent due to a broken thumb, there would be a huge mountain for them to climb on the Monday.

Next day, a sensational, maiden, forty-seven ball, one-day century by Ronnie Irani (101*) included 8 sixes and 5 fours. Mark Waugh scored 78 and Graham Gooch 51, to set the hosts a formidable task of having to score 304 to win the AXA game. They fell well short, but a highlight was provided by Michael Cawdron, making his first team debut on his old school ground. Batting at number nine, he scored fifty in 'an innings full of fine shots' recalled Mike Smith.

Overnight the boundary boards and divisions between various enclosures were dismantled and transported to Bristol for the following day's NatWest Cup quarter-final tie against Northamptonshire. This created a rather strange aura, a feeling of abandonment at the start of the last day's play, and there were murmurings of discontent amongst the crowd, some of whom felt the tie should be played on the College ground.

However, their mood soon changed when they were treated to some fascinating cricket by Alleyne and Symonds who set about their task in a positive manner. After an hour and a half Symonds was out for 57, and only 99 more runs were needed for victory. The captain continued with a full array of strokes, until he was eventually caught on 141. With the job virtually completed there were a few nerve-racking moments before Ball and Srinath saw the county home by three wickets, taking them to fifth place in the championship table. Reflecting on the many occasions he has played on the ground, Mark Alleyne recalls, 'This was one of my most special moments at Cheltenham, captaining Gloucestershire for the first time and winning the game.'

It had been another memorable conclusion to the Festival and David Foot wrote in *The Guardian,* 'The soul of this match had nothing really to do with corporate hospitality or delicately billowing canvas. It belonged quintessentially to a single performance, that of Mark Alleyne . . . There was nothing flamboyant because that is not the nature of the man. He is almost a reverent figure at the crease, still as one of those Chapel pews beyond the boundary.'

In November came the sad news that both Grahame Parker and Cyril Hollinshead had died. As secretary, Grahame Parker had steered the club through difficult times, while Cyril Hollinshead had been editor of the *Gloucestershire Echo* for twenty-nine years. He had attended the Festival on many occasions and once wrote:

'Festival cricket at Cheltenham in August - the very thought of it fires a train of memories; the flurry of flannels in the sunshine, the crowded stands, the gay arcs of tents with their chairborne critics, the connoisseurs by the sightscreens, glasses clinking in the marquees . . . once upon a time a band . . . and of course the backcloth of College buildings, Gothic and gracious.'

—— 1996 ——

The 1996 Festival saw Norman and Janet Walters running the club shop for the last time. Over the years, they had spent endless hours working voluntarily in the portakabin, selling hundreds of autograph books, mini-bats, sun hats, biros and chocolate bars. Norman recalls, 'Of all the many and varied jobs I did for Gloucestershire in more than a half-century - aided and abetted by Janet most of the time - none gave more satisfaction than starting and then running the shop.'

They had an unexpected break after two days, which was the time it took Leicestershire to win the match by 102 runs, putting them one step nearer to being crowned champions. Twenty-five wickets fell on an extraordinary first day. Mike Smith recalls 'the flat, perfect wicket' which defied criticism, although the TCCB had to be informed of the debacle which was due to good bowling and poor batting.

During Leicestershire's first innings, the Smiths were the men in charge. Ben was top scorer with 68* out of 159, while Gloucestershire's Mike found plenty of swing and ended with figures of 18-3-55-6. It took the visitors just twenty-seven overs to dismiss their hosts for 71 with Millns, Mullally, Simmons and Parsons sharing the wickets; but the day had not finished. By the time stumps were drawn, the visitors had lost another five wickets for 80 runs and Phil Simmons had collected a first day pair, courtesy of being trapped lbw twice by Mike Smith.

People were beginning to grumble because it looked as if the match would end very early leaving a Festival vacuum. They were right, for the visitors were bowled out for 150 and the hosts managed to last forty-two overs for their 136. Corporate entertaining suffered and Philip August estimated that around £7,000 of gate receipts would be lost. To lift spirits, two Gloucestershire XI's played a forty-over match on Saturday, with free admission for spectators.

In the AXA fixture on Sunday, the county made 284 - their highest score in the competition to date - with a rapid, unbeaten, ninety-five ball century by Mark Alleyne and 60 from twenty-seven balls by Andrew Symonds. However, they were pipped to the post by Leicestershire who won by six wickets, thanks to a sparkling 99* in seventy-five balls from Habib.

Tony Wright's benefit match provided rich pickings for autograph hunters and proved to be a day of great fun for players and spectators alike, with the beneficiary's Gloucestershire XI taking on a talented World XI in a match which reunited Mike Procter and Zaheer Abbas. Then followed a one day game when the county were beaten by 28 runs by South Africa 'A', for whom Herschelle Gibbs made 55 and Jacques Kallis 60, while left-arm leg spinner Paul Adams treated the crowd to his unique bowling action.

A sunny morning greeted everyone for the start of the match against reigning champions Warwickshire. Gloucestershire needed a win, and hopes were high that the Festival fortune would not desert them. Writing in the *Daily Telegraph,* Scyld Berry once said of Gloucestershire, 'Cheltenham is the ground where their cricket casts off the rather plain uniform it wears at the County Ground in Bristol and puts on its bright summer frock.' By the third evening, the local supporters were partying in their frocks, having trounced the opposition by an innings and 116 runs.

Batting first, Gloucestershire amassed 569 runs. At the end of play on the first day, they were 331 for 3, with Matthew Windows 162*. In making his maiden championship century, he had stood firm early on in his innings against the fiery bowling of Shaun Pollock and Gladstone Small and been given solid support by Tim Hancock (57) and Monte Lynch (69).

Windows, who added 22 to his overnight score before being dismissed, reflects, 'It was a shame I didn't get a double hundred . . . but Shaun Pollock was fresh in the morning.'

He may have captured Windows' wicket, but the South African could not contain the rampaging Andrew Symonds, who smashed 127 off one hundred and seven balls in his last innings for the county on the ground. Warwickshire were never in the hunt and apart from Dominic Ostler, who made 73 and 90, and a final flurry of runs from Pollock (53), their batsmen found Walsh's pace and bounce too much in both innings as he ended with match figures of 35.5-8-117-11. Next day rain spoilt the AXA match, and with no play on Monday the Festival fizzled out quietly.

—— **1997** ——

'Fortress Cheltenham' is how Mike Smith described the College ground for the latter part of the 1990s, and it was certainly the case for the next two Festivals when the county won all four championship matches and three out of their four AXA Life League fixtures. It was an auspicious welcome for the new club Patron, Lord Vestey.

With the 1997 Ashes series evenly balanced at a draw and one win each, England coach, David Lloyd, arrived on the ground for the first day of the Festival when the county's opponents were Derbyshire. The visitors won the toss and chose to bat, but they could not cope with Mike Smith's swing and bounce, and as a result of his devastating spell (12-1-47-6) they were dismissed for 120. Eight days later, Smith was playing for England at Headingley.

With Devon Malcolm fired up, also wanting to impress the England coach, Gloucestershire slumped to 16 for 3 as the pace bowler quickly removed Wright, Trainor and Lynch. Then followed one of the treats of the season as the county's overseas Tasmanian player, Shaun Young, joined the immortals of Gloucestershire cricket. In ten minutes short of six hours, with 39 fours and 2 sixes, Young scored 237, a feat described by David Foot in *Wisden* as 'a truly superb innings to live in memory with some of the timeless ones on the College ground'. Making his maiden championship century, then going on to his double hundred, he joined W. G. Grace, Wally Hammond, Charles Townsend and Zaheer Abbas, the only other county players to achieve double centuries on the ground. He featured in stands of 139 for the fourth wicket with Tim Hancock (54), and 244 for the fifth wicket with his captain, Mark Alleyne (97), who just missed out on his sixth century on the ground before his team reached 484.

Gloucestershire's burst of runs was as stunning as the blaze of colour produced by the floral displays in the town as part of its bid for the Britain in Bloom competition. More colour was being added by artist Jocelyn Galsworthy, on her first visit to the ground, who positioned herself by the scorebox on the pavilion side and proceeded to capture the scene.

Derbyshire fared much better second time around, and a defiant 94 from Kim Barnett held up the inevitable. But Smith, whose four wickets gave him ten in a match for the third time in the season, supported by Alleyne, Young and Lewis, bowled out the visitors on the third day and the county waltzed home to win by an innings and 35 runs, taking them to third place in the championship table.

There was more quick scoring on Sunday for the AXA game. Although Barnett made 99 for Derbyshire, Young, with 85 from sixty-one balls, helped by Lynch (54*), swept the home side to victory by 7 wickets with seven overs to spare. With a 49 run victory, Pakistan 'A' spoilt the county's roll the day before Durham came to town.

There was a sense of *déjà vu* for Festival goers the following morning, as the visitors won the toss, batted first and were skittled out for 86 before lunch. Alleyne (8.2-2-14-5) was the chief destroyer, supported by Young (10-4-9-3) and Lewis, who took 2 for 35, and to complete the picture Gloucestershire lost three quick wickets before starting to pile on the runs. Windows made 75 and Young 52, and through a rain-interrupted second day, Mark Alleyne (169) and Jack Russell (103*), making his first hundred in the championship for six years, heaped on the agony for Durham in a partnership worth 205. Declaring on 471 for 6, Alleyne left the visitors to face seventeen overs before the close, but the heavens opened much to their relief.

Starting the third day 382 behind, Durham's batsmen grafted

Cheltenham Cricket Festival Cheltenham College, by Jocelyn Galsworthy (1997)

From left to right, Peter West, Matthew Engel, Graeme Wright, Nico Craven, Frank Keating and David Foot at the launch of *Sunday, Monday or All Days*, at Wisteria Books (1998)

Chris Coley listening to Club Patron Lord Vestey (1998)

Right. Jocelyn Galsworthy at work (1997)

resolutely, with each partnership producing a few runs and frustrating their hosts. Lewis (81) anchored the innings for over four hours before David Boon (66) carried on. But by the close, Gloucestershire, despite having claimed the extra half an hour, had failed to complete the job with the visitors still there on 321 for 7.

Next morning, with rain in the air, Gloucestershire hearts fluttered, but they managed to capture the last three wickets before a deluge. Alleyne had taken four wickets to complete an outstanding all-round performance, recalling modestly, 'I was just taking Mike's wickets.'

Twenty-four points were safely in the bag and Gloucestershire were sitting proudly on top of the championship. They followed this with a convincing five wicket victory in Sunday's AXA game. The crowd were cock-a-hoop.

CHAPTER TWENTY-ONE (1998-2003)

APPROACHING THE
FESTIVAL CENTENARY

—— 1998 ——

Geoff Swift felt happy on the first day of the Festival. Sitting on a shelf in his office was the England and Wales Cricket Board Cup that he had won for preparing the best outground in England the previous year. There was every chance that it would be staying there for another twelve months.

In a low-scoring match, Sussex batted first and were bowled out for 191, with Walsh, Smith and Lewis sharing the wickets. By the close of play, the hosts were almost half-way to achieving a first innings lead, with Tim Hancock on 60*. He added 16 to his overnight score next day, while an eighth wicket partnership between Russell and Ball eventually enabled the county to reach 238.

Making his first visit to the ground, Neville Denson was inspired to write a poem entitled *Cheltenham Festival*:

Early arrived, I parked and wandered to the shops,
Picked up sweets and a paper, paid the lady what I owed.
'Enjoy the cricket, sir' she called, it caught me on the hop;
Smiling, I turned and said 'I didn't think it showed.'

Back in the ground, the College Chapel and Great Hall
Dwarf tents, marquees and like a stiff but kindly chaperone
Cast stern and watchful yet approving eyes on bat and ball,
On social chit-chat, cricket lore - and mobile phone.

'neath cloudless sky of Cotswold blue she looks around -
Bright dresses, shirt-sleeved gents in shorts add to this summer set;
Blazers, panamas, boaters, ties, dot colour to the ground:
I sense she's pleased the baseball cap's not master yet.

The midday sight and sound and smell of food and drink:
And books, old *Wisdens* telling tales of earlier Cheltenham days;
Jack Russell's paintings: time to paint the face some people think,
In oils or sun-block to keep out those harmful rays.

The regulars perambulate the ground, meet those
They haven't seen since festive, golden cricket days last year.
Oh yes, the cricket! A cover-drive - more poetry than prose.
''Gainst butress and spire it echoed' I seem to hear.

A superb shot and there are vital points at stake,
My guilt at being inattentive lessens as I see
The nation's finest writers on the game swap yarns and break
Their concentration for some joviality.

Tea in the New Club (which is old) then browsing at
Wisteria's books, transported back to days of endless sun,
When a finger always went high to an Evans' 'Howzat?'
And Bedser and Compton made quite sure that we won.

Play resumes, Courtney Walsh picks up a tennis ball,
He pockets it, looks skyward, feigning total innocence.
 An anxious wait for young boys each willing their hero tall
To toss it back; but Courtney strides out away from the fence -
Then quickly turns and bowls it back at last. It thrills them all.
What tales to tell when back at school - their joy's intense.

I leave, content the essence of the summer game,
So well loved for so long, remains alive and very well;
There's serious play but lightness too and it will stay the same
So long as Cheltenham can hold its magic spell.

Neville Denson was one of the guests at the launch of Nico Craven's thirtieth book, *Sunday, Monday, or All Days*, held during a sunny lunch interval. The celebration, spiced with speeches, nibbles and local wine, was held at the 'Wisteria bookshop', a 'venerable institution' according to Jamie Reid in *The Guardian*. Present were Peter West, David Foot, Matthew Engel, Frank Keating and Graeme Wright, each of whom had written a foreword to one of Craven's previous books, and they quizzed him to find out if this publication would really be his last, as he claimed.

When Sussex batted again, the Exiles' 'Player of 1997', Mike Smith (19-9-31-4), helped to keep their total down to 162, leaving Gloucestershire needing 116 to win. At the start of their innings, left-armer Jason Lewry produced two unplayable wicket-taking deliveries to complete a hat-trick, having previously dismissed Mike Smith to end Gloucestershire's first innings.

'One was a yorker,' according to David Foot in *The Guardian*, 'and the other slanted wickedly in the Cotswold breeze to produce such audible gasps that the nurses rushed to the ward windows of the hospital across the road to see what was happening. The batsmen, Nick Trainor and Dominic Hewson, certainly had no idea at all.'

Windows (60*) steered the county home to a seven wicket win, gaining twenty-one points and second place in the championship, putting extra emphasis on the visit of leaders Surrey the following week.

On Saturday, before the first of two AXA League matches played on consecutive days, a colourful five-over game took place to mark the one hundred and fiftieth anniversary of W. G. Grace's birth. Two teams, one led by Cheltenham Member of Parliament, Nigel Jones, posing as W.G himself, took to the field wearing Victorian cricket clothing, and their under-arm bowling was smashed all over the ground much to the amusement of the growing crowd.

A full house then watched Gloucestershire beat Sussex by 35 runs, but the following day, in front of another good crowd, they came unstuck against Northamptonshire, going down by 72 runs with five overs to spare.

Before Courtney Walsh's close-finishing testimonial match took place, a 'fastest bowler' competition was held. Ten 'quickies' took part and the winner was Devon Malcolm with one of his deliveries registering eighty-eight miles per hour. To round things off, Walsh took wicket-keeper Mark Alleyne by surprise when he bowled him an apple at eighty-one miles per hour.

The fun was over; Surrey had arrived on the ground hungry for points, and there was every indication that it would be a captivating contest. It lived up to all expectations from the moment Surrey won the toss, chose to bat and opener Ian Ward was dismissed for nought. The visitors then reached 297, based around an innings of 112 by their captain Adam Hollioake, while Mike Smith (19.5-2-66-6) made full use of the bouncy pitch.

Gloucestershire started reasonably well, with Cunliffe and Hancock putting on 53 for the first wicket. Hewson made a useful half-century,

Top. Jack Russell becomes a jockey (1999)

Middle. Gurkhas entertain the crowd (1999)

Bottom. Parachutists landing on the ground (1996)

Top. Shirt sleeves and sunhats prevail on the hospital side of the ground (2000)
Below. Looking towards the pavilion (2000)

before the gentle, rather dreamy, mood of the Festival was suddenly shattered. From 166 for 4, Gloucestershire collapsed in twenty-seven balls to 167 all out in twenty-three minutes. Martin Bicknell (14-5-34-5) and Saqlain Mushtaq (24-5-84-4) were the cause of the slump and they then sat back to watch their team mates build on the 130 run first innings lead. However, things did not quite go according to plan, for Courtney Walsh, in what was to be his last championship match on the ground, bowled as if he was playing for his place in the team. With all his characteristic fire, he skittled out the opposition for 135, ending with figures of 14-1-47-6. Gloucestershire needed 266 to win.

'On 163 for 6, Surrey were in the ascendancy,' reflected Mark Alleyne, but gradually Matt Windows (60) and Martyn Ball (48*) clawed their side back into the contest. The atmosphere around the ground was electric and Mike Smith, batting with Ball and dropped at square-leg just before the end, remembered 'the packed crowd willing us on'. Their exhortations worked, for the hosts won by two wickets and Matt Windows remembers seeing Courtney 'jumping off his seat with excitement'.

With a smile on his face, Mark Alleyne recalled, 'This was an important moment for us all, a turning point for Gloucestershire cricket. From then on, we started to win competitions.' After only a short time as coach, the approach and philosophy of John Bracewell was starting to show, and over the next five years his influence would be a key factor in the transformation of the team into one of the most competitive one-day sides in the country.

On the final day of the Festival, the county beat Surrey by twenty-two runs in the AXA game. Sponsors, Abbey Business Equipment, along with sixty other firms, had hired whole or part spaces in the ring of trim, white marquees over the last thirteen days and conducted business and entertained guests during another highly successful time for the county cricket club. Gate receipts were over £45,000, the team was now second in the championship and later, winning the outground award again, Geoff Swift's cup stayed firmly on the shelf.

—— 1999 ——

'Festival cricket, away from county headquarters, is where the heart of county cricket beats most strongly,' wrote Michael Henderson in *The Daily Telegraph*. 'It is where spectators loaf in deckchairs, munching sandwiches they have made themselves and napping between overs; where people renew friendships left off the previous summer; buy second-hand books from lovingly tended stalls; quaff pints, decent and otherwise, in tents; and generally rediscover why they fell in love with the game . . . The best of all is the College ground at Cheltenham. Good old "Chelters" never disappoints.'

On this occasion, he was wrong. For in 1999, there were several hundred despondent locals who left the ground after the second of the county's two championship defeats. Their run of victories had come to an end and they were sitting at the bottom of the game's four-day table. 'Fortress Cheltenham' had been breached. But Gloucestershire were flying high in one-day cricket and with a place in the Benson and Hedges Super Cup final, they were also proceeding smoothly through the NatWest Trophy rounds.

Invited to bat first, Worcestershire tortured their hosts before declaring on 591 for 7. There were three stylish centurions - Weston (139), Hick (122) and Solanki - whose 171 contained 6 sixes and 19 fours. Reflecting on the run-feast, Graeme Hick commented, 'It was an excellent hard, fast pitch with plenty of bounce . . . It is the best out ground pitch and much better than many county ground surfaces.'

In aid of Mark Alleyne's benefit fund, singer and songwriter Johnny Coppin, along with Sid Powell, Edward Gillespie and friends, gave an entertaining evening entitled *Gloucestershire Sport in Words and Music* in Big Classical. It proved to be far more harmonious than Gloucestershire's batting. Taking 6 for 101, Alamgir Sheriyar bowled Worcestershire to a first innings lead of 360 and Tom Moody duly enforced the follow-on. However, his hosts were not the push-over he had hoped for as Kim Barnett scored his maiden century for the county (106), while Ball (70*) and Lewis (62) featured in a ground record tenth wicket partnership for the county of 130. Needing 66 to win, Mike Smith quickly removed Worcestershire's first four batsmen; but the captain came in, steadied the ship and helped to steer his team to a five wicket success.

Next day, Gloucestershire hammered Yorkshire by 128 runs in a CGU National League match, thanks to Russell's 91* and Ball's 5 for 42. A week later, in the same competition, Mike Cawdron's 4 for 17 helped to give his side victory by three wickets against Warwickshire, the winning runs coming from Mark Alleyne's on-drive for six off the penultimate ball.

Having been beaten by Sri Lanka 'A', the county welcomed Durham for the final match, as they had done two years earlier almost to the day.

However, the result this time was a complete reversal of fortunes, with the visitors dealing their hosts an innings and 127 run defeat.

Durham's total of 552, their third highest score, included half-centuries from Lewis and Speight and 74 from Morris, while Speak (110) and Boon (139) featured in a record 192 run fourth wicket partnership for visitors to the ground. Gloucestershire never looked like getting anywhere near their target, and 5 for 78 for Brown in the first innings followed by 5 for 44 for Killeen in the second wrapped matters up in three days.

—— 2000 ——

Having finished bottom of the county championship the previous year, Gloucestershire were one of nine teams in the second division of the PPP Healthcare County Championship of 2000. The team arrived in Cheltenham on a high; one day cricket was proving to be their forte. They had already retained the Benson and Hedges Cup and there was excited talk of other trophies heading to Bristol. By the end of the season, through hard work and self-belief, the NatWest Trophy and the Norwich Union league title cup would both be sitting safely at Nevil Road.

The Festival's new sponsors were Cheltenham and Gloucester Building Society and it seemed like the ideal marriage - a leading national company based in the county linked to a well-established and popular local event. Roger Burden, their managing director, commented, 'A partnership between the Cheltenham Cricket Festival and C&G is a perfect match,' while Colin Sexstone, the county's chief executive was 'absolutely delighted that the most successful cricket festival in the country should be sponsored by a company of C&G's standing'.

Just before the Festival started the heavens opened, making preparations a nightmare for the organisers. As vehicles moved on and off the site churning up the ground, Chris Coley trudged round in his wellington boots, trying to keep a smile on his face, and eventually deciding to put down straw and woodshavings to allay the damage. When the Festival got underway the sun began to shine, and raincoats and umbrellas were replaced by shirt sleeves and sun hats.

Northamptonshire were the opening opponents and proceeded to make 543, their highest-ever score against Gloucestershire. Opening for the visitors, Adrian Rollins (63) and their Australian captain, Matthew Hayden (75), put on 131. Mike Smith likened Hayden's innings to Shaun

Young's huge score, remarking, 'They both used the bounce for their square-of-the-wicket shots.' Jeff Cook, an Australian born left-hander, also found it an enjoyable pitch on which to score runs, making 137 in four and a half hours, including 23 fours.

During lunch on the second day, Bryan 'Bomber' Wells and author Stephen Chalke launched their book, *One More Run.* Sitting and watching the match against Worcestershire the previous year, Stephen Chalke had quizzed, listened and recorded, as Bomber recalled the dramatic match against Yorkshire in 1957. He had also gathered contributions from former players and spectators present on the occasion. While tales included (and not included) in the book were still being exchanged, play resumed and although wickets were falling, the visitors were making rapid headway, each of their batsmen contributing to the huge total.

By the close, Gloucestershire, on 77 for 4, were facing an uphill struggle and they were bowled out quickly next day for 116. Following on, Dominic Hewson playing in front of his familiar old school pavilion clock, made a useful 57, while Ian Harvey scored a swashbuckling fifty. But the honours went to Jack Russell whose 110* lasted nearly five hours and ensured play went on into the last day. As those around him struggled against the spin of Graeme Swann (49.5-12-118-6) and Jason Brown (55-18-136-3), Russell stood firm. Finally, after a two hour stay at the wicket by Mike Smith, the visitors broke through and won by an innings and 99 runs.

A win against Worcestershire next day in the Norwich Union League kept the county on course at the top of the table, while a defeat at the hands of New Zealand 'A', followed by David Bridle's benefit day, preceded the arrival of Warwickshire.

'I can't believe there will be a bigger crowd for a championship game anywhere else this season,' said the county's chief executive, Colin Sexstone, when commenting about the Festival in the *Echo*. 'The numbers turning up for the Warwickshire game are tremendous. It's a tribute to the drawing power of the Cheltenham Cricket Festival. People come from far and wide and long may it continue.' Picking up their C&G 'goodie bags' once inside the ground, adults had paid £8, senior citizens £6 and under sixteens £2 at the gate, and with such a large number of spectators, it was hoped that the previous year's entrance receipts of £62,000 would be beaten.

Batting first, Warwickshire made 260 on the first day, with Harvey proving the most successful bowler, returning figures of 23-12-29-5.

Top. View from the balcony (1996)
Below. The Chapel end (2001)

Top. Tom and Ken Graveney (2001)
Below. The groundstaff: from left to right, Michael Broom, Andrew O'Brien,
Bob McInroy, Dennis Dunn, Simon McAulay (2002)

Windows (79) was the county's top scorer in their total of 254 and by the third day, the hosts having made 316, looked to have the upper hand for a final-day victory. When Gloucestershire batted, Allan Donald (19-11-22-1) and Ashley Giles (45-14-74-4) kept the runs down, and the visitors made no real effort in tempting their opponents to chase the target of 323 in the hope of capturing wickets. Long before the close the match fizzled out as a draw.

First-class entertainment on the final day of the Festival was provided by the Ghurka Brass Band on the outfield, playing a medley of tunes including *Don't Cry For Me Argentina,* while the Gloucestershire and Kent players went through the final stages of their pre-match practices. Kent made 199 from their forty-five overs, then Hewson and Harvey scored 72 in thirteen overs, leaving Russell to seal matters with a run-a-ball innings of 55*.

As another Festival came to an end, Colin Sexstone reflected, 'Cheltenham has a unique ambience. The secret of its success is the length, which must be protected, as nothing stands still and the structure of the game is forever changing.'

—— 2001 ——

It was always going to be difficult to follow their tremendous successes of the previous summer, and by the time the Festival arrived Gloucestershire's season seemed to be faltering. They were badly in need of some traditional Cheltenham tonic and, true to form, it materialized, with three wins and a draw amidst some glorious sunshine.

Table-leaders Sussex were the first opponents and having won the toss, Chris Adams invited his hosts to bat. 'It is a bold team that flies in the face of history, and usually a foolish one,' wrote Christopher Martin-Jenkins in *The Times,* when reporting the first day's play. 'Kim Barnett, Chris Taylor and Jeremy Snape made it a day to cherish for the many devotees of this great festival. Before the rounded mass of Cleeve Hill, the classical splendour of the College chapel and the ring of white marquees, they were bathed in unbroken sunshine and entertained by a constant ratatattat of boundaries, from the bats of Taylor and Snape in particular.'

Barnett's 79 was followed by a fifth wicket partnership of 204 between Snape (131) and Taylor (140) - later in the Festival to receive his county cap from chairman John Higson - as Gloucestershire reached 520.

On the third morning, Sussex were bowled out for 167 and started their follow-on, during which they performed with much more conviction. Chris Adams (123) and Richard Montgomerie (107), making his sixth century of the season, ensured that the game would go on until the final day and their hosts would have to bat again. Sussex were eventually dismissed for 375, with Ian Harvey returning figures of 23-11-33-5, leaving Hewson and Barnett to score the required runs, so taking the county to a ten wicket victory and their first championship win on the ground for three years.

Beyond the boundary boards at the Chapel end of the ground, curving round from the club caravan to the marquees which run parallel to Sandford Road, was Chris Coley's latest creation - a shopping mall of trade stands. It provided the perfect browsing and buying area for, amongst many others, Len Hartry, Festival devotee and avid cricket book collector. One of the tents was the ground headquarters for Mike Smith's benefit fund, where, a busy stream of his friends and supporters helped with various fundraising events throughout the Festival, the highlight being the auction of cricket memorabilia held in the College gymnasium. Unfortunately, the beneficiary was out of action with a back problem and was particularly disappointed not to be taking part. He claimed his two favourite places to play were Lords and Cheltenham: 'It is here that my heart always misses a beat for two reasons, the great atmosphere and warm sunshine.'

The next guests were Nottinghamshire for a Norwich Union League match, and after an early start, Richard Sharp, on duty at the Chapel Gate, had one of his busiest Festival days. A total of around £20,000 gate money was taken; money matters had come a long way from tales of farmers in olden days paying for their entry with a box of eggs.

Dominic Hewson (52) and Kim Barnett (100) opened the innings with a partnership of 124, and by the time Ian Harvey, with 6 fours and 2 sixes, had smashed 46, the county were well on their way to a big score. Batting alongside Martyn Ball at the end of the innings was all-rounder Mark Hardinges, making his first appearance on the ground, and his contribution to their partnership of 47 in four overs helped Gloucestershire reach 286 for 8, their highest league total to date. Nottinghamshire could only muster 170 and Hardinges has fond memories of his Cheltenham debut, which included taking a wicket. He found it exciting playing in front of a big crowd and enjoyed 'the good humour coming from the Montpellier Wine Bar'.

Next day, 1 August, the championship game against Hampshire

started and Tom Richardson took up his new post as the club's Chief Executive. Despite having won large amounts of prize money the season before, the finances of the club were not looking good and Richardson was faced with an immediate challenge of trying to put money matters back on an even keel.

The morning copy of *The Times* contained Alan Lee's running feature, *The Good Ground Guide*. At Cheltenham, although 'shelter from the sun' was at a premium and the scoreboards were considered 'rudimentary', access and signs, car parking, staff attitude, comfort, cleanliness, catering and bars all scored well. With ten out of ten for aesthetics and atmosphere, the Festival site, overall, received a glowing report:

'County cricket has only one proper Festival left, a sadness that illuminates the survivor ever more brightly . . . The stately chapel gives the College Ground its elegance, the imported marquees deliver its charm. No venue in the land evokes such unanimous affection, nor such protective instincts. Counties relish playing here, journalists compete for the coverage and spectators flock to the ambience of both town and ground.'

The visitors had just inflicted a first, first-class defeat upon the Australian tourists, but according to Ivo Tennant in *The Times,* Hampshire looked 'a bedraggled lot when they took the field'. Hit by a number of injuries, substitutes stepped in to fill the gaps and by lunch, when Nico Craven's thirty-first book was being launched, Matthew Windows (91) and Chris Taylor (56) were enjoying a profitable partnership. During the afternoon, Udal bowled thirty-two overs and took 4 for 76, and by the close Gloucestershire were all out for 334.

Rain prevented play the following day and the visitors were bowled out on the third day for 230. Then just after six o'clock, as the county's batsmen were building up a good lead, the town had an unexpected royal visitor. Following an accident while playing polo, HRH the Prince of Wales, under police escort, was whisked through the red traffic lights on Bath Road before arriving at the hospital. There he stayed overnight, leaving some wondering if he would pay the Festival a visit on Saturday morning, but instead he swept out of town to the Queen Mother's one hundred and first birthday party.

Meanwhile, at the Festival, Barnett went on to score 93 and the county's declaration left Hampshire needing 350 from sixty-five overs. They refused the challenge and luckily rain showed compassion on around 1,000 stalwart spectators, saving them from enduring a pointless afternoon's cricket.

Sunshine, breeze and clouds greeted 5,000 spectators to the ground next day for a memorable Norwich Union fixture, as the fast outfield and small boundaries helped to produce an action-packed, high-scoring match. 'Things happen so quickly at Cheltenham,' Martyn Ball commented and Ian Harvey's cameo in the sunshine of 67 in thirty-four balls started to prove the point. But there was more to come. Hitting 5 sixes and 10 fours, Matt Windows blasted 117 from ninety-four deliveries and with Taylor's 63, the county surpassed their score of the previous week to achieve a new record high of 344 for 6. Northamptonshire's brave attempt was kept in check by James Averis (9-1-56-5) and they finished up 83 runs behind their hosts.

Umpiring his last game on the ground before retiring at the end of the season, Ray Julian recalled, 'I saw over 600 runs scored that day . . . Players and umpires always look forward to coming to the Cheltenham Festival. It really is the place to be and may it continue for years to come.'

In October, having won the outground award yet again, Geoff Swift retired. As well as his responsibilities for the College grounds, he said he derived 'huge pleasure' watching the boys play on the wickets he had prepared for them, while 'doing the county square was a bonus'. Out of seven years, there was only one without an award. 'Quite good for an engineer,' remarked Geoff with a chuckle.

—— 2002 ——

Even the shrewdest of cricket brains was finding it difficult to make head or tail of the season's higgledy-piggledy first-class fixture list. It was as if a freak wind had rushed through the fixtures office at Lord's, blowing timetables and schedules into the air, and when the papers had settled back on the desk, nobody had checked their order before going to print. For the first time ever, the Festival started with a one-day match, making Cheltenham faithfuls feel doubly uneasy, for there was already a fragmented feeling of deep unrest in the club as certain dissatisfied players were airing their views over team selection, wages and contracts. Meetings took place and gossip was rampant. 'This is the sub-plot behind the Festival,' remarked Tom Richardson at the time.

Bert Avery, who had died peacefully at home in April, would certainly not have appreciated the discord on the ground. Described by Don Oslear as 'dear Bert Avery, the person who, for me, is Gloucestershire CCC', he

Top. A familiar Festival view (2003)
Below. Umbrellas up, as the old enemy returns. (2003)

Cheltenham collage

would, however, have enjoyed scoring as the Gloucestershire Gladiators got the Festival off to a flying start against the Hampshire Hawks.

After Hancock and Harvey had both been quickly dismissed by Mascarenhas, Spearman (107) - making an eye-catching first appearance on the ground - and Windows (76) put on 171 in twenty-seven overs as the hosts reached 296 for 9 in their forty-five overs. The visitors struggled from the start as Mike Smith captured early wickets, but half-centuries from Francis and Udal restored some respectability to their total and at the end they were 71 runs short of their hosts.

Glamorgan were the next opponents for a Frizzell county championship match and there were fireworks from the start of what can only be called Matthew Maynard's match. Firstly Michael Kasprowicz bowled Tim Hancock off his helmet, then he pole-axed fellow countryman Ian Harvey, while their wives were shopping happily together in town. Both batsmen ended up in hospital, but Taylor (126), Russell (84) and Fisher (79*) calmly steered their side to a first innings total of 438.

As the visitors steadily built their reply on the second day, hardworking committee member Michael Simpson was running a silent auction, which raised over £700 for the club's academy, helping the development of young cricketers. Meanwhile, for any youngsters watching, Matthew Maynard was providing a master-class in batsmanship out in the middle. Standing tall, punishing anything loose, his 140 kept Glamorgan within reach of their hosts at the end of first innings.

Former New Zealand Test opener, Craig Spearman, was given little support by his county colleagues when Gloucestershire batted again. Although he was caught off a huge towering six in the shopping mall by Sam Turvey, a keen spectator with a safe pair of hands, the opener went on to make 180* out of a total of 293, leaving the visitors 317 to win. With two overs to spare, helped by James (74) and Dale (49), Maynard's 118* saw Glamorgan home by 2 wickets in a thrilling finish.

In four championship innings on the ground, Maynard had scored four hundreds. 'It was a good cricket wicket,' he recalled, 'and a very special game for me as during the match I passed 20,000 runs for Glamorgan and recorded my fiftieth hundred in all first-class cricket. For these reasons alone, Cheltenham will therefore always hold very special memories for me.'

Complimenting the Glamorgan batsman, Mark Alleyne said, 'Matthew is a festival cricketer; this ground suits his style of play.'

'Each year Cheltenham improves,' commented Tom Richardson in the pre-festival booklet produced by sponsors C&G, and Derek Goddard in the *Echo* agreed. 'Value for money has never been higher at the Cheltenham Cricket Festival,' he said, pointing out that with a total of 1,466 runs having been scored, the match between Gloucestershire and Glamorgan had produced 'more runs than any other since the Festival started in 1872'. Paying tribute to the work of the groundsmen, Goddard concluded, 'Former Dowty Arle Court cricketer, Bob McInroy, is delighted with the way things have gone in his first year of preparing the wickets.'

Indeed this was reflected in the umpire's pitch report for the match, with favourable comments about the bounce, pace, consistency and turn, and the overall pitch-rating described as 'very good'.

'It's hard work and the jobs need to be done at the right time,' said Bob McInroy. 'Lots of TLC is required and we pay particular attention to detail . . . Watching the weather forecast and planning ahead is very important. In the spring the square is cut and lightly rolled, and in May the heavy roller introduced. In the middle of June we decide which strips to use for the Festival, and from then on the programme is to roll for twenty minutes each day provided the ground is damp and, if not, it is watered and rolled the next day . . . I try to get a good covering of grass to stop drying out and cracking, then we can produce hard, fast pitches.'

Dennis Dunn added, 'We used to box-mow the outfield, but now we use a Ransome floating triple, mowing two or three times a week before the Festival and every morning once it has started.'

During Martin Ball's benefit match, a players' meeting took place in Bristol, and with rumblings still afoot the committee acted before the start of the next match against Division Two leaders, Middlesex. Extended contracts were given to John Bracewell and Mark Alleyne, while neither Kim Barnett nor Jeremy Snape was selected to play. 'The committee is backing the coach,' said Tony Brown, 'otherwise player power will lead to anarchy.'

Middlesex spent all the first day, and some of the second, chasing leather over a hard, fast outfield that had seen no rain for just over a fortnight. Tim Hancock made 112, while former Hatherley and Reddings all-rounder Alex Gidman scored 94. Then sixties from Taylor and Alleyne and a half-century from Windows helped take Gloucestershire to a total of 494, as Abdul Razzaq ended up with 5 for 125.

At the lunch interval on the second day an announcement over the loudspeaker revealed that South African star, Jonty Rhodes, had been signed as one of the two overseas players for the following season. A feeling of great excitement immediately filled the ground and John Bracewell commented, 'Jonty is one of very few cricketers in the world who has the total pulling power of all age groups.' The committee had pulled off a great coup. By the close of play Middlesex looked rather shaky on 218 for 6.

Ivo Tennant wrote in *The Times* next day, 'With both bat and ball, Gloucestershire had a jaunty look about them maybe because of the news that the ebullient character Jonty Rhodes . . . would be flinging himself around in the field next year.' Rhodes was just the person they needed to keep up their spirits as some powerful batting by Paul Weekes (102), helped by wicket-keeper David Nash (43), ensured the visitors reached 363. Then, according to *Wisden,* 'Gloucestershire's early hold was loosened in the second innings by the magnificent Tufnell, who lured eight batsmen to their downfall.' The hosts were dismissed for 230 and Tufnell's figures of 39-12-66-8 were reminiscent of the old days when spin was king. Middlesex coach, John Emburey, commented on the pitch, 'It has bounce and turn. The wicket deteriorates at a good rate and sides with good spinners do well here.'

Needing 362 to win, Middlesex showed little interest in the target, batted carefully and earned a draw to keep themselves at the top of the table. It was not a wasted afternoon, for spectators were entertained by hard-hitting Ben Hutton who made 88, and there was warm applause at the fall of Andrew Strauss's wicket when the Middlesex captain provided Jack Russell with his one thousandth first-class dismissal for Gloucestershire.

'The Festival is more than a series of games of cricket,' reflected Tim Harman, chairman of the Cheltenham regional committee. Michael Simpson went one stage further: 'Cheltenham is part of the social scene of the year, along with Ascot, Glyndebourne and Henley . . . There is a family atmosphere.' Chelwood Gallery proprietor, Guy Vowles, agreed and complimented C&G on the entertainment for younger spectators such as face-painting, 'freebies' and the very popular game zone, with opportunities to play cricket and receive instruction from qualified coaches.

On Sunday, top of the table Gladiators played bottom of the table Sussex Sharks, but the game did not last very long. The visitors were bowled out in thirty overs for 116, Martyn Ball finishing with the impressive figures of 3.5-0-15-4, after the rot had been started by Harvey, Smith and Averis. With Spearman (24) and Harvey (68*) smashing 81 in eight overs, the hosts won by six wickets thus helping to ensure their passage to becoming league champions.

A defeat at the hands of the touring West Indies 'A' team completed the Festival, the same day as ninety-two-year-old Andy Wilson died. He was described in *Wisden* as 'one of those wicket-keepers, diminutive and undemonstrative, who are so efficient that their craftsmanship passes virtually unnoticed, though by no means unappreciated by fellow players and the county faithful'. He would be missed at the Festival, having attended it regularly as a journalist, observer, or lunch guest, since hanging up his gloves.

When the boundary boards and scoreboard had gone back to Bristol, there were about five weeks for Bob McInroy and the College groundstaff to turn the ground into three rugby pitches for the start of term. When the first showers of autumn had softened the ground, Bob, along with Michael Broom, Andrew O'Brien, Dennis Dunn and Simon McAulay, brushed, scarified, cut, spiked and top dressed the square with a high clay content loam, applied fertilizer and perennial ryegrass seed, so putting it to bed for the winter. As the hibernation period began, the outgrounds cup was once again awarded to this conscientious team.

—— 2003 ——

In his book *Rain Stops Play*, Andrew Hignell writes, 'While appearing on the surface to be a quaint reminder of the relaxed atmosphere and cosy informality of county cricket in the inter-war years, the Cheltenham festival is a most lucrative location for Gloucestershire CCC, and in the modern era of profit maximisation, a location they would not want to lose.'

It can be added that the Festival has played an important part in the financial success of many businesses in and around Cheltenham, helping to contribute to the figure of over £250 million generated annually by tourism in the Cotswolds.

At the start of the ninety-seventh Festival in July 2003, there was local support from residents and organisations for the *Don't Rubbish Cheltenham* campaign. The aim, to have the cleanest town in Britain by 2005, would be a further inducement to tourists, including Festival goers.

Heavy rain fell just before the event started and it was not long before Chris Coley, celebrating his silver jubilee as Festival co-ordinator, was throwing his hands up in horror when vehicles began to churn up the College ground.

For the opening game against Division Two leaders Worcestershire, the hosts were without Mark Alleyne, Mike Smith and Jack Russell, while the visitors were strengthened by the return, after a hand injury, of the former England batsman, Graeme Hick.

'All I've been hearing about since I started playing for Gloucestershire is the Cheltenham Festival,' said Jonty Rhodes, making his first appearance on the ground. So there was disappointment all round when, having faced some fiery deliveries from fellow-countryman Nantie Hayward, he was caught for 19 by wicket-keeper Steven Rhodes, off Australian pace-bowler Matthew Mason.

Making his Gloucestershire debut in place of Ian Harvey, who was playing for his country in a one-day series against Bangladesh, was Pakistan all-rounder Shoaib Malik who was dismissed in his twenties along with others in his team. Wickets kept falling and everything was going smoothly for Worcestershire until last man Jon Lewis joined another Festival newcomer, former Bournside School pupil Stephen Pope. In thirty-three balls, Lewis lifted the spirits of a rather solemn crowd, pulling and driving his way to 47, hitting 4 fours and 3 sixes, while Pope (17*), Jack Russell's understudy, had been at the crease for over an hour when his partner was finally dismissed. The county, having earlier been 117 for 5, had reached a respectable 271.

Next morning, bowling his second over in county championship cricket, Shoaib Malik dismissed Graeme Hick, thanks to a splendid catch at mid-wicket by Martyn Ball, and the visitors wobbled, losing 3 wickets for 20 runs in five overs. Worcestershire were on 103 for 4 and from the Chapel end, watching the intense, passionate battle taking place for runs and wickets, was E. M. Grace's grandson. As lunch arrived, he must have sensed the visitors gaining the upper hand; no more wickets had fallen and seventy runs had been added. Throughout the afternoon, spectators discovered that Worcestershire's tail was longer and had more of a sting than Gloucestershire's had the previous afternoon, as Solanki (35), Hall (73) and Rhodes (42*) supported the sterling work of their captain, Ben Smith (92). Standing in front of Wisteria Books, Graeme Hick watched as Worcestershire gained the ascendancy commenting, 'It didn't look good when we lost three quick wickets.' This prompted coach Tom Moody, standing alongside, to remark with confidence, 'We bat in depth.' Sure enough, by the close of play Worcestershire had reached 392 for 7.

Raining solidly, weather conditions were far from ideal next day when plans for more pedestrianisation, outside seating and *al fresco* dining areas in the town centre were under discussion. At the same time, the saturated College ground was not the picture Marie Journeaux had in mind when setting up her own corporate hospitality company the previous autumn. 'I am very pleased with marquee sales this year,' she said. 'Being here on the patch helps a great deal.' Her chart of marquee takers for the Festival showed very few blank spaces; today however, there would be some disappointed customers.

With the College Lawn car park closed because the surface was badly churned up, Worcestershire resumed their innings for another three quarters of an hour on Saturday morning and were finally dismissed for 439. Kabir Ali then bowled Gloucestershire's captain Craig Spearman in his first over and the hosts were nought for 1, still 168 runs behind.

While ominous-looking clouds began to fill the sky, Lisa Oversby, C&G's sponsorship and marketing services manager, explained about the company's enthusiasm for supporting the Festival: 'As a company we were late coming into sponsorship, we simply didn't need to, but now a name needs to be seen and for the last three years our relationship with the club has felt very comfortable. We work well together.'

As sponsors of the C&G competition (replacing the NatWest contest), the company's gleaming trophy was being proudly displayed at a stall in the mall. Spectators walking past were not to know that the two sides currently playing on the College ground would be locked in combat a month later in a Lord's final.

Former Worcestershire batsman, Philip Weston, and Jonty Rhodes were fighting doggedly for the hosts, and runs were coming slowly as Lisa Oversby confirmed that C&G had agreed to sponsor the Festival for another three years. This was good news; it meant their support for the various features and services on the ground would continue, and the striking lamppost banners on Suffolk Road and Thirlestaine Road were safe for a little longer. 'We are pleased to be able to support an event of national interest that happens locally . . . cementing our relationship with the local community,' said Lisa Oversby. 'But we mustn't let the Festival lose its charm by over manicuring it.' Working closely together, C&G has helped the county with objectives passed down from the England and Wales Cricket Board to encourage more families to watch cricket, hence the game zone and child-orientated goody bags.

At lunch, nearly one hundred Exiles, having made their annual pilgrimage to the Festival, gathered for an informal buffet. The following day, there was a repeat performance in the same marquee for the Gloucestershire CCC life members. Half an hour before tea, the rain returned. Rhodes was 58*, while Gloucestershire had slipped to 133 for 5, still 35 runs short of making their opponents bat again. Luckily for the hosts, the rain continued, forcing the game to end as a draw.

The ground was brimming with excitement next day for a top-of-the table National League clash against second placed Glamorgan. With conditions still wet underfoot after the recent two and a half inches of rain, the game started an hour late and third-placed Gloucestershire, still without Alleyne, but including Russell and Smith, bowled the visitors out for 197 in thirty-seven overs. Mark Hardinges and James Averis took three wickets each, as Jonty Rhodes pulled a thigh muscle while fielding and took no further part in the match, or sadly, the Festival.

Weston, Spearman and Gidman gave the county a flying start, before the game reached a nail-biting climax. Shoaib Malik provided sound support for Matt Windows (54*), who smashed Mike Kasprowicz to the mid-wicket boundary for his fifth four, gaining victory for the hosts by 7 wickets, with seven balls to spare. The win meant Gloucestershire leap-frogged Surrey and Glamorgan in the table to become the new leaders. When asked about the tense finish, Matt Windows modestly remarked, 'I felt everything was under control.'

On Monday, under a grey sky, the county, including New Zealand guest-players Craig McMillan and Chris Harris, were beaten by the wristy young strokeplayers of India 'A'.

'It is a pleasure to see them here,' said College master and former county player Martin Stovold, adding, 'You can't put a value on the Festival from the school's point of view.'

During a quiet moment, Chris Coley described by Lisa Oversby as 'the pillar of the Festival', reflected upon his own role:

'Once the College have broken up, we have access to the ground. The boundary line is marked by the groundstaff, and Attwools, who need ten days to erect their marquees, start pegging out the area. Then the seating, grandstands and boundary boards arrive.'

Chris Coley has 'a minimum twelve-hour day' for the duration of the Festival. First thing in the morning he starts by talking to the night security staff, before the council arrive to empty the rubbish bins. 'At eight o'clock the groundstaff arrive along with my team of eight Cheltenham College boys, whose first job is to help take the covers off. The boys then put the bins out around the ground and tidy up marquees ready for the day.' Just before play starts, it is time for the Festival co-ordinator to change and 'float round, trouble shooting'.

At lunch, helped by the College boys, raffle tickets for signed bats are sold in the corporate marquees, raising money for the county or beneficiary, with prizes presented at tea time. At the close of play, explains Coley, 'the lads help the groundstaff to cover up, supervise the scouts' litter-clearing and push the bins to the Chapel end, so they are ready for the council lorry next morning'. He sums up by saying, 'My job is to communicate between the College and the county and it's a lot easier when the sun has shone.'

Interest the following day centred on a Lord's Taverners match, for which the weather was most unkind. Eager autograph hunters darted round outside the pavilion, collecting the signatures of celebrities from various branches of sport and the media as they arrived for the contest between an International Rugby XI and The Lord's Taverners.

Play commenced under a cover of thick grey cloud, and by lunch the International Rugby XI, captained by J. P. R. Williams, had made 250 for 7 from their forty overs. Players and guests assembled in a marquee for lunch and it started to pour with rain. Envoys were sent out around the ground hunting for those huddled underneath umbrellas so they could be invited to the marquee for a post-lunch celebrity 'talking off-the-cuff' session.

When everyone was gathered, first up was Mike Gatting who was quizzed on his views about the morning's news of the resignation of England captain, Nasser Hussain. He was followed by author Leslie Thomas and Eddie Butler, John Taylor and Gary Newbon from the worlds of media and entertainment, all speaking on a variety of matters. The rain kept falling and it soon became evident that the Taverners' Test stars, Mike Gatting, Graham Roope, Bill Athey, Bruce French and Australian Ross Edwards, along with National Hunt racing's father-and-son act, Peter and Tom Scudamore, would not get a bat; but by now nobody seemed to mind, such was the mood in the marquee.

That evening, some three hundred and fifty guests sat down to enjoy a charity dinner and were entertained with a top-class cabaret by stalwart Lord's Taverners member and impressionist, Rory Bremner, and the charity's president, the musician, songwriter and entertainer, Richard Stilgoe. The day's programme had been arranged by Gloucestershire CCC and The Lord's Taverners and the money raised was divided evenly between the two parties. Gloucestershire's share was to be directed towards its youth development programme, while the Taverners' fifty per cent was to go, as always, towards 'giving young people, particularly those with special needs, a sporting chance'. 'It was a highly successful joint venture,' commented David Smith, Lord's Taverners western region treasurer.

Throughout the Festival there had been a major campaign selling office suites in the town's landmark tower block, the newly-named Eagle Tower. With its perfect view of the College ground, prospective purchasers looking round the building over the next five days would be able to catch glimpses of the final portion of the Festival, as Gloucestershire entertained Yorkshire in a promotion battle championship match and, to finish with, a National League fixture.

Only eleven overs were possible on the first day of the match. Having won the toss, stand-in captain Craig Spearman elected to bat, and within the first twelve balls, both he and his fellow opener Philip Weston were back in the pavilion, neither having scored a run. It was probably the best place to be, for rain kept falling and frustratingly prevented the game from progressing any further than 33 for 2 for the county. Even though there was little play, the staff of Cleeve Catering were kept as busy as usual, filling the players' plates with cereals, fruit, pasta, rice, salad, potatoes and meat and providing a constant supply of drinks.

Around half the scheduled number of overs were lost to rain next day and Bob McInroy and his staff kept rolling the covers on and off. In the dry spells, Gloucestershire moved to 201 for 6, and the crowd were entertained by some attractive batting from Matt Windows (73) and Alex Gidman (43), who added 69 at a run-a-ball for the fourth wicket.

Whatever was going on cricket-wise would not upset the celebrations taking place in marquee number seven for Ladies Day. Over morning coffee, a three course lunch and afternoon tea, professional ladies could mingle, socialise, watch cricket and do some business. As Lisa Oversby remarked, 'It is a day for business ladies, when the emphasis is on cricket and networking.'

In his match report for Friday's play, David Foot wrote in *The Guardian,* 'The umbrellas gave way to the cricket bats and Cleeve Hill, that towering blue-green fringe of the Cotswolds, came out from under the clouds. At last it was festival weather as the sun appeared.' Gloucestershire were bowled out for 263, with Steve Kirby (24-4-101-6) the most successful of Yorkshire's bowlers.

As the afternoon wore on, the Festival weather continued to improve with the stands filling up and warm smiles appearing on people's faces. Mark Alleyne had reason to feel pleased. Having not played any first-class cricket for three weeks, he had just come through a bowling fitness test and it was almost certain that he would be leading the side once again in the National League game on Sunday.

'Cheltenham is my favourite ground to play on, along with the aura of

Lord's,' said Alleyne, as he watched Martyn Ball capture another Yorkshire wicket. 'There is always a great atmosphere here; the seating is close to the action and we enjoy good support. Cheltenham is draining though; eleven days of intensive cricket takes it out of you.' When asked about the future of the Festival, he replied, 'Everyone is happy with the format at the moment. Cricket sells so well here . . . Cheltenham can be unforgiving, but it rewards accurate bowling and good batsmen. Over the course of a day, there is often a nice balance of runs scored and wickets taken and as the game progresses, the wicket turns.' How right he was, for at the close of play, Yorkshire had been dismissed for 226 with a balance of 37 runs in Gloucestershire's favour.

As the county's director of cricket, these were the final few days of Cheltenham for John Bracewell, who at the end of the season was to become New Zealand's national coach. In five years, by setting 'expectations and targets', John Bracewell had transformed his players into the winners of five limited-overs trophies. He spoke warmly of Cheltenham: 'It is one of the best pitches in England. The surface is good, so is the bounce. It is generally nice for batsmen, hard work for bowlers and it is spinning more each year.'

He had high praise for the setting and the knock-on effect it seemed to have on the players and officials. 'Cheltenham, more than anywhere, is where camaraderie of cricket overides everything else. Umpires, cricketers and coaches have a unified approach, there is no hostility or intensity of feeling that is the modern edge of the game. There is a greater acceptance and tolerance for things that may go wrong. Above all, there is fairness and fair play.'

Looking across the ground, he remarked, 'Perhaps it's the ambience of the place, the trees, the buildings, the history, that makes players a little more relaxed, but the cricket is as good and competitive as any in the county championship.' But with eyes fixed on the ring of marquees, he also spoke of the 'downside' which he didn't like: 'too many people hidden away in tents gossiping . . . dangerous talk, north versus south of the county manipulation'.

At half past eight on Saturday morning, with the sun shining, Simon McAulay was standing on the square holding one end of a long rope, with the other end attached to a tractor that Bob McInroy was driving round the boundary. The rope was knocking dew off the grass and before long the players emerged for their energetic warm-up routines. There was a lot of lost time to catch up on, but with promotion to Division One at stake, there were few risks taken and sadly the game petered out well before the end. The hosts made 284 for 6 declared, due largely to a 132 run second wicket partnership between Spearman (94) and Windows (57) and a dynamic 60 by Shoaib Malik, who hit four successive sixes and was then stumped going for the fifth.

'This Cheltenham wicket is as close to a South African one as you can get. It has more bounce than other English wickets and batsmen trust the pitch,' said Jonty Rhodes as he watched children enjoying themselves in the game zone. Of the Festival he said, 'There is lots going on and there is a nice contrast. On the field it is intense, while off it the atmosphere is relaxed.' It was a great shame that this *Wisden* Cricketer of the Year in 1999, one of the most exciting fielders in the world, had still not recovered from his injury. Set 322 to win, the visitors turned their noses up at the target, reached 75 for 2 and preserved their energy for the following day.

On Sunday morning Mike Broom stood on the square while it was the turn of Andrew O'Brien to drive the tractor on the 'dew run', before Dennis Dunn cut the outfield. All the marquees were booked and for Carol Cole, general manager of caterers Letheby and Christopher, there was a busy day ahead. In charge of the club's nominated caterers, Carol would be responsible for the reserved tables in the Hammond marquee and the Grace marquee restaurant, along with her staff of forty for the day, many of whom were local students. For the third occasion during the event she was also running the marquee taken by sponsors C&G, where later in the day a presentation would be made to Chris Coley for his outstanding contribution to the Festival. Used to catering for the large numbers at Cheltenham racecourse, Carol enjoyed 'seeing everyone relaxed' at the College ground. She smiled, saying, 'It's rather like running a small race meeting.'

Everything was peaceful at ten o'clock in the Montpellier Wine Bar marquee - the calm before the storm. In a couple of hours time it would be packed with real ale and lager drinkers, while wine and champagne would be available for those with a more sophisticated palate. Pimms in a jug was also becoming very popular, especially amongst the ladies. In the corner were tables reserved for lunch, and a quick look at the menu suggested that those who had booked were in for a tasty treat.

As always, there was a strange feeling on the last day of the Festival, a bit like the end of a school year - the excitement of moving on tinged with the sadness of farewells. Winning the toss, Matthew Wood chose to bat first and the visitors raced along to score 62 without loss in the first eight overs. Having lost their first wicket, according to David Green in

The Daily Telegraph, 'Yorkshire began to lose momentum and we had the now familiar spectacle of Gloucestershire's tight bowling, vivacious fielding and deadly throwing throttling an opponent's innings'. Seven wickets fell for 69 runs and in the forty-first over the visitors were dismissed for 183, as James Averis ended with the impressive figures of 8.5-1-50-4.

During the interval between innings, John Mace, the county's Duckworth-Lewis expert, could be seen patiently explaining the system to a young cricket enthusiast, Will Bain. He appeared to clarify key terms such as 'available resources', the factors that are taken into consideration when calculations are made in rain-affected matches, but there was no call for their use in the session of play that followed.

About a thousand spectators spilled onto the playing area of the ground. Some stared longingly at the pitch, dozens took part in small games of cricket, while others stood and talked or just admired this nugget of a festival, Lillywhite's legacy, shining brightly amidst the current furore calling for a radical shake-up in English cricket.

'We have built a garden party here and we must preserve the timelessness,' says Marie Journeaux, while Nico Craven feels, 'Cheltenham has kept the best of the old, but moved with the times.'

For some forty years, Derek Goddard has left his bike leaning against the chapel wall during the hours of play while gathering material for his *Echo* articles. In his early days of reporting, he wrote of the Festival, 'It is peaceful, it is still and above all it contributes to the sanity. It is unchanging and uplifting in a world that has become none of these things.' All these years later, he summarises the Cheltenham idyll as 'a fortnight out of real life'.

The county's patron, Lord Vestey, walking through the heaving crowd remarks, 'I have many happy memories of the Festival and Gloucestershire seem to do so well here.' With regard to the future of the event, he smiles and says, 'If it ain't broke don't mend it.'

The 2003 Festival draws to a close with Philip Weston (62) and Craig Spearman (93*) almost winning the match on their own, putting on 143 for the first wicket. Their lavish stroke play is a treat for the full house and keeps the College boys busy on the scoreboard.

As Matt Windows scores the winning run, loud, passionate West Country voices echo round the ground. It is all over for another year.

BIBLIOGRAPHY

Arlott, John, *Basingstoke Boy,* Willow Books, 1990.

Arlott, John, *Vintage Summer: 1947,* Eyre & Spottiswoode, 1967.

Association of Cricket Statisticians, *Gloucestershire Cricketers 1870-1979,* ACS, 1979.

Birkenhead, the Earl of, (Compiler), *John Betjeman's Collected Poems,* John Murray, 1963.

Caple, S. Canynge, *A History of Gloucestershire County Cricket Club 1870-1948,* Littlebury & Co., 1949.

Chalke, Stephen, talking with Bryan 'Bomber' Wells, *One More Run,* Fairfield Books, 2000

Craven, Nico, *Gloster's Centenary Cricket,* The Author, 1970.

Craven, Nico, *Best Out of Five,* The Author, 1975.

Craven, Nico, *Playing a Supporting Role,* The Author, 1981.

Craven, Nico, *Tea for Twenty Two,* The Author, 1983.

Craven, Nico, *Summer and Sunshine,* The Author, 1985.

Craven, Nico, *One Good Season Deserved Another,* The Author, 1987.

Craven, Nico, *Waiting For Cheltenham,* The Author, 1988.

Craven, Nico, *A Watching Brief,* The Author, 1995.

Craven, Nico, *Sunday, Monday, or All Days,* The Author, 1997.

Craven, Nico, *That Darn'd Elusive Championship,* The Author, 2003.

Gloucestershire County Cricket Club, *Yearbooks.*

Gower, David, *The Autobiography,* Collins-Willow, 1992.

Green, David, *The History of Gloucestershire County Cricket Club,* Christopher Helm, 1990.

Hammond, Walter, *Cricket My Destiny,* Stanley Paul, 1946.

Hart, Gwen, *A History of Cheltenham,* Leicester University Press, 1965.

Hignell, Andrew, *Rain Stops Play,* Frank Cass, 2002.

Hunter, A.A., *Records of Cheltenham College Matches against Public Schools 1856-1900,* Darter, 1901.

Illingworth, Ray, *The Tempestuous Years 1979-83,* Sidgwick & Jackson, 1987.

James, Henry, An Old Collegian, (Editor), *Scores of the Principal Matches played by Cheltenham College,* Darter, 1868.

Laver, Frank, *An Australian Cricketer on Tour,* Chapman & Hall, 1905.

Lillywhite, James, *Cricketers' Annual.*

Little, Bryan, *Cheltenham,* Batsford, 1952.

M.C.C., *Cricket Scores and Biographies.*

Miller, Douglas, *Cricket Grounds of Gloucestershire,* ACS, 2000.

Minute books of the College Council.

Minute books of Gloucestershire County Cricket Club

Minute book of the New Club.

Morgan, M.C., *Cheltenham College The First Hundred Years,* Sadler for the Cheltonian Society, 1968.

Pakenham, Simona, *Cheltenham A Biography,* Macmillan, 1971.

Parker, Grahame, *Gloucestershire Road,* Pelham Books, 1983.

Parker, Grahame, *100 years of Gloucestershire cricket,* Gloucestershire C.C.C., 1970.

Sampson, Aylwin, & Blake, Steven, *A Cheltenham Companion,* Portico Press, 1993.

Taylor, Alfred D., *Cheltenham Cricket Week 1878-1905,* Cheltenham Newspaper Co., 1906.

Ward, Paul, *Reminiscences of Cheltenham College, by an Old Cheltonian,* Bemrose, 1868.

Wisden Cricketers' Almanack, 1872 to present.

Contemporary reports in:

The Daily Telegraph; The Guardian; The Times.
The Financial Times; The Sunday Telegraph.

The Cheltenham Chronicle; The Cheltenham Examiner;
The Cheltenham Looker-On; The Gloucestershire Echo;
The Gloucestershire Graphic.

Bell's Life; The Field; Punch; Wisden Cricket Monthly.
Cotswold Life; Gloucestershire and Avon Life.

The Cheltonian.

STATISTICAL APPENDIX

COLLEGE GROUND, CHELTENHAM

Compiled by Keith Gerrish

Playing Record (1872 to date):	Played	Won	Lost	Drawn	Abandoned
County Championship	278	107	91	80	2
Other First Class	30	5	12	13	0
Total	308	112	103	93	2

First Match July 18, 19 1872   v Surrey
Last Match (to date) July 30, 31, Aug 1, 2 2003 v Yorkshire

Highest Innings Total
    Gloucs: 608-7d   v Sussex   1934
    Opponents: 607-6d   - Kent   1910

Lowest Innings Total
    Gloucs: 17   v Australians   1896
    Opponents: 27   - Surrey   1874

Highest individual score
    Gloucs: 318* W.G. Grace   v Yorkshire   1876
    Opponents: 229 J.E. Morris   - Derbyshire   1993

Best bowling in an Innings
    Gloucs: 10-113 T.W.J. Goddard   v Worcestershire   1937
    Opponents: 10-66 A.A. Mailey   - Australians   1921

Best bowling in an Match
    Gloucs: 17-89 W.G. Grace   v Nottinghamshire 1877
    Opponents: 15-184 W.H. Lockwood - Surrey   1899

Most Matches: 71   J.B. Mortimore
Most Runs: 2899   W.R. Hammond
Hundreds: Total: 217   (Gloucs 121, Opponents 96)
Most: 9   W.R. Hammond
Most Wickets: 409   C.W.L. Parker

Highest Wicket Partnerships - Gloucestershire:-

1st	169	G.M. Emmett & B.O. Allen	v Essex	1949
2nd	251	C.J. Barnett & W.R. Hammond	v Sussex	1934
3rd	269	B.O. Allen & W.R. Hammond	v Worcestershire	1937
4th	190	W.W.F. Pullen & E.M. Grace	v Middlesex	1884
5th	261	W.G. Grace & W.O. Moberly	v Yorkshire	1876
6th	245	P. Bainbridge & M.W. Alleyne	v Lancashire	1989
7th	131	F.J. Seabrook & W.L. Neale	v Leicestershire	1933
8th	127	M.W. Alleyne & C.A. Walsh	v Kent	1994
9th	129	H.V. Page & W.O. Vizard	v Nottinghamshire	1883
10th	130	M.C.J. Ball & J. Lewis	v Worcestershire	1999

Highest Wicket Partnerships - Opponents:-

1st	221	B.C. Broad & R.T. Robinson	- Nottinghamshire	1986
2nd	218	W. Bardsley & C.G. Macartney	- Australians	1921
3rd	224	G. Boycott & K. Sharp	- Yorkshire	1983
4th	192	N.J. Speak & D.C. Boon	- Durham	1999
5th	302*	J.E. Morris & D.G. Cork	- Derbyshire	1993
6th	206	J. O'Connor & J.W.H.T. Douglas	- Essex	1923
7th	128	W.G. Quaife & F.G. Stephens	- Warwickshire	1908
8th	134	Intikhab Alam & R.P. Baker	- Surrey	1977
9th	120	J. Langridge & M.W. Tate	- Sussex	1934
10th	157	W.E. Astill & W.H. Marlow	- Leicestershire	1933

Limited-over Records	Played	Won	Lost	Tied	No Result	Abandoned
Gillette/NatWest (1992)	**1**	**0**	**1**	**0**	**0**	**0**
Sunday League (1969 to date)	**59**	**35**	**21**	**1**	**2**	**4**
Other One-day (1995 to date)	**7**	**1**	**6**	**0**	**0**	**0**
Total	**67**	**36**	**28**	**1**	**2**	**4**

Highest Innings Total

Gloucs:	344-6	(SL)	v Northants	2001
Opponents:	303-7	(SL)	- Essex	1995

Lowest Innings Total

Gloucs:	99	(SL)	v Derbyshire	1993
Opponents:	85	(SL)	- Warwickshire	1973

Highest Individual Score

Gloucs:	117	M.G.N. Windows	v Northants	(SL)	2001
Opponents:	105*	G.A. Gooch	- Essex	(NW)	1992
	102	J.J.B. Lewis	- Durham	(SL)	1997

Best Bowling

Gloucs:	5-20	J.H. Shackleton	v Surrey	(SL)	1977
Opponents:	4-14	S.J. Base	- Derbyshire	(SL)	1993

Highest Wicket Partnerships - Gloucestershire:-

1st	151	Sadiq Mohammad & A.W. Stovold	SL	v Kent	1977
2nd	112	A.W. Stovold & K.M. Curran	SL	v Leics	1987
3rd	171	C.M. Spearman & M.G.N. Windows	SL	v Hampshire	2002
4th	155	M.G.N. Windows & C.G. Taylor	SL	v Northants	2001
5th	133	R.J. Cunliffe & R.C. Russell	SL	v Yorkshire	1999
6th	91*	R.C. Russell & M.W. Alleyne	SL	v Kent	2000
7th	48	D.R. Hewson & R.C.J. Williams	OD	v Sri Lanka 'A'	1999
8th	73*	C.G. Taylor & M.C.J. Ball	SL	v Worcestershire	2000
9th	68	M.J. Cawdron & R.C.J. Williams	SL	v Essex	1995
10th	37*	J.N. Snape & A.M. Smith	SL	v Hampshire	2002

Highest Wicket Partnerships - Opponents:-

1st	113	Ali Naqvi & Salim Elahi	OD	- Pakistan 'A'	1997
2nd	131	M.D. Moxon & R.J. Blakey	SL	- Yorkshire	1990
3rd	158*	C.J. Richards & M.A. Lynch	SL	- Surrey	1988
4th	143	A. Habib & G.I. Macmillan	SL	- Leicestershire	1996
5th	157	J.D. Ratcliffe & J.A. Knott	SL	- Surrey	1998
6th	95	Rana Qayyum & Azhar Mahmood	OD	- Pakistan 'A'	1997
7th	94*	S.C. Goldsmith & K.J. Barnett	SL	- Derbyshire	1991
8th	89	W.S. Kendall & S.D. Udal	SL	- Hampshire	2002
9th	27*	T.L. Penney & G.C. Small	SL	- Warwickshire	1996
10th	28	I.D.K. Salisbury & A.G. Robson	SL	- Sussex	1992

FIRST CLASS MATCHES AT CHELTENHAM COLLEGE

1	1872	Surrey	Won Inns & 37r	G 221	S 108 & 76
2	1873	Sussex	Drawn	G 424	S 212-5
3	1874	Surrey	Won Inns & 24r	S 27 & 73	G 124
4	1875	Sussex	Won 40r	G 130 & 234	S 204 & 120
5	1876	Yorkshire	Drawn	G 528	Y 127-7
6	1877	Nottinghamshire	Won Inns & 45r	G 235	N 111 & 79
7	1878	Sussex	Won Inns & 24r	G 198	S 29 & 145
8	1878	Yorkshire	Drawn	Y 212 & 20-2	G 173
9	1879	Yorkshire	Drawn	Y 135 & 63-1	G 269
10	1879	Nottinghamshire	Lost 6w	G 123 & 119	N 65 & 178-4
11	1880	Nottinghamshire	Drawn	N 272	G 172 & 171
12	1880	Surrey	Won 10w	S 285 & 117	G 351 & 52-0
13	1881	Yorkshire	Drawn	Y 267 & 194-3	G 254
14	1882	Middlesex	Lost 8w	G 144 & 176	M 228 & 94-2
15	1882	Yorkshire	Won Inns & 45r	G 256	Y 115 & 96
16	1883	Surrey	Lost 9w	S 261 & 20-1	G 109 & 171
17	1883	Nottinghamshire	Drawn	N 276 & 332-6	G 216
18	1884	Australians	Lost Inns & 136r	G 183 & 83	A 402
19	1884	Middlesex	Drawn	M 255 & 295	G 388 & 40-0
20	1885	Sussex	Lost 4w	S 300 & 239-6	G 159 & 376
21	1885	Surrey	Won 9w	S 198 & 116	G 277 & 38-1
22	1886	Australians	Lost 26r	A 119 & 114	G 74 & 133
23	1886	Yorkshire	Lost 5w	Y 167 & 52-5	G 85 & 131
24	1887	Lancashire	Lost 6w	L 252 & 103-4	G 132 & 219
25	1888	Australians	Won 8w	A 118 &151	G 209 & 61-2
26	1888	Middlesex	Lost Inns & 33r	G 115 & 147	M 295
27	1889	Surrey	Drawn	G 201 & 107	S 183 & 112-4
28	1889	Middlesex	Drawn	G 282 & 48-5	M 178 & 240-7d
29	1890	Middlesex	Won Inns & 22r	G 164	M 83 & 59
30	1890	Australians	Lost 8w	A 184 & 25-2	G 77 & 130
31	1891	Somerset	Lost Inns & 130r	S 255	G 25 & 100
32	1891	Middlesex	Drawn	G 145-6	
33	1892	Nottinghamshire	Drawn	N 429	G 146 & 196-5
34	1892	Surrey	Lost 10w	G 93 & 197	S 264 & 27-0
35	1893	Somerset	Lost 127r	S 197 & 270	G 166 & 174
36	1893	Australians	Lost 8w	A 207 & 37-2	G 109 & 131
37	1894	Surrey	Lost Inns & 49r	G 52 & 100	S 201
38	1894	Kent	Lost 84r	K 161 & 105	G 97 & 85
39	1895	Nottinghamshire	Won Inns & 93r	G 257	N 65 & 99
40	1895	Yorkshire	Won 7w	Y 221 & 143	G 219 & 147-3
41	1896	Kent	Lost 25r	K 190 & 178	G 202 & 141
42	1896	Australians	Lost Inns & 54r	G 133 & 17	A 204
43	1897	Kent	Won 63r	G 205 & 249	K 190 & 201
44	1897	Nottinghamshire	Won Inns & 40r	N 198 & 121	G 359-9d
45	1898	Kent	Won 27r	G 189 & 80	K 103 & 139
46	1898	Warwickshire	Won 5w	W 290 & 153	G 346 & 99-5
47	1899	Australians	Drawn	G 203 & 300	A 228 & 175-5
48	1899	Surrey	Lost 140r	S 292 & 211	G 207 & 156

49	1900	Yorkshire	Lost Inns & 44r	G 101 & 160	Y 305
50	1900	Essex	Won 2w	E 248 & 118	G 285 & 82-8
51	1901	Middlesex	Lost 4w	G 229 &148	M 87 & 291-6
52	1901	Kent	Drawn	K 155 & 17-0	G 204
53	1902	Yorkshire	Lost Inns & 102r	G 104 & 55	Y 261
54	1902	Australians	Lost Inns & 10r	A 312	G 152 & 150
55	1903	Kent	Won 219r	G 258 & 220	K 131 & 128
56	1903	Worcestershire	Won 100r	G 148 & 114	W 46 & 116
57	1904	Yorkshire	Drawn	Y 148 & 147	G 84
58	1904	Surrey	Lost 119r	S 206 & 91	G 79 & 99
59	1905	Australians	Drawn	A 195 & 77-1d	G 137 & 64-9
60	1905	Middlesex	Won 174r	G 148 & 231	M 100 & 105
61	1906	Kent	Lost 10w	G 220 & 156	K 245 & 132-0
62	1906	Sussex	Won Inns & 50r	S 63 & 164	G 277
63	1906	Worcestershire	Won Inns & 230r	G 523	W 147 & 146
64	1907	Kent	Won 7w	K 135 & 133	G 111 & 159-3
65	1907	Hampshire	Won 83r	G 131 & 237	H 165 & 120
66	1908	Warwickshire	Won 10w	W 286 & 206	G 473 & 23-0
67	1908	Hampshire	Lost 9w	H 332 & 35-1	G 166 & 198
68	1908	Yorkshire	Lost 182r	Y 219 & 222	G 83 & 176
69	1909	Australians	Drawn	A 215 & 247-8	G 411-8d
70	1909	Worcestershire	Drawn	W 292	G 198
71	1909	Essex	Drawn	G 162 & 91-0d	E 88 & 47-5
72	1910	Worcestershire	Won Inns & 63r	W 135 & 176	G 374
73	1910	Kent	Lost Inns & 242r	K 607-6d	G 168 & 197
74	1910	Surrey	Lost 4w	G 81 & 339	S 213 & 208-6
75	1911	Worcestershire	Won Inns & 69r	W 240 & 134	G 443
76	1911	Kent	Lost Inns & 94r	K 334	G 115 & 125
77	1911	Northamptonshire	Won 79r	G 134 & 141	N 139 & 57
78	1912	Kent	Lost 9w	G 129 & 87	K 122 & 95-1
79	1912	Australians	Drawn	A 256 & 67-7	G 150
-	1912	Surrey	Abandoned		
80	1913	Worcestershire	Won 129r	G 237 & 235	W 222 & 121
81	1913	Hampshire	Won 28r	G 169 & 152	H 196 & 97
82	1913	Warwickshire	Won 247r	G 328 & 172	W 134 & 119
83	1914	Nottinghamshire	Lost Inns & 69r	G 140 & 113	N 322
84	1914	Sussex	Drawn	G 278 & 256-8d	S 156 & 58-1
85	1914	Surrey	Lost Inns & 25r	G 182 & 110	S 317
86	1919	Warwickshire	Won 2w	W 252 & 100	G 252 & 102-8
87	1919	Worcestershire	Drawn	W 213 & 32-3	G 185
88	1919	Leicestershire	Won 8w	G 185 & 96-2	L 79 & 200
89	1920	Lancashire	Lost 10w	G 132 & 75	L 170 & 39-0
90	1920	Leicestershire	Won Inns 53r	L 54 & 83	G 190
91	1921	Lancashire	Lost 125r	L 201 & 250-8d	G 256 & 70
92	1921	Sussex	Lost 137r	S 245-9d & 147	G 149 & 106
93	1921	Australians	Lost Inns & 136r	A 438	G 127 & 175
94	1922	Essex	Won 6w	E 79 & 110	G 141 & 50-4
95	1922	Warwickshire	Won Inns & 163r	W 80 & 73	G 316-7d

96	1922	Kent	Lost Inns & 57r	G 53 & 138	K 248-9d
97	1923	Essex	Lost 6w	G 324 & 173	E 383 & 118-4
98	1923	Kent	Lost 10w	G 139 & 286	K 356 & 70-0
99	1923	Middlesex	Lost 8w	G 154 & 144	M 194 & 105-2
100	1924	Worcestershire	Won 91r	G 114 & 159	W 114 & 68
101	1924	Leicestershire	Won 7w	L 144 & 89	G 179 & 56-3
102	1924	Kent	Drawn	G 48 & 179-9d	K 76 & 67-4
103	1925	Hampshire	Drawn	H 244 & 244-6d	G 181 & 20-0
104	1925	Nottinghamshire	Lost 7w	G 66 & 89	N 122 & 36-3
105	1925	Kent	Lost Inns & 47r	G 71 & 300	K 418
106	1926	Australians	Lost 9w	G 144 & 178	A 287 & 39-1
107	1926	Nottinghamshire	Lost 224r	N 155 & 299-6d	G 128 & 102
108	1926	Surrey	Lost 97r	S 198 & 171	G 200 & 72
109	1927	Hampshire	Won 9w	H 219 & 93	G 295 & 18-1
110	1927	New Zealanders	Drawn	G 148 & 130-3	N 415-9d
111	1927	Surrey	Drawn	G 131-2	
112	1928	Essex	Drawn	G 315	E 177-2
113	1928	Surrey	Won 189r	G 304 & 319-9d	S 267 & 167
114	1928	Worcestershire	Won Inns & 168r	W 35 & 167	G 370-6d
115	1929	Sussex	Lost 1r	S 263 & 116	G 214 & 164
116	1929	Surrey	Drawn	G 186 & 339	S 286
117	1930	Warwickshire	Won 10w	W 120 & 107	G 201 & 29-0
118	1930	Surrey	Won Inns & 115r	S 79 & 155	G 349-8d
119	1930	Leicestershire	Won 8w	G 335 & 50-2	L 144 & 239
120	1931	Sussex	Drawn	G 104 & 3-1	S 173
121	1931	Surrey	Drawn	G 135	S 98-8
122	1931	Glamorgan	Drawn	Gm 111 & 76-3	G 175-8d
123	1932	Lancashire	Won 44r	G 378 & 165	L 276 & 223
124	1932	Essex	Won Inns & 12r	G 267	E 115 & 140
125	1932	Sussex	Lost 56r	S 133 & 141	G 86 & 132
126	1933	Worcestershire	Won 9w	W 193 & 205	G 253 & 146-1
127	1933	Leicestershire	Won 46r	G 278 & 340-8d	L 437 & 135
128	1933	Derbyshire	Won Inns & 85r	G 431	D 196 & 150
129	1934	Worcestershire	Drawn	G 254 & 234-6d	W 126 & 263-3
130	1934	Sussex	Won 7w	G 608-7d & 52-3	S 442 & 217
131	1934	Surrey	Won 279r	G 305 & 353-6d	S 261 & 118
132	1935	Worcestershire	Lost 8w	G 171 & 70	W 200 & 42-2
133	1935	South Africans	Won 87r	G 279 & 298	S 289 & 201
134	1935	Middlesex	Lost 4w	G 344 & 180	M 300 & 226-6
135	1936	Indians	Won 8w	I 154 & 260	G 313 & 104-2
136	1936	Surrey	Won 5w	S 210 & 270	G 193 & 289-5
137	1936	Sussex	Won 3w	S 266 & 164	G 257 & 174-7
138	1937	Worcestershire	Won 3w	W 310 & 202	G 196 & 317-7
139	1937	Derbyshire	Won Inns & 84r	G 392	D 228 & 80
140	1937	Sussex	Drawn	G 276	S 278-4
141	1938	Hampshire	Won 44r	G134 & 140	H 172 & 58
-	1938	Nottinghamshire	Abandoned		
142	1938	Worcestershire	Won 2w	W 270 & 180	G 204 & 250-8

143 1939	West Indians	Won 7w	W 162 & 220	G 152 & 231-3
144 1939	Derbyshire	Lost 1r	D 193 & 148	G 81 & 259
145 1939	Middlesex	Won 186r	G 214 & 327-7d	M 247 & 108
146 1946	Indians	Drawn	G 132-3d & 187	I 135-8d & 177-9
147 1946	Surrey	Won 55r	G 132 & 299-7d	S 140 & 236
148 1946	Worcestershire	Lost 10w	G 139 & 74	W 144 & 70-0
149 1947	South Africans	Lost 133r	S 225 & 248	G 185 & 155
150 1947	Middlesex	Lost 68r	M 180 & 141	G 153 & 100
151 1947	Glamorgan	Won 29r	G 172 & 138	Gm 156 & 125
152 1948	Northamptonshire	Lost 20r	N 177 & 208-4d	G 168 & 197
153 1948	Nottinghamshire	Won Inns & 98r	G 354-5d	N 168 & 88
154 1948	Surrey	Drawn	S 260 & 175	G 145 & 124-9
155 1949	Essex	Won 253r	G 349 & 250-8d	E 148 & 198
156 1949	Surrey	Lost Inns & 10r	S 374	G 168 & 196
157 1949	Glamorgan	Drawn	G 340 & 180-8d	Gm 170 & 180-3
158 1950	Middlesex	Drawn	G 440	M 296
159 1950	Worcestershire	Drawn	W 205-9d & 71-5d	G 70-6d & 111-5
160 1950	West Indians	Lost Inns & 105r	G 69 & 97	W 271
161 1951	Kent	Drawn	G 279 & 119-4d	K 234 & 66-3
162 1951	Glamorgan	Drawn	G 195 & 243-9d	Gm 289 & 63-2
163 1951	Worcestershire	Won Inns & 25r	W 318 & 74	G 417-8d
164 1952	Indians	Lost 6w	G 198 & 47-7d	I 138 & 108-4
165 1952	Leicestershire	Drawn	G 274 & 96	L 204 & 84-6
166 1952	Warwickshire	Drawn	W 104 & 164-6d	G 91 & 132-6
167 1953	Sussex	Drawn	G 385-7d & 154-9	S 209 & 344
168 1953	Worcestershire	Drawn	G 321-9d & 44-5	W 140 & 259
169 1953	Lancashire	Lost Inns & 19r	G 154 & 49	L 222
170 1954	Pakistanis	Drawn	G 143-9d & 42-2	P 176
171 1954	Derbyshire	Lost Inns & 52r	G 43 & 121	D 216
172 1954	Surrey	Lost 156r	S 143 & 278	G 153-8d & 112
173 1955	South Africans	Drawn	G 184 & 226	S 197 & 108-3
174 1955	Glamorgan	Won Inns & 9r	Gm 135 & 181	G 325
175 1955	Surrey	Lost 43r	S 180 & 77	G 135-9d & 79
176 1956	Sussex	Lost 10w	S 264 & 14-0	G 103 & 174
177 1956	Glamorgan	Won 68r	G 235-3d & 46-0d	Gm 87-3d & 126
178 1956	Kent	Won Inns & 75r	G 289-6d	K 45 & 169
179 1957	Sussex	Drawn	S 169	G 19-4
180 1957	Hampshire	Won 7w	H 125 & 66	G 177 & 15-3
181 1957	Yorkshire	Won 2w	Y 133 & 118	G 183 & 69-8
182 1958	New Zealanders	Drawn	G 106 & 160	N 127 & 10-0
183 1958	Glamorgan	Lost Inns & 41r	Gm 256	G 67 & 148
184 1958	Warwickshire	Drawn	G 265 & 71-0d	W 143-5d & 11-1
185 1959	Glamorgan	Lost Inns & 38r	Gm 371-9d	G 213 & 120
186 1959	Middlesex	Won Inns & 60r	G 290-9d	M 127 & 103
187 1959	Indians	Won 192r	G 318-9d & 186-4d	I 179 & 133
188 1960	Hampshire	Won 6w	H 315-5d & 116	G 255 & 182-4
189 1960	Middlesex	Drawn	G 221 & 280-9	M 320-6d
190 1960	Kent	Lost 156r	K 246 & 177-4d	G 140 & 127

191 1961	Glamorgan	Won 140r	G 166 & 177	Gm 123 & 80
192 1961	Lancashire	Lost 55r	L 233 & 219	G 142 & 255
193 1961	Kent	Lost 7w	G 165 & 178	K 276 & 71-3
194 1962	Pakistanis	Drawn	P 233 & 30-2	G 175-9d
195 1962	Lancashire	Won Inns & 73r	L 90 & 64	G 227-9d
196 1962	Nottinghamshire	Won 184r	G 205 & 232-5d	N 104 & 149
197 1963	Nottinghamshire	Won 104r	G 291 & 252-5d	N 292-5d & 147
198 1963	Worcestershire	Drawn	G 104 & 126-3	W 217
199 1963	Sussex	Lost 21r	S 196 & 124	G 231 & 68
200 1964	Warwickshire	Lost 5w	G 216 & 182-9d	W 101 & 298-5
201 1964	Glamorgan	Lost 110r	Gm 242 & 119	G 196 & 55
202 1964	Worcestershire	Lost 107r	W 143 & 281-4d	G 143 & 174
203 1965	Kent	Lost 55r	K 284-6d & 158	G 305 & 82
204 1965	Worcestershire	Lost 7w	G 210 & 173	W 253 & 131-3
205 1965	Sussex	Won 177r	G 370 & 146-5d	S 231 & 108
206 1966	Sussex	Lost 10w	G 149 & 96	S 202 & 44-0
207 1966	Surrey	Lost 7w	G 119 & 189	S 200-6 & 109-3
208 1966	Middlesex	Lost 9w	G 102 & 232	M 260 & 75-1
209 1967	Worcestershire	Lost 10w	G 123 & 155	W 247 & 35-0
210 1967	Pakistanis	Lost 49r	P 176 & 214	G 208 & 133
211 1967	Lancashire	Drawn	L 284 & 169-6d	G 264 & 132-9
212 1967	Leicestershire	Lost 6w	G 106 & 402	L 354 & 158-4
213 1968	Worcestershire	Lost 53r	W 224 & 166	G 179 & 158
214 1968	Sussex	Drawn	G 192-5d & 26-2	S 44-9d
215 1968	Surrey	Drawn	G 242 & 104-4d	S 176 & 43-6
216 1969	Worcestershire	Won Inns & 57r	W 98 & 103	G 258-4d
217 1969	Glamorgan	Lost Inns & 50r	G 73 & 160	Gm 283
218 1969	Warwickshire	Drawn	G 189	W 172-8
219 1970	Hampshire	Lost 4w	G 190 & 229	H 173 & 249-6
220 1970	Glamorgan	Lost 5w	G 324 & 152	Gm 356-9d & 124-
221 1970	Kent	Lost 1w	G 289 & 190	K 140 & 340-9
222 1971	Worcestershire	Drawn	G 213 & 210-8d	W 87 & 74-4
223 1971	Northamptonshire	Drawn	N 194 & 214	G 143 & 90-3
224 1971	Hampshire	Drawn	H 130 & 150-5d	G 97 & 132-9
225 1972	Lancashire	Drawn	G 218 & 174-9	L 354-7d
226 1972	Derbyshire	Won 5w	D 176 & 232	G 303 & 106-5
227 1972	Middlesex	Lost 6w	G 260 & 177	M 288 & 150-4
228 1973	West Indians	Drawn	G 213-9d & 93-7d	W 197 & 104-6
229 1973	Worcestershire	Won 138r	G 270 & 218-8d	W 135 & 215
230 1973	Warwickshire	Won 228r	G 325 & 205-6d	W 202 & 100
231 1974	Worcestershire	Lost Inns & 126r	W 390-5	G142 & 122
232 1974	Derbyshire	Drawn	G 279 & 238-2d	D 171 & 133-3
233 1974	Nottinghamshire	Drawn	G 282 & 7-1	N 172
234 1975	Kent	Drawn	K 257 & 357-6d	G 272 & 332-9
235 1975	Warwickshire	Won 4w	W 263 & 234	G 387 & 111-6
236 1975	Worcestershire	Lost Inns & 39r	W 297-9	G 68 & 190
237 1976	Glamorgan	Won 132r	G 339 & 253-4d	Gm 292 & 168
238 1976	Essex	Won Inns & 64r	E 160 & 167	G 391

239 1977	Surrey	Drawn	G 197 & 159-1	S 245
240 1977	Worcestershire	Won Inns & 35r	W 167 & 136	G 338
241 1977	Sussex	Won 8w	S 309-7 & 262	G 353-7 & 219-2
242 1978	Nottinghamshire	Drawn	N 221-8	G 7-0
243 1978	Glamorgan	Won 7w	Gm 144	G 146-3
244 1978	Hampshire	Drawn	G 151 & 219	H 189
245 1979	Yorkshire	Drawn	G 288-8	Y 303-8d
246 1979	Worcestershire	Drawn	G 308-8	W 142-9
247 1979	Surrey	Lost 1w	G 250-3d & 216-7d	S 200-5d & 267-9
248 1980	Hampshire	Won 197r	G 303 & 175-3d	H 178 & 103
249 1980	Worcestershire	Won 96r	G 178 & 177	W 111 & 148
250 1980	Middlesex	Won 6w	M 220 & 158-4d	G 109 & 271-4
251 1981	Surrey	Won 8w	S 160 & 170	G 166 & 165-2
252 1981	Hampshire	Won Inns & 86r	G 381-7d	H 174 & 121
253 1981	Kent	Drawn	K 310-6d & 276-6d	G 336-3d & 121-5
254 1982	Nottinghamshire	Lost 106r	N 197 & 284-6d	G 111 & 264
255 1982	Middlesex	Drawn	G 247 & 141-7	M 277
256 1982	Essex	Drawn	G 322 & 236-7d	E 303-9d & 107-5
257 1983	Glamorgan	Won Inns & 9r	G 376	Gm 204 & 163
258 1983	Warwickshire	Lost 4w	G 356-5d & 217-6d	W 303-9d & 271-6
259 1983	Yorkshire	Won 5w	Y 344-5d & 239-8d	G 307-6d & 280-5
260 1984	Sri Lankans	Drawn	G 278-4d & 116-6	S 286-1d
261 1984	Glamorgan	Drawn	Gm 258 & 243-6d	G 252-8d & 207-8
262 1984	Surrey	Drawn	G 280 & 225-6	S 367
263 1985	Leicestershire	Drawn	G 134 & 121-5	L 249
264 1985	Nottinghamshire	Drawn	N 216	G 15-0
265 1985	Warwickshire	Won 7w	W 127 & 211	G 253 & 86-3
266 1986	Hampshire	Won 17r	G 201 & 184	H 270 & 98
267 1986	Nottinghamshire	Drawn	G 345 & 249-5d	N 300-3d
268 1986	Middlesex	Lost 104r	M 349 & 68-1d	G 61-3d & 252
269 1987	Leicestershire	Lost 63r	L 367 & 235-3d	G 288 & 251
270 1987	Surrey	Won 52r	G 353-9d & 292-8d	S 330 & 263
271 1987	Kent	Drawn	G 436-7d & 130-7	K 323-8d
272 1988	Surrey	Lost 21r	S 312 & 115	G 163-9d & 243
273 1988	Warwickshire	Drawn	G 356-8d & 234-7d	W 307-7d & 191-8
274 1988	Yorkshire	Drawn	Y 367-8d & 104-4	G 214 & 404-6d
275 1989	Lancashire	Won Inns & 23r	L 93 & 278	G 394
276 1989	Middlesex	Lost 188r	M 222 & 206-7d	G 122 & 118
277 1989	Derbyshire	Drawn	D 448-9d	G 175-6
278 1990	Yorkshire	Drawn	Y 451-6d & 219-3d	G 574
279 1990	Northamptonshire	Won Inns & 128r	N 150 & 177	G 455-9d
280 1990	Surrey	Drawn	G 301 & 202-4d	S 200-6d & 302-9
281 1991	Glamorgan	Drawn	Gm 247 & 294-7d	G 140 & 346-9
282 1991	Sussex	Drawn	G 283 & F	S F & 199-7
283 1991	Worcestershire	Lost 108r	W 333 & 224-9d	G 241 & 208
284 1992	Yorkshire	Drawn	Y 364 & 30-2	G 257
285 1992	Hampshire	Drawn	H 167 & 274-8d	G 339-8d & 95-7
286 1992	Sussex	Won 4w	S 324 & 242-9d	G 221 & 346-6

287 1993	Derbyshire	Lost 7w	D 521 & 139-3	G 139 & 520
288 1993	Lancashire	Won 9w	L 294 & 213	G 450 & 58-1
289 1994	Yorkshire	Won 324r	G 291 & 484	Y 247 & 204
290 1994	Kent	Lost 50r	K 360 & 195	G 271 & 234
291 1995	Lancashire	Won 10w	L 231 & 117	G 265 & 84-0
292 1995	Essex	Won 3w	E 244 & 437	G 400 & 285-7
293 1996	Leicestershire	Lost 102r	L 159 & 150	G 71 & 136
294 1996	Warwickshire	Won Inns & 116r	G 569	W 216 & 237
295 1997	Derbyshire	Won Inns & 35r	D 120 & 329	G 484
296 1997	Durham	Won Inns & 28r	D 86 & 357	G 471-6d
297 1998	Sussex	Won 7w	S 191 & 162	G 238 & 118-3
298 1998	Surrey	Won 2w	S 297 & 135	G 167 & 266-8
299 1999	Worcestershire	Lost 5w	W 591-7d & 68-5	G 231 & 425
300 1999	Durham	Lost Inns & 127r	D 552	G 202 & 223
301 2000	Northamptonshire	Lost Inns & 99r	N 543	G 116 & 328
302 2000	Warwickshire	Drawn	W 260 & 316	G 254 & 237-5
303 2001	Sussex	Won 10w	G 520 & 23-0	S 167 & 375
304 2001	Hampshire	Drawn	G 334 & 245-6d	H 230 & 40-1
305 2002	Glamorgan	Lost 2w	G 438 & 293	Gm 415 & 320-8
306 2002	Middlesex	Drawn	G 494 & 230	M 363 & 265-5
307 2003	Worcestershire	Drawn	G 271 & 133-5	W 439
308 2003	Yorkshire	Drawn	G 263 & 284-6d	Y 226 & 75-2

CENTURIES FOR GLOUCESTERSHIRE (121)

Townsend, C.L.	135*	Australians	(2)	1899
Townsend, C.L.	129	Australians		1909
Hammond, W.R.	231	Derbyshire	(5)	1933
Allen, B.O.	128	Derbyshire		1937
Stovold, A.W.	102	Derbyshire		1974
Broad, B.C.	120	Derbyshire		1993
Young, S.	237	Derbyshire		1997
Alleyne, M.W.	169	Durham	(2)	1997
Russell, R.C.	103*	Durham		1997
Townsend, C.L.	123	Essex	(7)	1900
Smith, H.	149	Essex		1923
Sinfield, R.A.	114	Essex		1932
Zaheer Abbas	153	Essex		1976
Alleyne, M.W.	141	Essex		1995
Symonds, A.	123*	Essex		1995
Lynch, M.A.	111	Essex		1995
Crapp, J.F.	132	Glamorgan	(6)	1949
Milton, C.A.	106	Glamorgan		1959
Sadiq Mohammad	134*	Glamorgan		1976
Scott, R.J.	122	Glamorgan		1991
Taylor, C.G.	126	Glamorgan		2002
Spearman, C.M.	180*	Glamorgan		2002
Dipper, A.E.	100	Hampshire	(3)	1927
Young, D.M.	114*	Hampshire		1960
Broad, B.C.	116	Hampshire		1980
Milton, C.A.	110	Kent	(6)	1965
Bissex, M.	104	Kent		1970
Knight, R.D.V.	120	Kent		1975
Zaheer Abbas	111	Kent		1975
Zaheer Abbas	136*	Kent		1981
Curran, K.M.	119	Kent		1987
Dipper, A.E.	104	Lancashire	(5)	1921
Hammond, W.R.	164	Lancashire		1932
Bainbridge, P.	128	Lancashire		1989
Alleyne, M.W.	111	Lancashire		1989
Alleyne, M.W.	142*	Lancashire		1993
Seabrook, F.J.	110	Leicestershire	(2)	1933
Crapp, J.F.	110	Leicestershire		1952
Pullen, W.W.F.	161	Middlesex	(9)	1884
Grace, W.G.	127*	Middlesex		1889
Hammond, W.R.	124	Middlesex		1935
Crapp, J.F.	101	Middlesex		1939
Allen, B.O.	131	Middlesex		1950
Young, D.M.	140	Middlesex		1959
Graveney, T.W.	142*	Middlesex		1960
Procter, M.J.	134*	Middlesex		1980
Hancock, T.H.C.	112	Middlesex		2003
Barnett, C.J.	107	Northamptonshire	(3)	1948

Wright, A.J.	112	Northamptonshire		1990
Russell, R.C.	110*	Northamptonshire		2000
Grace, W.G.	119	Nottinghamshire	(7)	1895
Grace, W.G.	131	Nottinghamshire		1897
Crapp, J.F.	124	Nottinghamshire		1948
White, R.C.	102*	Nottinghamshire		1962
Young, D.M.	103	Nottinghamshire		1963
Curran, K.M.	117*	Nottinghamshire		1986
Bainbridge, P.	105	Nottinghamshire		1986
Hammond, W.R.	123	South Africans	(2)	1935
Sinfield, R.A.	102	South Africans		1935
Midwinter, W.E.	103	Surrey	(15)	1880
Grace, W.G.	104	Surrey		1885
Cranston, J.	111*	Surrey		1889
Jessop, G.L.	124	Surrey		1910
Hammond, W.R.	143	Surrey (2nd Inns)		1928
Hammond, W.R.	139	Surrey (1st Inns)		1928
Lyon, B.H.	189	Surrey		1934
Hammond, W.R.	108	Surrey		1936
Barnett, C.J.	101	Surrey		1946
Sadiq Mohammad	126	Surrey		1979
Procter, M.J.	102	Surrey		1979
Wright, A.J.	139	Surrey		1984
Bainbridge, P.	151	Surrey		1987
Curran, K.M.	101	Surrey		1988
Alleyne, M.W.	118	Surrey		1990
Townsend, F.	136	Sussex	(14)	1873
Thomas, F.E.	111	Sussex		1906
Langdon, T.	106	Sussex		1914
Barnett, C.J.	189	Sussex		1934
Hammond, W.R.	137	Sussex		1934
Lyon, B.H.	119	Sussex		1934
Parker, G.W.	102	Sussex		1937
Emmett, G.M.	116	Sussex		1953
Milton, C.A.	170	Sussex		1965
Zaheer Abbas	205*	Sussex (1st Inns)		1977
Zaheer Abbas	108*	Sussex (2nd Inns)		1977
Athey, C.W.J.	181	Sussex		1992
Taylor, C.G.	140	Sussex		2001
Snape, J.N.	131	Sussex		2001
Champain, F.H.B.	113	Warwickshire	(11)	1908
Langdon, T.	108	Warwickshire		1908
Dipper, A.E.	102	Warwickshire		1913
Dipper, A.E.	100	Warwickshire		1919
Dipper, A.E.	125*	Warwickshire		1922
Procter, M.J.	118	Warwickshire		1973
Stovold, A.W.	164*	Warwickshire		1983
Zaheer Abbas	109	Warwickshire		1983

Bainbridge, P.	119	Warwickshire		1988
Windows, M.G.N.	184	Warwickshire		1996
Symonds, A.	127	Warwickshire		1996
Townsend, C.L.	214	Worcestershire	(14)	1906
Sewell, C.O.H.	107	Worcestershire		1906
Roberts, F.B.	157	Worcestershire		1910
Roberts, F.B.	138	Worcestershire		1911
Dipper, A.E.	120	Worcestershire		1911
Dacre, C.C.R.	114	Worcestershire		1934
Barnett, C.J.	102*	Worcestershire		1934
Hammond, W.R.	178	Worcestershire		1937
Emmett, G.M.	146	Worcestershire		1951
Procter, M.J.	106*	Worcestershire		1973
Procter, M.J.	108	Worcestershire		1977
Sadiq Mohammad	102	Worcestershire		1979
Wright, A.J.	120	Worcestershire		1991
Barnett, K.J.	106	Worcestershire		1999
Grace, W.G.	318*	Yorkshire	(8)	1876
Moberly, W.O.	103	Yorkshire		1876
Hignell, A.J.	102	Yorkshire		1979
Romaines, P.W.	100*	Yorkshire		1983
Broad, B.C.	100	Yorkshire		1983
Bainbridge, P.	169	Yorkshire		1988
Bainbridge, P.	152	Yorkshire		1990
Alleyne, M.W.	109	Yorkshire		1994

CENTURIES FOR OPPONENTS (96)

Trumper, V.T.	125	Australians	(5)	1902
Ransford, V.S.	121	Australians		1909
Bardsley, W.	115	Australians		1912
Bardsley, W.	127	Australians		1921
Macartney, C.G.	121	Australians		1921
Wilkins, C.P.	111	Derbyshire	(5)	1972
O'Gorman, T.J.G.	124	Derbyshire		1989
Morris, J.E.	121	Derbyshire		1989
Morris, J.E.	229	Derbyshire		1993
Cork, D.G.	104	Derbyshire		1993
Boon, D.C.	139	Durham	(2)	1999
Speak, N.J.	110	Durham		1999
Perrin, P.A.	134*	Essex	(4)	1900
Douglas, J.W.H.T.	147*	Essex		1923
O'Connor, J.	128	Essex		1923
Robinson, D.D.J.	123	Essex		1995
Walker, P.M.	113	Glamorgan	(6)	1959
Khan, M.J.	157	Glamorgan		1970
Maynard, M.P.	129	Glamorgan (1st Inns)		1991
Maynard, M.P.	126	Glamorgan (2nd Inns)		1991
Maynard, M.P.	140	Glamorgan (1st Inns)		2002
Maynard, M.P.	118*	Glamorgan (2nd Inns)		2002
Day, S.H.	101*	Kent	(12)	1897
Humphreys, E.	162	Kent		1910
Mason, J.R.	121*	Kent		1910
Woolley, F.E.	148	Kent		1911
Hardinge, H.T.W.	129	Kent		1923
Woolley, F.E.	176	Kent		1925
Fagg, A.E.	107	Kent		1951
Richardson, P.E.	111	Kent		1961
Denness, M.H.	112	Kent		1965
Asif Iqbal, Razvi	109	Kent		1970
Cowdrey, M.C.	119*	Kent		1975
Benson, M.R.	159	Kent		1994
Eccles, J.	113	Lancashire	(5)	1887
Makepeace, J.W.H.	113	Lancashire		1921
Paynter, E.	103	Lancashire		1932
Collins, R.	100	Lancashire		1961
Lloyd, D.	104	Lancashire		1972
Coleman, C.A.R.	114	Leicestershire	(4)	1930
Astill, W.E.	156*	Leicestershire		1933
Berry, L.G.	128	Leicestershire		1933
Gower, D.I.	105*	Leicestershire		1987
O'Brien, T.C.	110	Middlesex	(8)	1884
Ford, F.G.J.	108	Middlesex		1889
Robertson, W.P.	110*	Middlesex		1901
Brown, S.M.	130	Middlesex		1950
Russell, S.E.J.	129	Middlesex		1960

Butcher, R.O.	173	Middlesex		1982
Gatting, M.W.	110*	Middlesex		1989
Weekes, P.N.	102	Middlesex		2002
Lowry, T.C.	101*	New Zealanders	(1)	1927
Cook, J.W.	137	Northamptonshire	(1)	2000
Barnes, W.	143	Nottinghamshire	(7)	1880
Selby, J.	100	Nottinghamshire		1883
Shrewsbury, A.	127	Nottinghamshire		1892
Walker, W.	105	Nottinghamshire		1926
Hill, N.W.	129	Nottinghamshire		1963
Robinson, R.T.	108	Nottinghamshire		1986
Broad, B.C.	105	Nottinghamshire		1986
Palairet, L.C.H.	100	Somerset	(1)	1891
Viljoen, K.G.	122	South Africans	(1)	1935
Wettimuny, S.	123*	Sri Lankans	(1)	1984
Read, W.W.	107	Surrey	(9)	1892
Brockwell, W.	167	Surrey		1899
Parker, J.F.	127*	Surrey		1948
Parker, J.F.	102	Surrey		1949
Barrington, K.F.	103	Surrey		1954
Knight, R.D.V.	142	Surrey		1984
Lynch, M.A.	114	Surrey		1987
Clinton, G.S.	102	Surrey		1988
Hollioake, A.J.	112	Surrey		1998
Newham, W.	141*	Sussex	(8)	1885
Vine, J.	101	Sussex		1921
Parks, J.H.	127	Sussex		1937
Suttle, K.G.	108	Sussex		1953
Parks, J.M.	102	Sussex		1956
Barclay, J.R.T.	105	Sussex		1977
Adams, C.J.	123	Sussex		2001
Montgomerie, R.R.	107	Sussex		2001
Smith, K.D.	109	Warwickshire	(1)	1983
Walcott, C.L.	126	West Indians	(1)	1950
Bowley, F.L.	101	Worcestershire	(7)	1919
Gibbons, H.H.I.H.	113*	Worcestershire		1934
Kenyon, D.	120	Worcestershire		1951
Turner, G.M.	181	Worcestershire		1974
Solanki, V.S.	171	Worcestershire		1999
Weston, W.P.C.	139	Worcestershire		1999
Hick, G.A.	122	Worcestershire		1999
Hirst, G.H.	108	Yorkshire	(7)	1900
Carrick, P.	128*	Yorkshire		1979
Boycott, G.	140*	Yorkshire		1983
Sharp, K.	121	Yorkshire		1983
Byas, D.	112	Yorkshire		1988
Metcalfe, A.A.	162	Yorkshire		1990
Moxon, M.D.	183	Yorkshire		1992

GLOUCESTERSHIRE FIRST-CLASS CAREER AVERAGES

BATTING

NAME	M	I	NO	Runs	HS	Avge	100	50	Ct	St
D.G. A'Court	2	3	1	7	7	3.50	-	-	-	-
T.M. Alderman	3	3	2	44	43*	44.00	-	-	1	-
B.O. Allen	32	55	0	1495	131	27.18	2	8	44	-
C. Allen	1	1	0	4	4	4.00	-	-	1	-
D.A. Allen	37	55	8	855	68*	18.19	-	3	24	-
M.W. Alleyne	35	60	5	2188	169	39.78	6	8	36	-
F.J. Andrew	1	0	0	0	0	-	-	-	-	-
M. Ashenden	1	1	1	7	7*	-	-	-	1	-
C.W.J. Athey	23	38	4	1101	181	32.38	1	5	26	-
J.M.M. Averis	4	3	0	8	8	2.66	-	-	2	-
A.M. Babington	3	3	0	73	58	24.33	-	1	2	-
Sir D.T.L. Bailey	9	16	3	278	77*	21.38	-	2	7	-
P. Bainbridge	27	42	5	1668	169	45.08	6	5	20	-
M.C.J. Ball	22	32	7	629	70*	25.16	-	1	37	-
S.N. Barnes	1	1	0	2	2	2.00	-	-	-	-
C.J. Barnett	40	70	5	2051	189	31.55	4	8	37	-
C.S. Barnett	28	47	4	900	67	20.93	-	5	11	-
E.P. Barnett	9	15	0	128	28	8.53	-	-	12	-
K.J. Barnett	4	8	1	408	106	58.28	1	3	2	-
C.F. Belcher	1	2	0	6	6	3.00	-	-	1	-
E.T. Benson	1	2	0	45	42	22.50	-	-	-	-
J.R. Bernard	3	4	0	33	16	8.25	-	-	2	-
J.G.W.T. Bessant	7	10	3	57	17*	8.14	-	-	4	-
D.G. Bevan	6	12	0	176	63	14.66	-	1	2	-
M. Bissex	22	42	6	776	104	21.55	1	3	15	-
B.S. Bloodworth	10	17	0	219	62	12.88	-	1	4	9
J.H. Board	43	69	4	1011	82	15.55	-	3	66	32
W.F. Boroughs	1	1	0	0	0	0.00	-	-	-	-
H.J. Boughton	1	2	1	28	16	28.00	-	-	1	-
J.J. Bowles	4	8	0	62	20	7.75	-	-	-	-
B.M. Brain	14	13	3	179	57	17.90	-	1	3	-
J.H. Brain	11	20	1	281	51	14.78	-	1	12	-
W.H. Brain	2	4	1	24	17	8.00	-	-	3	7
A.J. Brassington	14	14	3	49	11	4.45	-	-	30	6
A.N. Bressington	1	1	1	17	17*	-	-	-	1	-
B.C. Broad	14	25	1	848	120	35.33	3	3	12	-
A.H. Brodhurst	3	6	1	13	7*	2.60	-	-	-	-
A.S. Brown	56	95	9	1281	71	14.89	-	2	88	-
D.W.J. Brown	8	16	0	192	59	12.00	-	1	1	-
W.S.A. Brown	23	40	4	582	65	16.16	-	2	23	-
L.D. Brownlee	10	18	0	165	47	9.16	-	-	8	-
W.M. Brownlee	10	16	3	228	49*	17.53	-	-	5	-
J.A. Bush	18	24	6	142	32	7.88	-	-	25	12
R.E. Bush	1	1	0	0	0	0.00	-	-	-	-
I.P. Butcher	3	4	0	101	40	25.25	-	-	1	-
D. Carpenter	5	10	0	119	38	11.90	-	-	1	-

NAME	M	I	NO	Runs	HS	Avge	100	50	Ct	St
F.A. Carter	1	1	1	13	13*	-	-	-	-	-
M.J. Cawdron	1	2	0	20	18	10.00	-	-	-	-
F.H.B. Champain	22	38	1	732	113	19.78	1	2	21	-
H.F.B. Champain	1	2	1	12	11	12.00	-	-	1	-
J.H. Childs	29	24	14	91	34*	9.10	-	-	11	-
M.J. Church	2	3	0	27	22	9.00	-	-	3	-
B.F. Clarke	3	4	0	26	24	6.50	-	-	2	-
C. Cook	47	57	26	134	21*	4.32	-	-	11	-
K.E. Cooper	4	7	1	93	52	15.50	-	1	2	-
N.S. Cornelius	1	1	0	40	40	40.00	-	-	-	-
T.P. Cotterell	1	2	0	0	0	0.00	-	-	-	-
L.L. Cranfield	1	2	0	10	10	5.00	-	-	1	-
L.M. Cranfield	15	23	8	215	43	14.33	-	-	2	-
J. Cranston	15	21	4	383	111*	22.52	1	1	11	-
J.F. Crapp	38	67	1	2052	132	31.09	4	9	37	-
F.J. Crooke	1	1	0	20	20	20.00	-	-	-	-
A.C.M. Croome	6	9	0	42	22	4.66	-	-	4	-
R.J. Cunliffe	6	9	1	247	92*	30.87	-	2	3	-
E.J. Cunningham	3	6	1	88	61*	17.60	-	1	-	-
K.M. Curran	17	27	1	1083	119	41.65	3	5	17	-
F.A. Curteis	2	4	1	44	27*	14.66	-	-	-	-
C.C.R. Dacre	17	25	0	609	114	24.36	1	5	9	3
J. Davey	15	21	8	77	17	5.92	-	-	4	-
M. Davies	4	3	2	35	32*	35.00	-	-	2	-
R.P. Davis	2	1	0	23	23	23.00	-	-	4	-
B.F. Davison	2	1	0	0	0	0.00	-	-	1	-
R.I. Dawson	6	10	1	272	71	30.22	-	2	7	-
G.S. de Winton	2	4	0	93	80	23.25	-	1	3	-
E.G. Dennett	44	71	29	388	29	9.23	-	-	31	-
A.E. Dipper	46	82	7	2531	125*	33.74	6	12	21	-
J.H. Dixon	1	1	0	0	0	0.00	-	-	1	-
R.J. Doughty	1	1	0	6	6	6.00	-	-	-	-
B. Dudleston	3	6	0	108	47	18.00	-	-	2	-
M.S.T. Dunstan	1	2	0	42	38	21.00	-	-	-	-
E.D.R. Eagar	6	9	1	95	23	11.87	-	-	4	-
F.E. Ellis	2	4	1	49	21	16.33	-	-	1	-
G.M. Emmett	48	83	2	2095	146	25.86	2	13	27	-
R.J. Etheridge	1	2	1	16	12*	16.00	-	-	2	2
W. Fairbanks	7	10	2	78	29*	9.75	-	-	2	-
A.H.C. Fargus	2	4	0	17	8	4.25	-	-	-	-
J.J. Ferris	8	15	2	181	40*	13.92	-	-	3	-
C.R. Filgate	1	1	0	1	1	1.00	-	-	1	-
I.D. Fisher	3	5	1	147	79*	36.75	-	1	1	-
J.C. Foat	6	7	0	53	19	7.57	-	-	1	-
P.H. Ford	3	3	2	38	20	38.00	-	-	2	-
R.G. Ford	2	2	0	51	32	25.50	-	-	1	-
H.H. Francis	2	4	0	16	8	4.00	-	-	1	-
T.H. Gange	2	4	0	66	38	16.50	-	-	-	-

NAME	M	I	NO	Runs	HS	Avge	100	50	Ct	St
B.W. Gannon	4	5	3	7	5*	3.50	-	-	-	-
M.J. Gerrard	3	5	3	8	4*	4.00	-	-	1	-
A.P.R. Gidman	4	8	0	205	94	25.62	-	1	4	-
D.R. Gilbert	3	5	2	66	28*	22.00	-	-	1	-
W.R. Gilbert	15	21	1	429	95	21.45	-	2	16	-
T.W.J. Goddard	51	76	25	372	27	7.29	-	-	26	-
R.T. Godsell	3	6	0	31	14	5.16	-	-	1	-
H.S. Goodwin	8	15	2	88	26	6.76	-	-	11	-
F.W. Goodwyn	1	1	0	38	38	38.00	-	-	-	-
C.S. Gordon	1	1	0	12	12	12.00	-	-	1	-
E.M. Grace	36	58	1	1043	73	18.29	-	6	34	-
G.F. Grace	12	15	0	285	83	19.00	-	3	12	-
W.G. Grace Jnr	6	11	2	150	25	16.66	-	-	5	-
W.G. Grace	45	72	7	2290	318*	35.23	5	8	53	-
D.A. Graveney	47	58	19	750	43	19.23	-	-	28	-
J.K.R. Graveney	12	19	6	128	24*	9.84	-	-	6	-
T.W. Graveney	29	50	5	1466	142*	32.57	1	12	21	-
D.M. Green	9	16	0	537	92	33.56	-	4	8	-
M.A. Green	12	18	1	160	37	9.41	-	-	8	-
A.D. Greene	1	1	0	0	0	0.00	-	-	3	-
V.S. Greene	1	2	1	92	62*	92.00	-	1	-	-
T. Gregg	2	3	1	56	24	28.00	-	-	3	-
H.W.R. Gribble	5	7	1	34	13	5.66	-	-	5	-
E.L. Griffiths	3	5	2	70	25	23.33	-	-	1	-
J.V.C. Griffiths	5	7	3	74	27*	18.50	-	-	-	-
A.H. Haines	1	1	0	23	23	23.00	-	-	-	-
H. Hale	2	4	1	23	11*	7.66	-	-	1	-
I.E. Hale	1	2	0	0	0	0.00	-	-	1	-
J. Halford	3	3	1	52	42	26.00	-	-	2	-
W.R. Hammond	38	65	7	2899	231	49.98	9	12	55	-
T.H.C. Hancock	16	28	0	927	112	33.10	1	8	9	-
M.A. Hardinges	1	2	1	27	17	27.00	-	-	-	-
I.J. Harvey	7	13	2	183	52	16.63	-	1	6	-
Rev P.Hattersley-Smi	3	3	1	60	51*	30.00	-	1	1	-
D.G. Hawkins	12	19	2	256	37	15.05	-	-	5	-
R.W. Haynes	2	4	0	57	24	14.25	-	-	1	-
A.H. Heath	1	2	0	25	25	12.50	-	-	-	-
L.P. Hedges	8	12	0	89	20	7.41	-	-	4	-
W. McG.Hemingway	6	12	0	197	78	16.41	-	1	2	-
D.R. Hewson	6	12	1	226	67	20.54	-	3	4	-
A.J. Hignell	21	29	5	670	102	27.91	1	5	21	-
S.G. Hinks	2	4	0	110	64	27.50	-	1	3	-
G.D. Hodgson	11	18	2	670	82	41.87	-	7	9	-
V. Hopkins	3	5	2	25	9	8.33	-	-	8	2
H.J. Huggins	13	20	3	278	48*	16.35	-	-	5	-
A.D. Imlay	2	2	0	14	14	7.00	-	-	1	1
Imraan Mohammed	1	2	0	38	24	19.00	-	-	-	-
K.B.S. Jarvis	2	3	1	19	14	9.50	-	-	1	-

NAME	M	I	NO	Runs	HS	Avge	100	50	Ct	St
G.L. Jessop	41	70	2	1563	124	22.98	1	8	51	-
R.P. Keigwin	5	10	0	220	65	22.00	-	1	1	-
C.J. King-Turner	3	4	0	8	8	2.00	-	-	-	-
W.M.N. Kingston	1	2	0	21	17	10.50	-	-	-	-
E.M.M. Knapp	2	2	0	3	3	1.50	-	-	-	-
R.D.V. Knight	15	28	1	680	120	25.18	1	1	9	-
W. Knightley-Smith	3	4	0	64	56	16.00	-	1	2	-
G.J. Lake	1	2	0	15	15	7.50	-	-	-	-
G.E.E. Lambert	34	53	8	603	68*	13.40	-	2	24	-
R.J. Lanchbury	3	6	0	77	38	12.83	-	-	-	-
T.W. Lang	2	2	0	19	10	9.50	-	-	1	-
T. Langdon	29	53	2	939	108	18.41	2	1	13	-
D.V. Lawrence	20	26	4	145	34*	6.59	-	-	8	-
J. Lewis	12	18	2	236	62	14.75	-	1	6	-
J.W. Lloyds	18	28	2	673	94	25.88	-	4	16	-
A.J.H. Luard	2	3	0	12	6	4.00	-	-	-	-
M.A. Lynch	6	8	0	245	111	30.62	1	1	6	-
B.H. Lyon	29	51	5	1138	189	24.73	2	4	42	-
Shoaib Malik	2	4	0	80	60	20.00	-	1	-	-
T.G. Matthews	2	3	0	31	23	10.33	-	-	1	-
F.B. McHugh	9	12	5	26	12	3.71	-	-	-	-
R.G.W. Melsome	4	7	0	40	15	5.71	-	-	2	-
M.D. Mence	3	6	0	43	18	7.16	-	-	-	-
B.J. Meyer	41	67	19	625	63	13.02	-	1	68	14
W.E. Midwinter	8	11	0	348	103	31.63	1	1	8	-
R.F. Miles	5	6	1	46	30	9.20	-	-	1	-
P.T. Mills	32	49	10	383	54	9.82	-	1	17	-
C.A. Milton	61	111	5	2770	170	26.13	3	17	108	-
W.O. Moberly	15	21	0	404	103	19.23	1	1	9	1
E.R. Moline	1	1	0	3	3	3.00	-	-	-	-
F.G. Monkland	3	4	2	65	29	32.50	-	-	1	-
C.I. Monks	1	2	0	8	4	4.00	-	-	1	-
D.N. Moore	8	12	1	311	98	28.27	-	1	8	-
E.G. Morrison	1	1	0	2	2	2.00	-	-	-	-
J.B. Mortimore	71	118	16	1657	75	16.24	-	4	45	-
W.H. Murch	3	6	0	46	26	7.66	-	-	1	-
J.W.W. Nason	1	2	0	19	19	9.50	-	-	-	-
W.L. Neale	39	60	5	1295	96	23.54	-	7	19	-
R.B. Nicholls	55	103	4	2668	99	26.94	-	18	34	-
P.A. Owen	3	2	0	2	1	1.00	-	-	-	-
D.A.C. Page	9	16	1	301	45	20.06	-	-	10	-
H.V. Page	24	39	3	689	93	19.13	-	4	22	3
J.R. Painter	24	43	2	547	70	13.34	-	1	23	-
A.J. Paish	6	10	3	94	36*	13.42	-	-	3	-
C.W.L. Parker	66	96	26	821	49	11.72	-	-	32	-
G.W. Parker	14	23	1	354	102	16.09	1	-	15	-
M.D. Partridge	4	3	0	30	20	10.00	-	-	2	-
I.R. Payne	3	3	1	48	27	24.00	-	-	2	-

NAME	M	I	NO	Runs	HS	Avge	100	50	Ct	St
E. Peake	4	6	0	51	19	8.50	-	-	2	-
A.E. Penduck	1	2	1	5	5*	5.00	-	-	-	-
G. Pepall	1	1	0	1	1	1.00	-	-	2	-
R.W. Phillips	2	3	0	73	35	24.33	-	-	1	-
V.J. Pike	3	5	1	21	9	5.25	-	-	-	-
M.W. Pooley	2	4	2	71	25*	35.50	-	-	1	-
S.P. Pope	1	1	1	17	17*	-	-	-	1	-
M.J. Procter	32	54	6	1721	134*	35.85	5	8	40	-
C.T.M. Pugh	7	12	0	173	34	14.41	-	-	6	-
G. Pullar	1	1	1	62	62*	-	-	1	-	-
W.W.F. Pullen	14	22	1	441	161	21.00	1	1	13	-
O.G. Radcliffe	13	23	0	457	76	19.86	-	2	5	-
D.C.G. Raikes	2	3	0	23	23	7.66	-	-	4	3
J.N. Rhodes	1	2	1	77	58*	77.00	-	1	1	-
R.W. Rice	24	44	2	632	65	15.04	-	2	12	-
A.G. Richardson	4	7	0	144	51	20.57	-	1	1	-
T.M.N. Riley	1	2	0	19	19	9.50	-	-	1	-
A.W. Roberts	12	18	1	305	47	17.94	-	-	5	-
F.B. Roberts	25	40	1	821	157	21.05	2	1	23	-
F.G. Roberts	26	43	20	203	22	8.82	-	-	11	-
D.C. Robinson	12	22	2	248	74	12.40	-	1	12	2
F.G. Robinson	11	18	0	271	71	15.05	-	1	5	4
P.G. Robinson	5	8	1	145	43	20.71	-	-	5	-
P. Rochford	11	14	0	44	9	3.14	-	-	10	1
F.G. Rogers	2	3	0	44	40	14.66	-	-	2	-
J.A. Rogers	4	6	0	37	18	6.16	-	-	3	-
L.M. Roll	1	0	0	0	0	-	-	-	-	-
P.W. Romaines	23	42	1	1062	100*	25.90	1	5	13	-
W.H. Rowlands	9	12	1	139	33	12.63	-	-	6	-
R.C. Russell	42	63	17	1639	110*	35.63	2	9	143	9
S.E.J. Russell	9	18	1	302	51*	17.76	-	1	3	-
Sadiq Mohammad	28	49	5	1449	134*	32.93	3	7	35	-
E. Sainsbury	1	1	0	1	1	1.00	-	-	-	-
G.E. Sainsbury	8	5	3	15	13	7.50	-	-	2	-
M.G. Salter	7	13	0	153	39	11.76	-	-	8	-
C.J. Scott	21	36	6	262	32*	8.73	-	-	16	-
E.K. Scott	2	2	0	0	0	0.00	-	-	-	-
R.J. Scott	6	10	0	272	122	27.20	1	-	3	-
F.J. Seabrook	30	44	3	743	110	18.12	1	2	14	-
C.O.H. Sewell	27	48	2	1039	107	22.58	1	5	23	-
J.H. Shackleton	6	7	6	69	41*	69.00	-	-	4	-
D.R. Shepherd	34	58	7	1097	59	21.50	-	4	12	-
J.N. Shepherd	9	17	6	543	98*	49.36	-	4	7	-
D.P. Simpkins	1	2	1	1	1*	1.00	-	-	-	-
R.A. Sinfield	42	68	12	1445	114	25.80	2	2	10	-
A.M. Smith	16	24	5	83	15	4.36	-	-	5	-
D.R. Smith	33	50	11	502	61*	12.87	-	2	37	-
H. Smith	41	66	7	1259	149	21.33	1	10	40	25

NAME	M	I	NO	Runs	HS	Avge	100	50	Ct	St
J.N. Snape	4	7	0	185	131	26.42	1	-	2	-
C.M. Spearman	4	8	2	346	180*	57.66	1	1	5	-
E.J. Spry	4	8	1	27	22	3.85	-	-	-	-
J. Srinath	2	3	1	37	19	18.50	-	-	-	-
E.J. Stephens	15	19	2	296	48	17.41	-	-	13	-
F.D. Stephenson	1	2	0	15	15	7.50	-	-	-	-
A.W. Stovold	46	79	8	2220	164*	31.26	2	13	44	13
M.W. Stovold	6	7	2	83	39	16.60	-	-	1	-
G. Strachan	1	1	0	50	50	50.00	-	1	1	-
J.P. Sullivan	5	8	1	44	16	6.28	-	-	3	-
D. Surridge	2	3	0	2	2	0.66	-	-	-	-
R. Swetman	5	9	1	43	16	5.37	-	-	9	4
A. Symonds	4	6	1	312	127	62.40	2	1	5	-
H.W. Taylor	2	4	1	84	43*	28.00	-	-	-	-
C.G. Taylor	6	11	0	584	140	53.09	2	2	6	-
E.J. Taylor	6	8	1	77	25	11.00	-	-	2	-
F. Taylor	1	1	0	36	36	36.00	-	-	-	-
G.A. Tedstone	2	3	1	41	19	20.50	-	-	5	1
F.E. Thomas	3	4	0	274	111	68.50	1	2	4	-
P.L. Thorn	2	3	0	27	25	9.00	-	-	2	-
K.P. Tomlins	3	6	1	139	37	27.80	-	-	-	-
A.F.M. Townsend	1	2	0	25	16	12.50	-	-	-	-
C.L. Townsend	22	38	3	1130	214	32.28	4	3	27	-
F. Townsend	29	42	4	939	136	24.71	1	3	30	-
F.N. Townsend	2	4	1	29	26	9.66	-	-	3	-
N.J. Trainor	3	4	0	8	6	2.00	-	-	4	-
J.H.A. Tremenheere	1	1	0	7	7	7.00	-	-	-	-
W. Troup	6	12	2	219	51	21.90	-	1	1	-
P.H. Twizell	1	1	0	0	0	0.00	-	-	-	-
C. Tyler	2	2	0	22	22	11.00	-	-	2	-
P.I. van der Gucht	3	4	1	59	43*	19.66	-	-	6	4
J.T.C. Vaughan	3	5	2	121	80	40.33	-	1	3	-
M.J. Vernon	1	0	0	0	0	-	-	-	-	-
W.O. Vizard	2	3	1	50	49*	25.00	-	-	3	-
C.A. Walsh	24	32	7	418	66	16.72	-	2	8	-
B.T.L. Watkins	4	5	1	17	7	4.25	-	-	-	6
G. Wedel	3	6	1	40	12	8.00	-	-	4	-
B.D. Wells	16	23	7	174	42*	10.87	-	-	8	-
S.A. Westley	2	3	1	9	3*	4.50	-	-	1	-
W.P.C. Weston	2	4	1	53	28	17.66	-	-	-	-
R.K. Whiley	1	2	2	11	7*	-	-	-	-	-
R.C. White	9	16	1	333	102*	22.20	1	2	3	-
E.W.E. Wignall	1	1	0	0	0	0.00	-	-	-	-
A.G.S. Wilcox	3	6	1	48	22	9.60	-	-	1	-
A.H. Wilkins	6	6	1	50	23	10.00	-	-	5	-
J. Wilkinson	1	1	0	0	0	0.00	-	-	-	-
P.F.C. Williams	11	19	2	301	75	17.70	-	1	6	-
R.C. Williams	3	6	0	49	24	8.16	-	-	1	-

NAME	M	I	NO	Runs	HS	Avge	100	50	Ct	St
R.C.J. Williams	6	8	1	73	44*	10.42	-	-	23	1
A.E. Wilson	29	51	5	920	82	20.00	-	6	38	22
S.J. Windaybank	2	1	1	46	46*	-	-	-	-	-
A.R. Windows	15	27	1	209	48	8.03	-	-	6	-
M.G.N. Windows	19	35	3	1325	184	41.40	1	12	14	-
A.E. Winstone	4	6	0	30	12	5.00	-	-	3	-
R.B. Wood	1	2	1	6	3*	6.00	-	-	-	-
W.A. Woof	24	37	7	152	14	5.06	-	-	26	-
C.N. Woolley	1	1	0	22	22	22.00	-	-	-	-
S.H. Wootton	3	6	0	185	97	30.83	-	1	2	-
H. Wrathall	24	41	2	697	73	17.87	-	3	24	1
A.J. Wright	33	57	3	1505	139	27.87	3	7	30	-
G.N. Wyatt	1	2	0	4	3	2.00	-	-	-	-
D.M. Young	42	77	6	1774	140	24.98	3	5	8	-
S. Young	2	2	0	289	237	144.50	1	1	1	-
Zaheer Abbas	28	47	7	2186	205*	54.65	6	14	12	-
Extras				6317					23	
	3388	5428	692	109570	318*	23.13	121	431	2801	188

GLOUCESTERSHIRE FIRST-CLASS CAREER AVERAGES

BOWLING

NAME	Balls	R	W	Avge	Best	5w	10w	SR
D.G. A'Court	405	227	5	45.40	3-70	-	-	81.00
T.M. Alderman	509	294	16	18.37	4-81	-	-	31.81
B.O. Allen	6	7	0	-	-	-	-	-
D.A. Allen	6187	2361	113	20.89	6-25	6	1	54.75
M.W. Alleyne	2985	1625	53	30.66	5-14	2	-	56.32
F.J. Andrew	24	11	0	-	-	-	-	-
M. Ashenden	168	91	3	30.33	3-74	-	-	56.00
C.W.J. Athey	120	75	0	-	-	-	-	-
J.M.M. Averis	600	356	8	44.50	3-84	-	-	75.00
A.M. Babington	429	253	7	36.14	3-51	-	-	61.28
P. Bainbridge	1411	721	17	42.41	5-70	1	-	83.00
M.C.J. Ball	3694	1932	41	47.12	5-101	1	-	90.09
S.N. Barnes	120	48	1	48.00	1-19	-	-	120.00
C.J. Barnett	1756	681	22	30.95	3-49	-	-	79.81
K.J. Barnett	57	52	2	26.00	2-52	-	-	28.50
J.R. Bernard	114	46	2	23.00	2-37	-	-	57.00
J.G.W.T. Bessant	504	333	6	55.50	2-41	-	-	84.00
M. Bissex	2604	1203	53	22.69	7-50	4	1	49.13
J.J. Bowles	42	22	0	-	-	-	-	-
B.M. Brain	1514	669	32	20.90	5-46	1	-	47.31
J.H. Brain	180	96	5	19.20	4-54	-	-	36.00
A.N. Bressington	126	69	3	23.00	3-56	-	-	42.00
B.C. Broad	312	161	3	53.66	2-70	-	-	104.00
A.S. Brown	6201	2668	100	26.68	6-55	5	-	62.01
W.S.A. Brown	1548	608	24	25.33	4-39	-	-	64.50
W.M. Brownlee	814	526	16	32.87	6-84	1	-	50.87
J.A. Bush	88	37	0	-	-	-	-	-
M.J. Cawdron	168	70	3	23.33	3-70	-	-	56.00
F.H.B. Champain	72	37	0	-	-	-	-	-
J.H. Childs	5373	2414	95	25.41	6-69	4	-	56.55
C. Cook	9574	3088	185	16.69	7-64	13	1	51.75
K.E. Cooper	810	424	12	35.33	3-46	-	-	67.50
T.P. Cotterell	18	10	0	-	-	-	-	-
L.L. Cranfield	132	56	0	-	-	-	-	-
L.M. Cranfield	1568	744	33	22.54	5-60	2	-	47.51
J. Cranston	16	14	0	-	-	-	-	-
A.C.M. Croome	115	56	2	28.00	2-43	-	-	57.50
E.J. Cunningham	42	11	0	-	-	-	-	-
K.M. Curran	1502	900	24	37.50	4-37	-	-	62.58
F.A. Curteis	88	36	0	-	-	-	-	-
C.C.R. Dacre	30	14	0	-	-	-	-	-
J. Davey	1650	755	21	35.95	4-92	-	-	78.57
M. Davies	615	335	9	37.22	3-47	-	-	68.33
R.P. Davis	394	140	5	28.00	2-46	-	-	78.80
E.G. Dennett	10334	4175	280	14.91	8-69	29	13	36.90
A.E. Dipper	1128	578	31	18.64	7-46	3	1	36.38

NAME	Balls	R	W	Avge	Best	5w	10w	SR
J.H. Dixon	24	16	0	-	-	-	-	-
R.J. Doughty	150	103	2	51.50	2-70	-	-	75.00
B. Dudleston	42	27	0	-	-	-	-	-
F.E. Ellis	114	62	0	-	-	-	-	-
G.M. Emmett	366	171	7	24.42	4-58	-	-	52.28
A.H.C. Fargus	210	143	2	71.50	1-61	-	-	105.00
J.J. Ferris	773	432	14	30.85	3-41	-	-	55.21
I.D. Fisher	596	367	10	36.70	3-111	-	-	59.60
P.H. Ford	485	256	16	16.00	6-84	2	1	30.31
T.H. Gange	366	237	10	23.70	5-95	1	-	36.60
B.W. Gannon	617	373	11	33.90	3-47	-	-	56.09
M.J. Gerrard	352	269	3	89.66	2-25	-	-	117.33
A.P.R. Gidman	288	154	6	25.66	3-33	-	-	48.00
D.R. Gilbert	622	291	12	24.25	4-59	-	-	51.83
W.R. Gilbert	1419	579	38	15.23	6-51	1	-	37.34
T.W.J. Goddard	10781	4728	269	17.57	10-113	24	10	40.07
E.M. Grace	607	277	13	21.30	4-30	-	-	46.69
G.F. Grace	728	293	10	29.30	3-8	-	-	72.80
W.G. Grace Jnr	205	98	2	49.00	1-20	-	-	102.50
W.G. Grace	7316	2896	170	17.03	9-55	16	4	43.03
D.A. Graveney	7197	2982	122	24.44	8-85	5	2	58.99
J.K.R. Graveney	1046	510	23	22.17	6-45	1	-	45.47
T.W. Graveney	245	133	4	33.25	2-23	-	-	61.25
D.M. Green	66	20	0	-	-	-	-	-
M.A. Green	18	25	0	-	-	-	-	-
V.S. Greene	234	159	4	39.75	3-87	-	-	58.50
T. Gregg	64	39	0	-	-	-	-	-
J.V.C. Griffiths	282	134	7	19.14	2-23	-	-	40.28
H. Hale	40	19	4	4.75	4-13	-	-	10.00
W.R. Hammond	3475	1441	63	22.87	9-23	3	1	55.15
T.H.C. Hancock	132	87	3	29.00	1-4	-	-	44.00
M.A. Hardinges	48	60	1	60.00	1-60	-	-	48.00
I.J. Harvey	1165	483	26	18.57	5-29	2	-	44.80
D.G. Hawkins	432	245	10	24.50	6-81	1	-	43.20
R.W. Haynes	48	37	3	12.33	2-14	-	-	16.00
H.J. Huggins	1523	694	27	25.70	5-59	1	-	56.40
K.B.S. Jarvis	246	151	7	21.57	4-37	-	-	35.14
G.L. Jessop	4250	1719	91	18.89	8-29	4	-	46.70
R.P. Keigwin	210	120	4	30.00	4-40	-	-	52.50
R.D.V. Knight	638	331	12	27.58	3-18	-	-	53.16
G.J. Lake	120	59	2	29.50	2-59	-	-	60.00
G.E.E. Lambert	4472	2086	87	23.97	6-69	5	1	51.40
T.W. Lang	138	51	4	12.75	3-11	-	-	34.50
T. Langdon	36	34	0	-	-	-	-	-
D.V. Lawrence	3056	1942	72	26.97	7-47	3	-	42.44
J. Lewis	2093	1203	27	44.55	3-39	-	-	77.51
J.W. Lloyds	1461	916	24	38.16	5-37	1	-	60.87
B.H. Lyon	325	220	3	73.33	1-8	-	-	108.33

NAME	Balls	R	W	Avge	Best	5w	10w	SR
Shoaib Malik	396	146	5	29.20	3-76	-	-	79.20
F.P. McHugh	1224	404	21	19.23	6-41	1	1	58.28
R.G.W. Melsome	156	113	3	37.66	2-48	-	-	52.00
M.D. Mence	52	59	0	-	-	-	-	-
W.E. Midwinter	2296	609	27	22.55	5-81	1	-	85.03
R.F. Miles	565	204	9	22.66	4-18	-	-	62.77
P.T. Mills	5134	2119	100	21.19	6-38	6	-	51.34
C.A. Milton	246	96	3	32.00	1-7	-	-	82.00
J.B. Mortimore	13772	5224	267	19.56	7-35	15	2	51.58
W.H. Murch	380	275	10	27.50	4-67	-	-	38.00
W.L. Neale	375	257	6	42.83	3-28	-	-	62.50
R.B. Nicholls	24	22	0	-	-	-	-	-
P.A. Owen	342	239	4	59.75	2-37	-	-	85.50
H.V. Page	957	455	12	37.91	4-33	-	-	79.75
J.R. Painter	313	124	2	62.00	1-19	-	-	156.50
A.J. Paish	1321	518	30	17.26	7-93	3	1	44.03
C.W.L. Parker	16055	6621	409	16.18	9-35	38	15	39.25
G.W. Parker	384	142	4	35.50	2-9	-	-	96.00
M.D. Partridge	61	67	2	33.50	2-59	-	-	30.50
I.R. Payne	174	82	3	27.33	3-68	-	-	58.00
E. Peake	246	131	6	21.83	3-47	-	-	41.00
A.E. Penduck	66	32	0	-	-	-	-	-
G. Pepall	89	38	2	19.00	2-33	-	-	44.50
V.J. Pike	252	124	2	62.00	1-11	-	-	126.00
M.W. Pooley	246	113	3	37.66	2-56	-	-	82.00
M.J. Procter	4500	1881	110	17.10	7-16	6	2	40.90
W.W.F. Pullen	36	23	1	23.00	1-23	-	-	36.00
O.G. Radcliffe	251	147	5	29.40	4-24	-	-	50.20
A.W. Roberts	425	275	6	45.83	2-42	-	-	70.83
F.B. Roberts	666	392	4	98.00	1-14	-	-	166.50
F.G. Roberts	4395	1805	105	17.19	8-64	6	1	41.85
P.G. Robinson	168	101	2	50.50	1-5	-	-	84.00
J.A. Rogers	174	89	4	22.25	2-33	-	-	43.50
L.M. Roll	90	49	0	-	-	-	-	-
P.W. Romaines	25	39	0	-	-	-	-	-
W.H. Rowlands	24	2	1	2.00	1-2	-	-	24.00
Sadiq Mohammad	1132	598	22	27.18	4-51	-	-	51.45
G.E. Sainsbury	1296	661	16	41.31	3-53	-	-	81.00
C.J. Scott	2818	1154	57	20.24	6-42	1	-	49.43
E.K. Scott	210	101	1	101.00	1-42	-	-	210.00
R.J. Scott	498	292	5	58.40	2-39	-	-	99.60
F.J. Seabrook	48	34	0	-	-	-	-	-
C.O.H. Sewell	30	35	2	17.50	2-35	-	-	15.00
J.H. Shackleton	439	229	4	57.25	3-48	-	-	109.75
J.N. Shepherd	1987	853	35	24.37	7-64	1	-	56.77
D.P. Simpkins	12	15	0	-	-	-	-	-
R.A. Sinfield	5677	2321	105	22.10	6-43	7	1	54.06
A.M. Smith	2959	1609	72	22.34	7-70	5	1	41.09

NAME	Balls	R	W	Avge	Best	5w	10w	SR
D.R. Smith	4760	1986	91	21.82	6-44	4	-	52.30
J.N. Snape	276	141	1	141.00	1-91	-	-	276.00
E.J. Spry	210	164	3	54.66	3-84	-	-	70.00
J. Srinath	437	228	11	20.72	5-53	1	-	39.72
E.J. Stephens	114	77	1	77.00	1-12	-	-	114.00
F.D. Stephenson	156	69	5	13.80	5-69	1	-	31.20
A.W. Stovold	24	29	1	29.00	1-29	-	-	24.00
M.W. Stovold	6	3	0	-	-	-	-	-
G. Strachan	180	56	5	11.20	3-36	-	-	36.00
D. Surridge	402	166	3	55.33	2-51	-	-	134.00
A. Symonds	60	13	0	-	-	-	-	-
C.G. Taylor	147	132	3	44.00	3-126	-	-	49.00
P.L. Thorn	96	61	2	30.50	2-53	-	-	48.00
C.L. Townsend	3381	1798	117	15.36	9-128	12	5	28.89
F. Townsend	649	367	9	40.77	2-19	-	-	72.11
N.J. Trainor	30	27	0	-	-	-	-	-
P.H. Twizell	67	38	0	-	-	-	-	-
C. Tyler	186	94	2	47.00	2-27	-	-	93.00
J.T.C. Vaughan	174	92	0	-	-	-	-	-
M.J. Vernon	54	50	0	-	-	-	-	-
C.A. Walsh	4990	2550	152	16.77	8-58	13	6	32.82
G. Wedel	180	84	5	16.80	3-39	-	-	36.00
B.D. Wells	2843	1046	61	17.14	6-43	3	-	46.60
A.H. Wilkins	822	386	15	25.73	5-50	1	-	54.80
J. Wilkinson	165	57	4	14.25	4-57	-	-	41.25
P.F.C. Williams	30	31	0	-	-	-	-	-
R.C. Williams	431	281	6	46.83	3-13	-	-	71.83
A.R. Windows	658	262	11	23.81	5-36	1	-	59.81
M.G.N. Windows	6	0	0	-	-	-	-	-
W.A. Woof	5045	2177	113	19.26	8-125	10	1	44.64
C.N. Woolley	48	45	0	-	-	-	-	-
H. Wrathall	46	30	0	-	-	-	-	-
S. Young	354	144	10	14.40	3-9	-	-	35.40
Zaheer Abbas	36	6	0	-	-	-	-	-
Extras		4876	144	r/o				
	225317	105186	4719	22.29	10-113	278	72	47.74

INDEX

Abbey Business Equipment, 335
Abdul Razzaq, 348
Abel, R., 58, 92
Adams, C.J., 341-2
Adams, P.R., 324
Addrell, Revd, 131
Adhikari, H.R., 203-4
Adlard, Mr, 57
Aerial Derby, 128
Agg-Gardner, James, 37, 146
Albion Street, 55, 114, 135
Alcock, Charles, 26
Alderman, T.M., 297-9
Ali, Kabir, 352
Alim-ud-Din, 210
Allahakbarries, 141
Allan, Captain, 126-8, 133
Allen, B.O., 158, 163, 165,
  174, 176-7, 183-4, 186-7, 190,
  193-7, 199, 201
Allen, D.A., 206, 226, 229,
  237-9, 241, 245, 249, 256-7,
  259
Allen, G.O.B., 196
Allerton, Jeremy, 308
Alleyne, M.W., 294, 296, 300-1,
  305, 308-11, 315-7, 319, 322-4,
  326, 329, 332, 335-6, 347-8,
  351, 353, 355-6
Alston, Rex, 213
Alstone Baths, 162
Altham, H.S., 313
Amarnath, N.B., 184
American Wonders, 58
Amir Elahi, 172
Amiss, D.L., 262, 286
Andoversford, 183
Anstead, W.H., 25
Apple Centres West, 304
Archers, The, 201
Arle Court, 316, 348
Arlott, John, 183, 190, 208, 278
Armstrong, W.W., 98, 129, 132
Arnold, E.G., 113
Arnold, G.G., 270
Arsenal, 165
Ashleworth, 203
Ashton, C.S., 134
Asif Din, 298
Asif Iqbal, 253, 266
Assembly Rooms, 56-7, 73,
  82, 99
Astec Communications, 317
Astill, W.E., 161

Atherton, M.A., 300, 320
Athey, C.W.J., 275, 289, 291,
  293, 294, 296-7, 301, 304-6,
  308, 311-12, 354
Attewell, W., 70, 77
Attwoolls, 311, 353
August, Philip, 313, 324
Austin, I.D., 319-20
Australians, 32, 46, 56-7, 59-60,
  62-4, 66, 71-2, 78-9, 81-2, 89,
  91-3, 98, 103, 108, 110, 118-9,
  129, 131-2, 141, 143, 157, 184,
  291
Averis, J.M.M., 344, 349, 353,
  358
Avery, Bert, 238, 255-6, 260,
  344
Avon, river, 137
Babington, A.M., 307-8, 315
Bach Choir, 187
Bailey, M.J., 281
Bailey, Sir D.T.L., 197-8, 200-1,
  203
Bailey, T.E., 206
Bain, William, 358
Bainbridge, P., 271, 280-2,
  290, 294, 296, 298-9, 300, 305
Baker, Charles, 155
Ball, M.C.J., 301, 304, 311,
  316, 330, 335-6, 342, 344,
  348-9, 351, 356
Bannerman, A.C., 59
Bannister, J.D., 204
Baqa Jilani, 172
Barber, R.W., 235
Barclay, J.R.T., 271-2
Barclay, Kit, 272
Bardsley, W., 111, 119, 129,
  131
Barling, T.H., 172, 184
Barlow, Eddie, 305
Barlow, R.G., 61
Barnes, Revd R.Palmer, 198
Barnes, W., 42-3, 56, 69, 96
Barnett, C.J., 147, 152, 157,
  159, 161, 163, 166, 168, 170-2,
  176, 180-5, 187, 189-192, 245,
  264, 273
Barnett, C.S., 107, 111, 119,
  133-4
Barnett, E.P., 101
Barnett, K.J., 326, 336, 341-3,
  348
Barnwood, 113

Barratt, E., 55-6
Barrie, Sir James, 141
Barrington, K.F., 211, 240
Barron, W., 191
Barry, Revd Alfred, 21
Batchelor, Denzil, 247
Bates, W., 51
Bath Road, 18, 81, 185, 301,
  343
Bayshill House, 37, 62
Beach, Major W.W. Hicks, 198
Beach, Margaret A. Hicks, 95
Beaudesert School, 288
Beaufort, Duke of, 259
Bedser, A.V., 194, 211, 215
Bedser, E.A., 210
Beldham, G.W., 104
Bell's Life, 49-50
Bennett, H.W., 128
Benskin, W.E., 127
Benson, Archbishop, 85
Benson, M.R., 317
Bentall, Chris, 293
Berkeley Hill, 295
Berlin, Olympic Games, 173
Berry, G.L., 161
Berry, R., 208
Berry, Scyld, 324
Bethesda Methodist Church,
  198
Betjeman, John, 177
Bevan, D.G., 238
Bicknell, D.J., 306
Bicknell, M.P., 335
Billings, Mrs S., 178
Binks, J.G., 219
Bird, Dickie, 269
Birkenshaw, J., 243
Birmingham, 59, 73, 182
Bishop, Harold, 257
Bissex, M., 236, 238, 241, 243,
  245, 247, 251-3, 255-7
Blackburn, 162
Blakey, R.J., 298, 305, 310
Blind Beggars, The, 41
Blofeld, Henry, 256
Bloodworth, B.S., 135, 136, 140
Blue Hungarian Band, 103
Blythe, C., 105, 116, 119
Board, J.H., 70, 78, 96, 104,
  106, 108, 111, 208
Bolus, J.B., 232
Bonnor, G.J., 46, 57, 59, 85
Boon, D.C., 329, 337

Bosanquet, B.J.T., 97, 104
Boswell Cottage, 23
Botham, I.T., 307-8
Bournside School, 351
Bourton-on-the-Water, 131
Bowell, H.A.W., 109
Bowler, P.D., 304
Bowley, E.H., 151
Bowley, F.L., 121, 125
Boyce, K.D., 262
Boycott, G., 275, 277, 287-8
Bracewell, John, 335, 348-9, 356
Bradford, 77, 137, 239
Bradley, W.M., 81
Bradman, D.G., 155, 157, 192
Braham, Philip, 111
Brain, B.M., 248, 269, 275, 282
Brain, Christopher, 315
Brain, J.H., 58
Brain, S.A. & Co. Ltd, 315
Brain, W.H., 71-2, 315
Brassington, A.J., 265, 275-6, 278, 286, 290, 299
Brearley, J.M., 279, 284
Bremner, Rory, 321, 354
Bresslaw, Bernard, 224
Bridle, David, 260, 263, 286, 338
Briers, N.E., 296
Briggs, J., 61
Bristol Evening Post, 200
Bristol Rovers, 222
Bristol Times and Mirror, 115
Bristol, 81, 89, 96, 122, 128, 139. 144, 182, 201, 218, 236, 246, 256, 260, 263-4, 267, 272, 284, 295, 311, 322, 325, 337, 350
British Medical Association, 96
Britton, Jack, 272, 295
Broad, B.C., 277, 280, 282, 288, 291, 294, 314
Broadway, 141
Brockwell, W., 64, 73, 92
Broderick, V., 192
Brodhurst, A.H., 180-1
Brookes, D., 191-2
Brookes, Mr, 47
Brookes, Stan, 272
Broom, Michael, 350, 357
Brown, A.S., 217-8, 229, 235-6, 241, 244, 247, 251-2, 257, 262, 264, 267-9, 348
Brown, F.R.,172, 187, 259
Brown, J.F., 338
Brown, S.J.E., 337
Brown, S.M., 196
Brownlee, L.D., 108, 113-4
Bruen, A.S.F., 138
Bubble and Squeaks, 125
Bull, C.H., 167, 174
Buller, J.S., 174, 209, 214, 232, 252
Burden, Roger, 337

Burnaby, David, 111
Burnup, C.J., 79, 87, 106
Bush, J.A., 30, 48, 89
Buss, A., 234, 239
Butcher, A.R., 280, 307
Butcher, I.P., 291, 301
Butcher, R.O., 285
Butler, Eddie, 354
Byas, D., 298
Byrne, David, 311
Cadena Café, 126, 141
Caffyn, W., 21, 28
Cambridge, 131, 134, 149, 180
Cameron, H.B., 167-8, 173
Canada, 21
Canterbury Cricket Week, 23, 35, 45, 49, 78, 89, 97, 115, 159, 228
Cardiff, 56, 118, 248
Cardus, Neville, 131, 154, 248
Carlyon, Miss Kate, 44, 47
Carpenter, D., 209-10, 228
Carpenter, Robert, 21
Carr, A.W., 143
Carr, D.W., 115, 119
Carrick, P., 275, 298
Carter, R.G.M., 234, 241, 244
Carter, Revd E.S., 37
Cartwright, T.W., 249
Cass, G.R., 247, 262
Cave, H.B., 219
Cavendish House, 193, 236
Cawdron, M.J., 322, 336
Chalke, Stephen, 338
Challen, J.B., 67
Chambers, Mr, 76
Champain, F.H.B., 84, 89, 91-2, 107, 108-9, 114
Chapple, G., 320
Charlton Kings, 141, 186, 309
Charlton Park, 18
Chelt, river, 41
Cheltenham and Gloucester Building Society, 337-8, 348-9, 352, 357
Cheltenham Chronicle, 103, 105, 124, 158-9, 170, 172-3, 178, 184, 186, 201
Cheltenham Civil Defence Committee, 182
Cheltenham College Council, 31, 32, 39, 49, 84, 244
Cheltenham College, 17-19, 21, 25-32, 35, 52, 54, 57, 69, 71, 84-5, 108, 124, 127, 144, 173-4, 177, 182, 195, 213, 304, 314, 353
Cheltenham Corporation, 235
Cheltenham Cricket Festival, *passim*
Cheltenham Cricket Week, 31, 35, 37, 39, 41-2, 46-50, 54-5, 58-67, 71, 74, 77-8, 84, 86, 88-9, 93-99, 103-4, 107, 109-10, 273

Cheltenham Cyclist Club, 67
Cheltenham Everyman Theatre Association, 234
Cheltenham Examiner, 49
Cheltenham Festival of British Contemporary Music, 195
Cheltenham Festival of Literature, 195
Cheltenham Grammar School, 55, 73, 255, 284
Cheltenham Looker-On, 25, 30, 32, 48, 51, 72, 113, 116
Cheltenham Military Band, 60
Cheltenham Parish Church, 239
Cheltenham Police, 203
Cheltenham Saracens, 270
Cheltenham Spectator and Festival News, 307
Cheltenham Town CC, 101, 138, 269
Cheltenham Town Council, 37
Cheltenham Town F.C., 229
Chelwood Gallery, 349
Chesterfield, 161, 210, 265
Chesterton, G.H., 196, 207
Childs, J.H., 268-9, 271, 277, 280, 282, 286
Chipping Sodbury, 317
Chisselling, 51
Christiani, R.J., 199
Churchill, Winston, 161, 182, 264
Cirencester Grammar School, 126
Cirencester, 173
Clarence Hotel, 72
Clarke, Dr C.B., 180
Clarke, Jack, 244, 259
Clarke, R.W., 191
Clarke, S.T., 296-7
Clarke, Stanley, 155
Cleeve Catering, 355
Cleeve Hill, 52, 58, 114, 189, 214, 341, 355
Clift, P.B., 194, 200
Clifton College, 106, 226
Clifton, 29-30, 42, 56, 59, 62, 71, 149, 153
Clinton, G.S., 275, 297
Close, D.B., 218
Clydesdale Club, 18
Cobb, R.A., 295
Coco the Clown, 193
Cole, Arthur, 189
Cole, Carol, 357
Colesborne Park, 164
Coley, Christopher, 274, 276, 280, 305, 337, 342, 350, 353-4, 357
College Lawn, 108, 185, 206, 275
College Road, 125, 178
College, Old v Present, 37
Collins, R., 229
Colonnade, 97, 131

Colston's School, 277
Colwall, 155
Compton, D.C.S., 182, 187
Connor, C.A., 292
Conservative Club, 55
Constantine, L.N., 180
Contractor, N.J., 225
Cook, C., 184, 187, 189, 190,
192-4, 199, 200, 207, 215-6,
218-9, 224-5, 230-2, 234-5,
274
Cook, Dave, 299
Cook, J.W., 338
Cook, L.W., 126-7
Cook, T.E.R., 164-5
Coole, Thomas, 81
Cooper, K.E., 315-6
Cooper, W.H., 59
Coppin, Johnny, 336
Copson, W.H., 181
Cork, D.G., 314
Corn Exchange, 74
Cornelius, N.S., 114
Cornwallis, Captain, 140
Coronel, Vincent, 266
Corporation Band, 72
Cotswold Hospital Radio, 271
Cotswold Hunt, 74
Cotswold Life, 288, 313
Cottam, R.M.H., 257
Cotter, A., 104, 111
Coventry, Earl of, 136
Coventry, Hon. J.B., 137
Cowdrey, M.C., 216, 227, 266,
321
Cox, D.F., 214
Cox, G.(jun), 165, 173, 206
Craig, Douglas, 264
Cranfield, L.M., 165, 172-3, 192
Cranham Feast, 223
Cranston, J., 48, 64
Crapp, J.F., 172, 174, 177,
181-3, 185, 189, 191-4, 198,
204-7, 209, 211, 215-6
Craven, Nico, 168, 187, 249,
251-2, 255, 262, 265, 271,
277-9, 281-2, 285, 292, 298,
316, 322, 331, 343, 358
Crawford, J.N., 101
Cricket, 26
Croom, A.J., 154
Crosse, Edouard, 103
Cudgel Match, 37
Cunliffe, R.J., 320, 322, 332
Cunningham, E.J., 289
Curran, K.M., 291, 293, 294,
296-7, 299, 305
Curtis, T.S., 308
Cut off with a Shilling, 41
Dacre C.C.R., 145, 154-5, 159,
161, 163-4
Daily Telegraph, 272, 308,
314, 319, 324, 335, 358
Dale, A., 347
Daniels, Fred, 103

Daniels, Ken, 266
Daniels, Laura, 266
Darling, J., 89, 103, 108
Davey, J., 257
Davies, D.E., 194
Davies, H.D., 214
Davies, H.G., 200, 214
Davies, Hector, 172
Davies, M., 310-11
Davis, B.A., 252
Davis, E., 191,
Davis, R.C., 249
Davison, B.F., 269
Davy, E.F., 138
Dawes, Leo, 129, 136, 141
Dawson, R.I., 316
Day, S.H., 86, 97
de Ferrières, Baron C.C.A.,
35-7, 82
De Freitas, P.A.J., 296, 315
Deacon, Dennis, 299
Dean, H., 127
Deerhurst, 110
Denness, M.H., 236, 253, 266
Dennett, E.G., 88, 99, 101,
104-11, 113-4, 116, 118-9,
121, 123-4, 127, 129, 140-1,
174
Denning, Mr., 51
Denson, Neville, 330-1
Derbyshire, 161-2, 174, 181,
210, 257-9, 264-5, 304, 309,
314, 325-6
Devereux, L.N., 207
Devey, J.H.G., 87
Devil's Chimney, 144
Dexter, E.R., 235
Dickens, Charles, 23
Digby Colliery, 86
Dighton, Dr. A., 118
Dilley, G.R., 309
Dillon, E.W., 106
Dipper, A.E., 109, 116, 121, 123,
125-7, 133-6, 140-1, 143-6,
148, 151, 154, 158, 305
Dixon, A.L., 227, 237
Doctor at Sea, 234
Dodds, T.C., 193
Dodemaide, A.I.C., 308
Dodwell, Aimbury, 235-6, 249,
259
Doggart, G.H.G., 206
D'Oliveira, B.L., 237, 244, 263,
267
D'Oliveira, D.B., 308
Dollery, H.E., 205
Donald, A.A., 341
Donelan, B.T.P., 311
Douglas, J.W.H.T., 133-4
Dowty, 165, 274, 316
Dowty, Sir George and Lady,
227
D'Souza, A., 230
Du Boulay, A.H., 59
Ducat, A., 115, 123

Duckworth, G., 159
Duckworth-Lewis, 358
Dudderidge, Fred, 238
Duleepsinhji, K.S., 59, 151, 159
Dumbleton, 172
Dunn, Dennis, 348, 350, 357
Duraflex, 290
Durham, 326, 336-7
Dye, A.G., 224
Dye, J.C.J., 253
Dyer, D.V., 185
Dyke, Fred, 299
Eagar, E.D.R., 170, 173, 180,
217-8
Eagle Tower, 355
East Gloucestershire, 96
East, R.E., 269
Eccles, J., 61
Edgbaston, 87, 291
Edmonds, P.H., 260, 294
Edrich, G.A., 208, 235, 251
Edrich, J.H., 270
Edrich, W.J., 187, 190
Edward VII, 97
Edwards, R., 354
Eighty Eight Club, 299, 315
Elizabeth II, 222
Ellcock, R.M., 301
Elliott, M.T.G., 321
Ellis, Clive, 314
Elms, The, 155
Elwes, Lieut. Col. H.C., 164
Emburey, J.E., 278, 294, 300-1,
304, 349
Emmett, G.M., 171, 177, 180-1,
183, 192-4, 201, 203, 205, 208,
210-11, 213-6, 218-9, 225
Emmett, T., 30-1, 51, 61
Engel, Matthew, 331
England and Wales Cricket
Board, 330, 352
Essex, 94-5, 113, 133, 134,
146-7, 159, 168, 193, 267-9,
285, 294, 309, 312, 322
Etheridge, R.J., 219
Eton College, 18
Evans, E., 59
Evans, T.G., 216
Everyman Theatre, 234
Fagg, A.E., 200
Fairbrother, N.H., 320
Fairfield Avenue, 186
Fairford, 208
Family Jars, 44
Famous, The, 113, 236
Farjeon, Herbert, 313
Farrar, Gwen, 149
Fauconberg House, 37
Fauconberg, Lord, 62
Faulkner, Ken, 311, 321
Fay's Company, 58
Fazal Mahmood, 230
Feeney, Mr, 83
Felix N., 45
Felton, N.A., 305

Fender, P.G.H., 143-4, 147, 152
Ferris, J.J., 66-7, 70, 72, 76
Field, The, 49-50
Financial Times, 322
Fisher, I.D., 347
Fitton, J.D., 300
Fitzhardinge, Lord, 31
Fitzpatrick, Paul, 298
Flavell, J.A., 234, 236, 241
Fletcher, K.W.R., 269
Flint, John, 311, 321
Flowers, W., 56, 77
Foat, J.C., 270
Folland, Henry, 128
Follies, The, 119
Foot, David, 197, 225, 279,
288, 319, 323, 326, 331-2, 355
Ford, F.G.J., 64
Ford, P.H., 106
Forest of Dean, 32, 253
Foster, M.K., 136
Francis, J.D., 347
Freeman, A.P., 133-4, 137, 140
French, B.N., 354
Frost, M., 307
Fry, C.B., 106, 121
Fry's Ground, 157
Fullerton, G.M., 185
G.C.H.Q., 265
Galsworthy, Jocelyn, 326
Gange, T.H., 121
Garden Town of England, The,
64
Gardner, F.C., 205
Garrett, T.W., 59
Gatting, M.W., 278, 284, 294,
300-1, 354
Genevieve, 251, 286
George III, 37, 62
George V, 114
George, Mr, 32, 36, 42, 47, 51
George's Ltd., 97, 110, 125,
132,152
Ghulam Abbas, 243
Ghurka Brass Band, 341
Gibbins, Jesse, 316
Gibbons, H.H.I., 160-1, 163
Gibbs, H.H., 324
Gibbs, L.R., 249, 262
Gibson, Alan, 245, 256
Gidman, A.P.R., 348, 353, 355
Giffen, G., 57, 59, 72, 81
Gifford, N., 237, 241, 263,
267, 286
Gilbert, D.R., 306, 309, 321
Gilbert, W.R., 35-6, 44-6, 48,
52, 55, 58-9
Giles, A.F., 341
Gillespie, Edward, 336
Gillhouley, K., 232
Gilligan, A.E.R., 180
Gilligan, F.W., 146
Gladstone, William, 85
Gladwin, C., 210
Glamorgan, 190, 194, 200,

214-5, 222-3, 228-9, 235,
248-9, 252, 268, 274, 286,
289, 306-7, 347-8, 353
Glorious Glosters, 255, 257-60,
262, 265, 273
Gloucester Greats XI, 317
Gloucester, 59, 106, 164, 173,
228, 264
Gloucester, Bishop of, 85
Gloucestershire Aircraft
Company, 128
Gloucestershire and Avon Life,
273
Gloucestershire Artillery Band,
26, 28
Gloucestershire CCC, *passim*
Gloucestershire Echo, 62, 64,
73-4, 76-9, 89, 95, 132, 135,
138, 164, 170, 173, 186, 197-9,
201, 207, 212, 218, 225, 227-8,
232, 243-5, 247, 253, 259, 265-
4, 307, 312, 321, 323, 338, 348,
358
Gloucestershire Exiles, 158,
205, 265-6, 352
Gloucestershire Regiment, 1st
Battalion, 241
*Gloucestershire Sport in Words
and Music*, 336
Glover, A.C.S., 87
Goddard, Derek, 312, 348, 358
Goddard, J.D.C., 197
Goddard, T.L., 213
Goddard, T.W.J., 134, 136,
151, 153-4, 157, 159, 160-1,
163-6, 168, 170, 172-4, 176,
181-4, 187, 189, 190-4, 196-8
Golden Miller, 171
Gomez, G.E., 180
Gooch, G.A., 269, 312, 322
Gottingen, 270
Gough, Mrs Evelyn, 243
Gover, A.R., 172
Gower, D.I., 290-1, 296
Grace, Dr H.M., 23
Grace, E.M., 25, 27, 29-30, 34,
52, 57-8, 60, 64, 69, 78, 84,
107, 113
Grace, G.F., 25, 32, 42, 46, 49
Grace, W.G. (jun), 71-2, 82
Grace, W.G., 24-7, 29-32, 34-7,
39, 41-2, 46, 49, 51, 55-67, 69-
72, 74, 76-9, 81-6, 88-9, 107,
123-4, 127, 131, 136, 148, 162,
245, 270, 272, 279, 326, 332
Graham, J.N., 253
Grand Hotel, 31
Grant, R.S., 178
Graveney, D.A., 258-9, 262,
264-5, 267-8, 270, 272-3,
276-7, 280-2, 285, 288-9, 291,
293-4, 296, 298, 299, 300-1
Graveney, J.K.R., 178, 193,
196, 249, 258, 284,
Graveney, T.W., 178, 191-4,

198-9, 200, 203, 205-6, 208-9,
210, 213-6, 218, 223, 226-8,
234-5, 237, 239-40, 247-8, 258
Graves, P.J., 271
Gray, J.R., 226
Great Exhibition, 23
Green, D.M., 228, 244-5, 247,
249, 252-3, 298, 357
Greene, A.D., 46, 49
Greene, Revd J., 29
Greene, V.S., 296
Greenfield, Revd F.F., 37
Greenidge, C.G., 256, 293
Gregory, J.M., 131, 143
Gregory, R.J., 184
Gregory, S.E., 82
Greig, I.A., 305
Gretton, 74
Griffiths, David, 280
Griffiths, Miss Lydia, 103
Grimmett, C.V., 141, 143
Grundy, James, 21
Guardian, The, 288, 298, 323,
331-2, 355
Gunn, G., 122, 143
Gunn, J.R., 122
Gunn, W., 43, 56, 69, 76, 86
Hadlee, R.J., 284
Haig N.E., 135
Halfyard, D.J., 227-8
Hall, A.J., 351
Hall, L., 39, 51
Hall, Norma, 322
Halliday, Judith, 307
Hallows, C., 127
Hamer, A., 210
Hammond, H.E., 174, 197, 213
Hammond, W.R., 126-7, 131,
134-6, 138, 140, 144, 146-9,
151-2, 154-5, 158, 161, 163-4,
167-8, 170-2, 174, 176, 178,
180-4, 236, 264, 272, 279,
305, 326
Hampshire, 108-9, 116, 121,
137, 139, 144, 152-3, 176,
217-8, 226, 251, 256, 274-5,
277-8, 281, 292-3, 294, 310,
342, 343
Hancock, T.H.C., 314, 325-6,
330, 332, 347-8
Hanif Mohammad, 210, 239
Hanson, Canon, 239
Hardinge, H.T.W., 135
Hardinges, M.A., 342, 353
Hardstaff, J., (snr), 122
Harman, H.J., 128
Harman, Tim, 349
Harris, C.Z., 353
Harris, F.H., 94, 128
Harris, Lord, 65, 78-9, 124,
228, 313
Harrison, Ian, 197
Harrison, Mr, 83
Hartley, P.J., 310
Hartpury, 189

Hartry, Len, 342
Harvey, F.W.(Will), 189
Harvey, I.J., 338, 341-2, 344, 347, 349, 351
Harvi, Mr, 171
Hastings, 163
Hatherley and Reddings, 348
Hattersley-Smith, Revd P., 35
Hawarden, 85
Hawke, Lord, 95, 98, 101, 313
Hawkins, D.G., 228-9
Hay, Colonel, 133
Hayden, M.L., 321, 337
Hayward, Colonel, 128
Hayward, M., 351
Hayward, T.W., 73, 92, 101, 123
Hazare, V.S., 184
Headingley, 206, 287, 325
Headley, G.A., 178, 180-1
Headley, R.G.A., 235, 241, 244, 247, 262
Heap, J.S., 126
Hearne, A., 74, 97
Hearne, J.T., 69, 97
Hearne, J.W., 171
Hearne, W., 74
Hedges, B., 223
Hedges, L.P., 138, 145
Hegg, W.K., 319, 321
Hellens, 143
Hemingway, W.M., 79
Hemmings, Arthur, 172
Hemmings, E.E., 284
Henderson, Michael, 335
Henderson, Miss Lizzie, 44, 47
Hendren, E.H., 135, 170
Henson, Col H., 180, 186, 197, 203, 209, 212, 217
Hereford, 309
Herefordshire Beacon, 155
Hewitt, Chris, 307
Hewson, D.R., 332, 338, 341-2
Hick, G.A., 336, 351
Hide, J.B., 35
Higgs, K., 243
High Street, 82, 113
Highgate Cemetery, 29
Hignell, A.J., 265, 267, 269, 274-5, 281-2
Hignell, Andrew, 350
Higson, John, 341
Hill, A., 51
Hill, G.H., 222
Hill, Miss J., 72
Hill, N.W., 232
Hirst, G.H., 95, 98
Hitch, J., 165
Hitch, J.W., 116
Hitchcock, R.E., 235
Hitler, Adolf, 171, 173, 177
Hobbs, J.B., 115-6, 123, 143, 147-8, 152
Hodgson, G.D., 305, 307-8, 311, 314
Holder, V.A., 271, 278

Hollies, W.E., 192, 204
Hollinshead, Cyril, 323
Hollioake, A.J., 332
Holmes, E.R.T., 165
Hooman, C.V.L., 115
Hopkins, A. J., 98, 111
Hopkins, V., 172
Hornby, A.N., 61
Horton, H., 226
Hotel Majestic, 241
House of Lords, 31
Howard, N.D., 208
Howarth, Major Bell, 149
Howell, H., 125
Howell, Mr J., 178
Howell, W.P., 103
Howorth, R., 167, 184
Howse, Percy, 131
HRH the Prince of Wales, 85, 141, 343
HRH the Princess of Wales, 32, 292
Hubble, J.C., 135, 138
Hudson, Mr E.H., 44
Huggins, H.J., 88, 109-110
Hughes, S.P., 301, 304
Huish, F.E., 115
Humphreys, E., 115
Hussain, N., 312, 322, 354
Hutton, B.L., 349
Ibadulla, K., 235
Igglesden, A.P., 297
Illingworth, R., 218-9, 287-8, 320
Imperial Spa, 48
Imtiaz Ahmed, 209
Inchmore, J.D., 262, 278
India 'A', 353
India, 172, 293
Indian Police Service, 86
Ingleby-Mackenzie, A.C.D., 226
Insole, D.J., 193
International Cavaliers, 239
International Rugby XI, 354
Intikhab Alam, 241, 243, 280
Irani, R.C., 322
Iredale, F.A., 91
Irving, Charles, 217, 256
Jack Russell Arts, 310, 317
Jackson, H.L., 210
Jackson, Hon. F.S., 98
Jackson, P.F., 185
Jackson, V.E., 204
James Jimmy, 128
James K.D., 292, 293
James Lillywhite, Frowd and Company, 29
James Lillywhite's Cricketers' Annual, 26
James, S.P., 347
Jarrett, Michael, 247, 255, 259
Jarvis, A.H., 59
Jarvis, K.B.S., 300
Javed Miandad, 272

Jeeves, Percy, 121-2
Jelbert, Revd M., 198
Jenkins, R.O., 201
Jessop, G.L., 28, 73-4, 76-7, 84-7, 89, 91-2, 94-6, 98, 101, 104, 107-9, 111, 114, 116, 118-9, 121, 124, 137, 145, 148, 231, 266
Jesty, T.E., 281, 300
John Lillywhite's Cricketers' Companion, 27
John, V.B., 289
Johnston, Brian, 141, 143
Jones, A., 249, 268
Jones, A.N., 308
Jones, Brian, 249
Jones, E., 89, 92
Jones, Harry, 162
Jones, Nigel, 332
Jones, P.H., 229
Jones, S.P., 59-60
Jones, W.E., 200
Journeaux, Marie, 280-1, 305, 352, 358
Joy, R.C., 146
Joyner, Mr and Mrs Terry, 259
Julian, Ray, 320, 344
Kallicharran, A.I., 262, 267, 286
Kallis, J.H., 324
Kanhai, R.B., 262
Kardar, A.H., 209
Kasprowicz, M.S., 347, 353
Kay, Sir Brook, 46
Keating, Frank, 185, 189, 191, 279, 331
Keeton, W.W., 192
Keigwin, R.P., 131
Kennedy, A.S., 153
Kent, 30, 74, 78-9, 81, 84-7, 89, 97, 99, 103, 105, 108, 111, 114-6, 118, 124, 128, 129, 133-5, 137-9, 140, 163, 199, 200, 216, 227-30, 236-7, 252-3, 266, 270-1, 273, 282, 285, 296, 317, 319, 341
Kenyon, D., 196, 200, 234-5
Keyte, Vincent, 288
Khan, Imran, 262, 267
Kilburn, J.M., 65, 76
Killeen, N., 337
Kimpton, R.C., 174
King, Mr, 72
King-Turner, C.J., 134
Kirby, S.P., 355
Kitchen, Mervyn, 290
Knight, D.J., 123
Knight, R.D.V., 257, 265-6, 275-6, 289
Knightley-Smith, W., 215
Knott, F.H., 115
Kortright, C.J., 95
Kynaston, Revd Dr, 54
Ladies Day, 355
Laker, J.C., 192, 194, 214

Lamb, A., 84
Lambert, G.E., 178, 181, 190, 194, 196, 198, 203-5, 213-4
Lancashire, 61, 126-8, 139, 157-8, 208, 215, 230-1, 243-4, 257-8, 300, 315, 319-20
Lancet, 96
Lanchbury, R.J., 255
Langdon, T., 103, 109, 113, 123
Langridge, J., 151, 160, 164, 173-4
Langridge, J.G., 160, 164, 205
Lansdown, 165
Larwood, H., 139, 143, 320
Laver, F., 91-92, 103-4
Law, S.G., 321
Lawrence, D.V., 289, 291-4, 296-8, 305-7, 309, 315
Lawrence, Edwin, 26, 37, 50-2, 55, 59, 63-5, 69, 76, 79, 82, 87, 93-4, 113, 152
Lay, Ron, 235
Lea, Mrs, 186
Leach, Robert, 200
Leary, S.E., 253
Leckhampton, 131, 138
Lee, Alan, 320-21, 343
Lee, H., 135
Lee, Laurie, 129
Leeds, 111
Legge, Peter, 212, 280
Leicestershire, 124, 126-8, 137, 155, 157, 161, 204, 243-4, 269, 278, 290-1, 296, 324
Lemmon, David, 312
Lenham, L.J., 238
Lenham, N.J., 311
Leslie, Will, 95
Lester, G., 204
Letheby and Christopher, 357
Lever, J.K., 269, 285,
Lewis, A.R., 252
Lewis, Bill, 158, 160, 168
Lewis, J., 326, 336, 351
Lewis, J.J.B., 329-30, 337
Lewry, J.D., 332
Light, John, 205-6
Lilley, A.F.A., 87
Lilleybrook, 189
Lillywhite, Eliza, 54
Lillywhite, F.W., 17
Lillywhite, Fred, 19
Lillywhite, James, (jun), 27, 29, 36
Lillywhite, James, 17-9, 21, 23-32, 34-7, 39, 41-3, 46-7, 49-52, 54, 57, 59, 94, 101, 107, 113, 124, 147, 152, 162, 236, 310
Lillywhite, John, 19, 21, 29
Lillywhite's Guide to Cricketers, 27
Lipson, D.L., 171
Lloyd, C.H., 258
Lloyd, D., 243, 258, 325

Lloyds, J.W., 291, 294, 307
Loader, P.J., 215
Lock, G.A.R., 214, 243
Locke, Bert, 260
Lockwood, E., 31, 39
Lockwood, W., 70, 92, 93
Lockyer, T., 21
London, 92, 121, 165
Lord's Taverners, 321, 354
Lord's, 106, 135, 143, 151, 167, 186, 235, 263, 265, 270, 278, 286, 320, 344, 352
Loving cup, 37, 84
Luard, Capt. A.J.H., 70
Lucas, A.P., 95
Luckhurst, B.W., 266
Lumb, R.G., 275
Lynch, M.A., 280, 296, 306, 319-20, 322, 325-26
Lyon, B.H., 145-6, 148-9, 151, 153, 155, 157-8, 160-1, 163-4, 166, 168, 182
Lyons, J.J., 85
Macartney, C.G., 129, 131, 141
MacDonald, Ramsay, 158
Mace, John, 187, 358
Macready, William Charles, 23
Mad Hatters, The, 116, 119
Mailey, A.A., 129, 131-2, 143, 185, 313
Majid Khan, 249, 252
Makepeace, J.W.H., 126-7
Malcolm, D.E., 325, 332
Malvern College, 86, 209
Manchester, 154
Mankad, M.H., 183
Mann, F.T., 135
Mann, N.B.F., 185
Manning, Edgar, 36
March Hares, 111, 115
Margrett, Mr, 128
Marlar, R.G., 215
Marlborough College, 18-9, 26, 29
Marlborough Street, 147
Marlow, W.H., 161
Marriott, C.S., 138
Mars I, 128
Marshall, M.D., 292, 293, 310
Marshall, R.E., 226,
Martin, F., 87
Martineau, G.D., 165
Martin-Jenkins, Christopher, 313, 319, 341
Martin-Jones, David, 264
Mary, Queen, 133
Mascarenhas, A.D., 347
Maskell, Dan, 193
Mason, J.R., 79, 115
Mason, John, 272
Mason, M.S., 351
Massie, H.H., 85
May, P.B.H., 214, 229
Mayerl, Billy, 149
Maynard, M.P., 306-7, 347

MCC, 30
McAulay, Simon, 350, 356
McConnon, J.E., 200
McCrudden, Richard, 230, 232, 241, 244
McDonald, E.A., 129
McDonell H.C., 101
McDonnell, P.S., 59, 62
McEwan, K.S., 285
McGahey, C.P., 95
McGlew, D.J., 213
McGregor, G., 104
McHugh, F.P., 210-11
McIlwraith, J., 59
McInroy, Bob, 348, 350, 355-6
McKibben, T.R., 81-2, 84
McMillan, C.D., 353
Mead, C.P., 109, 139
Mead, W., 95
Melbourne Club, 60
Melville, A., 160, 164-5
Mendelssohn, Felix, 198
Mendis, G.D., 300
Merry, W.G., 279
Metcalfe, A.A., 305
Meyer, B.J., 222, 224, 248, 251, 253, 256-7
Michelmore, Cliff, 226
Mickleton, 61
Middlesex, 19, 45, 51, 58, 63-4, 66, 69, 76, 96-7, 104, 128, 135, 170, 182, 186-7, 189, 190, 195-6, 223-4, 227, 240, 248, 257, 260, 271, 273, 284-5, 294, 300-1, 304, 348-9
Midwinter, W.E., 32, 34, 42, 46, 49, 57, 59
Milburn, C., 249
Miles, Joe, 197
Mills, P.T., 88, 101, 108, 114, 127, 133, 135-9, 143-4, 162
Milns, D.J., 324
Milton, C.A., 199, 200-1, 204-5, 207, 209-11, 213-6, 218-9, 223-4, 232, 236, 238, 240-1, 244-5, 247, 249, 255, 258, 260
Milton, Jean, 217
Mitchell, T.B., 181
Moberly, W.O., 30, 41, 43, 48
Monks, C.I., 189
Montgomerie, R.R., 342
Montpellier Coal Exchange, 50
Montpellier Gardens, 42, 47, 57, 60, 63, 67, 89, 103, 111, 115-6, 119, 125, 138, 189
Montpellier Rotunda, 54
Montpellier Wine Bar, 315, 342, 357
Montpellier, 52, 272
Moody, T.M., 309, 336, 351
Moon, W.R., 69
Moore, D.N., 154, 160, 171-2, 195
Moore, John, 155, 195
Moore, Mervyn, 285

Moore, Roger, 290-1
Moore, Suzee, 291
Morgan, D.C., 210
Morley, F., 43
Morris, H., 289, 307
Morris, J.E., 304, 307, 314, 337
Mortimore, J.B., 198, 201, 204, 206-7, 211, 213, 215, 218, 222, 224, 228-30, 232, 234-41, 243, 245, 248, 251, 253, 255-6, 259, 262, 267
Moss, Johnny, 203
Moxon, M.D., 305, 309, 316
Much Marcle, 143
Mullally, A.D., 324
Mullan Shaun, 299, 315
Muncer, B.L., 190, 200
Municipal Orchestra, 126
Murch, W., 72
Murdoch, W.L., 57, 59, 67
Murray, A.R.A., 213
Murray, D.L., 262
Musgrove, Mr, 83
Mushtaq Mohammad, 230
Nash, D.C., 349
Nash, M.A., 248
Naval Engagements, 51
Neale, W.A., 145-146, 161, 165, 168, 173, 180-3
Neate, Horace, 164
Need, Geoffrey, 191, 203, 211, 292, 296
New Club, The, 60, 272, 279, 293, 322
New Education Fellowship Conference, 171
New York, 121
New Zealand 'A', 338
New Zealand, 145, 219, 347, 353
Newbon, Gary, 354
Newham, W., 58
Newman School of Dancing, 243
Newman, J.A., 145, 153
Newport, P.J., 308
Newstead, J.T., 110
Newton, A.E., 71
Newton, Alfred, 111, 116
Nicholas, F.W.H., 134
Nicholas, M.C.J., 293, 310
Nicholls, R.B., 222, 229-30, 232, 234, 237-9, 241, 245, 249, 252, 255, 258-9, 264-5
Nichols, G.B., 71
Niehaus, Dana, 185
Nine Points of the Law, 47
Noble, M.A., 91
Norman, Mr G, 118
Northamptonshire, 118, 191-2, 208, 256, 305, 322, 332, 337, 344
Northwick, Lord, 18
Norwich, 118

Nottinghamshire, 21, 28, 30, 32, 34, 41-3, 56, 66, 69-70, 76-7, 86, 96, 122, 136, 139, 143, 176, 224, 231-2, 265, 273, 284, 291, 293, 294, 342
Nutter, A.E., 191
Oakman, A.S.M., 234
Oates, T.W., 86
O'Brien, Andrew, 350, 357
O'Brien, T.C., 58
O'Connor, J., 134
O'Gorman, T.J.G., 304
Old Bath Road, 174, 178, 185
Old Stagers, 45, 78, 115
Old Time Music Hall, 236
Old Trafford, 208, 281
Oldfield, N., 191
Oldfield, W.A., 129
Ontong, R.C., 286
Opera House, 92, 119, 198
Ord, J.S., 205
Ormrod, J.A., 262, 278
Oslear, Don, 273, 281-2, 300-1, 344
Ostler, D.P., 325
Ough, Jean, 213
Oval, The, 25, 28, 46, 59, 71, 89, 98, 128, 146-8, 152, 157, 170, 172, 182, 184, 186, 192, 198, 203, 210, 227, 240
Oversby, Lisa, 352-3, 355
Owens, Jesse, 173
Owen-Smith, Dr H.G., 170
Oxford, 59, 108, 155, 209
Page, D.A.C., 163, 165, 167-8, 171, 173
Page, H.V., 55-6, 58, 61, 69, 128, 144
Pain, James, 60, 63
Painter, J.R., 59, 66, 70
Paish, A.J., 91-2, 96
Pakistan 'A', 326
Pakistan, 209, 229-30, 241, 257, 284
Palairet, L.C.H., 67, 71
Palmer, G., 57, 60
Palmer, Roy, 290-1
Parfitt, P.H., 227, 240
Parker, C.W.L., 89, 118, 121-2, 125-9, 131, 133-7, 139, 143-5, 147-9, 151-5, 157, 159, 160-4, 166-8, 170-1, 174, 184, 265
Parker, G.W., 158, 163, 166, 174, 185, 244, 248, 255, 263-4, 266, 269, 274, 284, 323
Parker, J.F., 192, 194
Parker, J.M., 262
Parker, Mary, 272
Parkhouse, W.G.A., 214
Parks, H.W., 160
Parks, J.H., 160, 164, 172, 174
Parks, J.M., 215
Parsons, G.J., 324
Partridge, M.D., 269-70
Pasley, Hamilton, 17

Pataudi (Nawab of), 183, 238
Pates, Mr, 140
Patesians Association, 270
Patterson, W.H., 79
Paynter, E., 159
Peach, H.A., 144
Peake, E., 62
Peate, E., 51
Perks, R.T.D., 167, 184-5, 207
Perrin, P.A., 95
Perry, Don, 249, 284, 292, 309
Perry, Fred, 193
Persse, H.W., 108
Pervez Sajjad Hassan, 243
Petra, Yvon, 193
Phebey, A.H., 227
Philadelphians, 96
Phillips, 285
Phillips, R.W., 249
Philo-Thespians, 36
Pike, A., 86
Pilling, H., 258
Pite, Mr, 177
Pitman, Alan, 249
Pittville Park, 107, 124, 189, 270
Pittville Pump Room, 235-6
Playground, 17, 19, 21, 30-1, 54, 96, 101, 124
Plough Hotel, 37, 41, 45, 48, 57
Plunket, Lord, 85
Pocock, N.E.J., 277
Pocock, P.I., 276, 280
Pollock, Mr, 36, 39
Pollock, S.M., 325
Pont, K.R., 285
Ponting, R.T., 321
Poor Relief Committee, 55
Pope, G.H., 181
Pope, S.P., 351
Postlip Mills, 57
Potter, Mrs, 73, 82
Poulton, Mrs, 260
Powell, Sid, 336
Prestbury Race Week, 171
Prestbury, 127, 146
Price, J.S.E., 260
Prichard, P.J., 312
Priors Farm, 186
Priory Parade, 118
Procter, M.J., 244, 247, 249, 251, 257-9. 262-3, 266-71, 275, 278-9, 282, 284, 324
Promenade Concert, 39
Promenade, 60, 85, 87, 124, 141, 178, 241
Public Schools XV, 143
Pugh, C.T.M., 228-30
Pullar, G., 243, 247-8
Pullen, W.W.F., 51, 58
Punch, 189
Quaife, B.W., 148, 161, 163
Quaife, W.G., 87-8, 109
Queen's Circus, 19, 23
Queen's Hotel, 27, 48-9, 59, 67, 72, 85, 208, 320

Radley College, 162
Raikes, D.C.G., 160
Ramadhin, S., 197-9
Randall, D.W., 273
Ranjitsinhji, K.S., 106
Ransford, V.S., 111
Read, H.D., 168, 170
Read, J.M., 64, 70
Read, W.W., 46
Redesdale, Lord, 31
Redmarley CC., 172, 185
Reid, Jamie, 331
Relf, A.E., 129
Rendcomb, 205
Repton School, 101
Rest of the World XI, 315, 317
Rhodes, J.N., 348-9, 351-3, 357
Rhodes, S.J., 351
Rhodes, W., 95, 98, 101, 109
Rice, C.E.B., 294
Rice, R.W., 77, 79, 81, 89, 91, 95
Richards, B.A., 251-2, 256
Richardson, A.W., 162
Richardson, P.E., 229
Richardson, R.B., 316
Richardson, T., 73, 78, 92
Richardson, Tom, 343-4, 348
Richmond, T.L., 139
Robert Macaire!, 47
Roberts, A.W., 113
Roberts, F.B., 111, 113-4, 116
Roberts, F.G., 61-2, 66, 96, 99
Robertson & Co., 131
Robertson, J.D., 182, 187
Robertson, W.P., 96-7
Robertson-Glasgow, R.C., 185
Robey, George, 132
Robins, R.W.V., 187, 189, 190, 196
Robinson, D.C., 136, 140-1, 143-4
Robinson, D.D.J., 322
Robinson, F.G., 124, 126, 129, 133
Robinson, P.E., 305
Robinson, R.T., 294
Rodney Road, 82
Rogers, Colonel, 82
Rogers, F.J., 136-7
Rolfe, Mr, 186
Rollins, A.S., 337
Romaines, P.W., 287, 289, 291, 293, 296, 298, 307
Roope, G.R.J., 276, 354
Root, C.F., 136
Rossiter, Dickie, 321
Ross-on-Wye, 155
Rowan, A.M.B., 185-6
Rowlands, W.H., 144, 146
Roy, P.K., 224
Royal Cheltenham Comedians, 41
Royal Cheltenham Wafer, 32
Royal Gloucestershire Hussars,

85, 258
Royal Hotel, 73, 78, 82
Royal Warwickshire Regiment, 122
Russell, R.C., 284, 286, 289, 296, 299, 300, 307, 310-11, 314, 317, 319-22, 326, 330, 336, 338, 341, 347, 349, 351, 353,
Russell, S.E.J., 227, 238,
Russell, W.E., 227
Ruston, Jim, 310, 317
Sadiq Mohammad, 257, 267-70, 272, 275, 277, 280-2, 285
Sainsbury, F.J., 49
Sainsbury, P.J., 218, 257
Salisbury, I.D.K., 311
Salter, M.G., 136
Sampson, Aylwin, 282
Sandford Fields, 18
Sandford Mill Farm, 185
Sandford Park, 189, 193
Sandford Road, 108, 185, 212, 280, 301, 342
Sandford Tithing, 18
Sandford, 41,
Sandham, A., 148
Santall, S., 87
Saqlain Mushtaq, 335
Sarwate, C.T., 183-4
Sayer, D.M., 228
Scarborough Festival, 60, 65
Scott, C.J., 181, 190-1, 200, 204
Scott, Dr H., 57
Scott, R.J., 307
Scudamore, Peter, 354
Scudamore, Tom, 354
Seabrook, F.J., 137, 147, 153, 157, 161
Selby, J., 56
Sewell, C.O.H., 77, 87, 104, 106-7, 115-6, 118-9, 123
Sexstone, Colin, 337-8, 341
Seymour, J., 115
Shackleton, D., 226
Shackleton, Howard, 126
Shackleton, J.H.S., 270
Shacklock, F.J., 70
Sharma, R., 304
Sharp, H.P.H., 187, 189, 190
Sharp, K., 287
Sharp, Richard, 245, 287, 342
Shaw, A., 42, 60
Sheather, Audrey Girl
Harmonists, 196
Sheffield, 39
Shelmerdine, G.O., 127
Shenton, Mr, 47
Shentons, printers, 194
Shepherd, D.J., 229, 235, 252
Shepherd, D.R., 245, 248, 252, 256-7, 267-9
Shepherd, J.N., 285-7, 289
Sheppard, David, Bishop of
Liverpool, 172, 180, 205-6, 217

Sheriyar, A., 336
Shirehampton, 111
Shoaib Malik, 351, 353, 357
Shrewsbury School, 155, 182
Shrewsbury, A., 32, 42, 56, 60, 69, 76, 86
Shropshire, 122
Shurdington Gaiety Girls, 243
Shurdington Road, 113
Shuter, J., 64
Shuttleworth, K., 243
Sidebottom, A., 299
Sills, Ron, 216
Silva, S.A.R., 289
Simmonds, W., 138
Simmons, P.V., 324
Simons, Amanda, 313
Simons, Barnaby, 313
Simons, Edward, 313
Simons, Emily, 313
Simons, George, 313
Simpson, Michael, 304, 347, 349
Sims, J.M., 182, 187, 190
Sinfield, R.A., 145, 148, 151, 154, 157, 159, 163, 165, 167-8, 170-2, 174, 176, 180, 182, 184
Singing Waiters, 243
Singleton, A.P., 185
Singleton's, 114
Skillicorne, Alderman W.N., 45
Slack, W.N., 284
Slingsby, John, 149, 157, 162, 170, 176
Small, G.C., 292, 325
Smith, A.M., 306-7, 312, 314, 320-22, 324-6, 330, 332, 335, 337-8, 342, 347, 349, 351, 353
Smith, Alderman and Mrs P.T., 198
Smith, B.F., 324, 351
Smith, C.L., 292
Smith, D., 181
Smith, D.M., 311
Smith, D.R., 218-9, 225, 231, 240, 244-5, 251
Smith, David, 354
Smith, H., 133-6, 146, 152-4, 157, 160, 208
Smith, K.D., 286
Smith, M.J.K., 222, 235
Smith, V.I., 185, 213
Smithson, G.A., 204
Snape, J.N., 341, 348
Snow, J.A., 239, 272
Society of Friends of the
Festival, 264, 266
Solanki, V.S., 336, 351
Somerset, 47, 49, 61, 67, 70-2, 76, 315
South Africa 'A', 324
South Africa, 152, 167, 170, 185, 192, 212, 231, 300

South of England XI, 26
South Western Convention of Bee Keepers, 160
Southampton, 116, 137
Southerton J., 25
Southwood, Revd T.A., 19, 31
Spa Entertainers, 138
Spa Orchestra, 189
Spa Quartette, 196
Spearman, C.M., 347, 352-3, 355, 357-8
Speight, M.P., 337
Spofforth, F.R., 57, 60
Sportsman, The, 123
Sportsman's Dance, 259
Spry, E.J., 88
Sri Lanka 'A', 336
Sri Lanka, 289
Srinath, Javagal, 319-21, 323
St Briavels, 32
St Paul's, 165
St Stephens, 270
Stanway House, 141
Staples, A., 143
Star Hotel, 224
Star, The, 168
Statham, J.B., 208, 229, 243
Steam Bread and Biscuit Works, 51
Stemp, R.D., 309
Stephens, E.J., 167
Stephens, G.W., 109
Stephenson H.H., 21
Stephenson, F.D., 285
Stevens, G.T.S., 135
Stewart, M.J., 215, 240
Stewart, R.W., 240
Stewart, W.J., 235
Stilgoe, Richard, 354
Stock Exchange, 94
Stoddart, A.E., 64
Stollmeyer, J.B., 180, 197-8
Stollmeyer, V.H., 180
Stovold, A.W., 264-5, 267, 270, 272, 274, 284-6, 289, 293-4, 297-9
Stovold, M.W., 274, 353
Strachan, G., 25-6, 28
Strauss, A.J., 349
Stroud Week, 228
Stroud, 284, 288
Strudwick, H., 143
Studd, C.T., 51
Subba Row, R., 211
Suffolk Road, 173, 352
Suffolk Square, 23
Sunday Telegraph, 298
Sunningend, 128
Supporters' Club, 205, 224
Surrey, 25-6, 28, 45, 46, 55-6, 58-9, 64, 67, 70, 73, 92, 101, 115-6, 119, 123, 128, 143, 145, 147-8, 152, 165-6, 172, 184, 192, 194, 210-11, 214-5, 239-40, 245, 269-70, 275-6,

280, 289, 296-7, 305-6, 319, 332, 335, 353
Surridge, W.S., 211
Sussex, 17, 19, 27-9, 35-7, 58, 105-6, 123, 128-9, 151, 158-9, 160, 163-5, 172-4, 180-1, 205-7, 215, 217, 234, 238-9, 245, 263, 271-2, 307-8, 311, 330, 332, 341-2, 349
Suttle, K.G., 206
Swan Hotel, 73
Swann, G.P., 338
Swansea, 59
Sweeting, Mr, 57
Swetman, R., 210
Swift, Geoff, 316, 320, 330, 335, 344
Swindon, 72, 92
Sydney Arms Hotel, 141
Symonds, A., 319-25
Tate, M.W., 160, 164
Tattersall, R., 208
Taunton, 67, 70, 159
Taylor, Bertram, 237
Taylor, C.G., 341, 343-4, 347-8
Taylor, J.M., 129
Taylor, John, 298
Taylor, L.B., 290
Taylor, Mr, 159, 162
Taylor, Tom, 45
Taylor, W., 265
Temple Meads, 178
Tendulkar, S.R., 309
Tennant, Ivo, 343, 349
Test and County Cricket Board, 260, 298, 313, 316, 324
Tetbury, 184
Tewkesbury CC., 110
Tewkesbury, 137, 154, 217
Thatcher, Margaret, 274
Theatre Royal, 41, 43, 47
Thirlestaine House, 18
Thirlestaine Road, 185-6, 280, 301, 352
Thomas, F.E., 106-7
Thomas, Harold, 222, 228, 230
Thomas, Leslie, 354
Thompson, Francis, 61
Thompson, G.J., 118
Thomson, A.A., 243
Thomson, N.I., 206, 234
Thornton, C.I., 65, 85
Tilley, Peter, 243
Time Magazine, 240
Times, The, 243, 247-8, 256, 293, 300, 320, 341, 343, 349
Titmus, F.J., 260
To Paris and Back for Five Pounds, 44
Tolchard, R.W., 269
Town Band, 36, 39, 67, 82
Town Hall, 99, 122, 126, 129, 132, 136, 140-1, 143, 149, 162, 171, 185, 189, 196, 203, 224, 237-8, 240, 243, 249, 258-9, 321

Townsend, C.L., 25, 71-2, 74, 76-9, 81-2, 86-9, 91-2, 95-6, 98-9, 104, 106-7, 109, 111, 127, 166, 272, 326
Townsend, F., 25, 27, 48, 52, 57-8, 71
Tozer, Victor, 255
Trades Union Congress, 158
Trainor, N.J., 325, 332
Tremenheere, J.H.A., 26
Tremlett, T.M., 292
Trent Bridge, 151, 241
Trott, G.H.S., 81-2
Troup, W., 86, 88-9, 94
Trueman, F.S., 218
Trumble, H., 81, 84
Trumble, J.W., 59
Trumper, V.T., 98, 110
Truscott, Rosemary, 273
Tubbs, Sir Stanley, 180
Tufnell, P.C.R., 349
Tunnicliffe, Mr, 164
Turn Him Out, 44
Turner, C.T.B., 66, 72
Turner, G.M., 255, 262-3
Turner, S., 285
Turvey, Sam, 347
Twenty-two Past and Present Cheltonians, 21
Twiselton, Frank, 264
Tyldesley, R.K., 126
Tyler, E.J., 69, 71
Tyler, Mrs, 19
Tyrolese Minstrels, 56
Tyson, F.H., 208
Udal, S.D., 343, 347
Ullyett, Roy, 168
Ulyett, G., 39, 51
Umrigar, P.R., 204, 225
Underwood, D.L., 237, 252-3, 282, 297
Union Club, 119, 138
United All-England XI, 21, 28, 35
Valentine, A.L., 198-9
Van der Gucht, P.I., 162
Vasconcellos, Josephina de, 255
Vaughan, J.T.C., 309, 312
Vaughan, M.P., 316
Venkataraghaven, S., 264
Venn, Jack, 272
Vestey, Lord, 321, 325, 358
Victoria ground, 136, 138-9, 149, 151-2, 203, 223, 235
Victoria, Queen, 61, 85, 97
Victory Club, 266, 270
Viljoen, K.G., 168
Vine, J., 129
Vizard, W.O., 56
Vowles, Guy, 349
Vowles, Mr L.T., 203
Voyce, Mr, 164
Voysey, Mrs, 186
Wade, H.F., 167
Wade, S., 61

Walcott, C.L., 198-9
Walker, I.D., 58
Walker, P.M., 222-3, 229, 252
Walker, W., 143
Walkley, Jim, 187
Walsh, C.A., 291-4, 297, 299, 300, 305, 309-10, 312, 314, 316-7, 319, 325, 330, 332, 335
Walsh, J.E., 204
Walters, C.F., 160
Walters, Janet, 200, 212, 272, 295, 323
Walters, Norman, 200, 205, 212, 272, 295, 310-12, 323
Waqar Younis, 306
Ward, A., 264
Ward, E.L., 168
Ward, I.J., 332
Ward, T.R., 317
Wardill, Major, 60, 91
Wardle, J.H., 218-9
Warner, A.E., 314
Warner, P.F., 104, 313
Warwick House, 118
Warwickshire, 87, 109, 121, 124-5, 128, 133, 152, 154, 204-5, 222, 234-5, 249, 255, 257, 262, 267, 286, 289, 291-2, 297-8, 324-5, 336, 338
Wasim Akram, 320
Wass, T.G., 122
Watkin, S., 307
Watkins, A.J., 200
Watkinson, M., 300, 319
Waugh, M.E., 322
Webb Brothers, 67
Webbe, A.J., 64
Webster, J., 191
Weekes, E., 198
Weekes, P.N., 349
Wellington College, 108
Wellington, Duke of, 82
Wells, A.P., 311
Wells, B.D., 131, 200-1, 203, 209, 210, 213-6, 218-9, 224, 231-2, 338
Wells, T.U., 196
Wemyss, Earl of, 141
Wensley, A.F., 158
West Ham, 227
West Indies 'A', 350
West Indies, 178, 180, 196-7, 260, 262, 285
West, Peter, 331
Westley, S.A., 249
Westminster Abbey, 97
Westminster School, 18
Weston, W.P.C., 336, 352-3, 355, 358
Weston-super-Mare, 200
Wettimuny, S., 289
Wheatley, Keith, 322
Whiley, R.K., 209, 210
Whitaker, J.J., 296
Whitbread, 270

White Heather, The, 92
White Viennese Band, 95
White, R.A., 224
White, R.C., 231-2
Whitebait at Greenwich, 41
Whitehead, Alan, 301
Whitney, M.R., 281
Whitticase, P., 296
Whysall, W.W., 143
Wilkins, A.H., 277
Wilkins, C.P., 259
Willey, P., 290, 296
Williams, C.B., 199
Williams, Harry, 224
Williams, J.P.R., 354
Williams, N.F., 304
Williams, O.J., 84
Williams, P.F.C., 134-5
Williams, R.C.J., 306
Willmott, Alderman H., 41
Wilson A.E., 171, 180, 183-4, 190-1, 194-5, 199, 206-8, 245, 265-6, 350
Wilson, G.A., 99
Wilson, H.L., 129
Wilson, P.H.L., 276
Winchcombe, 57
Windaybank, S.J., 281
Windows, A.R., 226, 228-30, 235
Windows, M.G.N., 226, 316, 326, 332, 335, 341, 343-4, 347-8, 353, 355, 357-8
Winrow, F.H., 192
Winter Garden, 39
Wisden Cricket Monthly, 319
Wisden Cricketers' Almanack, 27, 29, 60, 66, 69, 104-5, 110, 121, 143, 153, 160, 172, 193, 197, 204, 207-8, 210, 214, 216, 219, 227, 231, 257, 263, 266, 271, 276, 279-80, 282, 288, 290-1, 296, 305-6, 308-9, 310, 313, 326, 349-50, 357
Wisden, J., 21, 23
Wisteria Books, 295, 308, 312-3, 320, 351
Wodehouse, P.G., 121-2
Wolstenholme, Gerry, 307
Wolverhampton Wanderers, 125, 227
Wood, C.J.B., 126
Wood, D.J., 206
Wood, M.J., 357
Woodcock, John, 248, 293, 300
Woodfull, W.M., 163
Woodmancote, 172
Woodpeckers, 203
Wood's Glass Working Exhibition, 57
Woods, S.M.J., 61, 69
Woof, Philip, 151
Woof, W.A., 46, 49, 52, 55, 57-60, 62-4, 66-7, 74, 91, 95, 98, 126, 140, 151-2, 159, 173-4, 201

Wooller, W., 194, 200, 214-6, 223
Woolley, C.N., 111
Woolley, F.E., 111, 116, 133, 140
Woolmer, R.A., 266
Wooster, Bertie, 122
Wootton, S.H., 289
Worcestershire, 99, 105-7, 113-4, 116, 119, 124-5, 136, 139, 144, 148-9, 160, 163, 167, 170, 174, 177, 184, 196, 200-1, 207, 231, 234-7, 241, 244, 247-8, 255-6, 262-3, 267, 271, 275, 277-8, 308, 336, 351-2
Wrathall, H., 78, 84, 92, 99, 101, 103, 107
Wright, A.C., 137
Wright, A.J., 289, 290, 296-7, 301, 305-6, 308-9, 312, 314, 316, 321, 324-5
Wright, D.V.P., 199
Wright, Fred, 79
Wright, Graeme, 331
Wright, Kit, 246
Wright, W., 85
Wyatt, R.E.S., 200
Wynn, Mike, 274
Wynne, Madame Edith, 42
Yardley, W., 45
Yarnold, H., 185
Yeomanry Mess Room, 37
Yorkshire, 30, 35, 37, 39, 41, 47-8, 51, 60, 76-7, 94, 97-8, 101, 109-10, 121, 128, 160, 218, 239, 274-5, 286-7, 298-9, 304-6, 309-10, 316, 336, 338, 355-6, 358
Young Australians, 321
Young, D.M., 195, 198-9, 203, 208, 210, 213-5, 218-9, 222-4, 226-7, 230, 232, 234-5
Young, J.A., 187, 189, 190
Young, S., 325-6, 338
Ypres, 111
Zaheer Abbas, 257-8, 260, 266-73, 275, 279, 281-2, 284, 286, 288-9, 305, 317, 324, 326